Wittg

Meaning and Understanding

B

Essays on the
Philosophical Investigations

Volume 1

Wittgenstein
Meaning and Understanding

G. P. Baker & P. M. S. Hacker

Fellows of St John's College · Oxford

BLACKWELL
Oxford UK & Cambridge USA

British Library Cataloguing in Publication Data

Baker, G. P.
  Wittgenstein: meaning and understanding
  1. Wittgenstein. Ludwig. Philosophical investigations
  I. Title
  II. Hacker, P. M. S.
  III. Wittgenstein, Ludwig. Philosophical investigations
  149'.94   B3376.W563P53

ISBN 0–631–13071–3

Phototypeset in V.I.P. Bembo by
Western Printing Services Ltd, Bristol
Printed and bound in Great Britain by
T. J. Press (Padstow) Ltd., Padstow, Cornwall

For Anne and Sylvia

Contents

Preface to the Paperback edition

In 1980 we published a 692 page volume entitled *Wittgenstein – Understanding and Meaning, an analytical commentary on the* PHILOSOPHICAL INVESTIGATIONS. This consisted of detailed analysis of Wittgenstein's argument in the first 184 remarks of the *Investigations*. In the exegesis of Wittgenstein's text we analysed each remark, examined its role in his argumentative strategy, and, where it was illuminating to do so, traced its ancestry to Wittgenstein's voluminous *Nachlass*. Where necessary, we contrasted his arguments with those of the *Tractatus*, and where possible we identified his targets in the works of Frege and Russell. Interspersed at the appropriate places in the exegesis were seventeen essays surveying the central themes of this part of his book. Here we not only tried to give a synoptic view of his philosophical ideas, and to compare and contrast them with those of Frege, Russell and the *Tractatus*, but also to make clear their bearing on contemporary philosophical endeavours, in particular in philosophical logic and philosophy of language.

For the paperback edition we have split our original book into two, this volume consisting of the original essays and a companion volume of the exegesis entitled *An Analytical Commentary on Wittgenstein's* PHILOSOPHICAL INVESTIGATIONS. Each can be read and used independently of the other, although they are, of course, complementary.

Apart from structural alterations essential for the bifurcation of the original volume, the changes we have introduced are minimal.

First, internal cross-references within the original text have now been replaced by cross-references to the companion volume. In this volume references to *An Analytical Commentary on Wittgenstein's* PHILOSOPHICAL INVESTIGATIONS take the same form as in the original, viz. 'Exg. §n' refers to our exegetical remarks on the *Investigations* §n which are to be found under that heading in the companion volume.

Secondly, we have adapted the original Introduction to match it to each of the two volumes.

Thirdly, we have taken the opportunity to correct minor errors and typographical mistakes in the hard cover edition.

In the original edition we introduced our first substantial remarks on Frege with the following observation: 'Philosophers commonly assume that one of Frege's philosophical projects is to construct a general theory of meaning for a natural language. There are many reasons to doubt this assumption, but we shall not challenge it here. Rather, the picture of Frege's philosophy of language we shall present will conform to the standard average modern interpretation of his theories.' In the intervening years since we wrote this, we have come to realize, as we did not then, how deep the gulf is between the historical Frege and the 'standard average modern interpretation' of his mature theory. Had our book been on the *Tractatus*, which feeds so extensively on Frege's work (largely by way of critical reaction and far reaching modification), we would undoubtedly have had to rewrite it. As it is, we have now spelt out our conception of Frege's enterprise in *Frege: Logical Excavations*, and our original Galtonian picture of Frege as viewed by the moderns may stand. As long as it is appreciated what exactly it is, we still think it neither unfair not without substantial point. For Frege's impact upon late twentieth century philosophical logic has been largely via the standard average modern interpretation.

Two final points: first, through oversight we employed the abbreviation 'LA' for page references to Wittgenstein's *Lectures and Conversations on Aesthetics, Psychology and Religion*, and also for page references to Russell's 'The Philosophy of Logical Atomism'. Since the contexts in which the two books are referred to do not overlap, and since in each context it is clear to which writer and text we are referring, we have not rectified this regrettable ambiguity. Secondly, since we wrote the book various primary and derivative primary source material has been published. In particular, there is now available Wittgenstein's *Remarks on the Philosophy of Psychology* in two volumes, and his *Vermischte Bemerkungen (Culture and Value)*. This material was available to us in the form of the original manuscripts and typescripts, and was referred to, where necessary, by TS or MS number and page. We have not changed this. However, Desmond Lee's *Wittgenstein's Lectures, Cambridge 1930–32* and Alice Ambrose's *Wittgenstein's Lectures, Cambridge 1932–35* were not available to us. They contain much that is of interest and importance, and ideally we should have liked to incorporate references to remarks in these volumes that bear on the subjects we discuss. However, nothing in either book has led us to revise our judgment, and much in both volumes merely gives further confirmation to our interpretations. Consequently we have, with some slight regret, refrained from the luxury of dismantling set pages to insert references to these lecture notes.

G.P.B. & P.M.S.H.
Oxford, 1981

Acknowledgements

While composing this book we have been much assisted by institutions, friends and colleagues.

We are grateful to the British Academy for a generous grant for our research. Our publishers, Basil Blackwell Publisher Ltd., in particular Mr J. K. D. Feather and Mr D. Martin, have been most helpful in steering a difficult publishing project through all its stages. To our college, St John's, we are indebted for many facilities which eased and expedited our work. To Cornell University Library, and to the Bodleian Library, in particular Mr D. G. Vaisey and his staff, we are thankful for the services and space provided for us. To Mr C. Morgenstern we are most grateful for advice about lay-out and typography.

Mr J. M. Baker, Mr M. A. E. Dummett, Dr W. Künne, Mr B. F. McGuinness, Professor J. Meiland, Mr B. Rundle and Dr C. Wright all gave us generous help, advice, and criticism in reading and commenting on various parts of early drafts, raising numerous questions, answering queries and in general stimulating us into rethinking our position on many issues. Mr T. J. Reed put at our disposal his extensive knowledge of German literature and also aided us in translating difficult passages. Dr A. J. P. Kenny and Dr J. Raz read and commented on substantial portions of the text and gave us the benefit of much advice and constructive criticism. Above all we are indebted to Dr Joachim Schulte, who not only read the whole typescript and gave us extensive and penetrating criticisms of earlier versions, but also checked all our German transcriptions and translations. His help has been invaluable, his kindness memorable.

Finally, we are grateful to the Wittgenstein executors for permission to quote from the unpublished *Nachlass*. In particular we are indebted to Professor G. H. von Wright for his generosity in sending us the results of his extensive bibliographical research into the *Nachlass*, and for his kindness in answering numerous questions.

G.P.B. & P.M.S.H.
St John's College, Oxford
1978

Thoughts reduced to paper are generally nothing more than the footprints of a man walking in the sand. It is true that we see the path he has taken; but to know what he saw on the way, we must use our own eyes.

Schopenhauer

Introduction

The *Philosophical Investigations* was published a quarter of a century ago. It was hailed by some as the masterpiece of the 'first philosopher of the age'. Others have viewed it as a haphazard collection of perhaps profound, but at any rate exceedingly obscure, aperçus. Russell, at the other extreme, could see no merit in it whatsoever.

It is evident that the philosophical community is far from clear what it has received. Despite a veritable flood of secondary writings, there is little consensus on the main contour lines of the book, let alone upon details of interpretation. Although it is written in a lucid, non-technical style, and although individual remarks appear superficially clear (and often innocuous), the *Philosophical Investigations* is an exceedingly difficult book to understand. The welter of conflicting interpretations and contradictory evaluations bear witness to the fact that philosophers have found it baffling and opaque.

At the grand-strategic level some have argued that the *Investigations* is a further development of the philosophy propounded in the *Tractatus*, adding to and modifying, but by no means demolishing, the core of that work. Others have seen it as a wholly new departure, built upon the ashes of a magnificent failure. So its relation to its august predecessor, though crucial to its correct interpretation, is unclear. All agree that its structure is often non-sequential, but some claim that it is wholly lacking in order and that this indeed reflects Wittgenstein's repudiation of any systematicity in philosophizing. Others have discerned behind the apparently unruly organization a highly systematic philosophy, e.g., a generalization to philosophy of language of the principles of an intuitionist philosophy of mathematics. So it is unclear whether Wittgenstein propounds any integrated coherent philosophy—in method, in conception of the nature of the problems, or in their resolution. Many of Wittgenstein's remarks have a pronounced negative tinge. Some commentators hold that the *Investigations* is, as it were, a prolegomenon to any future philosophy—a prolegomenon which is followed by deafening silence. If the *Tractatus* was the swan-song of metaphysics, this seems the death-knell of philosophy. This is belied by the indisputable fertility of the book, most obviously in the philosophy of mind, which had changed but little since the eighteenth century. Is the *Investigations* intended as the final negation of all philosophy?

Similar polarization of views has occurred at the strategic level. Wittgenstein frequently appeals to our ordinary use of words (in contrast with philosophers' misuse). He has, by some, been classified (and abused) as an 'ordinary language philosopher' (and grouped with J. L. Austin). But for an 'ordinary language philosopher' he appeals remarkably infrequently to subtleties of idiom and usage beloved by Austinians. Again, he often raises questions of how language is learnt, how a child is taught to use a given expression. Is this not armchair learning theory? Would it not be preferable to substitute empirical data from psycholinguists? And how are considerations of learning and teaching furthered by constructing imaginary systems of communication and imaginary procedures for instructing imaginary half-wits to operate them? In his reflections upon meaning, he hints at numerous apparent equations: meaning is use, sense is given by assertion-conditions, how a sentence is verified will reveal what it means, etc. These are not obviously consistent, let alone equivalent. On top of this he denies the legitimacy in philosophy of *any* theories—but are *these* pronouncements not theories? Is not inconsistency here piled upon inconsistency?

The tactical level is no less baffling. Wittgenstein begins the book with a sketch of Augustine's remarks on how he conceived himself to have learnt language. What is the point of *that*? It was not part of Augustine's philosophy but of his autobiography, and it is not evidently a view any philosopher has adhered to. He criticizes ostensive definition at length, yet also argues that ostensive definition is as legitimate a form of definition as the most rigorous *Merkmal*-definition (even of numerals!). He embarks upon a long discussion of vagueness, in an apparent criticism of Frege. But what is his point? To add a smudge-operator to a neo-Fregean semantics? To insist that ordinary language is everywhere vague, and *then* to say that that is just as it should be? Between §§156 and 178 he interpolates a detailed discussion of reading. But what is the point of his showing that reading, deriving, being guided, etc., are family resemblance concepts? To many his philosophy of mind seems a form of behaviourism—neither original nor reputable.

At the level of interpretation of particular passages and lines, no less confusion reigns. Are his remarks on Frege's assertion-sign an agreement or disagreement with Frege? Can a supporter of phrastics and neustics invoke the footnote about sentence-radicals in favour of his theses or not? Is the single sentence about the standard metre being neither a metre long nor not a metre long a piece of wilful obscurantism (does he *really* mean to say that the metre bar has no length)?

These interminable controversies provided part of our motive in undertaking the task of trying to explain in detail, as well as delineate in general, the argument of the *Philosophical Investigations*. This perhaps betokens lack of adequate humility—rushing in (with the rest of the crowd) where the wise (if not the angels) wait. It has been suggested to us that it is too soon to embark on such a project. We were, however, emboldened by three considerations. First, the increased accessibility of the Wittgenstein *Nachlass* made some of our aims reasonably realistic. The *Nachlass* throws invaluable light not only upon particular passages of the *Investigations*, but also upon the development of Wittgenstein's thought after 1929. Secondly, if this kind of project were delayed for another half-century or more, the intellectual milieu and philosophical atmosphere of Wittgenstein's work (in particular Frege, Russell, the Vienna Circle), already increasingly remote for our generation, will be irremediably alien (cf. the fate of Kant's *Critique*). The risks of distortion and misunderstanding that we have had to run through lack of a longer perspective, though serious, must be balanced against the dangers of losing through the passage of time valuable information about, and sensitivity to, the problem-setting context of Wittgenstein's work. Finally, it is not unknown (here again Kant springs to mind) for great philosophical insights to be lost through misunderstanding, dogmatic misinterpretation, tides of fashion, and a naïve belief in progress. Although almost all Wittgenstein's philosophy bears directly upon central issues of current philosophical debate, usually negatively, much of it is ignored, to the detriment of the resultant 'theories'. Take, e.g., so-called 'philosophical semantics', thought by many to constitute the centre of the philosophical universe. If this activity is to be profitable, the semanticist must clarify (or at least consider!) what counts as 'giving the meaning' of an expression, how this is related to ordinary explanations and how those are related to meaning, since he aims to produce a theory of *meaning*. The concept of explanation cannot be allowed to take care of itself while the semanticist takes care of possible worlds, builds Chinese boxes of speakers' intentions, and 'postulates' abstract entities. Similarly, since such 'theories of meaning' purport to be systems of *rules*, we must first grasp the nature of rules, their role and application. It is foolish to concentrate exclusively on the precise formulation of meaning-rules and to ignore the issue of how grasping a meaning-rule is internally related to linguistic behaviour. Through misunderstanding or neglect, numerous controversies take place in blithe ignorance or disregard of powerful arguments in Wittgenstein's writings which, wholly or partly, undermine their presuppositions, methods, or putative resolutions. One of our hopes is that this study will go some way to remedy what seems to us a deplorable state of affairs. Whether Wittgenstein's arguments are correct or not, they should be confronted. They pose the questions to shake up the fashionable solutions to many of the problems of philosophy.

  This volume consists of seventeen essays bearing on the main themes discussed by Wittgenstein in §§1–184 of the *Investigations*. They also delineate, where relevant, the development of his views from 1929 onwards. Occasionally (e.g. in 'Ostensive definition and its ramifications', 'Proper names') we have tried to develop and extend ideas that are merely embryonic in his writings but whose implications seemed to us to merit more extensive examination. We have tried to make each essay as self-contained as possible, sometimes at the cost of a moderate degree of repetition. Nevertheless, there are multiple links between them. Early essays often draw blank cheques on later arguments, and arguments in later essays unavoidably presuppose points established in earlier ones. However, since the essays were originally written as accompaniments to the exegesis, now published as a separate volume, some matters that are examined in great detail in the exegesis are omitted from the essays. Consequently *some* of the evidence supporting our interpretations is not to be found here but in the companion volume *An Analytical Commentary on Wittgenstein's* PHILOSOPHICAL INVESTIGATIONS. The marked lacunae are but two: our detailed anatomization of Wittgenstein's criticism of Frege's distinction between sense and force occurs in a 16 page discussion of *Investigations* §22 and page 11 note, and our reasons for *not* pinning on Wittgenstein a 'cluster-theory' of proper names are spelt out in a seven page analysis of §79. These supplement the essays 'Uses of sentences' and 'Proper names' respectively.

The order of the essays reflects the order of the argument of §§1–184 of the *Investigations*; read sequentially they are intended to provide a reasonably comprehensive grasp of the salient themes in this part of the book. However, the reader may wonder why we stopped short at this point in the *Investigations*. Considerations of space apart, many reasons justify this decision. This dividing line corresponds most closely to the 1937 version (PPI), which ends at PI §189, and to that extent forms a unitary fragment. Consequently, the vast majority of the sources antedate 1938. The sequel raises a host of fresh problems needing detailed treatment. First, one must consider the various plans for the continuation of PPI, in particular Wittgenstein's work in philosophy of mathematics. Why was this originally conceived to belong here, and why did Wittgenstein change his mind? Secondly, one must consider the further attempts to complete the book (i.e. the 1943 and 1945 versions), as well as the compilation of *Bemerkungen I* (TS. 228) and its cannibalization for the final version of the *Investigations*. Thirdly, the source material for the sequel, especially §§198–427, dates largely (though not exclusively) from 1938–45, in particular 1944–5, hence presents a new set of 'archaeological' problems. These three reasons concern the structure and history of the book.

Nevertheless, since §§143–242 surely form the heart of the argument of the *Investigations*, should we not then have continued until §243? Historical reasons apart, two further considerations militated against this.

Although §§143–242 form an integral unity, the sequel to §242, i.e. the private language argument, is a crucially important and immediate application of the conclusions drawn from the rich argument of those hundred sections. So it would be no more justifiable to stop at §243 than at §184. Secondly, the sheer number of central philosophical topics so densely packed in §§185–242 (e.g. necessity and possibility, rules and their application, identity, agreement in judgements and definitions) require such detailed consideration and necessitate drawing so heavily from sources in Wittgenstein's philosophy of mathematics, as to make it quite impracticable to try to encompass all this in the scope of one volume.

If we are right in considering §§143–242 as the core of the book, and liken it to a mountain range that must be crossed before Wittgenstein's philosophy can be understood (and, among other things, the famous private language argument seen aright), then this volume, *Wittgenstein–Understanding and Meaning*, can be seen as taking us to the top of the mountain passes. A subsequent volume, to be entitled *Wittgenstein–Meaning and Mind* (occasionally referred to in the text as 'Volume 2') will pick up the threads and attempt to unravel the mysteries enveloping Wittgenstein's discussions of what it is for something to follow from, be derived from or necessitated by, a rule. And it will then go on to apply these insights not only to obtain a better grasp of meaning and understanding but also to cast fresh light on philosophy of mind. For the time being, a synoptic view of what has been achieved up to this point in the *Investigations* is adumbrated in the concluding essay of this volume: 'Meaning and understanding'.

Three final points: use, grammar, and criteria. Given the prominence of the slogan 'meaning is use', it may seem surprising that we have no essay on the subject of the use of words in general. It has rightly been remarked that the term 'use' *in vacuo* is too nebulous to give much guidance. But Wittgenstein's employment of the term is by no means nebulous: in each context his point is clear. Relative to each context, we have tried to explain in detail what he meant. If that enterprise is successful, there is nothing more to be said. For it should be clear enough that the whole of this book and its companion volume of exegesis is, either directly or obliquely, concerned with exploring the significance and ramifications of Wittgenstein's revolutionary association of the meanings of linguistic expressions with their uses in the actions and transactions of human beings. Secondly, Wittgenstein's use of the term 'grammar' is unusual and idiosyncratic. It will be scrutinized in detail in Volume 2. In the meantime we have followed his use. Thirdly, the controversial term 'criterion' is frequently invoked in the following pages. Our employment of it is not intended to be arcane or theory-laden, and in these respects is intended to match Wittgenstein's own use. By it we mean something that is *a priori*, defeasible evidence for something else. Doubtless much seems problematic here, and to the extent that this is so we have in fact drawn a blank cheque upon Volume 2, in which the topic will be thoroughly discussed. We would have liked to consider everything at once. But because of 'merely medical limitations', we have had to content ourselves with a linear exposition. Clarifying the concept of a criterion cannot be done successfully prior to (independently of) a correct conception of meaning, and, conversely, this conception turns on the notion of criteria of understanding. Wittgenstein's philosophy is like a stone arch; each stone supports all of the others—or, at least, nothing stands up until everything is in place. What we have tried to do in this volume is to prepare the place for each stone, although of course not everything is yet in place.

Abbreviations

1. *Published works*

The following abbreviations are used to refer to Wittgenstein's published works, listed in chronological order (where possible; some works straddle many years). The list includes derivative primary sources, i.e. Waismann's books,[1] and lecture notes taken by others.

NB   *Notebooks 1914–16*, ed. G. H. von Wright and G. E. M. Anscombe, tr. G. E. M. Anscombe (Blackwell, Oxford, 1961).

PT   *Prototractatus—An Early Version of Tractatus Logico-Philosophicus*, ed. B. F. McGuinness, T. Nyberg, G. H. von Wright, tr. D. F. Pears and B. F. McGuinness (Routledge and Kegan Paul, London, 1971).

TLP   *Tractatus Logico-Philosophicus*, tr. D. F. Pears and B. F. McGuinness (Routledge and Kegan Paul, London, 1961).

LF   'Some Remarks on Logical Form', *Proceedings of the Aristotelian Society*, supp. vol. ix (1929), pp. 162–71.

WWK   *Ludwig Wittgenstein und der Wiener Kreis*, shorthand notes recorded by F. Waismann, ed. B. F. McGuinness (Blackwell, Oxford, 1967).

PR   *Philosophical Remarks*, ed. R. Rhees, tr. R. Hargreaves and R. White (Blackwell, Oxford, 1975).

LE   'A Lecture on Ethics', *Philosophical Review* 74 (1965), pp. 3–12.

M   'Wittgenstein's Lectures in 1930–33', in G. E. Moore, *Philosophical Papers* (Allen and Unwin, London, 1959).

PG   *Philosophical Grammar*, ed. R. Rhees, tr. A. J. P. Kenny (Blackwell, Oxford, 1974).

GB   'Remarks on Frazer's "Golden Bough"', tr. A. C. Miles and R. Rhees, *The Human World* no. 3 (May 1971), pp. 28–41.

BB   *The Blue and Brown Books* (Blackwell, Oxford, 1958). Occasionally 'Bl.B.' and 'Br.B.' are used for special reference.

[1] For the history of the composition of these books and their importance for the study of Wittgenstein's philosophy, see G. P. Baker, '*Verehrung und Verkehrung*: Waismann and Wittgenstein' in *Wittgenstein: Sources and Perspectives*, ed. G. Luckhardt (Cornell University Press, Ithaca, 1979).

LPE   'Wittgenstein's Notes for Lectures on "Private Experience" and
       "Sense Data"', ed. R. Rhees, *Philosophical Review* 77 (1968),
       pp. 275–320.

EPB   *Eine Philosophische Betrachtung*, ed. R. Rhees, in *Ludwig Wittgen-
       stein: Schriften 5* (Suhrkamp, Frankfurt, 1970).

RFM   *Remarks on the Foundations of Mathematics*, ed. G. H. von Wright,
       R. Rhees, G. E. M. Anscombe, tr. G. E. M. Anscombe, revised
       edition (Blackwell, Oxford, 1978).

LA   *Lectures and Conversation on Aesthetics, Psychology and Religious
       Beliefs*, ed. C. Barrett (Blackwell, Oxford, 1970).

LFM   *Wittgenstein's Lectures on the Foundations of Mathematics, Cambridge
       1939*, ed. C. Diamond (Harvester Press, Sussex, 1976).

PI   *Philosophical Investigations*, ed. G. E. M. Anscombe and R. Rhees,
       tr. G. E. M. Anscombe, 2nd edition (Blackwell, Oxford,
       1958).

Z   *Zettel*, ed. G. E. M. Anscombe and G. H. von Wright, tr. G. E. M.
       Anscombe (Blackwell, Oxford, 1967).

C   *On Certainty*, ed. G. E. M. Anscombe and G. H. von Wright, tr.
       D. Paul and G. E. M. Anscombe (Blackwell, Oxford, 1969).

RC   *Remarks on Colour*, ed. G. E. M. Anscombe, tr. L. L. McAlister and
       M. Schättle (Blackwell, Oxford, [1977]).

EMD   *Einführung in das mathematische Denken*, F. Waismann (Gerold,
       Vienna, 1936).

IMT   *Introduction to Mathematical Thinking*, F. Waismann, tr. T. J. Benac
       (Hafner, London, 1951).

PLP   *The Principles of Linguistic Philosopy*, F. Waismann, ed. R. Harré
       (Macmillan and St Martin's Press, London and New York,
       1965).

LSP   *Logik, Sprache, Philosophie*, F. Waismann mit einer Vorrede von
       M. Schlick, herausgegeben von G. P. Baker und B. McGuinness
       unter Mitwirkung von J. Schulte (Reclam, Stuttgart, 1976).

Reference style: all references to *Philosophical Investigations* Part I are to
sections (e.g. PI §1), except those to notes below the line on various pages.
References to Part II are to pages (e.g. PI p. 202). References to other
printed works are either to numbered remarks (TLP, PT) or to sections
(Z) signified '§'; in all other cases references are to pages (e.g. LFM 21 =
LFM page 21).

2. *Nachlass*

All references to unpublished material cited in the von Wright catalogue
(*Philosophical Review* 78 (1969), pp. 483–503) are by MS. or TS. number

followed by page number. Wherever possible, we make use of the pagination or foliation entered in the original document (although these numerations follow no uniform pattern). For memorability, we have introduced the following special abbreviations.

Manuscripts

Vol. I refer to the eighteen large manuscript volumes (= MSS. 105–22)
Vol. II written between 2 February 1929 and 1944. The reference style
etc. Vol. VI, 241 is to Volume VI, page 241. References to Vol. X, Um. refer to W.'s pagination of the *Umarbeitung* of the 'Big Typescript'. The *Umarbeitung* begins on folio 31^b of Vol. X and is consecutively paginated 1–228.
C1 refer to eight notebooks (= MSS. 145–52) written between 1933
to and 1936. The reference style C3, 42 is to C3, page 42.
C8

Typescripts

EBT 'Early Big Typescript' (TS. 211): a typescript composed from Vols. VI–X, 1932, 771 pp. All references are to page numbers.
BT The 'Big Typescript' (TS. 213): a rearrangement, with modifications, written additions and deletions, of EBT, 1933, vi pp. table of contents, 768 pp. All references are to page numbers. Where the numeral is followed by 'v.', this indicates a handwritten addition on the reverse side of the TS. page.
PPI 'Proto-Philosophical Investigations'[1] (TS. 220): a typescript of the first half of the pre-war version of the *Philosophical Investigations* (up to §189 of the final version, but with many differences); 1937 or 1938, 137 pp. All references are to sections (§).
PPI(R) R. Rhees's pre-war translation of PPI (TS. 226): this goes up to PPI §95 (= PI §107), and is extensively corrected in Wittgenstein's hand; 1939, 72 pp. All references are to sections (§).
PPI(A) a fragmentary carbon copy of PPI consisting of part of a rearrangement of PPI §§96–116 with renumberings, corrections and additions in Wittgenstein's hand. It is not cited in the catalogue. All references are to sections.
PPI(B) a 137-page typescript (not cited in the catalogue) consisting of the four-page 1945 preface and a carbon copy of PPI with renumberings, corrections and additions in Wittgenstein's hand. PPI(B) §§109–48 consists of a rearrangement of PPI §§93–116, which correspond to PPI(A). PPI(A) and (B) were compiled sometime between 1939 and 1945. The fragments of PPI(A) are nearly identi-

---

[1] Our title.

cal with the corresponding parts of (B). The corrections throughout PPI(B) are generally closely followed in TS. 227 (the final
typescript). (Where the fragmentary PPI(A) differs from (B) it is
(B) that is followed in TS. 227.) All references are to sections.

PPI(I)   The so-called 'Intermediate Version', reconstructed by von
Wright; it consists of 300 numbered remarks; 1945, 195 pp. All
references are to sections (§).

B i   *Bemerkungen I* (TS. 228), 1945–6, 185 pp. All references are to
sections (§).

3. *Abbreviations for works by Frege*

BG   *Begriffsschrift, eine der arithmetischen nachgebildete Formelsprache des
reinen Denkens* (Halle a/S., 1879).

FA   *The Foundations of Arithmetic*, tr. J. L. Austin, 2nd edition (Blackwell, Oxford, 1959).

FC   'Function and Concept' ⎤   in *Translations from the Philosophical*
CO   'On Concept and Object'⎟   *Writings of Gottlob Frege*,
SR   'On Sense and Reference'⎟   ed. Peter Geach and
N   'Negation' ⎦   Max Black (Blackwell, Oxford, 1960).

GAi,ii   *Grundgesetze der Arithmetik, begriffsschriftlich abgeleitet*, Band I,
1893, Band II, 1903 (Hermann Pohle, Jena).

FG   *On the Foundations of Geometry and Formal Theories of Arithmetic*, ed.
and tr. E.-H. W. Kluge (Yale University Press, New Haven, 1971).

T   'The Thought', repr. in *Philosophical Logic*, ed. P. F. Strawson
(Oxford University Press, London, 1967).

NS   *Nachgelassene Schriften*, ed. H. Hermes, F. Kambartel, F. Kaulbach
(Felix Meiner Verlag, Hamburg, 1969).

4. *Abbreviations for works by Russell*

PrM   *The Principles of Mathematics*, 2nd edition (revised) (Allen and
Unwin, London, 1937).

PM i   *Principia Mathematica*, Vol. i (with A. N. Whitehead), 2nd edition
(Cambridge University Press, Cambridge, 1927).

PP   *The Problems of Philosophy* (Home University Library, London,
1912).

OK   *Our Knowledge of the External World as a Field for Scientific Method in
Philosophy*, revised edition (Allen and Unwin, London, 1926).

LA   'The Philosophy of Logical Atomism', in *Logic and Knowledge,
Essays 1901–1950*, ed. R. C. Marsh, pp. 175–281 (Allen and
Unwin, London, 1956).

ML   *Mysticism and Logic* (Longmans, Green, London, 1918).
IMP   *Introduction to Mathematical Philosophy* (Allen and Unwin, London, 1919).
AM   *Analysis of Mind* (Allen and Unwin, London, 1921).

I

AUGUSTINE'S PICTURE OF LANGUAGE:
das Wesen der Sprache

1. *Introduction*

The *Investigations* opens with a quotation in which Augustine describes how he learned language as a child. Wittgenstein detects in this description a picture of the essence of human language: the individual words of a language are names of objects and sentences are combinations of names. He extracts from Augustine's description of learning a language what he refers to as 'Augustine's conception of language' (PI §4; BT 25) or 'Augustine's description of language' (PI §§2 f., 32; BT 27; EPB 117).

For the purpose of introducing a discussion of meaning, this sketch of a picture of language is too bare. Wittgenstein develops it immediately. He treats the idea that every word is the name of an object as the root of a more complex conception, articulated in three theses: (i) every word has a meaning; (ii) this meaning is something correlated with the word; (iii) it is the object for which the word stands. This triad of theses is not the only possible way to articulate the idea that every word names an object. But they are an integral part of what Wittgenstein calls 'Augustine's conception (or description) of language'.

Wittgenstein makes at least two further immediate extensions of the initial sketch. First, Augustine's conception is equated with the thesis that ostensive definition is the fundamental form of explaining the meaning of a word (BT 25, cf. PLP 94). This is a natural interpretation of Augustine's description of learning language, and it might seem a corollary of taking the meaning of a word to be the object named by it. This thesis informs Wittgenstein's description of the slab–game (PI §§2, 6). It also motivates the lengthy discussion of ostensive definition. Secondly, Augustine's picture is equated with the thesis that every sentence is a description of something; or, alternatively, that naming and describing constitute the two essential functions of language. This might seem a corollary of treating sentences as combinations of names, since the uniform structure of sentences does not provide for differentiation in function. Though this thesis is not explicit, it underlies the discussion of the uses of sentences (PI §§18 ff., 363) and various remarks about descriptions (PI §§180 f., 290 f., 585). According to Wittgenstein, Augustine's picture includes the claims that ostensive definition and describing belong to the essence of language, even though these theses are extensions of the original bare sketch.

Just what belongs to an Augustinian picture of language? What are its limits? These questions have no precise answers. None are needed, and none would be appropriate. A philosophical picture (or 'theory') can be known only by its fruits. What matters is how it is applied, what consequences are squeezed out of it. The idea that every word is a name and every sentence a combination of names says nothing about what words or sentences mean, what it is to understand an expression, or what it is to explain its meaning. At best, the picture suggests answers to these questions. Therefore, an examination of it must start by elaborating the picture, filling in necessary details, and extracting their implications. Wittgenstein mentions many theses that seem natural ingredients of any more fully worked-out version of the initial bare sketch, and he examines and criticizes these in different writings. Criticism of these theses will constitute cogent criticism of the initial picture only to the extent that they are natural developments of it; i.e. only to the extent that we are inclined to acknowledge that these must be what was really meant by thinking of words as names and sentences as combinations of names. As long as *most* of the theses are acknowledged as integral parts of this initial picture, effective criticisms of them will undeniably undermine Augustine's picture even if there is a margin for dispute about precisely which theses belong to this picture and which are external to it. In this case nothing will turn on how these disputes are resolved. If Wittgenstein's subsequent discussion is to be related to his opening presentation of Augustine's picture, then we cannot say that this picture includes nothing apart from the initial pair of theses. But once we include more in 'Augustine's picture of language', there is no unequivocal boundary separating what falls within it from what falls without. At best we can articulate a number of theses that seem entirely natural supplements of the original pair—a normal form of the Augustinian picture.

This would have a diagnostic function. Numerous sophisticated accounts of meaning are unconsciously rooted in the Augustinian picture, and this manifests a disease of the intellect. This will have *many* symptoms. But a philosopher need not exhibit all of them to be diagnosed as suffering from this disease. Rather, the disease manifests itself in a syndrome of symptoms. Comparison with the normal form of the Augustinian picture facilitates identification of those exhibiting a form of this syndrome. Developing the normal form might also have a therapeutic role.

We are inclined to be captivated by simple pictures, either consciously or unconsciously. It seems illuminating to think of all words as names. The application of this picture we leave to take care of itself. *Somehow* (though we know not how) this *must* account for how words are understood, how they are explained, how they fit together into sentences, etc. *Simplex sigillum veri*: part of the charm of the picture is its simplicity and naïvety.

As soon as we reflect on how to apply the primitive picture, to work out the *details* of its application, we encounter difficulties. It is part of the magic of the picture that we meet these difficulties not by jettisoning the picture itself but by introducing refinements and qualifications. We deal with problems *seriatim*, erecting ever more complex and sophisticated structures. As we pile epicycle on epicycle, the sheer ingenuity of the construction exercises its own fascination. Moreover, the greater the elegance of the developed 'theory', the more closely it approximates to the ideal of a scientific theory—an ideal towards which we are all attracted. If philosophy is in pursuit of knowledge, must it not take the form of a *theory?*

The fact that the *Investigations* opens with an exposition of Augustine's picture of language is itself important. It reflects a watershed in Wittgenstein's attempts in the 1930s to organize his remarks into a publishable book. The 'Big Typescript' and its three revisions (Vols. X–XI, MS. 140, and Vol. XII) begin differently. The opening chapter in each of them consists in a discussion of meaning and understanding, in particular of what it is to understand a sentence. They argue that meaning something and understanding are not mental events that give life to the dead signs of language (cf. BB 1). Conceived as mental events, meaning (*Meinen*) and understanding drop out of a proper philosophical account of language (BT §1 ff.). Wittgenstein then indicates a correct conception of understanding and explanation. Augustine's picture is introduced and discussed only in the second 'chapter', after this preliminary. By contrast, the *Brown Book* (with its revisions, MS. 141, EPB) and the *Investigations* (in all its versions) open with the discussion of Augustine's picture. What motivated this change of strategy must be a matter of conjecture. It *might* have been that Wittgenstein was struck by the misleadingness of his starting by saying that meaning and understanding drop out of the consideration of language when in the sequel he argued that questions about meaning should be treated as questions about understanding. (The paradox is only apparent, of course: understanding 'drops out' only when misconceived as a private mental event, whereas properly understood it is the key to a correct account of meaning. But, though only apparent, the paradox might well obstruct a reader's vision of Wittgenstein's argument.) Whatever its motivation, the change of strategy is noteworthy.

2. *The Augustinian picture*

A prerequisite to an examination of Augustine's picture of language is to elaborate the idea that all words are names, all sentences combinations of names. This is necessary to assess the extent to which this picture informs theories of meaning which Wittgenstein was criticizing, and hence to judge the consequences of his criticisms of its fundamental aspects. Its elaboration into a set of more detailed theses is guided by two principles. First, these theses should be natural, smooth extensions of the primitive picture. Secondly, they should be directly related to arguments in Wittgenstein's writings. This leaves some room for disagreements, but nothing important should turn on their resolution.

Augustine's conception of language is an *Urbild*. The family of philosophical accounts of meaning that grow out of it are full-blown 'theories'. This family we will call 'the Augustinian picture'.

(A) Word-meaning and ostensive definition

(i) Any significant word signifies something. Its meaning is what it stands for or signifies. It is assigned a meaning by correlating it with an object. Such a correlation gives it a meaning by making it into a name of an object. It represents the object that it stands for. If a word signifies nothing, it is meaningless. (TLP 3.203; PI §§1, 40–3; PLP 311 ff.; PM i.66; LA 200 f.)

(ii) Explanations of meaning can be roughly divided into verbal and ostensive definitions (BB 1). Since verbal definitions merely explain one expression by means of others and hence constitute connections within language, ostensive definitions provide the only possible means for correlating words with things. Only an utterance of the form 'That is . . .', together with the gesture of pointing at something, can be used to correlate a word with a thing (PLP 95, 277 f.). There must be ostensive definitions in *every* language[1] (PLP 107, cf. BT 46). They are necessary for language to represent reality.

(iii) The thesis that all words are names is equivalent to the thesis that the fundamental form of explanation of words is ostensive definition, that ostensive definitions are the foundation of language (BT 25, cf. PLP 195f.). The meaning of every expression can be immediately or proximately explained only by means of ostensive definitions. Hence there must be a whole system of ostensive definitions in every language. (PLP 107; 'die primäre Sprache'; cf. BT 46–56.)

(iv) Every ostensive definition forges a link between language and the world (PLP 107; WWK 246; BT 54). It generates a tie between a word and a thing (BT 173). By means of any ostensive definition 'we seem to pass beyond the limits of language and to establish a connection with reality itself' (PLP 277; BT 42, cf. 172; cf. also WWK 249).

---

[1] Cf. B. Russell, *An Inquiry into Meaning and Truth* (Allen and Unwin, London, 1940), pp. 65, 290.

(v) Any details about the method used to correlate a word with a thing are irrelevant for considering its meaning. All that matters is the bare fact that it *is* correlated with a particular object.[2] The rest is of merely psychological or historical interest (cf. PT 3.202111).

(vi) An ostensive definition (like a stipulative verbal definition) forges a timeless link between a word and a thing. Any given thing either is or is not identical with the thing timelessly correlated with a particular word by a particular ostensive definition. This is independent of whether we can settle this question, of whether we can reidentify this object, *a fortiori* of how we might try to reidentify it. The same is the same—the rest is a matter of psychology (cf. PI §377).

(vii) The meaning of a name is invariant in all its applications, whatever the context of its occurrence. It always stands for the same object. (It has a meaning independently of the sentences in which it occurs (cf. PM i. 66).)

(B) The 'completeness' of ostensive definition

(i) It must be possible for an ostensive definition of an unanalysable word to be a complete explanation of the meaning of this word; for it to be final and unambiguous. Otherwise, ostensive definition could not provide the foundations of language. If every ostensive definition were ambiguous or left open questions about the application of the defined word, it would require supplementation, and, unless this were itself further ostensive explanation, something other than ostensive definition would be necessary to secure the foundations of language. Any attempt to supplement an ostensive definition of a primitive expression must be either redundant or inconsistent with the meaning already assigned to it.

(ii) Any final, unambiguous ostensive definition must completely determine what counts as a correct use of the defined expression (and what counts as an incorrect use). It must settle all aspects of the use of the definiendum. Therefore any principles governing this use must 'flow' from it, i.e. from the fact that this expression is thereby correlated with a particular thing (BT 164–6; PLP 61 f.). This can be represented by the analogy of meaning-bodies (*Bedeutungskörper*) (BT 166 f.; PG 54; PLP 234–7). The rules for correct use of a word express the nature of what is correlated with it as its meaning, just as the combinatorial possibilities of a set of coloured triangles would be determined by the invisible glass prisms of which each triangle was a single painted face. Meaning-rules express the geometry of meaning-bodies. The meaning of a word determines its whole use, and an ostensive definition completely determines its meaning.

---

[2] Ibid., p. 294.

(iii) Since they flow from the essential nature of the thing correlated with the word, meaning-rules express the essential features of the world. This guarantees a metaphysical harmony between language and the world. The essence of language *is* the essence of the world (cf. BT 62 f., PI §96).

(iv) Necessary truths fall into two classes, analytic and synthetic. Analytic truths follow from verbal definitions of their constituents, i.e. they can be transformed into logical truths by means of verbal definitions. Unless this is possible, a necessary truth is synthetic. Consequently, if there are any necessary truths concerning the referents of indefinables, these must be synthetic. They reflect the essential natures of the objects correlated by ostensive definitions with these words (just as laws of physics describe the physical properties of objects). If, e.g., an ostensive definition gives a full and final explanation of each colour-word, then the necessary truth that nothing is red and green all over must flow from the nature of the colours red and green. Each of these colours must, as it were, get in the other's way so that both cannot simultaneously occupy the same position, just as two people cannot sit on a single chair (LF 169; PR 106 f.; cf. PrM 233). (The 'completeness' of ostensive definitions of primitive expressions seems to make room for synthetic necessary truths (cf. PLP 59, PrM 233).)

(v) Ostensive definitions do not respect differences of logical type or category. Words of different kinds can be so defined, e.g. proper names, adjectives for perceptual qualities, action-verbs, and sortal nouns (BT 25; PI §1). Category-differences, hence the combinatorial possibilities of words, must flow from the essential natures of the objects correlated with words. It is part of the nature of a tone, e.g., that it has a pitch but not a colour, that it makes no sense to say of a particular tone that it is red, but does make sense to say that it is higher than middle-C. The 'logical grammar' or 'logical syntax' of language is something given by the logical structure of the world (TLP 2.01231, 2.0131, 2.0141, 4.123–4.1241; WWK 240).

(C) 'Psychological' aspects of word-meaning

(i) Understanding a word consists in correlating it with the object that is its meaning, i.e. in associating a word with a thing. (If a word is correlated with nothing, there is no such thing as understanding it.) Giving a word a meaning and meaning something by a word are both correlative to understanding. To give a word a meaning is to bring it about that the word is understood in a particular way, i.e. that it is correlated with a particular object. To mean something by a word is to intend that it be understood in a particular way, i.e. that a particular object should be associated with it.

(ii) Since understanding seems to be a mental activity, we are inclined to characterize the content of understanding as being 'in the mind'. Understanding consists in a *mental* association of a word with an object (cf. LA 186 f., 204 f.). The word is correlated with its meaning by means of the *intention* that it should stand for this thing. The mechanism of the correlation is itself a mental one; hence, the correlation itself is 'psychological' (NB 99, cf. BT 12 f., 173). Understanding is, as it were, a form of mental pointing at an object, a way of projecting language on to the world. (So too, therefore, is meaning something by a word.) Meaning and understanding are activities separate from the physical activity of uttering or writing words; they take place in the medium of the mind, give life to language (BB 3 f.; BT 1, 13; cf. PG 41, 44 f.).

(iii) Understanding consists, either immediately or proximately, in acquaintance with things. Ostensive definition presupposes confrontation with the thing named by the defined word, since otherwise it could not effect an association of this thing with the word. If ostensive definition is the foundation of language, then acquaintance is the foundation of understanding (LA 201, 204 f.). (Cf. Russell's principle of acquaintance, PP 58, LA 193–6.)

(iv) There can be no understanding of an indefinable (unanalysable) word without acquaintance with the correlated thing (LA 197, 201).[3] If acquaintance requires a mental representative of the object of acquaintance, then every simple idea presupposes a corresponding experience or impression. Each distinct kind of word presupposes a corresponding kind of experience; e.g. perceptions for perceptual properties, and 'logical experience' for logical indefinables.[4]

(v) There are no degrees of understanding primitive words. Either one grasps the meaning of such a word fully or one does not know its meaning at all. The association of a word and a thing is either right or wrong. There are no degrees of acquaintance with the thing named by a primitive word. (A contrary impression might arise from conflating acquaintance with a thing and knowledge of its external properties. These are logically independent. Acquaintance does not amount to knowledge of all the truths about a thing (OK 144 ff., cf. TLP 2.01231, LA 204).)

(vi) Acquaintance with the thing that is its meaning must give a full understanding of a word. A person must be able to 'read off' from his acquaintance with this object the whole of the 'logical grammar' of the correlated word. He must be able to recognize what are the principles governing the correct use of the word on the basis of a careful scrutiny of the object. A full understanding of the word must be encapsulated in his acquaintance with the thing; ready, as it were, to be extracted by mental

---

[3] Cf. also B. Russell, 'Theory of Knowledge' (unpublished manuscript in the Russell archives at McMaster University, 1913?), p. 305.

[4] Ibid., p. 181.

alchemy (cf. PG 50, BB 39 f.). For if the logical grammar of a word is laid up in the nature of the correlated object, and if understanding a word presupposes a grasp of its logical grammar, then this knowledge must be laid up in that acquaintance the object of which gives a complete understanding of the word (a form of harmony between language and thought).

(vii) Complete understanding of an unanalysable word is achieved at a flash, if at all. It consists in becoming acquainted with the object named. This is conceived as an instantaneous mental event (especially since it is independent of knowing external truths about the object of acquaintance). Since it gives full understanding of the word, it must determine the entire future use of the word. Hence, it seems, a momentary event has effects that unfold only over an indefinitely extended period. Accordingly, it is natural to treat the correct applications of a word and explanations of the rules for its proper use as 'symptoms' of (i.e. inductive evidence for) the prior occurrence of an instantaneous mental event (BT 150 f., 164 f.; PG 44 f., 49 f.).

(viii) The counterpart of the possibility of instantaneous understanding ought to be the possibility of instantaneous loss of understanding. Someone might suddenly forget the meaning of a word, i.e. forget what it is correlated with. (On the other hand, it seems that his ability to use the word correctly might soldier on unaffected. Having read off the rules of use from the nature of the object, he might retain them (by 'habit' memory) after having lost his grip on the correlation between the word and the object.) (Cf. BT 179–81.)

(ix) Understanding a word does not presuppose possession of any method for reidentifying the object correlated with it as its meaning, nor does it presuppose the ability to reidentify this object. Whether an object is the same as one previously pointed at in a particular ostensive definition is itself an objective question, quite independent of whether anyone has a method for deciding it incontrovertibly (cf. PI §377).

(x) A person's explanation of the meaning of a word need not exhibit the content of his understanding of it. An explanation is merely a means of bringing it about that someone correlates a particular word with a particular object. Explanations would be otiose if administering a drug to a person brought it about that he correlated words and things correctly (cf. BT 176–9).

(xi) The teaching and learning of language is a matter of establishing correct correlations between words and things (as Augustine describes). The fundamental form of teaching is ostensive definition. What is fundamental to language-learning must be the ability to interpret ostensive definition correctly (BT 25; PI §1, 32).

(xii) Successful communication consists in common pairings of words and things by both speaker and hearer. A speaker means a particular word in a particular way by correlating it with a particular thing and intending his hearer so to correlate it. The hearer understands it as it was meant if he correlates it with just this particular thing. (To the extent that it is impossible to prove that there are any shared correlations, there is scope for scepticism about the possibility of communication.)

(xiii) Only the thing that is correlated with a word is its meaning; all its other mental associations are irrelevant. This principle is compatible with different degrees of anti-psychologism. Indeed, it is neutral between realism and idealism. At one extreme would be the thesis that the object named by a word is *never* in the mind, although understanding the word consists of a mental correlation between the word and the object. On this view, mental images, emotive tone, feelings, etc., are never relevant to understanding words (cf. FA p. x). At the opposite extreme would be the thesis that only an object in the mind can be named by a word, since a mental correlation can hold only between mental objects. On this view, some (perhaps all) words might stand for mental images, and all must signify objects 'given in experience' ('directly present to the mind') (PP 46–51; LA 201).

(D) Sentence-meaning and 'generative' explanation

(i) Sentences[5] are combinations of names. In normal written and spoken language they are strings or concatenations of words; hence they are linear combinations of names (TLP 4.22).

(ii) Sentences must be composite. Except when elliptical (e.g., one-word answers to WH-questions), a sentence must contain two or more significant constituents. In a relatively uninflected language, it normally consists of two or more words, and hence is visibly composite (TLP 4.032; PLP 317–20).

(iii) The meaning of a sentence is determined by the meanings of its constituents (cf. TLP 3.318, 4.024–4.03). Its meaning is a function of the meanings of the names out of which it is composed; or its meaning is composed out of these meanings in accordance with the mode in which the names are combined together. (It is natural to construe this fundamental principle as the claim that the meanings of words are logically prior to the meanings of sentences in which they occur as constituents, that names have meanings by themselves, independently of sentences (cf. PM i. 66).)

(iv) The thesis that sentences are combinations of names has commonly (e.g. in classical empiricism) been taken to imply that there is nothing to explain about sentence-meaning apart from the meanings of

---

[5] In this exposition, we use 'sentence' to translate *Satz*. This sounds strained to the ear attuned to distinguishing sentences, statements, propositions, etc. So would any other uniform translation of *Satz* (e.g. 'proposition'), yet uniformity is desirable to avoid splitting up what is a family resemblance concept (cf. 'Family resemblance', pp. 205ff.).

the constituent names. However, taken together with the thesis that the meaning of a sentence is composed of the meanings of its constitutent names *in accordance with their mode of combination*, it leads to the thesis that the fundamental form of explanation of a sentence is a 'generative' explanation, i.e. an explanation of each of its constituents together with an explanation of how it combines them. Assuming that each of its constituents is explained, there is nothing to explain about a sentence apart from its logical form (cf. TLP 4.02–4.027).

(v) The meanings of its constituents (together with its form) correlate a sentence with a possible state of affairs (NB 38; PT 4.11), i.e. with some arrangement of the things that are individually correlated with its constituent names. The sentence asserts that the correlated things are arranged in a certain way. This correlation of sentences with possible states of affairs is derived from the correlation of names with things. (Hence, it is natural to assume that a sentence cannot be explained by ostension (cf. PLP 282 f., 291).)

(vi) The truth-value of a sentence is determined by whether or not the possible state of affairs correlated with it is actual. It is true if there is a corresponding fact, false if there is not (TLP 4.05–4.06, 4.25, 4.41; PP 123, 128 ff.). The meaning of a sentence determines only what must be the case for it to be true. Its truth or falsity depends on what actually is the case (except for certain 'degenerate' or 'trivial' sentences expressing analytic propositions).

(vii) The meaning of a sentence does not (typically) depend on its truth-value. It depends on what things are correlated with its constituent names, but not on whether these things are in fact arranged as the sentence says that they are (TLP 4.061, cf. 4.024).

(viii) The meaning of a sentence depends only on the correlations of its constituents with things and on its form; everything else is irrelevant. In particular, its meaning is independent of its method of verification and of the grounds for judging its truth-value (cf. BG §4; FA p. vi, §61; TLP 4.024).

(E) The 'completeness' of generative explanations of sentences

(i) The 'generative' explanation of a sentence must be a complete explanation of its meaning. It must be final and unambiguous. It must settle all questions about the use of the explained sentence, at least in so far as these are dependent on meaning. Otherwise, word–explanations would not constitute the foundation of language (cf. TLP 4.024–4.03).

(ii) Logical relations or inferential connections between sentences depend on their meanings. Consequently, they must be determined by generative explanations of sentence-meanings. If its logical consequences are to be visible in its explanation, a sentence must be so explained that those consequences are contained in the explanation (archetypally as the separate conjuncts of the full generative explanation). They must be exhibited as parts of the sentence at the first level of analysis. Moreover, since logical relations are independent of subject-matter, they must depend only on the form of a sentence. Therefore, there must be a uniform analysis of any sentence of a given form into a set of sentences that exhibit the logical consequences common to any sentence of this form. (The analysis of a particular sentence just consists of filling this form with the appropriate content, i.e. the explanation of each of its constituent names.) (TLP 5.11–5.132; OK 53, 66 f.)

(iii) Not every combination of names need be meaningful. Whether a particular combination is meaningful depends solely on the form of the combination and the categories of its constituent names. Given a particular significant combination of names, the substitution for any of its constituents of a word of the same category yields a meaningful sentence. Conversely, if replacing one word in a significant sentence by some other word yields a meaningless combination of names, these two words must belong to different logical categories. Any principles of significance for combinations of names must be systematic and general (GA i. §§28–32; PM i. 47–9, 95; cf. BB 83 f., PLP 96 f.).

(iv) Sentences are put to various uses: as orders, statements, questions, warnings, etc. These differences in use cannot readily be accounted for in terms of differences in their constituents. Consequently, unless they can be shown to flow from differences in sentence-form, they must be held to have no relevance to sentence-meaning. This is the standard conclusion. All sentences have a uniform function from a logical point of view. They are all descriptions (NB 38; TLP 4.023). They state how things stand with respect to each other (PT 4.11; TLP 4.022, 4.03). They 'assert' (in a 'logical sense') that the things correlated with their constituent names are arranged in certain ways (PrM 35; cf. TLP 4.022, 5.124). The general form of a sentence is 'This is how things stand' (TLP 4.5). Their uniformity of logical function is derivative from the uniformity of function of the names of which they are composed. As naming is to words, so describing is to sentences (cf. PI §§24, 26 f., 291). Differences in the uses of sentences are all 'psychological' (NB 96, cf. PM i, 92).

(F) 'Psychological' aspects of sentence-meaning

(i) Understanding a sentence consists in understanding its constituent words and its logical form (OK 52 f.; TLP 4.024 f.; LA 193). This is readily conceived of as calculating the meaning of a sentence from the meanings of its constituents and the rules of a logical syntax. Accordingly, it is possible to understand a novel sentence provided that it is a combination of familiar names in a familiar logical form (TLP 4.027 ff.).

(ii) Understanding a sentence is a mental activity. This activity is complex and articulated. Its ingredients are the mental correlations of its constituents with what they name and the apprehension of a logical form. Together these activities constitute an association of the sentence with a possible state of affairs. Understanding a sentence is an activity separate from hearing or uttering the sentence.

(iii) The mental activity of understanding a sentence mediates between language and action. It is conceived as an intermediate stage between hearing a sentence and acting on it. *Before* a person can obey a command, he must understand it; once having understood it, he then decides whether to comply (BT 15–17; PG 46; BB 3,12; cf. PI §451).

(iv) Understanding a sentence consists in knowing what it describes, i.e. what possible state of affairs would make it true. Its truth-conditions are what is understood in understanding it (TLP 4.024).

(v) Understanding a sentence does not (typically) require knowing its truth-value, i.e. knowing whether the possible state of affairs described by it is actual (TLP 4.024).

(vi) Understanding a true sentence does not presuppose acquaintance with the fact that makes it true. Understanding it does not require any experience other than what is required for understanding its constituents and its form. (The capacity to envisage possibilities is limited only by the initial supply of significant words and logical forms. The mind resembles a kaleidoscope.) (Cf. PM i. 43, TLP 4.024.)

(vii) Understanding a sentence is independent of the ability to frame a mental image of the possible state of affairs that would make it true. Otherwise, a generative explanation of a sentence could not be a complete explanation of its meaning, nor would giving such an explanation settle conclusively whether a person understood the sentence (cf. FA §58).

(viii) Knowing how a sentence combines understood words in an understood form must constitute a complete understanding of the sentence. In particular, this must give a full knowledge of its entailments and its logical relations with other understood sentences; also a full knowledge of the relevant principle of significance governing which combinations of names form significant sentences. (What understanding a logical form consists in is unclear.)

(ix) Understanding a sentence is independent of knowing its force or the use to which it is put (either in general or on a particular occasion of its utterance).

(x) Judging that a sentence is true (or false) is a mental act over and above understanding the sentence. Asserting (or denying) a sentence is an outward expression of this interior mental act (PLP 300–3; PI §22; PM i. 92; GA i. §5).

(xi) Understanding a sentence is independent of knowing what would constitute good grounds for judging it to be true or false, or any method for verifying or falsifying it (BG §4; FA §47).

(xii) A person's explanation of the meaning of a sentence need not exhibit the content of his understanding of it. Nor need a person who understands the explanation understand the sentence explained. The explanation explains what is understood in understanding the sentence only if it is a correct generative explanation; it must show how the meaning of the sentence is derived from the meanings of its constituents and its form. Most explanations are defective when measured against this standard; e.g. an explanation by paraphrase, by drawing a picture of what is described, or by describing how to verify the sentence (PI §§70, 353).

(G) Philosophical morals

(i) Philosophical analysis is simultaneously a clarification of language and the world. Its aim is to discover the essence of language, which is also the essence of the world (cf. LA 178 f., 270).

(ii) Language would be perspicuous to the extent that differences in grammar exactly corresponded to differences in the logical form of sentences. It is natural that philosophy should aim at maximizing the perspicuity of language by introducing a logically correct notation (*Begriffsschrift*) and explaining how to substitute it for our ordinary forms of expression (an 'ideal language') (cf. TLP p. x, LA 197 f., PR 52).

3. *Augustine's picture: a proto-theory or paradigm*

Under Wittgenstein's general supervision, our careful tending of the seed of Augustine's picture of language has produced a striking specimen in the garden of philosophy—a whole *Weltanschauung* encompassing language, the mind, and the world (the Augustinian picture). Wittgenstein did not admire this plant, though he thought it to be of colossal importance. He saw it as a weed, so important a weed that much of the *Investigations* constitutes an elaborate campaign to eradicate it. Such an expenditure of effort would have been ridiculous unless Wittgenstein had thought that the Augustinian picture was a pernicious and widespread weed.

The Augustinian picture looks like a widely ramifying philosophical theory centred on a comprehensive theory of meaning. But what is its importance? Have major philosophers advanced this theory in its fully developed form? Even superficial acquaintance suggests that it fails to square in all important respects with the accounts of meaning criticized in the *Investigations*, viz. those of Frege, Russell, and the *Tractatus*. Does this deprive it of interest? Only if it is regarded as one possible theory of meaning among the many thrown up in the history of philosophy. But it can be seen differently, as the full flowering of certain propensities in philosophical thinking which are expressed in a variety of ways in accounts of meaning that are superficially quite different from each other. It is important in so far as it embodies a conception of meaning that informs a range of major accounts of meaning. The fact that nobody has made explicit the Augustinian picture of language does not rob it of interest. On the contrary. It is characteristic of a *Weltanschauung* that it has no owner or author; that it is the common property of many individuals. Moreover, its articulation is a particularly difficult task to the extent that its influence is widespread. For the easiest way to recognize intellectual influences is to note the oddities that they lead to. What is pervasive and thus seems normal is difficult to distinguish from brute fact. Consequently, we must not conclude from the fact that no philosopher has explicitly advanced the fully developed Augustinian picture that it is of negligible importance.

Augustine's picture of language might be represented not as an explicit theory, but rather as a proto-theory that shapes the development of many philosophical theories of meaning. It is like an invisible force, evident only in its visible effects; like a prevailing wind that affects the growth of a tree, it might show itself only in the asymmetric shape that it gives to explicit theorizing. Indeed, such a view is suggested by Wittgenstein's characterizing its central tenets as a picture (*Bild*) of the essence of language. For it is pictures that take us in (PI p. 184) and hold us captive (PI §115), and the primary aim of philosophical therapy is to immunize us against pictures which try to force themselves upon us (PI §425), from which we cannot turn our eyes, even though they fail to provide solutions to our problems (PI §352). The adoption of a picture is often the first step in intellectual inquiry, and it is apt altogether to escape our notice (PI §308). Here we speak of names and objects, leaving the nature of the objects quite undecided, open to future investigation; but this seemingly innocent move commits any resultant theory to a particular way of looking at language, because we have a definite conception of what a name is and what it is to get to know objects better (comment on PI §1 in the style of PI §308). Augustine's picture of language is just such a picture or proto-theory, easily mistaken for a harmless manner of speaking or a description of indisputable facts until its subtle effects are made visible and brought to our attention. (A similar influential proto-theory is the conception of the contrast between the mental and the physical as the contrast between the inner and the outer.)

Alternatively, we might see it as a paradigm towards which theories gravitate: as the philosophical counterpart of a scientific paradigm (in Kuhn's sense). It establishes the intellectual climate within which proceeds a whole style of investigations into meaning. It motivates and directs inquiry, influencing what are perceived to be the problems requiring explanations and what would count as satisfactory solutions to them. In Russell's view, e.g., if every word were clearly a name whose meaning was the object named, philosophers would have nothing to discuss. Fortunately this prospect of unemployment is remote, just because many expressions, e.g. definite descriptions, so conspicuously resist this treatment; Russell's theory of descriptions is an intellectual triumph because it shows how to reconcile certain notoriously recalcitrant phenomena with the paradigm. More generally, the ingenuity of investigators and the sophistication of theories are judged by their success in accommodating everything to the adamantine standards set by the paradigm. At the risk of anachronism, we could describe Augustine's picture of language, according to Wittgenstein's view, as a paradigm underlying the bulk of the major investigations into meaning. In criticizing it from many angles, he aimed at effecting, as it were, a 'scientific revolution' in philosophy, i.e. at breaking the grip of a paradigm that bedevils our reflections on meaning.

Had Wittgenstein given a single systematic exposition of the Augustinian picture, he might have described his activity as the presentation of an *Übersicht* of a whole family of theories of meaning (see 'Übersicht', pp. 542 ff). Its value rests in its giving a deeper understanding of these theories, an insight into what unifies them in spite of superficial differences. (Its value would not be diminished by its failing to qualify as a complete theory of meaning itself, nor by the fact that the theories of which it gives a surview contain many elements not even mentioned in it.) The worth of the Augustinian picture is its power to illuminate the theories of meaning of which Wittgenstein apparently intended it to give an *Übersicht*, viz. the theories of Frege, Russell, and the *Tractatus*. Hence this is what we have to investigate in order to clear the ground of houses of cards.

4. *Frege*

Philosophers commonly assume that one of Frege's philosophical projects is to construct a general theory of meaning for a natural language. There are many reasons to doubt this assumption, but we shall not challenge it here. Rather, the picture of Frege's philosophy of language we shall present will conform to the standard average modern interpretation of his mature theories.

It would be a parody of Frege's account of meaning to describe it as perfectly exemplifying the Augustinian picture of language. But equally superficial would be a contemptuous repudiation of the suggestion that it conforms with this picture. Frege's semantics seems to accord, if not with the letter, at least with the spirit of the picture.

The prosecution would argue that Frege treats virtually all words as names and all sentences as combinations of names, acknowledging only minor deviations from this norm. His taking words to be names is manifest in his conception of reference (*Bedeutung*). Any significant word must have a reference (on a given occasion of its use) if a sentence in which it occurs is to bear a truth-value. (More accurately, any expression with a sense must have a reference if a sentence in which it occurs has a truth-value. Some expressions, e.g. the copula (with an adjective) or a bound variable, do not have senses, though they contribute to the thought expressed by a sentence (cf. FG 67).) The assignment of a truth-value to the sentence depends only on what the reference of each constituent word is, i.e. on what it stands for. If we ignore words whose reference is context-dependent (e.g. demonstratives and personal pronouns), we can for 'scientific' purposes treat every word as a name, which is fully understood by anybody who knows what it signifies. (Context-dependent expressions, according to Frege, cannot, strictly speaking, be said to have a sense, or, at any rate, a complete sense. Only taken in context do they have a sense, which varies with the context.) In so far as our interest is in the question of the truth and falsity of statements, every word is a name. Frege never calls into question the use of words as names. Instead, he argues about what particular words stand for, i.e. what kinds of things they are names of (e.g., whether numerals are names of first-level concepts, second-level concepts, or objects). Although words are classified into logical types, this differentiation is superimposed on a fundamental uniformity of function: each word must have reference in any sentence bearing a truth-value. This encapsulates the basic idea of the Augustinian picture, viz. that only names can figure in descriptions of how things are. By treating all words as names, Frege also treated sentences as combinations of names. (Not every combination of names constitutes a sentence; distinctions of logical type, e.g. first-level concept/object, are invoked to differentiate well-formed sentences from nonsense.) In his later writings, Frege explicitly assimilated sentences to names by taking them to be complex names of truth-values. This seems natural only to the extent that he had already treated sentences as parallel to those combinations of names (e.g. 'the satellite of the earth') that he called 'complex proper names'. Such arguments establish a *prima facie* case for Frege's subscription to the Augustinian picture of language.

It is comparatively easy, however, to construct a first line of defence against this charge. Indeed, little more is needed than to emphasize the importance of points brushed aside by the prosecution as minor deviations.

(i) The thesis that every significant word has a reference is a mere truism. The reference of any expression just is its semantic role, the part it plays in determining the truth-value of any sentence in which it occurs. To say that a word is significant is just to say that it plays some part in fixing the truth-value of sentences where it occurs non-vacuously, and this, in turn, is just what it means for the word to have a reference. Hence

Frege's doctrine is not a commitment to any theory, merely a definition of his technical term 'Bedeutung'.

(ii) Frege's distinction between sense and reference blocks the ascription to him of the Augustinian conception of names. On that view, a name is not merely any word correlated with an object, but a word whose meaning *is* the object correlated with it; hence, a word whose meaning is fully grasped simply in virtue of its correlation with this object. This is precisely what Frege rejects in introducing his distinction. His notion of sense, not his notion of reference, is what approximates to the concept of meaning. By implicitly taking the sense and the reference of any expression to be distinct, he tacitly denies that the meaning of any word is the object named by it. He certainly denies that the meaning of *every* word is what it stands for. At least some words in a natural language may have sense but lack reference. Moreover, the sense/reference distinction is invoked to account for the possibility that a person may understand each of two names that stand for a single object without knowing that they stand for the same thing. This presupposes that the correlation of a name with the object that it names does not (always) give a complete grasp of its meaning. Consequently, Frege's use of the sense/reference distinction is incompatible with the claim that he treats every word as a name according to the Augustinian picture.

(iii) Even if the term 'name' in the Augustinian picture meant simply any word with reference, Frege would not concede that it made sense to claim that every word is a name. To do so would violate his distinction between concept and object (FA p. x) and, more generally, his distinction between expressions of different logical type. What he calls a proper name has as its reference (if it has one at all) an object, whereas what he calls a concept-word (a predicate) has as its reference a concept. Since there is no relation that holds between a word (a proper name) and an object which can intelligibly be said to hold between a word (a concept-word) and a concept, it follows that there is no such thing as *the* relation of a word to its reference, hence no such thing as *the* relation of naming. There are as many relations as there are logical types. At best there is a formal analogy between the distinct relations of proper names to objects, of predicates to first-level concepts, of quantifiers to second-level concepts, etc. (Just as there is only a formal analogy between identity for objects and 'identity' for concepts.) Therefore, the thesis that every word is a name is either false or nonsensical.

(iv) The Augustinian picture implies that the meaning of a word is invariant, whatever the context of its utterance. Its meaning is laid down once for all by correlating it with an object; its sole function, in any context, is to stand for this object. This conception of the context-invariance of meaning is a generalization of the idealized picture of proper names summarized in the slogan *unum nomen, unum nominatum*. It is at variance with Frege's account of sense. Expressions whose reference depends on the context of their use (e.g. demonstratives and personal pronouns) do not have a sense. Only the expression *together with its context* has a sense. Given this treatment, the fact that context-dependence is a fundamental feature of language is a major obstacle to taking Frege to subscribe to the Augustinian picture. (And so too is his treatment of expressions in oblique contexts.)

(v) It would be misleading to ascribe to Frege the thesis that sentences are combinations of names. He had an explicit concern with the structure of sentences and with its contribution to understanding sentences and to determining their truth-values. Since the expression 'combination of names' obscures the importance of structure, Frege's view might better be couched as the thesis that sentences are articulated structures composed of names.

(vi) Ostensive definition is a central element of the Augustinian picture, but Frege does not even mention the subject.

These defences do not deprive the prosecution of room for manoeuvre. Despite the distinction between sense and reference, it seems that the Augustinian picture of meaning underlies Frege's semantics. The concept of sense for a word is explained as the 'mode of presentation of its reference'. The sense of a name is the means for determining for any given object whether or not it is the referent of the name (a 'criterion of identity'); the sense of a first-level predicate is the means for determining a concept as its referent and thereby for determining of any given object whether or not it falls under this concept; etc. It is characteristic of Frege's account of sense that reference plays an essential part in what it is to grasp the sense of an expression. Though sense is distinct from reference, the two concepts are internally related. Explanation (or stipulation) of the sense of an expression must give a means for determining its reference. The explicit model for Frege's account is the proper name; its sense is grasped by somebody who knows what has to be the case for any given object to be its reference. It is problematic whether his account of sense can be extended from proper names to other parts of speech (first-level predicates, sentence-connectives, quantifiers, and other second-level predicates . . .). A negative verdict should be returned if there is nothing, e.g., that plays a role in what it is to grasp the sense of a predicate which corresponds to the role of the object in what it is to grasp the sense of a name. (This is a refinement and sharpening of the familiar criticism of using universals to account for the meanings of general terms, viz. that there is nothing to which predicates stand in the relation that proper names stand to particulars.) Frege does not hold that the sense of any word *is* its reference, nor even that its reference determines its sense. None the less, his theory of meaning is a refinement of the Augustinian picture. It conforms to the basic principle that reference must be ascribed to any expressions which function as significant units of sentences of a language. This has the customary consequence, the requirement of a baroque ontology. The 'realm of reference' includes, as well as objects, concepts and relations of various levels (NS 209 f.); the population of objects is swelled by such 'entities' as numbers, classes, directions of lines, and truth-values. All of these are required to assign meaning to predicates, numerals, class-names, etc. In short, Frege's semantics seems intended to salvage the Augustinian picture. His solution to its difficulties involves making it more complex by the superimposition of an extra tier; a 'realm of sense' complements an already overpopulated 'realm of reference'. Far from jettisoning the Augustinian picture, he strives to save it by refinements and qualifications, by adding new degrees of freedom to the construction of theories on this basis (e.g. the possibility of meaning without reference). The underlying continuity is his conviction that the concept of sense cannot be explained independently of reference, where reference is conceived of as a timeless correlation between a word and an entity (of an appropriate type).

Summing up, the prosecution might argue that not only is Frege's semantics a version of the Augustinian picture of language, but also it is not obviously even an *improved* version. It purchases its plausibility at the price of mystery. Notoriously, there is no clear account of the criteria for identity of sense, even between names. By Frege's own standards, this deprives the expression 'the sense of x' of any (clear) meaning and makes his semantics defective from a scientific point of view. His introduction of sense also generates a host of fresh problems in working out the Augustinian picture, because the relation of the sense of a sentence to understanding, knowledge, and judgement is altogether obscure. Although the sense of a sentence 'determines' its reference (truth-value) however the facts may fall out, it is not clear how my grasping the sense of a sentence is supposed to be related to my ability to judge whether it is true or false, since Frege has no account of what 'complete knowledge of the facts' might be. Conversely, it seems that I may be able to use a word correctly as regards both syntax and the ability to make correct judgements incorporating it, yet not grasp its sense correctly. Many people who can count and do elementary arithmetic do not, e.g., understand that the reference of '0' is the extension of the concept 'equal to the concept "not identical with itself"' (FA §74); hence they do not grasp its sense even though they use the numeral '0' correctly. There are two conflicting ideas in Frege's semantics. On the one hand, the sense of a word is something transcendent. It settles, quite independently of us, what applications of the word are correct, and thereby it constitutes an objective standard against which to judge whether someone understands the word correctly. On the other hand, the sense of a word is what we

understand in understanding it, what we explain in defining it. If sense is
to explain away his puzzles about how language is used (e.g. the
possibility of cognitively non-trivial identity-statements), then it must be
immanent and accessible to us. By failing to resolve the tension between
these lines of thought, Frege's theory of meaning raises more problems
than it solves.

Frege's distinction between sense and reference might appear to put his
theory of meaning well outside the target area of Wittgenstein's attack on
the Augustinian picture of language. This is an illusion. It is not safe, as it
were, from ricochet. Frege's semantics is an uncommonly luxuriant
specimen of the weed Wittgenstein is eager to root out.

5. *Russell*

Despite its considerable changes, Russell's philosophy of language
conforms closely to the Augustinian picture. Russell's account of meaning is the product of scientific method in philosophy not only in the
respects that he indicated, but also in that it is the progressive elaboration
of a theory within the gravitational field of a paradigm which determines
both what is seen as problematic and what counts as an acceptable
solution.

The Principles of Mathematics starts from the assumption that every
word occurring in a sentence must have some meaning (p. 42). '*Words* all
have meaning, in the simple sense that they are symbols which stand for
something other than themselves' (p. 47). If an expression is definable,
then its analysis will explain what it stands for in terms of expressions
whose meaning is presumed to be known. Indefinables cannot be so
explained; to grasp their meaning is to become acquainted with what
they stand for. In some cases this acquaintance will presumably be
effected by ostension, e.g. for such terms as 'red'. In other cases,
ostension seems impossible, e.g. for indefinables of logic. 'The discussion
of [logical] indefinables . . . is the endeavour to see clearly, and to make
others see clearly, the entities concerned, in order that the mind may have
that kind of acquaintance with them which it has with redness or the taste
of a pineapple' (p. xv).

Adherence to the Augustinian picture of word-meaning has its characteristic expression in Russell's early work: the claim that logical principles governing words flow from the nature of the objects correlated with
them as their meanings. This is explicit in his account of how to
construct a philosophical grammar. Unlike ordinary grammar, it is to
classify expressions into types, not by superficial appearances (noun,
adjective, adverb, etc.), but by the characteristics of the entities which
expressions stand for. It requires, e.g., the distinction between proper and

general names 'or rather between the objects indicated by such names' (p. 43); and similarly the distinction between things and concepts (p. 44). To construct its categories we must penetrate the surface of grammar and see through to the nature of the entities named by words. The same activity is necessary to discern the principles of synthetic incompatibility that form an important part of general logic; e.g. the impossibility of the coexistence of red and green at the same spatio-temporal place (p. 233).

At this stage Russell seems aware of only two problems in the Augustinian picture of word-meaning. One is the meaning of the copula; Russell treats it very obscurely as a unique form of relation (p. 49). The other is the analysis of what he calls denoting. In the sentence 'I met a man', the words 'a' and 'man' both stand for concepts, not for things, and yet the sentence asserts a relation between me and a thing, not between me and a (complex) concept (p. 53). The solution to this puzzle is given by the notion of denoting. The phrase 'a man', as well as having meaning (i.e. standing for a complex concept), denotes a thing (person) in the sentence 'I met a man'. In such cases the thing denoted is 'connected in a certain peculiar way with the concept' (p. 53). To avoid misunderstanding we must distinguish what a complex term means (stands for) from what it denotes. A simple term, by contrast, cannot stand to a thing in this mysterious relation of denoting. Russell construes Frege's terms 'Sinn' and 'Bedeutung' to correspond to his terms 'meaning' and 'denotation', and criticizes him for making a distinction in the case of simple names which is applicable only to complex ones (p. 502). Russell's thesis that the denotation of a complex name is not its meaning does not constitute a rejection, but rather a refinement, of the thesis that the meaning of a word is the object that it stands for. (He accepts, e.g., the characteristic paradox that any genuine identity-statement is trivial, admitting exceptions only for the case of denoting concepts (p. 64).)

In this early book, Russell accepts without discussion that sentences are combinations of names. They are complex. They correspond to propositions which consist of two or more constituents (p. 44). (A 'proposition' does not consist of words, but contains the entities indicated by words (p. 47).) This generates two puzzles. First, a worry about how it is possible to make a false judgement or to assert something false, since there is no 'proposition' (complex of objects) to correspond to what a false sentence says (cf. p. 40). Second, a puzzle about how a proposition differs from the aggregate of its constituents, about where the unity of a proposition is to be found. The constituents of the proposition 'A differs from B' are merely A, difference, and B. 'Yet these constituents, thus placed side by side, do not reconstitute the proposition' (p. 49). Russell feels that the solution lies in distinguishing a verb used as a verb from the verb considered as a term in the proposition, but he despairs of giving a clear account of this distinction (p. 50) and hence of the copula (p. 49). This whole concern arises from the presumption that a sentence is a combination, a laying side by side, of names.

At first glance, the later development of Russell's theory of meaning seems to be a gradual retreat from this rigorous adherence to the Augustinian picture. The recognition of incomplete symbols is just the admission that not every expression that occurs in a sentence functions as a name; in a true sentence not every expression need stand for a constituent of the 'proposition' or fact making it true. Russell progressively enlarged the class of incomplete symbols; first he added definite descriptions; then class-concepts or class-names; then most ordinary proper names and demonstratives; and finally logical constants. Does this not *prove* that he moved further and further away from the Augustinian picture?

This conclusion is profoundly mistaken. The recognition of incomplete symbols is only a superficial departure from the Augustinian picture making possible a full, rigorous adherence to it. Russell emphasizes the contrast between appearance and reality in our conception of language. It *seems* as if not every word has as its meaning something that it stands for. Hence, it *seems* that not all the components of sentences conform to the Augustinian picture. But, in fact, the apparent components of sentences, i.e. ordinary words, are not their *real* components. These must be discovered by logical analysis. Complex terms, i.e. definable expressions, must be eliminated by substituting for them their definitions. This process must continue until they are all analysed into their indefinable components. Thereafter, incomplete symbols must be successively removed by substituting for them whole sentences that are equivalent in meaning to the originals but free from the symbols to be eliminated. Only at the end of this process are the real components of a proposition revealed. Of them it is true that their meanings are the objects that they stand for. The Augustinian picture fits the fully analysed proposition, but not sentences before analysis. Russell's express commitment to this view is the principle of acquaintance: every proposition which we can understand must consist wholly of (real) constituents[6] with which we are acquainted. Prior to working out the theory of descriptions, he would have had to supplement this principle with an account of the obscure relation of denoting. For a complete understanding of a sentence of the form 'The Φ-er Ψ s' would require not only acquaintance with Φ, Ψ, (and *the*), but also knowing what the complex term 'the Φ-er' denotes. Consequently, the identification of definite descriptions as incomplete symbols removed the major obstacle to the claim that the Augustinian picture gives a complete account of language in its fully analysed form. This is why the theory of descriptions was a liberation for

---

[6] For Russell the 'constituents' of a proposition are the meanings (entities) named by the expressions in the fully analysed sentence expressing that proposition.

Russell. To criticize this theory because it launches a search for the logically proper name is a serious misunderstanding. The idea of a logically proper name, i.e. of a name whose meaning is the object named, is the core of the Augustinian picture, and this is what generated the problem to which the theory of descriptions is the triumphant solution because it allows the elimination from an account of meaning of the relation of denoting. Russell's treatment of incomplete symbols is the essential step in vindicating the principle of acquaintance and hence the thesis that language conforms to the Augustinian picture.

While the conception of words as names manifests itself most strikingly in Russell's principle of acquaintance, it also underlies his exposition of the theory of types, his conception of philosophical analysis, his doctrine of universals and even his causal theory of meaning.

(i) On his view, the distinction of logical types must rest on the properties of the objects which words stand for. It constitutes a sort of ultra-physics. Establishing that a word functions as a predicate is finding out that some property is correlated with it as its meaning; 'exists' is not a predicate because what it is correlated with is not a property (of objects). That a predicate cannot take itself as argument rests on the fact that no property of objects is also a property of properties. The theory of types is a system of statements of such basic facts. From it we derive a system of rules about which combinations of signs constitute meaningful sentences; e.g., that it is nonsense to put a function as its own argument. (Wittgenstein objected that Russell appealed to the meaning of signs when establishing the rules for them (TLP 3.331). Even though Russell accepted this criticism and later adopted as his official view that 'the theory of types is really a theory of symbols, not of things' (LA 267), he none the less explained the theory of types exactly as before, appealing to such necessities as that of distinguishing between classes and particulars (LA 260). His acceptance of the Augustinian picture made it impossible for him to conceive of developing the logical grammar of an expression otherwise than by appealing to the nature of the object for which it stands.)

(ii) The proper business of philosophy is analysis. Breaking up what is correlated with a word into its logical constituents will be mirrored in a definition of the word in terms of words standing for these constituents, while a correct definition of a word must correspond to the anatomization of what it stands for into its logical constituents. The analysis of the meaning of a word corresponds to the logical structure of the correlated object. Therefore, philosophical analysis clarifies both language and the world. The phrase 'logical atomism' summed up Russell's commitment to this conception of analysis. He never abandoned this view, though he dropped the label.[7]

---

[7] Russell, *An Inquiry into Meaning and Truth*, p. 322.

(iii) Russell seems never to have had any doubt about the need for universals in a correct account of language. For this reason he never presents much argument for the existence of universals, and his considerations of alternative views are shallow and question-begging. He assumes that the only possible way of assigning meaning to general words is to treat them as *names*. Therefore, he needs to postulate something (universals) for them to be names of. In the sentence 'I am in my room', the word 'in' obviously has a meaning: 'it denotes a relation that holds between me and my room . . . The relation "in" is something which we can think about and understand, for [otherwise], we could not understand the sentence "I am in my room"' (PP 90). Consequently, the only possible argument for the elimination of universals is the claim that language can be constructed without the use of any general words. This Russell rightly judges to be impossible (PP 95–7). Only somebody in the grip of the Augustinian picture could advance these remarks as *arguments*. This background is evident too from the role that universals are meant to play. Russell uses them to extend the correspondence theory of truth to *a priori* statements. The sentence '2 + 3 = 5', e.g., is about the numbers 2, 3, and 5, and it is true in virtue of the relations between them. This account of truth gives universals a second role independent of the theory that they are the meanings of general words. Only if a term cannot stand for an object unless this object is its meaning does the correspondence theory of truth even seem to require completion by the recognition of universals.

(iv) Russell's later causal theory of meaning in *Analysis of Mind* and *An Inquiry into Meaning and Truth* starts from the idea that the meaning of a word is something correlated with it for which it stands. The theory gives an explanation of what kind of correlation this is (AM 189): viz. that the name-relation is a causal relation between words and things (AM 197). It demystifies the nature of the mental association between names and the objects named, comparing this to the correlation of experiential stimuli and behavioural responses familiar from experiments in psychological conditioning (AM 191, 199). Without the background of the Augustinian picture, Russell's elaboration of his causal theory would make no sense at all.

The conception of sentences as combinations of names is equally prominent throughout Russell's writing. It is explicitly formulated in his principle of acquaintance and also in his correspondence theory of truth with its associated metaphysics. A fact is a complex object composed of simple objects (PP 129; PM i. 43). A sentence, when fully analysed, consists of simple signs (primitive concepts), and hence it is a complex composed of simples. It is true provided that the complex object composed of the simple objects correlated with its names according to its form actually exists, i.e. if there is a 'corresponding' fact; otherwise, it is false

(PP 128; PM i. 43; LA 182). The correspondence between a sentence and the fact that makes it true depends on the composition of sentences out of names (LA 195, 197). The clarification of the different logical forms of combinations of names into sentences causes Russell considerable difficulties and receives increasing attention in his writings. He is embarrassed about how to account for the difference in 'sense' between 'aRb' and 'bRa': is it a difference in the constituents of these sentences or in their forms? (Cf. PP 127 f.) He thinks of a logical form as something simple (cf. NB 18, 121); hence he conceives of understanding the form of a sentence on the model of acquaintance with an object (cf. LA 219, 224–6). One of the most important and difficult tasks of logic is to clarify the logical forms of problematic sentences (OK 60, 67 f.). Russell urges logicians to pool their experience in the construction of an inventory of logical forms (LA 216). His underlying idea is that understanding a sentence is simply a matter of acquaintance with each of its (real) constituents and its logical form, i.e. a combined grasp of form and content (OK 52 f.).

To state that Russell's general account of language conforms to the Augustinian picture would be too weak. The whole purpose of his successive theories of meaning is to *prove* that language really does so. This conformity is deep, not apparent, and must be demonstrated. Philosophical analysis of language is what reveals it. The principle of acquaintance sums it up. Finally, the Augustinian picture informs Russell's conception of an ideal language: that would be a language in which conformity to it was *visible* because no sentence would appear except in completely analysed form. The Augustinian picture functions as a norm of representation in Russell's description of language.

6. *The* Tractatus

Superficially, the *Tractatus* presents a version of Augustine's picture of language. The signs occurring in a completely analysed proposition, apart from logical operators, are names (TLP 3.201 f.). 'A name means an object. The object is its meaning [*Bedeutung*]' (TLP 3.203). Every proposition is a truth-function of elementary propositions, i.e. it is constructed from them by means of logical operations (TLP 5), and 'an elementary proposition consists of names. It is a nexus, a concatenation, of names . . . It consists of names in immediate combination' (TLP 4.22 f.). Consequently, the very possibility of propositions is based on the principle that signs go proxy for objects (TLP 4.0312; NB 37). Analysis reveals the hidden conformity of every possible language with the Augustinian picture in spite of the appearance of divergence. Every proposition really consists of *names* and is a *description* of a possible fact

(TLP 3.144, 4.01, 4.023, 4.024). Hence the general form of a proposition is: 'This is how things stand' (TLP 4.5).

Whether there is a gap here between appearance and reality is a deep issue involving a host of familiar controversies. The problems ramify, extending from the foundations of logic to the nature of the world. It would be absurd even to try to give here a definitive proof that the *Tractatus* conforms to the Augustinian picture of language. Instead, we shall simply attempt to show that this is a plausible view of the book. In writing the *Investigations*, Wittgenstein makes it clear that he then regarded the *Tractatus* in this light.

The *Tractatus* looks like the working out of a simplification of Frege's theory of meaning along the lines suggested by Russell. Russell had identified Frege's distinction between sense and reference with his own distinction between what a word means (what it stands for) and what it denotes. Consequently, the elimination of the relation of denoting by means of the theory of descriptions amounted, in his view, to a proof that a complete theory of meaning can dispense with Frege's notion of sense. In a fully analysed sentence, each word has only *Bedeutung* ('reference'), not 'sense'; i.e. its meaning is the object that it stands for. This is the thesis of the *Tractatus*: each constituent of an atomic proposition has only *Bedeutung*, not *Sinn* (TLP 3.3), and its meaning (*Bedeutung*) is the object that it stands for (TLP 3.203). A parallel simplification is applied to Frege's account of sentences: an elementary sentence has *Sinn*, but no *Bedeutung* (TLP 3.3). (That a name has meaning (*Bedeutung*) depends on its being correlated with an object. That an elementary sentence has meaning (*Sinn*) depends on its correlation *qua* fact with a possible state of affairs (*Sachverhalt*), of which it is the logical picture. Since it makes no sense to assert that a relation holding between certain *objects* holds also between certain *facts*, there is no such thing as the *Bedeutung* of a sentence (TLP 3.144, cf. NB 93).) An elementary sentence consists only of names in immediate combination, and its sense is a function of the meanings of its constituents (TLP 3.318). The totality of possible worlds is the totality of the combinatorial possibilities of the existence or non-existence of states of affairs (*Sachverhalten*); hence it is the totality of the combinatorial possibilities of the truth or falsity of elementary propositions (each of which is independent of every other one) (TLP 4.26). Therefore, if the sense of a sentence is completely determined by specifying its truth-value in every possible world, then every sentence can be analysed as a truth-function of elementary sentences (TLP 4.2, 4.3, 4.4). As a consequence, analysis will reduce any sentence to a truth-function of elementary sentences each of which is a concatenation of names. The *Tractatus* thus demonstrates that any possible language, when fully analysed, conforms exactly to the Augustinian picture. With the sole exception of logical operators, the analysed form of any sentence will be a combination of words whose meanings are the objects that they name.

Although the strategy of the *Tractatus* mirrors Russell's, its scope and method seem inspired by Frege's anti-psychologism. Wittgenstein draws a very rigid boundary between logic and psychology and excludes from discussion everything characterized as psychological. This includes all of the 'psychological' aspects of the Augustinian picture. In particular, Wittgenstein excludes any serious consideration of what it is to explain or understand a word or a sentence, what it is to mean something, how names are correlated with objects, how objects are reidentified, how propositions are verified, and how sentences function in communication (e.g. the differences between questions, commands, and assertions (cf. NB 96)). His contempt for 'psychological' issues is perhaps most notorious in the fact that he left the notion of object shrouded in obscurity. In complete ignorance of what objects are, how can they play any role in what we explain when we explain the meanings of expressions or in what we understand when we understand a word or a sentence? The exclusion of all matters of 'psychology' differentiates Wittgenstein's logical atomism from Russell's. It also makes it pointless to search the *Tractatus* for many of the theses characteristic of the Augustinian picture. At best they are counterfactually in the *Tractatus*; i.e. they would have been what Wittgenstein would have said had he thought it necessary to discuss such matters. (He later identified some of these tacit 'psychological' theses (cf. PI §81, BT 253).)

The *Tractatus* is a vindication of the Augustinian picture of language. It is a synthesis of the best in Russell and Frege, marrying the economy of Russell's account with the austerity of Frege's. It is *a priori* and dogmatic. It assumes that Augustine's picture does depict the essence of language, and it then argues that every possible language, every possible world, every possible thought *must* have a certain structure in order for this picture to be correct. In taking logic as the basis of metaphysics (NB 93), Wittgenstein projected the Augustinian picture on to reality: he literally remade the world in its image. No wonder he later identified dogmatism as the intellectual sin of the *Tractatus* (WWK 182–4).

II

EXPLANATION

1. *Introduction*

From the very beginning the *Investigations* highlights the notion of explanation (of words) and also the associated concepts of teaching and training. Wittgenstein thus seems to stress three apparently pedagogical concepts. Training or drill is noted as a foundation of explanation (Z §419, PI §86), rule-following (PI §§143 ff.), and mathematical calculation (LFM 58 ff.). How words are taught and learnt is treated as an important component of concept-clarification. Scrutiny of explanations is the regular route for establishing truths about the meanings of expressions (e.g. the account of family resemblance concepts and the private language argument). Practices of explaining words are even studied as independent language-games (PI §28, cf. §49, PLP 94 ff.). Wittgenstein's investigation of meaning gives prominence to how speakers *learn* to use expressions.

This fact is widely noted but little understood. Current philosophers are apt to see it as a defect in at least one of three ways. First, it infects semantics with a primitive learning-theory. Wittgenstein's account of language-learning was arm-chair speculation and has long since been superseded by advances in psychology based on detailed empirical experimentation. Secondly, it introduces empirical data which are in principle irrelevant to philosophical theories of meaning. In particular, it conflates genetic investigations (the natural history of concept-acquisition) with concept-analysis. Thirdly, it is a sophisticated form of psychologism and therefore illegitimate. Both teaching and learning are internally related to the concept of understanding, and understanding is a paradigmatic psychological phenomenon. Focussing on explanation threatens to visit all these defects simultaneously on Wittgenstein's account, for an explanation is a mere means for producing understanding and hence belongs among the causal antecedents of language-use.

Deflecting these criticisms at a superficial level is simple. Yet it amounts to a poor exposition of Wittgenstein's thought. It would treat his remarks on training, teaching, and explanation as at best infelicitous expressions of profounder truths, thereby depriving them of any rationale or justification as if they should be passed over in embarrassed silence. This would fail to clarify why he saw these remarks as *virtues* of his discussion of meaning.

The emphasis on explanation in the *Investigations* is clearly deliberate and certainly not an optional extra to Wittgenstein's whole account of meaning. Indeed, he harped on the internal connection of word-meaning and explanation. Meaning is what is explained in giving an explanation of meaning (PG 68 f.). Less platitudinously, meaning is the correlate of understanding and understanding the correlate of explanation (BT 11). The meaning of an expression is not something deeper and more theoretical than what is patent in the accepted practice of explaining this expression; and this practice, like any normative practice, must be familiar to its participants, open to inspection, and surveyable. Spelling out the relations between explanation, understanding, and meaning is a central theme of the *Investigations*. This essay breaks the ground by a preliminary exploration of the concept of explanation.

One initial caveat is necessary. It concerns an ambiguity in 'Erklärung' ('explanation'). In the sense in which sciences explain phenomena, there are, according to Wittgenstein, no explanations in philosophy. The sense of 'explanation' in which explanations of word-meanings are spoken of is quite different from its counterpart in science. Scientific explanations are empirical, refutable by the facts, revisable in the light of new discoveries, and never in principle (but only provisionally, historically) final. Explanations of meaning (in the 'material mode') are not empirical, not discovered or modified in the light of new evidence, and hence final. The former are nomological, the latter normative. Whether, grammar apart, philosophy contains any explanations, will be discussed elsewhere ('The nature of philosophy', pp. 280f.). It is important to keep these two senses of 'explanation' apart.

There is a further important point concerning Wittgenstein's use of 'explanation'. Commonly, although not uniformly, he contrasts *Erklärung* with *Definition*. *Definition*, in these contexts, is taken to be a *Merkmal*-definition, and hence a special case of explanation (*Erklärung*). One of the cardinal sins of philosophers is to think that the only legitimate form of *Erklärung* is *Definition*. This wars with the principle that meaning is what is given by explanations of meaning; *Definition* is only *one* form of explanation, which does not have special privileges.

2. *Training, teaching, and explaining*

Despite the prevalence of the accusation that he engages in illegitimate armchair learning theory, Wittgenstein unequivocally repudiates genetic analysis. 'Learning a language *brings about* the understanding of it. But that belongs to the past history of the reaction' (PG 41). An *explanation* of the operation of language as a psychophysical mechanism is philosophically irrelevant (PG 70), for we are not interested in empirical facts (considered as empirical facts) about language (PG 66); they have no bearing on our concerns. For all philosophy is concerned, our actual knowledge of language might well be innate; that would not affect our use of language. 'It may be all one to us whether someone has learned the language or was perhaps from birth constituted to react to sentences in German like a normal person who has learned it' (PG 188, cf. BB 12). Although it seems paradoxical, it is conceivable that understanding should occur without any teaching whatever. 'Teaching as the hypothetical history of our subsequent actions (understanding, obeying, estimating length, etc.) drops out of our considerations' (BB 14). No matter whether our current mastery of the use of an expression (or language as a whole) was learnt, acquired as a result of a brain operation, or innate, the criteria for whether one understands the expression (language) are wholly unaffected. 'The way in which language was learnt is not contained in its use' (PG 80).

Why then is Wittgenstein interested in teaching? 'Am I doing child psychology?' he queries (Z §412); 'I am making a connection between the concept of teaching and the concept of meaning.' There is an obvious connection between the two concepts. For *what* is taught in language-teaching is the use (meaning) of expressions. To the extent that the teaching is not only training (e.g. to repeat the series of numerals), but also involves *explanation* (e.g. ostensive definition), the internal relation is even more evident, for not only is the object of teaching to teach the meaning, but the method of teaching is to give an explanation of the meaning. However, Wittgenstein's interest in teaching ramifies in various directions. We shall enumerate five.

(i) Teaching contexts serve to highlight the presuppositions of a linguistic competence, as well as their contingency. Explanations of meaning given in teaching do not function in a linguistic vacuum. The explanation of the meaning of an expression in a language is itself given in language. There is no extra-linguistic Archimedean point from which words or language can be explained (PG 40). Language must speak for itself. Consequently, grammatical explanations presuppose a background of prior understanding, a partial linguistic competence. With language-*learners* such as we, explanation has a pedagogical role only after brute training has laid the foundations of elementary linguistic skills (Z §419). (With creatures having innate mastery of language, explanation would have no pedagogic role, but would have a function in determining criteria of understanding and so settling, in dispute, whether certain disagreements were over definitions or judgements, meaning or truth. That is, its role would be the same as its role in the non-pedagogic transactions of mature language-users.)

The basic linguistic training undergone prior to teaching and explaining involves a host of presuppositions. These concern both the natural order of things (broadly speaking, the continuation of those regularities of co-existence and succession that are observable by us as we tread our path in the world) and the order of human nature. A wide range of discriminatory abilities, recognitional reactions, imitative propensities, and behavioural patterns are part of the natural history of mankind. Were these different in certain imaginable ways we would have a radically different language, or none at all. Philosophers often forget that a language is part of the history of a form of life. This oversight does not have merely trivial consequences. Examination of teaching contexts helps remind us how much is taken for granted for explanation to be possible.

(ii) Explanation explains only within a language (PLP 126). A person can only understand an explanation *as* an explanation once he can frame questions of the form 'What does . . . mean?' or 'Does he mean . . . by . . .?' Explanations are correlates of requests for explanations of meaning, unclarity or doubt about meaning, and misunderstanding about meaning (PG 62; PI §27). This is one aspect of the fact that explanations of meaning 'belong to grammar'. They give an array of intra-linguistic articulations rather than connecting language to reality or stating contingent truths about sounds or signs. They presuppose considerable knowledge (with us, acquired through drill and training) in order to get a grip. One can, by means of explanations, extend the nascent network of the learner's language, but only if it is there to be extended.

(iii) Teaching gives a primitive language-game in which a word is used (LA 1), and is useful in destroying misconceptions. Thus it is salutary to be reminded that one is not shown a dream when one is taught to say 'I dreamt'. Similarly, the order of teaching cannot be contrary to the order of logical priority, if any (e.g. the relation of '. . . is F' and '. . . seems F' (Z §§413 f.)).

(iv) Teaching brings to the fore the purposes of explanation, and hence the standard of satisfactoriness of explanations (see below). We give explanations to teach the use, to avert a particular misunderstanding, or to establish a shared understanding of a given expression. In order to achieve these goals, it is neither necessary nor possible that every conceivable misuse or misunderstanding be brought to light and explicitly excluded or cleared up. In giving an explanation of a term like *Satz* ('sentence with a sense' or 'proposition'), it is not necessary thereby to distinguish *Sätze* from cabbages. Nor is it, *pace* Frege, a defect in an explanation of 'number' that it will not 'decide for us' whether or not Julius Caesar is a number (FA §56). This viewpoint is not a matter of liberal tolerance, nor of willingness to abide by pedagogic sufficiency. It is rather rooted in Wittgenstein's conception of the point of explanation, the criterion of completeness of explanation, and the onus of proof in disputed cases.

One might object that this conception of explanation is too pragmatic. After all, when philosophers raise questions about the definition of 'a right' in jurisprudence, the explanation of 'person' in ethics or philosophy of mind, or 'colour' in epistomology, their questions are not guided by such pragmatic considerations. This is correct. What is doubtful, however, is whether their quest is really for an explanation. Commonly what they need is an *Übersicht* of explanations which are perfectly well known (see 'Übersicht', pp. 305 ff.)—and an *Übersicht* of explanations, or even a synopsis of explanations, is not itself an improved explanation which is in competition with our common-or-garden variety. Occasionally, especially, e.g., in legal philosophy, philosophers seek a regimentation (e.g. of the concept of legal right) for more or less practical purposes. But this, again, is not an explanation of the meaning of our term in current legal discourse, but a stipulation to be justified by certain purposes. Moreover, such considerations are very marginal indeed in the heartland of philosophy (philosophy of language, metaphysics, epistemology, philosophy of mind).

(v) The importance of scrutinizing teaching does not consist in what it shows about learning, but what it shows about *what* is taught. In teaching, unlike mere training, we explain the meanings of words. Meaning is what is given by an explanation of meaning (PG 59; PI §560), and explanations of meaning are characteristically given in teaching to those who have mastered enough of the language to ask for them. Explanations of meaning are normative. As *causes* of understanding they are indeed irrelevant; but as *rules*, standards of correctness that enter into the criteria of understanding, their relevance to philosophy is paramount.

Explanations given in teaching (or the giving of which provides criteria of understanding) display three further crucial features.

(i) They bring to light what it is that we, in our linguistic transactions, call 'an explanation of meaning'. This has three significant corollaries, two positive, one negative. (a) We are forced to attend to the diversity of types of explanation of word-meaning, e.g. ostensive definition, definition by reference to samples (canonical or optional), explanation by example, contextual definition, and to the nature and diversity of explanation of sentence-meaning, i.e. simple paraphrase (which need not involve strict synonymy), paraphrastic *contrast* (which may be supplemented by, e.g., ostension), contextual amplification. (b) The normativity of explanations of meaning is emphasized, for just as giving a correct explanation of a word is a criterion of understanding it, so too an explanation provides a standard (though not necessarily an application rule) by appeal to which members of a speech-community judge correctness of use. (c) Negatively, scrutiny of our common practice of explanation of words serves as a corrective to the semanticists' subliming the notion of explanation. A Fregean would say that an explanation is a rule fixing the contribution an expression makes to determining the truth-conditions of any sentence in which it occurs. Thus an explanation of a first-level concept-word 'Φ' is a rule determining for any object

under any possible conditions whether it has the property Φ (GA ii. §56).
But *this* explanation of 'explanation', though it purports to set out
necessary and sufficient conditions for a statement to be an explanation of
meaning, is at odds with our ordinary notion of explanation. If the
meaning of 'explanation' is itself what is explained in our actual
explanations of 'explanation' (of word-meanings), then this Fregean
account is a distortion of our concept. One kind of explanation of
'explanation of meaning' is by example; we may cite all the variety
mentioned in (a) above, and more, as examples of explanation of
word-meaning. Not only do we not give a Fregean explanation of
'explanation of meaning', but, more importantly, we would not acknowledge its correctness. It is too restrictive, failing to include much that we
manifestly classify as explanation. Moreover, on this explanation of
'explanation', numerous expressions cannot be explained by us. Frege,
thus interpreted, does not set standards of explanation that are too high
for us mere mortals (appropriate, as it were, only for God and the
angels), rather he sets standards that are absurd. Just how deeply this
redefinition of 'explanation' distorts a philosophical surview of language
will come to light later.[1]

(ii) Consideration of teaching contexts highlights what a *successful*
explanation is, and what it is for it to be complete. The latter issue is, of
course, the positive correlate of the rejection of the Fregean ideal. The
notion of a complete explanation needs re-examination (see below).
What it is for an explanation to be successful must obviously be
understood in terms of its fulfilling the purposes of an explanation in
language-teaching and in clarifications of meaning. It is successful to the
extent that it averts a specified misunderstanding, confirms a shared
understanding, or teaches the use of an expression. Whether it is
successful depends on the learner's subsequent use of the expression
explained and on whether this use manifests understanding of the
expression and hence understanding of the explanation of it. An explanation may be complete without being successful, and successful without
being complete. This is partly clarified by a third feature.

(iii) Explanations may be final but are not infallible (any more than a
final court of appeal is infallible). An explanation, according to Wittgen-

---

[1] Wittgenstein did not lack sympathy for the Fregean vision. After all, he had once
succumbed to a version of it. Nor was he even as late as 1930 altogether immune to the
intoxicating power of a sublimed conception of explanation:

Ich kämpfe immer wieder—ob erfolgreich das weiss ich nicht—gegen die Tendenz in meinem eigenen
Geiste an in der Philosophie Regeln autzustellen (zu konstruiren), Annahmen (Hypothesen) zu machen
statt nur zu sehen was da ist (Vol. IV, 160).

(I struggle again and again—whether successfully I do not know—against the tendency in my own mind
to set up (construct) rules in philosophy, to make suppositions (hypotheses) instead of just seeing what is
there.)

stein's generous conception of a rule, gives a rule for the use of the expression it explains (although by no means always an application rule). But it does not *apply* the rule it specifies. The finality of a rule consists in there being no further rule guiding us in applying it.[2] But, of course, it does not follow that no mistakes, let alone misunderstandings, are possible. An ostensive definition of 'red' is, in the appropriate context, with an appropriate sample, both final and complete. But it does not apply itself; it will not distinguish red from orange. Where rules come to an end, there their application waits. It is a bridge that can, as it were, only be crossed in practice, not in theory (EBT 112). On the one hand, explanation of word-meaning *is* explanation of word-application (Vol. VI, 217); on the other, only the application of language can show how it is applied (Vol. VI, 70). The tensions between these complementary ideas are frequently evident. They will, however, only be faced head-on in Volume 2.

3. *Explanation and meaning*

Meaning is what is given by explanation of meaning. The importance of this truism cannot be overestimated.

First, it enables us to side-step talk about meanings, with all the confusion invited by that noun. Explanations are, as it were, 'concrete', and do not so easily mislead us, in the way 'meaning' does, to chase shadows (Vol. XII, 32). The dictum could be interpreted: 'Let's only bother about what's called the explanation of meaning, and let's not bother about meaning in any other sense' (PG 69).

Secondly, the dictum returns us to our ordinary linguistic practices, including our practices of explanation. Applied to the term 'explanation' itself, it prevents us from subliming the notion of explanation into an arcane ideal. We have a well-established *practice* of explanation. This in itself lays important restrictions upon what an explanation *is*—restrictions which we will merely enumerate for the moment. (i) Explanation must be general: the grounds for an assertion, for example (PG 228), must hold not only for *this* person and *this* occasion, but quite *generally*, although they are not, of course, indefeasible. Grounds and justifications here are grammatical (not inductive) and are given in explanations. (ii) Explanations must be public: 'If I need a justification for using a word, it must also be one for someone else' (PI §378). This is a distinct point

---

[2] Of course, if the explanation employs words that are not understood by the hearer, those words may in turn be explained. But *those* explanations are not rules for the application of the rule in the statement of which these words occur. That there are further explanations in *this* dimension does *not* show that a rule is not final, i.e. that a further rule mediates between the explained expression and its application.

from generality. It rules out, for example, the appeal to subjective perceptions (which is not ruled out by the generality requirement) as grounds for assertion. 'I could not apply any rules to a *private* transition from what is seen to words. Here the rules really would hang in the air; for the institution of their use is lacking' (PI §380). (iii) Explanations, unlike causes, come to an end; i.e. the practice of explanation has limits (which may shift). (iv) Where explanations end lies consensual action, an agreed practice of *applying* a term in a given way. Explanations do not apply themselves, but there exists a public practice of applying the explained expressions *in accord with* the explanation (i.e. there are criteria determining accord and discord, and a practice of appeal to the rule given by the explanation). (v) For a language to exist there must be agreement in definitions, hence consensus in accepting certain types of explanation as criteria of understanding, the satisfaction of which establishes such agreement (PI §241). (Each of these different points will be discussed later.)

Thirdly, the dictum is one move in the exhaustive campaign waged against the calculus model of language (meaning) and its correlate, the mental (or neural) model of a *mechanism* of understanding. Explanations, on Wittgenstein's conception, must be immanent—accessible to us and surveyable by us. This is not guaranteed by the calculus model nor required by the mechanism picture of understanding. But unless explanations are thus accessible there would be no criteria of understanding other than correct use. Thus explanation would become detached from understanding (and what are ordinarily conceived as explanations would be merely heuristic). It would at least make sense to possess ineffable understanding of word-meaning, for the real, ideal, explanation may not yet have been discovered, and may indeed transcend the powers of the human intellect. But, Wittgenstein insists, a meaning or sense that cannot be explained does not concern us, for one cannot act in contravention of it (Vol. IV, 259). Explanation is not bringing something hidden to light, merely displaying (but not making) a move in a game we constantly play.

4. *Explanation and grammar*

That grammar is autonomous, arbitrary, not justified by reference to reality is a deep leitmotiv of Wittgenstein's later work. That explanations are intralinguistic (even though they often, as in ostensive definition, include partly concrete symbols) is merely an aspect of this general thesis. They belong to grammar. Giving an explanation consists in displaying some of the connections in the grammatical reticulation of rules. Explanations are rules, but, of course, not always or even usually application rules. Their normativity consists in the fact that a rule given by an acceptable explanation provides a standard to judge correct uses of an expression. This may be by way of *grounds* of application, legitimacy of *substitution*, or *criteria of understanding*.

A corollary of the contention that meaning is what is understood when one understands an expression and what is explained in an explanation of meaning is that the age-old dogma that language contains 'indefinables' must be re-examined. What does it mean to say that an expression is indefinable (BT 256 ff.)? That it is not defined by *Merkmale*? Or that it cannot be explained? The former is unobjectionable, but trivial. The latter is incoherent, for there can be no ineffable meanings in a language.

The classical requirement that definition be a kind of analysis, that it give necessary and sufficient conditions for the application of an expression, was the product of philosophers' pipe-dreams. It is an illusory ideal that stands in the way of a correct grasp of our form of representation. First, definitions of a term that analyse it into a conjunction of characteristic marks (*Merkmal*-definition) are only one kind of definition in terms of necessary and sufficient conditions (definitions *per genus et differentiam* are merely a limiting case of *Merkmal*-definitions). Other kinds are prominent, e.g., in mathematics ('prime number') and genealogy ('grandfather'); here necessary and sufficient conditions are given by employing expressions of generality. Secondly, definition by necessary and sufficient conditions is only one kind of explanation of meaning, and by no means privileged. It is important to note that contrary to philosophical dogma, different explanations of one and the same term may be equally legitimate. One can define an elephant by genus and differentia, but an ostensive definition at the zoo is not less correct (nor is pointing at a mere picture of an elephant!). A seemingly crude explanation such as 'It is a large, grey, thick-skinned animal with a long trunk and huge flapping ears' is none the worse *qua* explanation of word-meaning, no matter how painful to a zoologist's ears.

Not only may the same term be explained in different ways, but different terms may be peculiarly suited to one kind of, or a narrow range of, explanation. When this is so, this feature of the appropriate mode of explanation often reveals important facets about the type of the expressions. Thus names of perceptual qualities are explained by samples, days of the week by enumeration, prepositions by contextual paraphrase, etc.

It is worth noting the wide diversity of types of explanation of meaning and reflecting on the oddity of philosophers' insistence that *Merkmal*-definition is uniquely appropriate, the rest being mere approximation to this ideal. We must recognize explanations of words by reference to samples (cf. 'Ostensive definition and its ramifications' pp. 102 ff.). Such definitions may involve a canonical sample (the standard metre), or an optional sample, whether it is also a standard one (any kilogram weight) or not (any coloured object). It may involve ostension (if an observable sample is available), sampling the sample (e.g. tasting a

lemon), or 'manufacturing' the sample (e.g. a musical note with a tuning
fork). Equally it may involve locating a possible sample or giving
instructions for its production. Quite a different kind of explanation is
encountered when we deal with family resemblance terms (cf. §§65 ff.).
These we explain by means of paradigmatic examples, typically with a
similarity rider. The examples may vary from person to person and time
to time. If A explains a family resemblance concept 'Φ' by reference to
examples a . . . d 'and other like cases', and B explains 'Φ' by reference to
examples e . . . h 'and other like cases', it does not follow that their
understanding of 'Φ' (its meaning) differs as long as citing a . . . d and
citing e . . . h are both criteria for understanding 'Φ' and so acknowledged in the general practice of explaining 'Φ'. There are many other
types of equally legitimate explanation: locative explanations, ostension,
truth-table explanation of logical connectives, contextual paraphrase,
explanation by enumeration, explanation by examples together with a
generative rule, and others. Only dogmatism blinds us to the richness
and diversity of our actual practices of explanation.

One reason for our failure to examine and take seriously different
kinds of explanation is dogmatism about adequacy of explanation.
According to this dogma, an explanation of a concept is *complete* if and
only if it unambiguously determines of any object whether or not it falls
under the concept. Similarly, an explanation is *successful* if and only if it
enables the hearer to decide of any object whether or not it falls under the
concept (given the facts). Judged by these standards of adequacy, most
actual explanations, indeed many *kinds* of explanation, are defective, i.e.
neither complete nor successful. We are apt therefore to dismiss them as
incorrect.

We must carefully distinguish correctness from completeness and
from success. Successfulness is an external pedagogical property of
explanations. A has successfully explained to B what 'Φ' means to the
extent that his explanation enables B to go on and make at least those
applications of 'Φ' which in the practice of the language would be
justified by reference to that explanation. Correctness and incompleteness, by contrast, are internal normative properties of explanations. An
explanation may be correct but incomplete. It is perfectly correct to say
that justice is, *inter alia*, paying one's debts. Socrates is wrong to reject
this explanation altogether; rather, he should point out its limitations,
remind us that justice also takes other forms. We may call this feature
'incompleteness'. It does not consist in the fact that the explanation will
not decide for us whether the number two is just! Rather, it consists in
the fact that there are legitimate standard applications of the term which
we do not take to be explained by this explanation. One could not justify
the application of 'just' or 'unjust' to strict liability in the penal code by
reference to Cephalus' explanation. But giving a correct explanation *is* a

criterion of understanding, whereas failing to give a complete explanation is *not* a criterion for failing to understand. Indeed, in many circumstances, giving a correct but incomplete explanation is a criterion of understanding, or, at least, of partial understanding. Only if Cephalus were to give an incorrect explanation of 'just' or were to misuse it would there be grounds (albeit themselves defeasible) for Socrates to deny that he understands it.

What then is a *complete* explanation? Clarifying this involves noting three features of the general idea of completeness. (i) 'Complete' and 'incomplete' are correlative terms. It only makes sense to say of an X that it is incomplete if it makes *sense* to say that it is complete; i.e. there must *be* specifiable criteria of completeness for X. (ii) 'Complete' and 'incomplete' are relative terms. There is no absolute standard of completeness. Rather, what counts as a complete X depends upon what X is, and what criteria we fix for a complete X (if any). (iii) Incompleteness is in general a defect relative to the purposes by reference to which particular criteria of completeness are fixed. Note the parallels with the concepts simple/complex and exact/inexact. In particular, it is remarkable that inexactness, like incompleteness, is in general a relative defect, but neither feature is uniformly so. An inexact or incomplete X may suit our purposes perfectly in a given context.

How do these considerations bear upon the idea of completeness of explanation? A complete explanation of an expression is an explanation that may legitimately be invoked as a standard of correctness for the application of that expression in normal contexts. Relative to this standard of completeness, explanations may be incomplete in failing to provide as general a standard of correct use. An incomplete explanation may be perfectly adequate in certain contexts, e.g. when only one aspect of an expression is in view, or when establishing a rough and ready understanding is sufficient for purposes at hand. The completeness of an explanation of meaning is not (*contra* Frege) a feature of the *form* of the explanation (e.g. laying down necessary and sufficient conditions of application). It is rather a feature of the *normative role* of the explanation in the practice of using the expression, and of the role which *giving* that explanation has in establishing understanding. Thus, e.g., an ostensive definition of 'red' is not incomplete because it provides no application rule (grounds of application, or justification), nor because it fails to explain uses such as 'He saw red and lashed out in fury'. So too, a *Merkmal*-explanation of 'bachelor' is not incomplete because it does not budget for 'bachelor of arts'. And an explanation of a family resemblance term by paradigmatic examples is complete, even though its rider 'and other like things' does not specify the rough borderlines of the concept.

It might seem that the lexicographer or grammarian gives the only really complete explanations of the meanings of expressions. Most speakers, one might think, can give only incomplete explanations of the meanings of words they use and understand. It is the task of lexicographers to discover or assemble the complete explanations. This is fallacious. For a comprehensive synopsis of different explanations of subtly divergent uses of an expression is not a more general (hence complete) explanation of any particular use. The lexicographer's concatenation of explanations is not a unitary explanation that serves as a standard of correct use for every application of its explanandum. (An explanation of how to castle in chess is not incomplete for failing to mention all the other rules governing the movements of the king and rooks.)

The explanation of completeness clarifies why giving even a complete explanation does not guarantee understanding. The learner must also grasp the method of projection of the explanation. Pointing at a scarlet rose and saying 'That colour is red' will not delineate the boundaries of the concept. 'Only the application of language can show how it is to be applied' (Vol. VI, 70). But the explanation is not incomplete for lack of a rule stating how it is to be applied; the learner must learn the application from our practice (and even if we had a supplementary rule here, he would still have to learn how to apply *it*—from our practice). Consequently, giving even a complete explanation is only a *criterion* (defeasible evidence conferring certainty *ceteris paribus*) of understanding, and not a sufficient condition of understanding. For a person may give a correct and complete explanation of 'X', and yet regularly misapply 'X' in some standard context, e.g. he may define 'red' correctly, but go on to call orange objects red, or he may explain 'game' by saying that rugby, cricket, and football, and other like things, are games, and then deny that chess is a game. He has not bridged the gap between explanation and application, i.e. he does not employ the explanation as a rule guiding the application of the term it defines to those cases to which we apply it, applications which we take to be explained and legitimized by that explanation.

There can be more than one complete explanation of an expression, even in a single context. Pointing at scarlet or maroon objects in explanation of 'red' gives an equally correct and complete ostensive explanation of 'red'; cricket, chess, and tiddlywinks, or rugger, draughts, and poker are equally good paradigms in a family resemblance explanation of 'game'. What the different complete explanations of the same expression share is a common status in the practice of explanation. Giving any correct explanation is a criterion of understanding, and if it is complete it can equally be appealed to as a standard of correctness of use in all normal cases.

Must every significant expression in a language have a complete explanation? It seems that there are numerous counter-examples to this claim, e.g. applicatives, prepositions, and many adjuncts, disjuncts, and conjuncts constitute obvious ones (to take only one example, the preposition 'on': 'on the table', 'on the agenda', 'on the air', 'on call', 'on further reflection', 'on Monday'). In cases such as these (and they are legion), we manifest our understanding by contextual paraphrastic explanation. There is no explanation of the meaning of 'on' *simpliciter*, yet it makes a significant contribution to phrases and sentences in which it occurs.[3] If asked for *the* meaning of words such as 'on', 'well', 'rather', 'so', 'yet', we typically respond by asking for the context of their occurrence.

Does this not show that there are no complete explanations for such expressions? The case rests on a misunderstanding. On the one hand, we can and do give complete explanations of the various phrases to which these prepositions, etc., contribute. On the other hand, we do not give *any* explanation, either complete or incomplete, of such an expression in isolation. *There is no explanation* which fulfils the role of standard of correct use for an expression of the kind in question in all standard contexts. This fact is indeed reflected in our hesitation to say of such expressions that they have *a* meaning. On the one hand, they clearly make a non-trivial contribution to contexts in which they occur (which we can readily explain); on the other, there is no general explanation of what they mean (not even by way of a general rule specifying their systematic effect on the context of their occurrence). There is nothing here that we do not know, nor any reason for thinking that our understanding outstrips our ability to explain. Although there is no (complete or incomplete) explanation which functions as a standard of correct use for every context of occurrence of these kinds of words, it does not, of course, follow that for every context of occurrence there is not a complete explanation. Indeed, we should reflect on the bizarreness of the idea that explanation (*in grammar*) might not be complete. Does this mean that our use of the expression is governed by rules (standards of correctness) of which we are ignorant? Or is it that we know them but cannot articulate them? Do they then 'act at a distance' by metaphysical or metapsychical means? The idea is as absurd as the thought that our rules for a game might be incomplete, even though we can all play it perfectly well.

5. *Explanation and understanding*

The concept of understanding and its relations to meaning and explanation lie at the heart of Wittgenstein's philosophy of language. Is he therefore guilty of not separating the psychological from the logical, the

---

[3] This has non-trivial consequences for the principle that the sense of a sentence is composed of the senses of its constituents, and that we understand a sentence in virtue of understanding its constituents and structure.

ve from the objective? The accusation rests upon a misunder-
ıg of what is wrong with psychologism. Frege's repudiation of
.ologism is associated with the correct insight that meaning is
objective, public, and communicable. Ideas, which were, for the
'psychological logicians', the gold backing for the currency of words, are
identifiability-dependent on their owners, hence not objective or capable
of being shared. Indeed they are only communicable on condition that
the words designating them have a meaning that is objective and hence
distinct from the ideas designated. Meanings are not psychological
objects. This appropriate criticism of the Cartesian and empiricist
heritage, however, in no way justifies the contention that no psychological concept is pertinent to a correct surview of meaning.

In particular, since its meaning is what is understood when a person
understands an expression, the concept of understanding is indeed
pertinent to our investigation. While the psychological accompaniments
of understanding are irrelevant, the criteria of understanding are not.
They show the grounds for ascribing understanding to a person, for
attributing to him a grasp of the meaning of a given expression. Hence
the concept of understanding gives us leverage upon that of meaning.
Since the criteria of understanding establish the possibility of a shared,
agreed, understanding of an expression and since the object of understanding is thereby shown to be objective and communicable, introduction of the concept of understanding does not involve us in 'subjectiv-
ism', but sustains the objectivity of meaning which the anti-
psychologism was concerned to preserve.

Explanation is internally related to understanding. Not everything that
brings about or promotes understanding is an explanation. If, miracul-
ously, we had a drug which had the effect of producing knowledge of
French in its taker, taking the drug would not be a kind of explaining,
nor giving it a kind of teaching (B i. §34; PLP 126). A good spanking
may hasten learning, but it is not an explanation. Explanation gives the
content of understanding, i.e. the meaning of the expression understood
by the speaker (to be understood or acknowledged by the hearer). Hence
explanation would still be necessary to specify *what* is understood even if
the understanding were innate or induced by drugs. To repeat: meaning
is what is given by an explanation of meaning; so what is understood
when the explanation is grasped is the meaning.

The understanding with which we are concerned is the correlate of
explanation (PG 60). To understand an expression is to know what it
means. But if one knows what a given expression means, must one be
able to *say* what it means, i.e. answer the question 'What does it mean?'?
By definition a competent speaker uses his language correctly. But may
not his ability to use language outstrip his ability to explain that use? And
if he can give explanations of a sort, may they not merely point, hint at,

show the path towards correct use or proper explanation, and hence be 'scientifically speaking' inadequate?

This was indeed Frege's view and is still widespread. If the concept of explanation is sublimed, as in Frege's philosophy, then there is no reason why explanation should be the correlate of understanding: 'Often it is only after immense intellectual effort, which may have continued over centuries, that humanity at last succeeds in achieving knowledge of a concept in its pure form, in stripping off the irrelevant accretions which veil it from the eyes of the mind' (FA p. vii). And when we come to 'indefinables', the best we can do, in Frege's view, is 'to lead the reader or hearer by means of hints, to understand the words as intended' (CO p. 43).

Nothing could be further from Wittgenstein's conception of the matter. Explanations are not discoveries. What is understood by speakers of the same language is a shared, common, public meaning. There are no such things as ineffable meanings, nor is understanding a concealed inner mechanism. A competent speaker understands the expressions of his language. What are the criteria of his understanding? Wittgenstein emphasizes two: correct use of the expression, i.e. use in accord with the general practice, and giving correct explanations of that use, i.e. correct explanations of meaning. The two criteria are logically independent yet related.

They are related in the following way. The expression 'to know what "X" means' must be construed as containing an indirect question; i.e. 'what "X" means' is not a relative clause standing for some object that *is* the meaning of 'X'. Hence to know what 'X' means is to be able to answer the question 'what does "X" mean?' If a person understands the expression 'X', then he knows what it means, and if he knows what it means, then he can, standardly, answer the question 'What does it mean?', i.e. explain what it means. This point applies equally to sentences and to words or phrases. In the case of words, a competent speaker who uses 'X' correctly can explain the use of 'X', minimally, simply by invoking examples of its use. Many words can be explained perfectly well by spelling out series of appropriate examples of their applications (EBT 514; PG 119 f.). Examples are not a kind of hocus–pocus, nor are they mere hints at explanations (PG 273). Equally, if an appropriate instance is available, someone can use it as a sample to give an ostensive definition. For if he is able to say of the red object that it is red, then he may define 'red' by saying of the colour of that object that it is red. *Pari passu*, ostensive definition is not an 'aid' to understanding, but is a rule, belonging to the symbolism, for the use of the word defined (Vol. VI, 213). Further, if no sample is available, but a person knows where one is, he can give a locative explanation; and so on. These connections between ability to use and ability to explain depend upon a humdrum interpretation of what is an admissible explanation.

Though correct use and correct explanation (the two criteria of understanding) are thus connected, they are nevertheless independent. It does not *follow* from the fact that someone has used 'X' correctly in a given sentence that he will, on demand, explain it correctly. He may explain it incorrectly, thus casting doubt upon his understanding of 'X'. Yet, normally, if he in general uses 'X' correctly in various typical contexts, he will also give a correct explanation of 'X'.

The other side of the coin shows the same relatedness and independence. A person may give a correct explanation of 'X', and if he does he will normally also use 'X' correctly. Giving a correct explanation is a criterion of understanding. If he explains 'circle' as 'a plane figure each point of which is equidistant from a given point', or as 'the shape of a tenpenny piece', or as 'that figure over there', he will normally use the term 'circle', correctly in sentences such as 'The circle over there is too small', or 'Can you draw a circle here?' But though explanation and use are thus connected, they are independent. He may not know how to *apply* the rule he has given in his explanation in the correct (accepted) way. He may give a correct ostensive definition of 'violet', but go on to call indigo objects violet. He may use 'yellow' as we use 'something yellow', and hence give the same ostensive definition as we do, but use the expression defined differently (Vol. XII, 118). Thus his incorrect use will defeat the criterial support given by his correct explanation to the assertion that he understands the meaning of 'X'. Indeed, it will manifest his not actually understanding the explanation.

Now let us revert to the question of whether there may not be a gap between a person's understanding and his ability to explain what it is that he understands, between his knowing what 'X' means and his being able to say. We must admit the possibility of defective explanations, e.g. by giving poor examples in explaining a family resemblance concept or borderline paradigms in ostensive definition. Equally, one must budget for common forgetfulness or lack of linguistic self-consciousness, e.g. leaving a very important aspect of use unmentioned (similar to explaining the moves of the chess king, but forgetting the castling rule). Thus it would be common to explain 'nearly' as having much the same meaning as 'almost', quite forgetting their uses after negation. Even more obvious would be the difficulty in explaining the meanings of prepositions, concessive conjuncts, dummy sortal nouns, etc., in either a complete or synoptic way. That, one is inclined to think, is the grammarian's task. Does it then follow that we sometimes know what 'X' means, but cannot explain its use? Or that we know what we mean by what we say (in uttering a sentence containing 'X') but cannot explain what we mean? But then what does knowing what 'X' means consist in? We are imposing the wrong picture upon the concepts. First, it is our giving a *correct* explanation that is a criterion of understanding, and that need not

Explanation

be a *synopsis* of use. Most of us would be stumped to answer the question 'What does "at" mean?'—and would characteristically respond 'In what context?', or 'What particular phrase do you have in mind?' We may not be able to give a synopsis of use, but it does not follow that we cannot explain. No competent speaker would normally have any difficulty in giving a paraphrastic explanation of 'at 2.00', 'at Carfax', 'at school', 'aimed at the bird', 'alarmed at the commotion', 'left it at that', etc. It is these latter exercises that constitute criteria for understanding—not a metalinguistic synopsis. Secondly, we must consider what are the criteria for a person's being able, or not being able, to give a certain explanation. Clearly, the mere fact of not giving a particular explanation does not establish inability to give it. If a person is stumped for a reply to a request for an explanation, and we suggest one to him, and he sincerely responds 'Oh yes, of course; I should have thought of that'—we would frequently be willing to claim that he would have been able to explain if . . . We will normally be satisfied with his acknowledging the correctness of correct explanations. Thirdly, we must recall the large variety of generally acceptable explanations. That a person cannot explain 'circle' as 'the locus of points in a plane equidistant from a given point' (an inability explained by lack of knowledge of elementary geometry and its terminology) does not show that he cannot explain what 'circle' means, and does not support the contention that such a person's understanding (ability to use) outstrips his ability to explain. If he points at a circular figure and says 'That ↗ [shape] is a circle', he *has* explained the term. Finally, we can see that one source of the idea of knowing but not being able to say is the traditional idea that some words name 'simple ideas' or 'indefinables'. Everyone knows, one might think, what 'red' means—but no one can say. Does one depend here upon an elucidation 'relying upon an understanding willing to meet one half-way'? This notion rests on too restrictive a conception of saying or explaining. Ostensive definition by reference to a sample *says* what red is, explains what 'red' means. The sample together with the deictic gesture is a symbol. Similarly, under-standing of a family resemblance concept is not ineffable. We all know what 'justice' means, what games are, what moral value is, and we know how to say these things too. Not by 'essentialist' *Merkmal*-definitions, but by explanations by examples together with similarity clauses. These do *say* what 'games', 'justice', 'moral value' mean.

We need have no qualms about meanings being ineffable or under-standing being opaque. There are no discoveries in philosophical gram-mar, although a philosopher strives for an *Übersicht* of language. In this essay we have tried to state a case. In the rest of this book we shall try, with refinements and qualifications, to argue for it.

LANGUAGE-GAMES

1. *The emergence of the game analogy*

Although the notion of a language-game is introduced only in the *Blue Book*, the idea has a clear ancestry in Wittgenstein's earlier thought. For it can be traced back, through various transformations and reorientations, to the repudiation of the thesis that atomic propositions are logically independent of each other. This thesis was a cornerstone of the *Tractatus*. The existence of a logical dependence between propositions was there taken to be a mark of internal complexity. If 'p' entails 'q', then some constituent of 'p' must, it seemed, be complex, for that the sense of 'q' is contained in the sense of 'p' is explained by the fact that some component of 'q' is a characteristic mark of some component of 'p'. So when all complexity is eliminated by analysis, the resultant elementary propositions are logically independent.

This thesis of independence was the first acknowledged flaw in the foundations of the logical atomism of the *Tractatus*. In 'Some Remarks on Logical Form', Wittgenstein admitted that he had earlier thought statements expressing the degree of a quality to be analysable into a 'logical product of single statements of quantity and a completing supplementary statement'. This, he now realized, was false. As elaborately argued in *Philosophical Remarks* Ch. VIII, expressions for determinates of a single determinable occurring in elementary propositions vitiate the independence thesis. That B is red implies that B is not green, yellow, etc., and this cannot be accounted for in terms of truth-functional composition.

In the *Philosophical Remarks* Wittgenstein tried to budget for this incoherence by introducing the notion of a *Satzsystem*. Propositions are conceived of as belonging to systems, i.e. sets of propositions between the members of which relations of exclusion obtain which are not consequences of truth-functional combination, but of the concept-words occurring within the atomic proposition. This manoeuvre enabled Wittgenstein to continue to cling to one of the fundamental principles that had informed his earlier philosophy: namely that language is a kind of calculus. It is a logico-syntactical system of formation- and transformation-rules together with assignments of meanings to the indefinables (the 'axioms' of the calculus). These jointly determine the meaning of every well-formed sentence of the language. Together with the appropriate facts, this calculus determines unequivocally the truth-value of every such sentence. We shall later scrutinize in detail the calculus model, and Wittgenstein's criticisms of it.

At the same time an important analogy crops up in Wittgenstein's reflections on language, namely that between language and chess. It is worthwhile tracing its source back to the controversy between Frege and the formalists, to note Wittgenstein's reasons for resuscitating the analogy, to examine the various ways in which he exploited it, and finally to see how he poured new wine into this old bottle when the calculus model was repudiated.

Thomae (quoted by Frege: GA ii. §88) argued that arithmetic is a game with contentless signs played according to combinatorial rules. Numerals are thus akin to chess pieces; both are merely external signs for, foci of, a set of rules. Wittgenstein discussed the formalists' conception of arithmetic, their use of the chess analogy and Frege's reactions to this (WWK 103 ff., cf. 124, 150 f., 163, 170). Frege presents two alternatives: either mathematics is about signs, ink marks on paper, or it is about what those signs represent, namely numbers. But, Wittgenstein argues, this is a false dichotomy. This is clarified by the formalists' chess analogy. For a game of chess is not 'about' chess pieces (if the queen is carved so as to appear fierce she will not be any more powerful in the game). But the pieces do not go proxy for anything. They have no *Bedeutung*. One could say that the 'meaning' of a chess piece is the sum of rules that determine its possible movements. But equally correctly, that it has no meaning. Similarly, Frege is right that the sign '0' does not have the property that when added to the sign '1' it yields the sign '1', but wrong to infer that '0 + 1 = 1' is therefore 'about' numbers. The chess analogy suggests an alternative conception: namely that numerals used in sentences of pure arithmetic have no meanings. Only the applications of arithmetic give it any meaning. The sentences of pure arithmetic are in effect *rules*. They govern the use of numerals in sentences of applied arithmetic.

Already at this stage Wittgenstein utilizes the analogy more extensively than did the formalists. Chess can usefully illuminate features of logical syntax. If language is conceived as a logico–syntactical calculus, chess can bring to light the following features. (i) Its rules, like the rules of chess, have no foundations and cannot be justified by reference to reality. Its rules are autonomous; nothing dictates them.[1] (ii) Its rules are arbitrary and could be different; change the rules and you merely change the game. 'Losing Chess' is a different game from chess. (iii) The logical syntax of a word determines its place in grammar, and is akin to the rules determining the possible moves of a chess piece. All that is lacking is the

---

[1] In Vol. IX, 234 Wittgenstein remarks that Frege suggested that there could be people who are only acquainted with the first five cardinal numbers, but the rest of the series exists irrespective of their, or our, knowledge. Do the rules of chess also exist independently of us? See also TS. 219, 8: the analogy with chess illustrates the autonomy of language, for it diminishes the temptation to conceive of meaning as an object which can be pointed at.

assignment of meaning, i.e. a method of application. (iv) It is the method of application that differentiates language (and applied mathematics) from chess (and pure mathematics).

The sting lay hidden in the last two points. When the implications of the seemingly innocuous rider concerning the application of signs in a calculus became clear to Wittgenstein, he attacked the calculus model of language. But the chess analogy remained useful. Whether language is a calculus or not, (i) the outward similarity of words is comparable to that of chess pieces, and no less misleading (PG 59); (ii) the combinatorial possibilities of words are comparable to the possible configurations of chess pieces; (iii) the use of a word in an utterance is like the use of a chess piece in a move; (iv) the meaning of a word is (up to a point) analogous to the powers of a chess piece; (v) just as a chess piece has significance only in the context of a move, and a move is a move only in a game, so too, correctly understood,[2] a word has a meaning only in the context of a sentence and a sentence is a sentence only in a language; (vi) understanding a word is not a mental state, event, or process, but (with qualifications) an ability to use it in certain ways for certain purposes, just as knowing how to play chess is knowing how to move the pieces in conformity with the rules of chess in pursuit of the goal of winning—in both cases a technique is mastered (MS. 166, 28 f.).

The analogies are important, but they must not overshadow the dissimilarities between language and a calculus. Their importance only became clear to Wittgenstein in the mid-thirties. Here we will provisionally list some of the misleading features of the calculus model. (i) It has no internal association with action and behavioural response, or at least none that appears on the surface. (ii) It suggests a system of rules covering all possible cases, whereas our language, as Wittgenstein came to see, does not lay down rules which will dictate a result for every conceivable circumstance. (iii) It obscures philosophical problems concerning the application of rules, the fact that rules do not determine their own application and that although there may be rules guiding the application of rules, this process does not terminate in rules which univocally determine their own applications. (iv) It misconstrues the principle that a word has a meaning only in the context of a sentence and concurrently totally distorts the nature of understanding. It is false that a complete understanding of language is derivable from knowledge of definitions and forms alone. (v) It idealizes syntax by encouraging the myth of 'logical form' that will be perspicuously displayed by 'logical syntax' and provide a univocal method of distinguishing sense from nonsense. (vi) it is not readily adaptable to the facts that we explain different expressions in different ways, and that radically different explanations are equally

---

[2] See 'A word has a meaning only in the context of a sentence', pp. 166 ff.

correct for one and the same univocal expression. (vii) It opens up, at least potentially, a gap between the internal relations set up within the calculus (the intra-calculus explanations) and the common-or-garden explanations that we accept in our linguistic practices as criteria of understanding. (viii) Consequently, it raises a serious problem of 'fit'. Given a model calculus of a language, what features will show it to be correct? If the intra-calculus explanations of meaning diverge from our ordinary explanations of meaning, what independent data can vindicate the model?

These considerations are among those that led Wittgenstein to abandon the calculus conception of language (although, to be sure, not *every* feature of it was jettisoned). This (negative) development, however, took some years. His abandonment of the *Satzsystem* conception, on the other hand, was rapid. Its range of application was narrow (determinates of determinables) and even within its range it failed to capture the rich, untidy conceptual articulations (between, e.g., 'red' and 'seeing red', first- and third-person uses of the latter expression, different tenses, 'appearing red' and 'appearing red to X', etc.). As Wittgenstein attended more to the philosophical significance of the activities and behaviour of which the use of language is an integral part, the conception of language as a calculus was seen to be less fruitful. It needed to be replaced by something much looser and more flexible.

The new move was to draw analogies between the idea of language and that of a game. It was made early and hesitantly, and coexisted for a long while with the calculus conception:

Wer etwas dagegen hat, dass man sagt, die Regeln der Grammatik seien Spielregeln, hat in dem Sinne Recht, dass das was das Spiel zum Spiel macht, die Konkurrenz von Spielern, der Zweck der Unterhaltung und Erholung, in der Grammatik abwesend ist, etc. Aber niemand wird leugnen, dass das Studium des Wesens der Spielregeln für das Studium der grammatischen Regeln nützlich sein muss, da *irgend* eine Aehnlichkeit zweifellos besteht. Es ist überhaupt besser, ohne ein gefasstes Urteil oder Vorurteil über die Analogie zwischen Grammatik und Spiel, und nur getrieben von dem sicheren Instinkt, dass hier eine Verwandtschaft vorliegt, die Spielregeln zu betrachten. Und hier wieder soll man einfach berichten, was man sieht und nicht fürchten, dass man damit eine wichtige Anschauung untergräbt, oder auch, seine Zeit mit etwas Überflüssigen verliert.

Man sieht dann vor allem, wie der Begriff des Spiels und damit der Spielregel ein an den Rändern verschwimmender ist. (EBT 578.)

(If anyone objects to saying that the rules of grammar are rules of a game, he is right in the sense that what makes a game into a game, the competition of the players, the purpose of entertainment and relaxation, is absent from grammar, etc. But no one will deny that the study of the nature of rules of games must be useful for the study of grammatical rules, since *some sort* of similarity undeniably obtains. It is on the whole better to reflect on rules of games without any fixed opinion or prejudice about the analogy between grammar and game, but merely to be driven by the certain instinct that there is here a kinship. And here again one should simply report what one sees, and not fear that one is thereby undermining an important aspect, nor that one is wasting one's time on irrelevance.

One sees then above all how the concept of a game and with it that of rules of a game are blurred at the edges.)

From this tentative step a great deal was to follow over the next few years. For the notion of a game carries with it a wide range of desiderated associations that may fruitfully illuminate the concept of language. Games are free creations of the human mind, autonomous and rule-governed. The rules of a game do not budget for every conceivable circumstance, but are not therefore deemed incomplete. The foundation of the ability to play a game lies in training; the ability to play it is mastery of a technique. Playing games is a human *activity*, and its existence presupposes common reactions, propensities, and abilities. The 'gap' between rules and their application, which is bridged by training and familiarity with the practice of playing, is in plain view. The goal of a game, to the extent that it is a winning or losing game, is determined by the game (by what counts as winning or losing) and is not extraneous to it (PG 184), even though one may play for pleasure, fame, or money.

Furthermore, the concept of a game, which became Wittgenstein's favoured example of a family resemblance concept, itself exemplifies these important features of family resemblance that characterize the concepts of language, proposition, and rule. It is not a sharply defined concept, given by *Merkmale*, but is explained by reference to overlapping central cases linked in various complex and often tenuous ways with large numbers of different cases. It can be, though need not be, indefinitely extended, for there is no determinate set of necessary or sufficient conditions which an activity must satisfy in order to be a game.

With this significant shift the chess analogy did not lose its point. It remains a fruitful analogy, not because chess is a calculus, but because it is a game. Indeed, it becomes a more useful analogy in the new context since it preserves, *qua* analogy, many of the valuable features that were captured (even though distorted and exaggerated) by the calculus conception of language.

2. *The idea of a language-game*

The emergence of the game analogy led to the development of the idea of a language-game and hence a novel technique of philosophical analysis which may be called 'the language-game method'. The idea of a language-game is introduced[3] in the *Blue Book* (17):

> I shall in future again and again draw your attention to what I shall call language-games. These are ways of using signs simpler than those in which we use the signs of our highly complicated everyday language. Language-games are the forms of language with which a child begins to make use of words. The study of language-games is the study of primitive forms of language or primitive languages. If we want to study the problems of truth and falsehood, of the agreement and disagreement of propositions with reality, of the nature of assertion, assumption and question, we shall with great advantage look at primitive forms of language in which these forms of thinking appear without the confusing background of highly complicated processes of thought. When we look at such simple forms of language, the mental mist which seems to enshroud our ordinary use of language disappears. We see activities, reactions, which are clear-cut and transparent. On the other hand we recognize in these simple processes forms of language not separated by a break from our more complicated ones. We see that we can build up the complicated forms from the primitive ones by gradually adding new forms.

Having thus introduced, explained, and given point to the novel notion, Wittgenstein, surprisingly, does not employ it in the *Blue Book*.

The quoted passage suggests an *analytic-genetic* method which is later repudiated. It is no part of the conception of a language-game in the *Investigations* that it is a form of language with which a child begins to make use of words, although *some* invented language-games might be (cf. PI §7(b)). Two considerations militate against the analytic-genetic conception. (i) It has all the misleading implications of 'armchair learning theory' (cf. 'Explanation', pp. 29 ff.). (ii) The implicit picture in the *Blue Book* is of an unchanging core of elementary skills, which children acquire, and upon which more complex and sophisticated skills are grafted. This is correct *for us*: the child learns to use expressions which have multiple connections in the web of our language, and it begins with those which are presupposed by the more complex ones (e.g. it learns to use 'red' before 'looks red', 'red block' prior to 'image of a red block', etc.). But if we want to invoke imaginary language-games for philosophical purposes by comparing our use with analogous uses of a *primitive* language in a *simpler* context, then we must not look at child-learning situations which are simply *fragments* of a larger whole which is itself the source of our puzzlement. In the *Investigations*, the emphasis rightly shifts to 'primitive languages' and away from how a

---

[3] It is worth comparing the PG discussion (PG 57 = Vol. X, Um. 36) of the builders' language-game with the PI version. One can see here how far Wittgenstein had progressed in his method of analysis.

child learns a part of our language. The important feature of these primitive languages is that they are complete in themselves. By contrast, when we teach a child a fragment of our language we conceive of what it learns as a part of a greater, integrated whole, and hence as fragmentary. Its extension, when learnt, is viewed as a completion of *our* language, rather than an extension of an independently complete language. So we do not treat what is initially learnt as altered by subsequent learning, but rather we see the child as having an incomplete mastery of a greater whole, the rest of which is yet to be learnt. That is, we commonly view the child's learning from the perspective of the complete mastery of the language which we are aiming at. We distinguish here criteria for a partial mastery of a language (or part of it) and criteria for complete mastery. But in the complete language-games of the *Investigations*, addition and modification may change the original base. Adding pawns to a proto-chess is not merely expanding the game, but inventing a different game, for it changes the range of possible moves and configurations.

It is only in the *Brown Book* (1934–5) that the language-game *method* achieves maturity (and perhaps is used to excess). There is no deep difference between its use there and in the *Investigations*. The purpose of this technique is succinctly stated (PI §§5, 130). The difficulty in philosophy stems in part from our lack of a surview of our language (cf. 'Übersicht', pp. 305 ff.). Invented language-games are useful in so far as they are surveyable (PI §5(a)). Since we are not concerned with completeness or exactness (Z §§464 f.), we can ignore the objections that invented language-games are not exactly like ours and that calling fragments of our language 'language-games' is misleading since they are incomplete. Our whole interest lies in seeing connections, analogies, and disanalogies that will display the articulations of our language which give rise to, and resolve, philosophical problems. Such problems do not arise through imprecision and insufficient detail, and are not resolved by accumulation of exhaustive detail and 'scientifically' precise statements. Detail and precision are, tautologically, only necessary where needed, and that is not everywhere. Invented games need not be isomorphic with corresponding parts of our language. They illuminate both by similarity and difference, by showing, in a simple context, some feature which is analogous to a characteristic of our language, but which is there isolated from the confusing surroundings of its ordinary use. It also shows thereby, e.g., what complex concepts have a place in the *description* of our language, but not in the primitive context, and why. By setting up different grammatical structures from ours, we can soften our prejudices and dogmatism (that our grammar is correct, or the best), lay bare philosophical myths (that grammar is justified by reference to reality), and undermine facile generalizations.

3. Invented language-games

Wittgenstein's invented language-games display many features which are given varying prominence for philosophical purposes at hand. A language-game contains the following.

(i) Words, and sentences formed from them according to combinatorial rules: the vocabulary is given and its use in speech acts (moves in the language-game) specified.

(ii) Instruments (PI §§291, 569; BB 84): in the *Brown Book* Wittgenstein calls (a) gestures, as used in teaching the use of 'there', (b) patterns, whether samples, words, or figure drawings, and (c) pictures in a table which correlates words and pictures, 'instruments'. This accords with his favoured tool analogy for words. Most importantly, it extends the concepts of language and grammar to include elements hitherto regarded (by linguists and philosophers) as extraneous. This is a remarkable innovation (cf. 'Ostensive definition and its ramifications' pp. 102 ff.).

(iii) Context (*Zusammenhang*): it is important to distinguish the generality of the notion of context that is being used and the purpose for which it is brought into view. Like any other game, a language-game is 'played' in a setting. Wittgenstein's stress on the context of the game appears to be motivated by the wish to bring to the fore elements of linguistic activities which, while not obviously involved in the explanation of the meaning of constituent expressions (hence unlike instruments), are nevertheless pertinent to their meaning. At its most general the notion of context encompasses the presuppositions of meaning. If the context were significantly different, the game would not be played, for it would be pointless (C §617). Every game has its normality conditions the obtaining of which are presupposed by the game (Z §350). These may be very general features of the natural world, e.g. rigidity and non-elasticity of material objects and rods, without which no measuring would occur, and equally general features of man, e.g. agreement in responses (to injury, colour, pointing, etc.). They may, however, involve more specific features, peculiar to a very particular language-game of, say, a small linguistic group, e.g. interests and values (Z §380), special activities such as battles (PI §19), building (PI §2), contests (BB 110), as well as the availability of particular types of object (e.g. building stones, colour samples, etc.). We must distinguish context understood as presupposition of the *existence* of a game, as presupposition for the *actual playing* of that game on a given occasion, and as the colouring, as it were, of the game.

(iv) Activity of the game: this feature is related to the former. It is in the activities constitutive of a language-game that the point and purpose of linguistic expressions is evident. Concentration upon the activity which is the 'playing' of a language-game highlights the diversity of linguistic symbols, emphasizes their normal contexts of use, their normal (diverse) purposes, and the normal justifications for their use.

(v) The use, purpose, role and function of instruments, words, sentences (and occasionally even language-games themselves): these are crucially important features. We have here a family of concepts which plays a central role in Wittgenstein's philosophy. In his view the cardinal error of twentieth-century philosophy has been the focus upon form and structure of expression rather than upon these features (LA 2).

(vi) Learning games: we do learn games and the foundation of this learning is training (Z §§387, 419). In many of his invented language-games Wittgenstein sketches the different kinds of training necessary for a participant to be able to play (e.g. memorizing words, memorizing the sequence of natural numbers, learning the practice of comparison of samples, or the method of projection of a pattern, etc.). This highlights the nature of rule-following, and the way in which the 'gap' between rules and their application is bridged. It emphasizes the presuppositions of explanation and the prerequisites of doubt and question. It is a crucial component of the claim that all explanation comes to an end. By illuminating the difference in kinds of training for the use of different words, it clarifies the logical diversity of kinds of words (numerals, colour-words, names of material objects, etc.).

(vii) Completeness: Wittgenstein commonly emphasizes that his invented games are not fragments of a language, but should be considered as complete (PI §§2, 18; BB 81). Although not all of them are so characterized, those which are conceived as complete are especially useful as objects of comparison. Obviously, they lack features which are possessed by the analogues, in our language, of the elements in the primitive language (e.g. a number system consisting of '1, 2, 3, 4, many'). But they serve to isolate features which are obscured in the welter of conceptual connections of our complex language.

4. Natural language-games

Notoriously 'language-game' is also used to designate fragments of our actual linguistic practices. Wittgenstein speaks of 'the language-game with' words, e.g. 'game' (PI §71), 'proposition', 'language', 'thought', 'world' (PI §96), 'pain' (PI §300), 'read' (PI §156); also of language-games surrounding characteristic linguistic acts or activities, e.g. lying (PI §249), telling (PI §363), giving orders and obeying them, describing the appearance of an object, or giving its measurement, reporting an event, etc. (PI §23), telling a dream (PI p. 184), confessing a motive (PI p. 224); and also of more complex activities into which language is

woven, but which are not merely speech-acts or activities, e.g. constructing an object from a description, forming and testing hypotheses,
presenting results of experiments in tables and diagrams (PI §23),
making inductive predictions (PI §630). Occasionally, the term is used
even more generously, e.g. the language-game with physical objects or
sense impressions (PI p. 180) or with colours (Z §345).

The various elements previously isolated with respect to imaginary
games apply (with the exception, usually, of completeness) to actual
language-games. To the extent that isolation of a natural language-game
is possible, it is a matter of highlighting, bringing to the fore, features of
linguistic activity so firmly embedded in our daily practices that we no
longer notice them. Thrust forward in this way, we can more readily
scrutinize the familiar, see its dependence upon the texture from which
we have removed it, compare it with imaginary games deliberately
different in significant ways.

If the similarities between the artificial language-games and such a
fragment of language are sufficiently striking and extensive, it is natural
to extend the term 'language-game' by applying it also to the fragment
itself. This is a familiar development of language. Compare, e.g., the
penetration of the hydrodynamic terminology into electrodynamics in
virtue of the complex analogies between the behaviour of fluids and
electricity. We all speak of 'electric *current*' (or of electricity as 'current');
and it is immediately intelligible to characterize voltage as electrical
pressure or amperage as the rate of flow of electricity. The whole point
lies in constructing illuminating comparisons in order to dispel confusion. The measure of its success is the degree of naturalness in describing
puzzling fragments of our language as language-games. Yet, like all such
analogical developments of language, the transference of terminology
carries with it attendant dangers. We are moving in the realm of analogy;
language is not a game, nor typically are the activities into which its use is
woven.

IV

THE USES OF SENTENCES

1. *Introduction*

In §§18–27 Wittgenstein examines the second main ingredient of the Augustinian picture of language, that all sentences are mere combinations of names and function as descriptions. Like the preceding remarks, these are tentative and exploratory. They do not give a definitive refutation of this aspect of the Augustinian picture, nor do they track down the source of this illusion of insight. Still less do they sketch out a general account of how sentences are used and of how knowing how a sentence is used is related to understanding it. Nevertheless, the indisputable content of these sections is the suggestion that Augustine's picture of language gives a mistaken answer to the question 'What is a sentence (*Satz*)?', i.e. that describing is no more part of the essence of language than naming. This claim, if it can be substantiated, has radical consequences; for the thought that statement-making is the essential function of language is deeply rooted in philosophical theories of language.

In part because of the absence of a fuller treatment of the topic of using sentences, in part because of a tendency in his interpreters to consider each of his remarks in isolation from its argumentative context, and in part because of independently generated interest in 'speech-acts', these few sections of the *Investigations* have become a focus of controversy. Some have viewed them as arguing that the picture theory of meaning of the *Tractatus* can be salvaged by treating it as a theory of sense which must now be supplemented by a theory of mood or force. So what is understood in understanding a token-sentence can be split up into understanding the sentence-radical (which gives the 'descriptive content' of the sentence) and knowing the semantic mood (which gives its 'force'). Others have interpreted the argument as denying that it is possible to explain the use of sentences by distinguishing the theory of meaning from the theory of force. Some invoke these sections to support the claim that the examination of 'speech-acts' belongs to the theory of meaning (that 'illocutionary force' is part of meaning), while others deny the legitimacy of so doing. The general import of Wittgenstein's remarks here is by no means obvious.

In this essay we attempt to clarify §§18–27(a) in three respects: (i) to fill in a more detailed argument against the thesis that all sentences are descriptions; (ii) to indicate Wittgenstein's diagnosis of the roots of this illusion; and (iii) to sketch what he saw to be the correct conception of the relation of sentence-meaning and the uses of sentences.

2. Descriptions and facts

The Augustinian picture builds on the fundamental idea that all sentences are descriptions. Is this proto-picture not *obviously* incorrect? Surely the most cursory reflection, stimulated by the list of language-games in §23, shows it to be false. Indeed, it seems that a language might contain no descriptions at all; e.g. it might consist wholly of orders (§18) or questions and answers (§19).

Although this is an error, and indeed an obvious one, this conception of sentences will not be eradicated by the technique of confronting it with a truism. For philosophers have not *argued* themselves into it—*a fortiori* they have not done so through ignorance of this truism. Instead, they have taken this proto-picture as the starting point for their reasoning and then elaborated a fuller account of sentence-meaning to defend it against obvious objections.

One line of defence of Augustine's proto-picture is to admit that sentences have different uses, but to ascribe this to the fact that they are descriptions of different kinds of facts. The expression of a rule does not describe what is the case ('reality') but rather what ought to be the case (PLP 143). A request describes the speaker's desire (Vol. XI, 82). A question sometimes describes the speaker's state of ignorance (PI §24), sometimes his desire to be informed of something (EBT 598; PI §24; PLP 407). A speaker's justification of his action describes a connection between his action and something else, e.g. a desire or order (cf. PI §487). A description of a house in a novel describes a fictional fact, not an actual fact (cf. Vol. XII, 216). There seems no limit to the number of kinds of facts that we can distinguish, and hence no doubt that differences in the uses of sentences can always be represented as differences in the kinds of description that they express.

Wittgenstein makes many remarks that point to defects in this development of the Augustinian picture.

(i) The point of calling a sentence a description is presumably to characterize it as having a particular use. But even what are ordinarily called descriptions have a variety of different uses (PI §§24(b), 290 f.; Vol. XII, 215 f.). Further extension of 'description' (e.g. by treating rules as descriptions of normative facts) aggravates this problem. Consequently, even if all sentences were descriptions, it would not follow that they had a uniform use (EBT 575 f.; RC §336).

(ii) If every possible sentence in any conceivable language were a description, i.e. if there were no such thing as a sentence which did not function as a description, the term 'description' would not have its customary meaning since it would be extended to cover what are ordinarily *not* counted as descriptions (e.g. rule-formulations, questions, commands, curses). Moreover, the thesis that no sentence could fail to be a description makes the claim that every sentence is a description vacuous.

(iii) Treating every sentence as a description distorts the connection between understanding a sentence and reacting to it. If what a person communicates in saying something is a description of some fact, then understanding what he says is simply a matter of taking in the information contained in his description. What we do in response to this information is, it seems, something altogether independent (cf. PI §363). On this view, we must understand an order *before* we can obey it; understanding what we have been told to do is a mental event, for the occurrence of which our behaviour is at most a symptom. Similarly, our comforting someone who says 'I am in pain' is alleged to be appropriate only because he has conveyed to us the information that he is hurt and because we know that certain sorts of treatment alleviate pain; our behaviour in such a case is based on an inductive inference (cf. Z §§537 ff.). This account distorts the fact that certain behavioural responses to an utterance are criteria for understanding it (or misunderstanding it). Thus, it overlooks the fact that some responses to utterances are 'primitive', i.e. not grounded in inferences (cf. Z §§540 ff.).

(iv) Because the concept of description is internally related to others (e.g. the concepts of beginning and ceasing to have a property, of truth, of evidence), characterizing a sentence as a description has logical consequences (cf. Z §549). The consequence of calling every sentence a description is a budget of paradoxes. False analogies generate apparent problems, and mythical entities or processes are called into existence to solve them. 'My door is open' is a paradigmatic description; 'When was it opened?' is a sensible question in response to it, and this has an unproblematic answer (though perhaps not known to me). Compare the sentences 'It is true that my door is open' and 'It is true that my door will be repainted next year'. Do these describe particular statements as being true? If so, does it make sense to ask when they did (or will) *become* true? and when they did (or will) *cease* to be true? We might counter these questions by saying that truth is a peculiar kind of property (a 'timeless' property) of statements, so that these questions are out of order. But would it not be better to deny that 'It is true that p' *describes* something (as being true) and to say instead that the sentence is equivalent to 'p' (cf. PLP 28 ff., PI §136)? Similarly, someone can sensibly ask 'How do you know that your door is open?', and this has unproblematic answers (e.g. 'I can see that it is'). Compare the sentences 'I have a toothache' and 'I am angry'. Are these descriptions? If so, what do they describe? And how do I know that they are true? We might answer that they describe *states of mind* (a sensation and an emotion respectively) and that we know whether these descriptions are true by *introspection*. Wittgenstein criticizes both of these philosophical moves and traces them in part to the dogma that these sentences *must* function as descriptions (PI §§304 ff., 587, pp. 221 f.). We need to recognize the differences between expressions of inner states (pain, anger, love, pity, etc.) and descriptions of them (LPE 302, 319; PI §244, p. 189); also to note that the same type-sentences may now be used for the one, now for the other purpose (cf. PI §586, p. 189, PLP 289). To call all sentences descriptions involves assimilating all sentences to a single paradigm in spite of their manifest diversity. Confusion could be avoided only if we kept in mind the grammatical differences between different kinds of descriptions. But then these sentences in their different uses would be descriptions in different senses of the word 'description' (EBT 575 f.), and that would be another way of saying that it is pointless to group them together under the heading 'descriptions'.

The conclusion to be drawn from these criticisms is parallel to Wittgenstein's verdict on the thesis that all words are names. Just as we can explain a word by means of a sentence of the form '"X" signifies . . .', so we can explain any sentence by means of a sentence of the form '"p" describes the fact that . . .'. Yet assimilating the descriptions of the uses of sentences in this way cannot make the uses themselves any more like one another; for, as we have seen, they are absolutely unlike (cf. PI §10). So, too, when we say 'Every sentence in language describes something', we have so far said nothing whatever (cf. PI §13).

3. Disguised descriptions and analysis

The previous considerations might wean someone from the idea that every sentence is, as it stands, a description of some fact. This need not, however, eradicate Augustine's proto-picture, but might instead lead to a more subtle defence of it. Despite appearances, every sentence is essentially a description. This becomes clear only when it is suitably transformed. Analysis is indispensable for revealing its true form. The proto-picture of language as consisting of names combined into descriptions can be vindicated only by appeal to analysis.

Analysis of sentences might take either of two forms, leading to slightly different developments of the Augustinian picture.

(i) It could transform any given sentence of whatever grammatical form into an equivalent sentence that had the same use and yet the form of a description (a declarative sentence). The analysis of the sentence-question 'Is it the case that p?' might be, e.g., 'I would like to know whether it is the case that p' (EBT 598, cf. PI §24). Similar procedures of translation would have to be specified for every kind of sentence.

(ii) Analysis might extract from every sentence, whatever its use, something which functions as a description. What analysis exposes is the crucial fact that sentences with different uses may have an identical descriptive content. The Augustinian picture is correct provided that understanding the content of a sentence gives a *complete* grasp of its *meaning*; differences in the uses of sentences are psychological, i.e. they depend on speakers' purposes and the conventions for conveying them to an audience (e.g. the moods of verbs, word-order, intonation). Frege, e.g., claimed that a single 'content of judgement' was shared by the assertion that p, the question whether p is the case, the assumption that p, and the antecedent in the assertion that q if p (cf. Exg. §22). The essential differences among the uses of a given content of judgement turn on the occurrences of distinctive acts of mind overtly expressed via grammatical conventions. The young Wittgenstein generalized this thesis: 'Assertion is merely psychological. . . . Judgement, command and question all stand on the same level; but all have in common the propositional form. . . . What interests logic are only the unasserted propositions' (NB 96). This enabled him to reach the conclusion that the essential function of sentences was describing, i.e. that the general form of the proposition is 'This is how things stand' (TLP 4.5).

Against the Augustinian picture incorporating analysis in the first form, Wittgenstein now suggests the following criticisms.

(i) Since any given sentence and its paraphrase as a description must have the same use, the possibility of paraphrasing all sentences into a uniform form does not show that they have a uniform use. Indeed, to the extent that they have different uses, it serves only to disguise these differences (cf. PI §§10, 13). One attaches the wrong significance to the possibility of certain grammatical transformations if one argues that all sentences function in a single way (cf. PI §24).

(ii) It is an illusion to think that the possibility of paraphrasing every sentence into a description proves that understanding non-descriptive uses of language is not fundamental for understanding language. Consider the paraphrase of 'Is it the case that p?' into 'I would like to know whether it is the case that p' or 'I do not know whether it is the case that p'. Each of these 'descriptions' contains an indirect question. How is *it* to be understood (cf. EBT 598)? Would it not have to be explained by reference to the corresponding direct question? If so, can the paraphrase be an *analysis* of the original question?

(iii) Even if every sentence could be paraphrased as a description with the same use, that would not show that descriptions are the *fundamental* form of sentences, nor that anybody who utters a sentence always *means* what is stated in its descriptive paraphrase (cf. PI §§60, 63). In these ways too, one is tempted to attach the wrong significance to the possibility of certain grammatical transformations (cf. PI §24).

Against the elaboration of the Augustinian picture by means of analysis in the second form Wittgenstein's criticisms are more extensive.

(i) The idea that an assertion *contains as a part* a descriptive content shared with other uses of sentences (e.g. questions and commands) is a mistake. This mistake stems from misinterpreting the possibility of paraphrasing sentences used to make assertions into 'that'-clauses preceded by an operator 'It is asserted . . .' or 'It is the case . . .', and the correlative possibilities of paraphrasing interrogative sentences used to ask questions into 'that'-clauses prefixed by 'Is it the case . . .', and imperative sentences used to command into 'that'-clauses prefixed by 'Make it the case . . .' (PI §22(a)). Independently of this possibility of paraphrase, there is no such thing as 'the descriptive content of a sentence' to play the requisite role of expressing the sense of a declarative sentence while being in principle unfit for expressing its 'force', i.e. of being used, as a declarative sentence is used, to make an assertion. Like Frege's 'assumption', the descriptive content of a sentence would have to be a dependent entity. So it must be represented by an expression that cannot be used in isolation to make assertions, ask questions, issue orders, etc. (i.e. by a 'sentence-radical' (PI p. 11 n.)). Hence it cannot be represented by a sentence. The only obvious[1] candidate for so expressing the descriptive content of a sentence is a 'that'-clause. Two considerations support this choice. First, 'that'-clauses appear in the above paraphrases of sentences used to assert, question, or command into noun clauses prefixed by an operator. Secondly, a 'that'-clause is often used in oratio obliqua to report what someone has asserted, ordered, etc., and hence it seems to express *what* was asserted or ordered (i.e. a descriptive content which may be common to assertions, orders, questions, etc.). But the meaning of a 'that'-clause cannot be identified with the meaning of any sentence. Indeed, Frege acknowledged this point by identifying the reference of a 'that'-clause with the *sense* of the sentence contained in it. This non-equivalence of meaning is manifest in the fact that a 'that'-clause, not being a sentence, cannot be used to make a move in a language-game. So, again, what expresses the descriptive content of a sentence (a thought, assumption, or content of judgement) cannot be a sentence, but if it is not a sentence, its sense cannot be the sense of a sentence.[2]

---

[1] A slightly less obvious candidate would be a complex gerund. Russell, in 'Theory of Knowledge', opted for this form of words as the expression of a proposition, which is itself an incomplete symbol, needing completion. The proposition, thus conceived, is the primary object of understanding when the use of a sentence is grasped. It is what is common to assertion, hypothesis, expression of volition, etc. Judging, doubting, wanting, supposing, suspending judgement, etc., are different mental relations to the proposition that is grasped or understood. ('Theory of Knowledge', pp. 196ff., 204, 213, 215, 273f.)

[2] For a more detailed discussion of Wittgenstein's objections to Frege's analysis cf. Exg. § 22 and Exg. p. 11 n.

It should be noted that this objection does not *prohibit* stipulative introduction of an assertion-sign to flag sentences, whether atomic or compound, that are used assertively. The assertion-sign could be given various roles, e.g. as a punctuation mark to indicate the beginning of a sentence, thus distinguishing the linguistic unit being used to make a move in the language-game from subordinate elements within that unit; or, to distinguish an assertion from a fiction (PI §22(c)–(d)). Nor does the objection deny the possibility of paraphrasing declarative and inter-rogative sentences into 'that'-clauses plus an operator. The objection is to the contention that every sentence used to make an assertion contains a descriptive content which is the sense of the sentence and which is common to this assertion, to the order given by uttering a corresponding imperative, to the question asked by uttering a parallel interrogative sentence, etc. In addition, the objection warns us against misinterpreting the significance of the possibility of paraphrase.

(a) That we can paraphrase sentences into 'that'-clauses plus the appropriate operator no more shows that every assertion, question, or command, etc., contains a description in the form of a 'that'-clause than the possibility of paraphrasing every statement into the form of a question followed by a 'Yes' (e.g. 'Is it raining? Yes!' = 'It is raining') shows that every statement contains a question (PI §22(b)).

(b) It would be mistaken to think that the paraphrase provides a uniquely perspicuous expression of an assertion, request, question, etc., a form of words that necessarily carries its use upon its face. 'I would like to know whether p is true', 'You ought to go home', or 'The chess queen stands upon its own colour at the beginning of the game' are declarative sentences, but paraphrasing them into 'It is the case that I would like to know whether p is true', 'It is the case that you ought to go home', and 'It is the case that the chess queen stands upon its own colour . . .' does not render their meaning more perspicuous. It merely serves to obscure their use by a canonical form.

(c) We should not follow Frege and Russell in thinking that projecting the assertive use of sentences on to the articulated form of assertion-sign and sentence-radical is also an anatomization of the act of asserting into two components, e.g. entertaining and judging (PI §22(c)).

(d) Since an asserted sentence, a question, etc., need contain no 'that'-clause, the thesis that every assertion, question, etc., has a descrip-tive content is most naturally construed as the claim that the act of making an assertion, asking a question, etc., consists in part in the relation of a speaker to an abstract entity. The idea informing such a picture is that there is a distinct act ('entertaining a thought') that is an ingredient in every act of using a sentence to assert something, to ask a question, to formulate a rule, etc.; or, that there is a distinct act ('understanding the propositional content') that is an ingredient in the full understanding of a sentence used to make an assertion, etc. The thesis of common content thus reinforces the Platonistic temptations to reify propositions and also supports a misguided conception of the use and understanding of sentences (cf. PI §§22(c), 363). Temptation and misconception alike must be resisted.

(ii) The idea correlative to the thesis of a common descriptive content is that assertions, assumptions, questions, requests, orders, etc., are differentiated only by reference to speakers' intentions or mental acts of meaning (*Meinen*). The general background for this erroneous idea is the conception that sentences are dead signs if divorced from their backing of thought; that mental states or processes behind the expression and accompanying its utterance or its being heard are what give life to a sentence (BB 4 f.; PLP 283). Wittgenstein advances many arguments against the thesis that meaning and understanding are mental states or processes accompanying speaking and hearing sentences (cf. 'Understanding and ability', pp. 331 ff.). The life of signs lies in their use (BB 4). This general outlook applies to the differentiation of assertions, assumptions, orders, predictions, etc. Differences between them are differences in the practice of using sentences, viz. in the circumstance in which they are uttered, in the explanations given of them, in the different justifications for their utterance, and in the different practices of reacting to them. Whether an utterance is an assertion depends, e.g., on whether there is the possibility within the language of characterizing it as true or false or the possibility of using it in the calculus of truth-functions (PLP 288), but not on whether its utterance is accompanied by the mental act of 'judging'. It also depends on the circumstances of the particular utterance, e.g. whether the speaker is acting on the stage or reading a book aloud (Vol. XII, 321). That 'Light' functions now as an order, now as a report, is manifest in giving contrasting explanations of the utterance, e.g. 'Bring me a light' and 'The light is already switched on' (BT 201 ff.). The terms 'assertion', 'command', 'promise', etc., are characterizations of the *uses* of sentences (PI §21), and there are behavioural criteria for whether somebody has asserted, commanded, or promised something.

Wittgenstein's verdict is that in neither form does analysis reveal that describing is the essential function of sentences. It cannot, by exposing a deep uniformity beneath 'superficial' differences in use, vindicate the proto-picture of sentences as descriptions.

4. *Last refuge*

One might nevertheless think that something can be salvaged from the wreck of the Augustinian conception of sentence-meaning. In view of the foregoing criticisms we might relinquish the claim that every sentence contains a description, but still insist that description or assertion is necessarily fundamental to language. The Augustinian conception of sentences would be treated as a defective expression of the underlying idea that the information-conveying function of language *must* have a certain logical priority. The argument rests on the need (in any language-game beyond the most primitive) for explanations of expressions, even if their standard use (as in the builders' game) is to give orders. Viewed from the Augustinian perspective, this elevates the form of explanation 'This is ξ' (i.e. ostensive explanation) to an indispensable articulation of language. Since this *is* the form of the declarative sentence and since it *seems* to be used assertively, this may appear to justify a residuum of the original contention.

There is much wrong with this argument. It is, however, totally undercut by pointing out, as Wittgenstein does, that the explanation 'This is A' is not an application of 'A', not an assertion that something has the property A, but a grammatical sentence that has only the form of an assertion (cf. 'Ostensive definition and its ramifications', pp. 95 f.). Moreover, one could equally well introduce ostensive definitions in the imperatival form: 'Let "A" stand for this $\nearrow$!'

There seems to be another line of tactical retreat from the Augustinian picture of sentence-meaning. The thesis that all sentences contain descriptions is again treated as a defective formulation of an underlying truth. The basic idea is that every sentence is really a combination of names: its use flows from the meanings of its constituents and its structure. The notion of descriptive content mistakenly inserted an intermediary between the use of a sentence and its construction out of its constituents. Provided that the words and structure of a sentence directly determine its use, the notion of descriptive content can be cheerfully discarded. There seems to be a strong argument in support of this conclusion: how can we conceivably understand a sentence, including its use, except through understanding its constituents and its structure?

Though seductive, this argument too is futile (cf. 'A word has a meaning only in the context of a sentence', pp. 154 ff.). The different grammatical forms with which we are acquainted are each shared by utterances with a multitude of different uses, while any 'form' that is hidden cannot be part of an account of what we understand in understanding a sentence. The myriad uses of sentences are not mirrored, but rather concealed, by the limited variety of forms of sentences. Where this is the source of philosophical problems, enlightenment may come from careful and subtle differentiation of uses of sentences. Bedazzled by form, philosophers are often blind to the uses of sentences.

e illusion of uniformity

Augustine's proto-picture of language depicts a fundamental uniformity in the use of sentences. Unless philosophers were moving in the field of force of some powerful sources of illusion, it would seem inexplicable that they should have defended this counter-intuitive conception. Wittgenstein emphasizes two centres of intellectual gravitation: one is the tendency to assimilate expressions exhibiting apparent common form, the other the tendency to compensate for distortions thus introduced by treating essential differences in how expressions are used as differences in speakers' states of mind. He thereby relates the illusion that all sentences are essentially descriptions to other diseases of the understanding.

(i) Different versions of the Augustinian picture differently misconstrue the possibility of certain grammatical transformations, e.g. the possibility of writing an explanation of every sentence in the form '"p" describes the fact that . . .' or of paraphrasing every non-declarative sentence in the form of a declarative sentence (e.g. 'p?' as 'I would like to know whether p'). We are inclined to see the essence of all language in these accidental features of the grammar of English (or German), to take certain paraphrases to reveal the real structure of our thought.

(ii) The significance of the possibility of such transformations rests on the significance we attach to uniformity in forms of expression. We are impressed, e.g., by the possibility of paraphrasing every kind of sentence as a declarative sentence; we see possession of the form of a declarative sentence as an important feature of a sentence. This attests to our facility in discerning a particular form and to the difficulty of apprehending other features of expressions. We can 'take in' the form of a sentence at a glance, but not the situations in which it is correct to use it nor the range of uses that it has (cf. PI §520, MS. 136, 118, TS. 229, §1578).

(iii) Concentrating on forms of expressions is dangerous in so far as we *assume* that identity of use follows from identity of form. This is a major source of misconceptions in philosophy.

If I had to say what is the main mistake made by philosophers of the present generation, . . . I would say that it is that when language is looked at, what is looked at is a form of words and not the use made of the form of words (LA 2).

We are as much misled by form, by grammatical analogies, in reflection about sentence-meaning as we are in thinking about word-meaning (PI p. 224).

Vorsichtig wie auf brüchigem Eis, muss man vorwärts gehen; überall nach der Verwendung fragen, nirgends dem Schein des Ausdrucks trauen. Denn jeder der geläufigen Ausdrücke legt eine andere als die tatsächliche Verwendung nahe. (Vol. XII, 217.)

(One must go forward carefully, as over thin ice; always to inquire into the application, never to trust in the appearance of an expression. For every one of our familiar expressions suggests an application different from its actual one.)

We use such words as 'assertion', 'question', 'command' as descriptions of grammatical forms of sentences, although their primary application is to uses of sentences (cf. PI §21). We are inclined to think that there are only as many uses of sentences as there are distinct grammatical forms of sentences (cf. PI §23(a)), overlooking the fact that a single form may have a variety of uses (PI p. 188). Hundreds of misleading analogies converge to hide the diversity of uses of sentences from our view; seduced by form, we treat as descriptions many sentences which are not descriptions at all (cf. Vol. XII, 217).

(iv) The Augustinian picture accounts for differences in the uses of sentences in terms of speakers' performances of different mental acts. This account manifests both our craving for generality and a typical response to its frustration. We are not satisfied by an explanation of such a term as 'assert', 'command', 'praise', 'wish', which takes the form of describing the various (defeasible) criteria for its application. Instead, we insist that there *must* be something common among all acts correctly characterized, e.g., as 'asserting something' (BB 17). This common ingredient is not readily apparent. Since we cannot specify any one overt act that is common to every act of asserting something, we declare that a single mental act corresponds to the word 'assert' and that it occurs whenever someone asserts something (cf. PI §36).

(v) Making assertions, issuing commands, etc., are intentional acts. But we are inclined to misconstrue intentions as acts or states of a person's mind. Hence we think that what is essential to making an assertion is something behind and on a different level from uttering a sentence in certain observable circumstances, that whether or not uttering a sentence constitutes an assertion depends on whether or not it has the requisite mental backing.

(vi) We are inclined, in philosophy, to dismiss descriptions of grammar, since we hanker after explanations on the model of science. So, instead of describing different uses of sentences and the circumstances of their employment in order to obtain an *Übersicht* of those linguistic practices and transactions that perplex us with respect to the uses of sentences, we introduce abstract entities to *explain* the possibility of false belief, of supposing something without asserting it, of denying what somebody else asserts, etc.

Many of what Wittgenstein identifies as the characteristic sources of philosophical confusion about meaning are visible in the elaboration of the Augustinian conception of sentences.

6. Sentences as instruments

The Augustinian picture of language contains a captivating account of the meaning and use of sentences. Breaking its hold on our thinking will be partly a matter of criticizing arguments in defence of the view that all sentences are descriptions, and partly a matter of criticizing the background conception of the mind and its role in language use. But these criticisms may not suffice. Equally important is a competing picture, something to guide our thinking about sentences in the right direction and to prevent backsliding into familiar patterns of thought. This too Wittgenstein provides: 'Look at the sentence as an instrument, and at its sense as its employment' (PI §421, cf. §§291, 569).

The meaning of a sentence, like that of a word or phrase, is internally related to the criteria for understanding it. These are of two main types: explaining it and using it correctly. The form of explanation typical for sentences is paraphrase: the sentence to be explained is replaced by another sentence that dispenses with a problematic expression, an opaque construction, or an uncertain use. (Note that it is not a necessary condition for a paraphrase to manifest understanding that it be synonymous with the original sentence. Treating someone's giving the paraphrase 'I want to know whether p' as a criterion for his understanding the question 'Is it the case that p?' (cf. PI §24, BT 202 f.) does not presuppose that these type-sentences are synonymous.) The use of sentences has two aspects, and these are reflected in a subdivision of the criteria of understanding. One concerns producing a sentence in appropriate circumstances, the other reacting to a sentence in a way appropriate to the circumstances. Both kinds of criteria are important. The first kind connects the grounds of an assertion with its meaning and the 'truth' of avowals of inner states with speakers' behaviour. The second kind is prominent in Wittgenstein's descriptions of language-games. One point of stressing that speaking a language is part of a pattern of activity is that how people react to utterances manifests whether and how they understand them. Whether the assistant in language-games (2) or (8) understands the builder is to be seen from what he does; what mental processes accompany what he does are typically irrelevant.

Wittgenstein's earlier employment of the principle of verification had emphasized one aspect of a typical use of declarative sentences, i.e. one kind of criterion of understanding such sentences. It had highlighted the internal connection between the meaning and the assertion-conditions of declarative sentences. His mistake had been to exaggerate the uniformity of use of declarative sentences (distinguishing only 'propositions', 'hypotheses', and mathematical propositions (M 261 ff.)) to oversimplify the connection between assertion-conditions and sentence-meaning, and to exaggerate its importance by neglecting non-assertoric uses of sentences and other criteria of understanding. Describing how to verify a sentence is merely one criterion of understanding it and hence one contribution to its grammar (PI §353). One of Wittgenstein's main purposes in introducing language-games was to redress the balance by stressing non-assertoric uses of sentences and by calling attention to the fact that reactions to utterances function as criteria for understanding uttered sentences (TS. 219, §1577). All this is conspicuously neglected if we think that 'The whole point of communication [lies] in this: someone else grasps the sense of my words—which is something mental: he as it were takes it into his own mind. If he then does something further with it as well, that is not part of the immediate purpose of language' (PI §363).

Just these features of the use of language are emphasized by conceiving of sentences as instruments. How we use sentences in discourse with others and how we respond to these sentences when uttered by others manifests how we understand them; this point about criteria of understanding is a crucial part of the idea that speaking a language is part of a form of life. In place of the venerable picture that speaking consists in conveying thoughts from one person's mind to another's, Wittgenstein substitutes a new picture: speaking is akin to the activity of playing a game. Using sentences for the various purposes of discourse consists in making and reacting to moves in the language-game, i.e. in producing and responding to utterances of sentences. To use a sentence to assert or to order, etc., presupposes mastery of techniques, viz. of the language-games of assertion, command, etc. So too does understanding these uses of sentences. Only by means of a sentence can a person make a move in the language-game (PI §49), and understanding (or meaning) a sentence presupposes mastery of the relevant language-game (cf. PI §199).

This conception of understanding sentences is parallel to Wittgenstein's conception of understanding words. Understanding a word is a matter of knowing how to use it correctly, i.e. of having a mastery of its use (*Gebrauch*). Using it correctly is a criterion of understanding it. Similarly, understanding a sentence seems a matter of having a mastery of its use (*Verwendung*), and using it correctly is a criterion of understanding it. In view of this parallelism the contention that the meaning of a word is its use in the language (PI §43) would have as its counterpart the thesis that the sense of a sentence is its use (PI §421) or its role in the language (cf. PG 130, BB 42, PI §§21, 199).

Like the counterparts for words, both the comparison of sentences with instruments and the thesis that the meaning of a sentence is its employment crystallize and clarify Wittgenstein's whole outlook on language. There are three respects in which this elucidation is especially prominent.

(i) This picture of the use of sentences unifies and renders perspicuous his objections to the account of sentence-meaning embodied in the Augustinian picture of language.

(ii) The slogan that the sense of a sentence is its use gives a synopsis of Wittgenstein's tactics in dealing with specific problems about understanding sentences. In particular, he treats identity (and difference) in use as a criterion for identity (and difference) of sense. Close similarity in their uses justifies saying that 'I believe that it's going to rain' is similar in meaning to 'It's going to rain' (PI p. 190) and 'He says it will rain' to 'He believes it will rain' (PI p. 192). We might even say that the sentence 'He can continue the series 1, 5, 11, 19, 29 . . .' in certain circumstances has the same meaning as 'He knows the formula $a_n = n^2 + n - 1$', because here they have the same use (BB 115). Conversely, 'Human beings believe that twice two is four' and 'Twice two is four' do not have the same sense because they have entirely different uses (PI p. 226). Wittgenstein treats lack of clear use as a criterion for denying a clear sense to a sentence (or to a picture). The questions 'Is the visual image of a tree simple or composite?' and 'What are its simple component parts?' have no clear use, i.e. no clear sense (PI §47). The sentences 'Men have souls' and 'Consciousness awakens at a particular level in the evolution of the higher animals and men' have no clear sense because the pictures that they depict have no clear applications (cf. PI §422, p. 184). Wittgenstein frequently criticizes 'philosophical sentences' by investigating their uses. In some cases, they have no clear use; the Law of Excluded Middle, e.g., is often cited where it amounts to nothing more than a picture having no clear application (PI §352, cf. §426). In other cases, philosophers distort the ordinary uses of sentences and hence their senses; a philosopher may, e.g., suppose that the sentence 'I see this' expresses a deep truth even though it is deprived of its customary use (BB 174), or that the sentence 'This is how things are' expresses the essence of language even though it is ripped out of the only context in which it has a use (PI §134). Misapprehensions about the use of a sentence amount to misapprehensions of its sense. These apparently diverse remarks are given unity by the slogan 'The sense of a sentence is its use, its role in language.'

(iii) The comparison of a sentence to an instrument or tool, and its use to the use of a tool, provide an illuminating picture in terms of which to view the relation between the form and use of sentences. The analogy between words and tools was invoked by Wittgenstein in order to emphasize the fact that words of a given form, i.e. grammatical category, may have very different uses, and that it is the latter, not the former, which must be grasped in order to comprehend correctly the notion of the meaning of a word. The same analogy serves the identical purpose in respect of sentence-meaning. The use of an instrument is not a *part* of the instrument, and there is no such thing as incorporating its use into the instrument. Of course, one can stipulate that certain tools be used only for such-and-such purposes, and prohibit their use for other purposes. One may even stick labels on tools saying what uses are authorized. So too with sentences. Their form may indicate their standard use, but the use of a sentence does not *flow*, independently of us, from its form. Indeed, in many cases, the form of a sentence (like the grammatical category of a word) may be wholly misleading with respect to its use (e.g. arithmetical sentences, first-person present-tense psychological sentences, deontic sentences), and sentence-tokens of the same type-sentence may, in varying circumstances, be used very differently. We sometimes embody explicit markers of standard use in sentences, as with explicit 'performatives' but even this does not *guarantee* the use of the sentence (e.g. the common frequentative use of sentences having the form of a performative). No matter how we 'improve' the form of a sentence (e.g. by paraphrase into a canonical form of mood-operator plus sentence-radical), its use on a particular occasion does not *follow* from its form. This has two important corollaries. (a) The classification of sentences as assertions, commands, questions, etc., is a classification of uses not of forms. (b) Understanding an utterance implies mastery of the practice in which this sentence is used as an instrument.

There are, however, serious problems about the remark 'Look at the sentence as an instrument, and at its sense as its employment [*Verwendung*]' (PI §421). First, characterizing a sentence as an instrument seems more problematic than comparing words with tools. Instruments, like tools, are typically employed not just on a single occasion, but repeatedly. Although some sentences are used on many occasions, many are not; there is no *practice* of using many typical type-sentences. This does not, however, undermine the point of Wittgenstein's analogy. Calling a sentence an instrument is intended merely to emphasize its role in a particular language-game; to highlight its instrumental functions, or the way that it is woven into a whole pattern of activity. Speaking is not typically an idle exercise, but is undertaken for particular purposes. Orders, threats, questions, even descriptions, are typically addressed to an audience for the purpose of bringing about or modifying responses, both verbal and non-verbal. An order or a rule may be likened to a guiding gesture, a description to an architect's plan or a cross-sectional diagram with measurements (PI §291). Though 'once-off' affairs, these may naturally be called instruments. Secondly, the notion of use (*Verwendung*) is rather nebulous. (a) Use can be either specific or generic. A sentence used to assert that Hannibal crossed the Alps might be said to have the same use as one used to assert that passion-flowers blossom in the autumn; or they might be said to have different uses. The context of a remark usually makes this clear; e.g. specific use is in question in the argument that 'I believe it's going to rain' and 'It's going to rain' have the same sense (PI p. 190) and in the comment that rules of inference give

sentences their meaning because they are rules for the use of these signs
(RFM 179 f.). Generic use is sometimes indicated by the term 'Verwen-
dungsweise' (e.g. PI §23). (b) 'Use' or 'application' ('Verwendung' and
'Anwendung') are variable in scope. Sometimes they contrast with 'explanation' ('Erklärung'): whatever is not part of the explanation of an
expression belongs to its application (PLP 13). Often, however, their
scope is narrower: the proof of a theorem is contrasted with its
application (RFM 165), the justification for the Law of Excluded Middle
with its use (cf. PI §352), or the justification for taking a picture as the
interpretation of a sentence with the application of this picture (PI §§377,
422). In these latter cases, the connection between the sense of a sentence
and its use is meant to draw attention specifically to the fact that reactions
to utterances are often criteria of understanding them. (c) Understanding
an utterance presupposes mastery of the technique of using sentences of
this kind. The principles for individuating or demarcating language-
games being unclear, it is obscure what the scope of this mastery is. To
the extent that language-games merge into each other, one might even
claim that 'to understand a sentence means to understand a language' (PI
§199). Wittgenstein himself deflates the hyperbolic comment by
equating understanding a language with having mastery of a technique.
What we require is only criteria for failing to have mastery of specific
techniques for using sentences.

To compare a sentence with an instrument is merely to draw an
analogy. That it limps in certain respects does not prevent it from being
genuinely illuminating in others. In particular, the analogy draws
attention to aspects of sentence-meaning conspicuously neglected or
indeed obscured by philosophers who have developed in various ways
the Augustinian picture of language. It forces us to attend to the relation
between the form of a sentence and its use. It focuses upon the
complexity of the criteria for understanding sentences. It highlights the
integration of the use of sentences into the multifarious activities of
language-users. It emphasizes the extent to which understanding sentences is part of the mastery of a complex practice.

7. The uses of sentences

Wittgenstein's account of the meaning of sentences emphasizes that
understanding an utterance presupposes understanding (knowing) how
the uttered sentence is used, i.e. that grasp of sense presupposes the
mastery of the techniques of using sentences and of the differentiation
between these techniques. A competent speaker of our language must
know what it is to use a sentence to make an assertion, to issue an order,
to ask a question, to formulate a rule, etc., and also what it is to accept,

reject, or suspend judgement about an assertion, to obey or disobey an order, to answer or fail to answer a question, etc. There must be criteria for performing these actions, as well as criteria for a person's having a mastery of these practices.

Three points are crucial for the clarification and differentiation of fundamental uses of sentences.

(i) Making assertions, issuing orders, asking questions, etc., are intentional actions for whose performance by a person there must be behavioural criteria. Although these acts can be performed without saying anything (e.g. an assertion may be made in response to a WH-question by pointing or an order given simply with a gesture), they are standardly performed by uttering sentences. Moreover, if the terms 'sign' and 'sentence' are construed generously enough to cover 'utterances' consisting of gestures, samples, drawings, etc., these acts are invariably performed by 'uttering' sentences and hence may be termed '*speech*-acts'. The characterization of the corresponding intentional actions of rejecting assertions, obeying orders, answering questions, etc., will always involve response to an uttered sentence, and for these actions too there will be behavioural criteria. Criteria for both kinds of actions will be defeasible, depending on circumstances. Declaiming on a stage in the course of a play, e.g., standardly defeats the claim that the actor has made an assertion by uttering a declarative sentence (although the character in the play has made an assertion); but even this defeating circumstance is itself defeasible (a point exploited by certain playwrights, e.g. Pirandello, for dramatic effects).

(ii) In many languages (verbal) sentences may have various grammatical forms. We distinguish declarative, interrogative, imperative, and optative sentences. Whether someone who utters a sentence makes an assertion, issues an order, asks a question, etc., depends not only on the context of his utterance, but also on its form. Indeed, uttering a sentence-question in an appropriate context is a criterion for asking a question. Like other criteria, this one is defeasible. In appropriate circumstances, someone who utters a sentence of this form makes an assertion (viz. by asking a 'rhetorical' question). Moreover, not uttering a sentence of this form is not a sufficient condition for failing to ask a question. A person might well ask a question by uttering an appropriate declarative sentence (e.g. 'I would like to know whether it is raining') or even by uttering an inappropriate one (e.g. 'It is raining'), provided he satisfied criteria for intending to ask a question in uttering this sentence. Finally, he might ask a question or make an assertion by means of a gesture or drawing, in which case the question about the *grammatical form* of the sentence uttered, still less about its anatomization into mood-operation and sentence-radical, would not even arise. The defeasibility of the inference from a person's uttering a sentence of a particular grammatical form to his using this sentence in a particular way is part of the concepts of making assertions, issuing orders, formulating rules, etc. Accordingly, there is no such thing as writing such a use of a sentence into its form.

(iii) Differentiation of the acts of using sentences tempts one in the direction of a certain mentalist mythology. To issue an order, one might think, must involve meaning the uttered sentence as an order; while obeying an order presupposes understanding the order as an order. Similarly, one must mean an assertion as an assertion, a question as a question, etc., as well as understand an assertion as an assertion, a question as a question, etc. These claims might be taken as restatements of the fact that such acts as making assertions or obeying orders are intentional. But they are potentially misleading. Neither meaning nor understanding an order as an order is a mental accompaniment of speaking or hearing an utterance (PI §20). The claim that a person is issuing or obeying the order to slope arms does not rest on his satisfying criteria for expressing or grasping an imperative force-indicator together with his satisfying criteria for meaning or understanding a particular descriptive content (RFM 116), still less with there being merely inductive evidence that he interprets this order as the order to slope arms. Consequently, we cannot take meaning (or understanding) an order as an order to be one separable ingredient in every complex act of issuing (or obeying) an order. What appears to be a harmony between mental accompaniments of using sentences is nothing more than contingent regularities between the practices of explaining sentences, of producing them, and of reacting to them. (These are the analogues for sentences of the agreement in definitions and agreement in judgement that underpin the criteria for understanding words.)

From the point of view of the meaning of sentences and the criteria for understanding them, what is crucial is a grasp of their uses, especially of the fundamental differences in use marked by such terms as 'assertion', 'command', 'question', 'wish', 'request'. It is important to note that such differences correspond only roughly, if at all, to differentiation in the grammatical forms of sentences. In particular, two tokens of the same type-sentence may be used in quite different ways, and tokens of type-sentences differing in form may have an identical employment. In place of the classification of sentence-types by reference to their gram- matical forms, Wittgenstein substitutes classification of utterances by reference to the criteria for using sentences in different ways. Like the segregation of words into categories, such classification will be relative to our purposes in setting it up; it will depend on the nature of the language investigated and the activities of the language-users (cf. PI §§18 f.); and, finally, it will need to be modified over time in so far as linguistic practices evolve (PI §23).

8. *Assertions, questions, commands make contact in language*

The various fallacies and misleading temptations scrutinized above arise not merely because of the ready surveyability of form as opposed to use, nor simply because of our natural inclination to impose a Procrustean uniformity upon dissimilar phenomena. Rather, these reasons seem to be vindicated by the fact that the distinctions they lead to appear fruitful in resolving pressing and otherwise intractable philosophical problems.

We have seen that postulation of a common content, the 'assumption' or 'thought', was intertwined with a mentalistic interpretation of the acts of asserting, questioning, commanding, etc. The difference between asserting and supposing something, according to this view, consists in the different mental relations to this abstract object. Hence, the reason why a parrot's uttering 'p' is not an assertion that p is that the parrot does not perform the mental act of judging the thought that p to be true. But once we realize the chimerical nature of this abstract object, it is easy to see this mythology of mental acts for what it is. A person's uttering 'p' constitutes an assertion, not because it has the backing of an accompanying mental act, but because his utterance is a use of a sentence in appropriate circumstances by a person who has mastered a practice and is familiar with the language-game in which this technique is at home. The parrot's utterance is not an assertion, but not because we conjecture that it does not accompany its squawks with acts of judgement, rather because it does not play this, or any other, language-game, or indeed is not master of any technique of using sentences (PI §§25, 344).

It is, of course, true that uttering a sentence 'p' is not the same as asserting that p. But it does not follow that asserting that p involves doing something *more* than uttering the sentence 'p'. Asserting that p does not consist in mouthing the sentence 'p' while simultaneously doing something else, e.g. judging. (Just as uttering the formula of a series is not the same as being able to continue the series, but being able to continue is not something behind the utterance of the formula, something of which the utterance is a mere symptom (BB 113).) It is not a hidden accompaniment of the spoken sentence that determines whether it is an assertion, but the circumstances of its use.

This point can be highlighted by means of the analogy between a sentence and a picture. A picture on its own does not tell us whether it represents what happened, what ought to have happened, what was dreamt or wished. But no mental supplementation will make a picture reveal its secrets. It is rather the way a picture is used, in appropriate circumstances (e.g. as illustration in a story book as opposed to an instruction manual), that renders it the representation that it is (B i, §209).

It seemed to Frege that we must recognize the existence of an abstract entity, the thought or assumption, in order to provide for the possibility of entertaining, supposing, or hypothesizing a thought without asserting it. But we need not postulate any abstract entity to *explain* how this is possible. What we must do is to bring to the fore the *expression in language* of such putative mental relations to these alleged entities. We express a supposition or hypothesis that p with sentences such as 'Suppose that p were the case, then . . .', or 'If p were the case, then . . .'. A criterion (although not the only criterion) for wondering whether p is *saying* 'I wonder whether p' or asking 'Is it the case that p?' Is there any further mystery? Of course, what A supposes may be identical with what B asserts. But this does not require postulating a common *object* to which the two people are differently related (see below).

It might be thought that unless we postulate abstract entities expressed by sentences, and introduce explicit mood-operators signifying force, we cannot explain the non-triviality of inference by *modus ponens*, the possibility of negation, and other logical operations. Thus it might be argued that if 'p' means the same both times in 'm; if m then p; therefore p' it seems that there is no inference, for the assertion 'p' is already part of the premises. If it does not mean the same, then the inference is invalidated by the ambiguity of 'p'. But introducing an assertion-sign to mark the distinction between the content and the act of assertion clears this muddle up. The content asserted in the conclusion '⊢p' occurs also in the premise '⊢(if m then p)', but is not there asserted.

Of course, this distinction between force and content generates new problems. What is it, in ordinary language, that 'carries assertive force'? How can we get by without an assertion-sign? How should assertoric, interrogative, imperative, etc., force be distributed among the constituents of molecular sentences? Nevertheless, we think, the first steps towards the light have been taken. The remaining problems are merely technical.

In fact, the very first step already contained the error from which the problems flow. The error is the failure to realize that to assert, to question, or command, etc., are *uses* of sentences. From this followed the attempt to embed the use *in the symbol used*. This produces absurdity, e.g. Frege's attributing extraordinary properties to '⊢': *it* asserts something (FC 34 n.), it *contains the act of assertion* (GA i. §5). But a sign is not a use, and no sign can contain its use. Of course, there are markers of use in language, e.g. the mood of the verb, the explicit performative, intonation-contours. Although we could introduce markers of use as prefixes to sentences (PI §22), such markers are neither necessary nor sufficient for a given use of a sentence to be of a particular kind.

It is an illusion that without a special assertion-sign we cannot explain the non-triviality of *modus ponens*. Of course, the two occurrences of 'the grass will grow' in the argument 'If it is raining, the grass will grow; it is raining; therefore, the grass will grow' have the same meaning in so far as an explanation of the meaning of the one will serve equally well for the other, though this will be only a partial explanation of the conditional sentence. Equally obviously, the first occurrence of this sentence in the argument is not uttered assertively; i.e. in saying 'If it is raining, the grass will grow', one is not asserting that the grass will grow. One is using the molecular sentence to assert a conditional. But if an assertion-sign were indispensable for making this point, how could its use be *explained*? Puzzlement about *modus ponens* can only be cleared up by clarifying the criteria for making an assertion. The assertion-sign can at most have the role of marking a distinction with which we are already familiar (PI §22(c)–(d)). This redundancy of the assertion-sign is apparent from philosophers' prohibition on placing '⊢' in the antecedent of an asserted conditional. The reason for this, of course, is that the antecedent is not asserted. But, impeccable argument though this is, it makes grasping the differentiation of what is asserted from what is not asserted a precondition for mastering the correct use of the assertion-sign. If the assertion-sign were indispensable for explaining the non-triviality of *modus ponens*, then we would not be able to understand this explanation.

The thesis that every sentence contains a descriptive content has a deep attraction to philosophers. Not only does it vindicate, in a sublimed form, the Augustinian conception of sentence-meaning with its attendant stress on the descriptive role of sentences, but it seems to explain the nature of otherwise baffling internal relations. It must be possible, Frege insisted, for two people to believe the same thing, so *what* is believed cannot be an idea, which is identity-dependent on its owner, but must rather be something objective. This objective entity must also be something to which various people can stand in different relations, for what A believes may be identical with what B supposes, conjectures, or entertains. Moreover, although what A believes may be identical with what B supposes and C conjectures, A does not believe, B does not suppose, and C does not conjecture, *a sentence*. But this is readily explained by supposing each sentence to have as its sense a descriptive content which is what is severally entertained, supposed, believed or conjectured. Similarly, what A asserts may be identical with what B asserts, even though they do not utter the same sentence. So *what* they assert must be something else, i.e. an 'assumption' (PI §22(a)). Finally, what A orders B to do is precisely what B does when he obeys A's order, and also precisely what B *does not do* if he disobeys. What B queries when he asks whether p seems to be exactly what A asserts when he answers that p is the case, and also what he denies when he answers that p is not the case. These internal relations are made perspicuous, it seems, when we realize that A's command to B has the same content (hence can be expressed by the same sentence-radical but with a different mood-operator) as the assertion that described B's fulfilment of the command, and differs from the description of B's non-fulfilment of the command only in that the latter sentence-radical is the negation of the former. Similarly, a sentence-question contains the same descriptive content as its affirmative answer, only it asks whether 'that is how things are' and its answer asserts that that is how things are.

It is, of course, true that *what* several people believe when they believe the same thing is not a private object; also, that believing, wondering, supposing are not (except trivially) relations between a person and a sentence; and that the harmony between a command and its fulfilment is not contingent. But it is not true that what is believed is a public object, that believing is a relation between a person and a non-sentential abstract object, that the harmony between command and its fulfilment can only be explained by postulating an assumption, thought, or content of judgement that is expressed by a sentence-radical shared by a canonical formulation of the command and the assertion of its fulfilment.

Frege's explanation of these internal relations is analogous to the idea that the expectation that p must, in some mysterious fashion, contain a shadow of a future fact in virtue of which the fact that p will constitute a fulfilment of the expectation that p (Vol. XI, 116 f.). This comparison calls attention to Wittgenstein's dissolution of the puzzle of the intentionality of expectation. The expectation that a gun will go off does not already contain in a mysterious way the future fact that the gun will go off. That I expected the shot to be louder than it was does not mean that it made more noise in my expectation (or imagination). Nor does the fact that the gun's going off fulfils my expectation that it will go off consist in the obtaining of a peculiar relation between an external event and an internal one. Rather, expectation and its fulfilment make contact in language. It is a grammatical truth that the fact that p is what fulfils A's expectation that p; also that expecting that p is expecting the fulfilment of the expectation that p (PR 65 ff.; PG 157).

Frege's puzzle about the apparent common content of assertion question, and supposition is resolved by pointing out that assertion, question, supposition, command, etc., *make contact in language*, not via an extra-linguistic entity. The idea that there is some common *thing*, a thought or assumption, which A and B severally assert, suppose, or query (perhaps by uttering quite different sentences) stems in part from confusing the 'what' of a relative clause with the 'what' of an indirect question. The translation into Latin of 'I told you what he said' would contain an indirect question. This points towards a correct conception of the assertion 'What A asserted is what B believes', viz. that this is not the assertion of an identity between the (abstract) thing which A asserted and the thing that B believes, but rather the assertion that the same answer (e.g. in the form of a 'that'-clause) can be given to both the question

'What did A assert?' and 'What does B believe?' The connection is set up *in grammar*, e.g. in the conventions for oratio obliqua, and not via a postulated extra-linguistic entity. So, too, it is indeed not a contingent fact that the command that A bring it about that p is fulfilled by A's bringing it about that p. But this is simply because the command to bring it about that p is equivalent to the command to bring about the fulfilment of the command to bring it about that p, and it is a logical truth that A's bringing it about that p is the fulfilment of the command that A bring it about that p. The answer to the question 'What is the fulfilment of the command to bring it about that p?' is a *grammatical transformation* of the command to bring it about that p (PLP 119). Command and its satisfaction make contact in language. No extra-linguistic entity is needed to mediate between command and what counts as its satisfaction, nor any sentence-radical to mediate between the expression of a command and the assertion of its fulfilment.

Of course, one can paraphrase commands and descriptions of their fulfilment into a canonical form in which the canonical sentences have a common feature. 'Make it the case that p' and 'It is the case that p' have in common *the sentence* 'p'. But that does not mean that the unparaphrased command and description of its fulfilment have anything in common. *Pari passu*, if there *is* any common object to the question 'Is it the case that p?' and the assertion 'It is the case that p', it is merely the humble sentence 'p' that occurs in both (EBT 598; BT 206; Vol. XI, 86 f.; Z §684; cf. Exg. §22 (2, iv)). Of course, not even this is necessary (e.g. 'Was A tired at midnight?', 'He was weary then.'). But the absence of a common sentential component does not imply the presence of a common non-sentential component.

For each of these various puzzles Wittgenstein's strategy of focusing upon the uses of *sentences* undermines philosophical theories erected to *explain* how we can, mysteriously, do many of the mundane things we do do with language. It explains away the mystery by clarifying the grammatical articulations that gave rise to the impression of mystery.

V

OSTENSIVE DEFINITION AND ITS RAMIFICATIONS

1. Introduction

Wittgenstein explored the nature of ostensive explanation in unparalleled detail. He also clarified the related phenomenon of the role of samples in the explanation and application of expressions. His remarks on these topics are some of his most important and original contributions to philosophy. They also lay the foundations for his criticisms of logical atomism and of the possibility of a private language.

Paradigmatic examples of ostensive explanations involve a gesture of pointing and the utterance of a sentence of the form 'This is . . .' or 'This is called ". . ."'. Someone might explain 'red' by pointing to a red object and saying 'This is red', or he might explain 'dog' by pointing to a spaniel and saying 'This is a dog'. Such typical ostensive explanations make use of particular indicated objects as samples. Others, however, do not do so; someone might point to a person and say 'This is N.N.', and this is naturally (though misguidedly) described as an ostensive definition of the name 'N.N.', although no sample is involved. In all of these cases there is the temptation to infer that what is pointed at in explaining an expression 'x' *is* the meaning of 'x'. How else would pointing at something constitute (the operative part of) an explanation of (the meaning of) 'x'? This misconception of ostensive explanation is one of the tap-roots of the Augustinian picture of language. Indeed, Wittgenstein equates the idea that all words are names with the idea that ostensive definition is the fundamental form of explanation or the foundation of language (BT 25). The meaning of the name 'N.N.' is not the person pointed to in ostensively explaining who N.N. is (i.e. the bearer of 'N.N.') (PG 63 f.), nor is the meaning of 'red' what is pointed to in ostensively explaining what 'red' means. Unclarity about ostensive definition was something that Wittgenstein later identified as a main source of the errors of the *Tractatus*:

Unklar im Tractat war mir die logische Analyse und die hinweisende Erklärung. Ich dachte damals, dass es eine 'Verbindung der Sprache mit der Wirklichkeit' gibt. (WWK 209f.)

(In the *Tractatus* I was confused about logical analysis and ostensive definition. I thought at that time that there is a 'connection between language and reality'.)

This shift of viewpoint, in particular the repudiation of the idea of 'connections' between language and reality, marks a dramatic change.

Hence his remarks on ostensive explanations and the uses of samples are pivotal for his reassessment of logical atomism.

Although ostensive definition has been extensively discussed over the past fifty years, the focus of these philosophical discussions has been much narrower than Wittgenstein's. Two issues have usurped attention: first, what kind of thing it is that an ostensive definition correlates with an expression, especially whether this is public objects or private experiences; and, secondly, whether any ostensive definition definitively correlates anything with an expression, i.e. whether an ostensive definition ever definitely fixes the meaning of an expression. (Both of these issues are much debated in neoclassical empiricism.) Wittgenstein's remarks are usually interpreted as important contributions to these debates. Indeed, by many, they are seen to settle both issues: the private language argument settles the first and the doctrine that every ostensive definition can be misinterpreted settles the second. This is a mistake. His intention was to criticize the whole framework of thought about language within which these controversies arise. Wittgenstein's description of the role of ostensive explanations and samples reorients our viewpoint, undermines these traditional questions, and replaces them by quite different questions and answers. Failure to appreciate this means missing the point of a sizeable chunk of his remarks, especially his account of the autonomy of grammar.

Wittgenstein's examination of ostensive definition is inseparable from criticisms of his logical atomism. The whole edifice of the *Tractatus* was balanced on the support of the analysability of colour-exclusion. Once Wittgenstein acknowledged that the mutual exclusion of parallel determinates under a determinable could not be analysed, he had to relinquish the thesis that atomic propositions are logically independent of each other (LF 167 ff.). Lexically indefinable determinates, e.g. colour-predicates such as 'red' or 'green', are explained by reference to samples (PR 73), and the mutual exclusion of parallel determinates generates an internal relation between atomic propositions (LF 168).

These early insights were, however, only the beginning of a tortuous path to clarity. Although Wittgenstein now regarded samples as belonging to language, he retained the idea that symbols explained ostensively constituted the foundations of language. He toyed with the idea of a 'primary language' concerned only with unowned sense data; its words would be explained by private (mental) ostensive definition, and hence its samples would be mental (e.g. images (PR 73)). According to this conception, primary language is the foundation for our public language ('secondary language'), whose words would be explained by means of analyses into expressions in the primary language (cf. WWK 45, PR 51, 84). Wittgenstein also considered another version of a foundation-theory of language: here the primary language was conceived as a system of gestures (and material props, e.g. samples), and this underlay the secondary (word-)language by providing the backing for the ostensive definitions (cf. BT 4 ff., Vol. X, Um. 63, PG 88 ff.). The 'Big Typescript' and its revisions criticize and repudiate any such suggestion that ostensive definitions or samples are the essential foundations of language. This radical break with empiricism is maintained throughout his subsequent writings.

Wittgenstein's reflections on the mutual exclusion of parallel determinates traced out an equally zigzag course to his ultimate conclusion. These internal relations among atomic propositions cannot follow from the ostensive explanations of the determinates. That would presuppose that some sense could be made of what it is for a truth to follow from the meanings of its unanalysable constituents. But this cannot be done; it would require the intelligibility of the notion of meaning-bodies (BT 166 ff.; PG 54 ff.). Hence Wittgenstein initially suggested treating the internal relations among atomic propositions as independent ingredients of the grammar of their constituents. Propositions predicating parallel determinates (e.g. lengths, shapes, or colours) of a single object form a system of propositions (*Satzsystem*) each of which is incompatible with every other one (WWK 63 ff., 73 ff.; PLP 59). Understanding this feature of the grammar of such determinates is independent of understanding the ostensive explanations of them; it is a distinct convention about how they are to be used (PLP 61 ff.). But this conception, too, is mistaken. It is incompatible with our taking someone's giving a correct ostensive definition of 'red' as a criterion of his understanding 'red', and with our typically treating ostensive definitions as *complete* explanations of expressions. Wittgenstein ultimately came to the conclusion that the mutual exclusion of parallel determinates (and, more generally, internal relations among determinates) is an aspect of the practice of ostensive explanation: viz. we do not accept as correct an ostensive definition of 'green' by reference to any sample whose use we acknowledge as correct in giving an ostensive explanation of 'red' and vice versa. Hence colour-exclusion is a feature of the practice of explaining colour-words by the use of samples. It turns on the admissibility or inadmissibility of simultaneous use of objects as samples in explaining different expressions (cf. RFM 75 f.). This account of colour-exclusion is a particular application of Wittgenstein's account of the 'objective necessity' of colour-geometry. The apparent necessity of such principles as that white is lighter than black merely reflects our conventions for the use of samples in explanation of meaning. Our rules for the use of 'white', 'black', and 'lighter than' interlock in the use of samples: any pair of samples that we accept as explaining 'white' and 'black' respectively we also accept in explaining 'lighter than'. This insight is a major advance on the traditional empiricist treatment of ostensive definition, resolving the difficulty of whether propositions expressing the 'geometry of colour' are analytic or synthetic *a priori*.

The task of elucidating Wittgenstein's ultimate conception of ostensive explanation and the uses of samples in grammar must draw on his more developed remarks, not on his subsequently discarded ones. Consequently, discussions antedating the 'Big Typescript' must be set aside as being impregnated with the notions of primary language and *Satzsysteme*. Although there is continued development in his thoughts, the differences among his remarks on the nature of ostensive definitions and samples are thereafter largely matters of detail. Hence we draw on the 'Big Typescript' and subsequent writings to clarify the account of the *Investigations*. In developing his ideas, we later extend them in some ways not authorized by his remarks. We also limit our attention to the case of ostensive definition by reference to samples.

2. *The range and limits of ostensive explanations*

It is commonly supposed that an ostensive definition of an expression is acceptable only *faute de mieux*. If, e.g., it is possible to give a *Merkmal*-definition of a concept-word, then only this can be countenanced as a proper explanation. Consequently, ostensive definitions are treated by philosophers as being correct only for unanalysable expressions.

This general prejudice in favour of *Merkmal*-definitions is one of Wittgenstein's chief targets; it is the object of his attack in the discussion of family resemblance and determinacy of sense (PI §§65–88). The correlative prejudice against ostensive explanations is itself challenged. Wittgenstein emphasizes the possibility of using ostensive definitions to explain a wide range of expressions. These include colour-nouns and colour-adjectives (e.g. 'red', 'violet'), proper names of persons or things (e.g. 'N' 'Mont Blanc'), names of stuffs (e.g. 'sugar', 'iron'), names of shapes (e.g. 'cube', 'arch'), names of kinds or species (e.g. 'dog', 'pencil', 'chair'), names of activities or actions (e.g. 'lifting', 'sleeping'), names of conditions (e.g. 'rain'), and perhaps even names of holidays or days of the week (e.g. 'The Day of Atonement', 'Monday'). Giving ostensive definitions of such expressions is a correct way of explaining them. Pointing at a tennis ball and saying 'That is spherical' is a correct explanation of 'spherical', even though it is possible to give a *Merkmal*-definition of the word. Over a wide range of words ostensive explanations are equipollent with various forms of verbal explanations, including *Merkmal*-definitions. Giving any correct explanation, whatever its form, is a criterion of understanding.

It is important to note that Wittgenstein does not aim to show that ostensive definitions are defective by comparison with other forms of explanations of words. On the contrary, his purpose is to prove that they are not especially privileged; in particular, that they do not lay the foundations of language. Ostensive definition is demoted to the ranks, not cashiered. It is a perfectly legitimate and unambiguous (though misinterpretable) way of explaining the meanings of *many* expressions. The fact that any ostensive definition can be misinterpreted does not demonstrate that every one is incomplete.

Wittgenstein, in emphasizing the wide competence of ostensive definition, also challenges the dogma that there are many kinds of words not susceptible to ostensive definition. He declares that one can ostensively define numerals and points of the compass (PI §28), even logical connectives (PG 61; PLP 105). This seems disputable. A philosopher might object that numerals are second-level predicates or names of 'abstract entities'; in neither case do they stand for something perceptible, and hence they cannot be explained by ostension. Equally, one might claim that directions can be referred to only by a complex singular term formed from an operator 'the direction of ξ' applied to a singular term designating a line; hence, too, that understanding the name of a direction presupposes understanding this functional expression and its arguments. Finally, there is simply nothing to point to in explaining a logical operator; even if it were conceded, e.g., that 'and' is the name of a relation between propositions, this is not something that can be picked out by a gesture!

Wittgenstein's treatment of numerals (PI §§28 ff.) is typical of his reaction to such philosophical dogmatism. Philosophers conclude that something is impossible although its occurrence is visible and familiar to them. For we do accept as perfectly exact an ostensive explanation of 'two', e.g. pointing at a pair of nuts and saying 'That is called "two"' (or perhaps 'That is a pair' or 'The number of these is two'). What must be removed are the obstacles to accepting such an explanation at its face value. One objection is that an ostensive explanation of 'two' might be misinterpreted, e.g. as a proper name of this particular pair of nuts. To this there are two ripostes. First, *every* ostensive definition is open to misinterpretation (PI §28) (and so indeed is *every* explanation of whatever form (PI §87)); hence, this objection would have no special relevance to whether numerals can be ostensively defined. Secondly, what *can* be misinterpreted need not *be* misinterpreted; a person may well learn how to use 'two' correctly from this ostensive explanation, and whether he does so will be manifested by his subsequent applications of 'two'. An explanation is correct provided that giving it is accepted as a criterion of understanding the expression it explains, and that people normally react to it in the appropriate way (PI §87), and this holds in particular for ostensive definitions. A second philosophical objection is that numerals stand for abstract entities or second-level concepts. To this the reply is

that one is misled by the conception of meaning as naming. To say
that a numeral is the name of a number (or, worse, of an abstract entity)
merely invokes a form of representation ('the word . . . signifies . . .';
cf. Exg. §§9 f., 13) which is at best empty, at worst exceedingly misleading in various ways. First, it imposes a spurious uniformity on a
diverse range of expressions (e.g. '2', '½', '0.5', '0.333 . . .', '$\sqrt{2}$', 'π',
'2 + 2i', 'π'''). Secondly, treating numerals as names of second-order
properties would obscure the important differences between numerals
and expressions of generality (e.g. between 'three' and 'there is . . .').
Above all, what must be grasped in understanding numerals is their *use*,
not their meanings conceived of as entities which, by artificial manipula-
tions of formal concepts, one can represent them as 'standing for'.
Therefore, there is no reason why ostensive definitions should not
explain how to use numerals. And it is noteworthy that the category of
the expression explained by ostension is shown by the accompanying
training (e.g. memorizing the number-series and learning to carry
through 1:1 correlations), not by supplementary explanations employing
formal concepts (e.g. a second-level predicate) (BB 79).

Parallel responses are appropriate to the similar philosophical objections that directions and logical connectives cannot be defined ostensively. Calling 'North' the name of a direction does not settle how it is to
be used or distinguish its use from the use of other names of directions
(e.g. 'the zenith', 'left', 'up', 'straight ahead'). By contrast, it is readily
explained by pointing and saying 'That is North'. Understanding
'North' does not require knowledge of how to use the functional
expression 'the direction of ξ', but only being able to apply 'North'
correctly; e.g. understanding is manifested by obeying the order to go
North or by giving a correct answer to the question whether some
person went North. Similarly, categorizing 'and', 'or', and 'not' as logical
connectives, operations, or proposition-forming operators on propositions does not settle how they are to be used or distinguish them from
expressions used very differently (e.g. 'It is true that . . .', 'It is necessary
(possible) that . . .'). Wittgenstein asserts that one can explain their
meanings by gestures: 'and' by a gesture of gathering together (BT 42;
PG 53), 'not' by a gesture of rejection or exclusion (BT 34, 42; PG 58, 64;
PI §550), and 'or' by presenting alternative choices in a gesture (PLP
105). One might ostensively explain negation, e.g., by saying 'No more
sugar' and taking the sugar away (PG 64), or by drawing a figure and
saying 'Look, this point is in the circle, that one is *not*' (PLP 105). We
might even conclude 'Negation . . . is a gesture of exclusion, of rejection'
(PI §550). Certainly, explanation of it by gestures is no more problematic than its explanation by a truth-table, for that too is simply a pattern of
signs whose meaning lies in its use and this use is analogous to the use of
the gesture of rejection or denial (PG 55, 58).

The range of expressions ostensively definable is very much wider than philosophers have recognized. One might object, however, that Wittgenstein reaches this conclusion only by distorting the concept of ostensive definition. Does, e.g., the possibility of explaining negation by a gesture of exclusion show that the word 'not' can be given an ostensive definition? By extending the concept of ostensive definition beyond its normal frontiers, Wittgenstein perhaps makes assertions about the competence of ostensive explanation that are only superficially at odds with philosophical orthodoxy.

Although there is some justice in this objection, it misrepresents the concept of ostensive definition. The boundaries of this concept are, in Wittgenstein's view, less clear than commonly thought. Indeed, it is itself a family resemblance concept (PLP 104 ff.). There is a range of paradig-matic examples of ostensive definitions, and surrounding these are many explanations differing in numerous different ways from the central cases. The class of ostensive definitions has no 'natural frontiers'; it merges imperceptibly into explanations of different forms that might, for certain purposes, be treated as distinct. It is important in philosophy to note that no gulf separates ostensive definitions from *Merkmal*-definitions; there is a continuous spectrum of connecting links. Provided this point is acknowledged, where the boundary of ostensive definition is drawn matters relatively little.

Central cases of ostensive explanations involve three elements: a deictic gesture, something pointed at, and a verbal formula (especially 'That is . . .' or 'That is called ". . ."'). Among them would be the explanation of 'red' by pointing at a red book and saying 'That is red', that of 'metre' by pointing at a metre-stick and saying 'The length of this is one metre', that of 'dog' by pointing at a bull-dog and saying 'That is a dog', and that of 'N.N.' (or of who N.N. is) by pointing at someone and saying 'He is N.N.'. These paradigms resemble each other in many respects. These respects become fewer and more attenuated as we move away from the central cluster towards the peripheral cases.

(i) What counts as a deictic gesture, i.e. as pointing? Clearly I can point to a colour-patch, a particular dog, some nuts, or a point of the compass. But can I point to a sound, a smell, or a day of the week? I can call attention to a tone with a gesture; e.g., I might say 'Listen, that is C flat', indicating a particular note by jerking my extended index finger or pointing in the direction from which the sound is coming (PLP 104 f.). I might say 'Smell, this is putrid', having something that smells putrid on the end of my index finger and putting this under another's nose. The limits of what counts as pointing are unclear and perhaps unimportant for philosophical purposes. The explanation of an olfactory or tactile pro-perty by means of a sample seems essentially parallel to the explanation of a colour-word. Indeed, we might concentrate on the similarities by

letting pointing drop out of consideration altogether. Under the
umbrella of ostensive definition we could encompass the explanation of
colour-words or shape-words by means of a chart correlating words and
samples or pictures (PLP 107 f.).

(ii) What counts as something pointed at? Clearly I can point to a
particular object, but can I point to its colour, shape, texture, weight,
length or number? Or can I point to a point of the compass, an action
(e.g. lifting a weight), or an activity (e.g. playing football)? There the
gesture of pointing is clear-cut, but not so the question what is pointed
to. Of course, we contrast pointing to the colour of a book with pointing
to its shape. But in both cases is not the book what we really point to,
though in the first we use it as a sample for explaining a colour-word and
in the second as a sample for explaining a shape-word? The parallel
treatment of numbers, directions, actions, and activities seems impossible. When, e.g. I point to the North, does this mean that I am really
pointing to some object, say a tree on the horizon, which I am using as a
sample (of the direction North?)? An alternative account might exploit
the greater powers of mental archery. The physical gesture of pointing
might be replaced by the speaker's intention, for he can certainly *mean* a
number, a colour, a shape, a direction, an action, or an activity in
ostensively explaining a word. This would liberalize the range of things
that can be 'pointed at', but at the price of requiring an explanation of
what it is to mean the colour rather than the shape of a book or the
number rather than the configuration of some nuts (cf. Exg. §§33 ff.).
The question is what are the possible substitution-instances of 'x' in the
expression 'pointing to x'. But once formulated, this seems idle for
clarifying ostensive explanation. What is crucial are the facts that
pointing North and saying 'That is North' is a correct explanation of
'North' and that this explanation is very similar to the paradigmatic
ostensive definitions of 'red' or 'dog'.

(iii) What counts as an admissible form of words in an ostensive
definition? The paradigm formula is 'This is . . .'; e.g. I point to a red
patch and say 'This is red'. Equally appropriate would be the sentence
'This colour is red'. But what about uttering the formula 'This is called
"red"'? ' "Red" means this colour' (cf. Vol. X, Um. 42)? Or even ' "Red"
means the same as "This ↗ colour" [pointing at the red patch]'? These
formulations might seem inadmissible, e.g. because they mention the
word 'red' instead of using it. Further problems arise from extending the
verbal formula. What if I say '*This* and *this* and *this* are red'? Or '*This* is
red, and *that* is not red'? (cf. EBT 145). Or '*This* is red, and so too is
anything that resembles it'? Or, perhaps, 'This is red, and anything else is
red that resembles this more closely than it resembles *that* [a sample of
orange] and *that* [a sample of purple]'? With many sortal nouns one could
even spell out the relevant respects of resemblance; e.g. 'This is a Bearded

Warbler, and so too is any warbler resembling it in having a decurved bill and a broken eye-ring'. Here, it might seem, the ostension and the specimen would drop out of the explanation altogether, since the similarity-clause amounts to a definition *per genus et differentias*. And what of the explanation of 'game' by a set of paradigms picked out ostensively? Is this an ostensive definition, an explanation by examples and a similarity-rider, or both? The principles for the individuation of explanations are unclear, and so too the principles for determining of explanations complex in form whether they count as ostensive definitions. What is clear, however, is that characteristic features of simple paradigmatic ostensive explanations are present in varying degrees in more complex explanations and that there are many kinds of explanations transitional between paradigmatic ostensive definitions and paradigms of other forms of explanation (e.g. *Merkmal*-definition).

These questions expose some ways[1] in which ostensive definitions shade off into explanations of other types. But there are other kinds of borderline cases, for ostensive explanations also shade off into things which are not explanations at all.

(i) The vagueness of the boundary separating explanation from teaching and training (cf. 'Explanation', pp. 30 ff.) is equally apparent for ostensive definition. There are primitive forms of ostensive teaching that precede ostensive definition in the order of learning (cf. Exg. §6). Where such training ceases and ostensive explanation begins is not sharply determined (PG 62).

(ii) How an expression is explained seems to shade off into the mere history of how it was learnt. If an explanation is internally related to the meaning of an expression, it must somewhere 'enter into' or be 'involved in' applications of this expression. (In grammar there is no action at a distance (PG 81).) This is a general problem about characterizing explanation, but it seems particularly urgent in respect of ostensive definitions (cf. PG 80 f.). If I explain 'metre' by pointing at a metre-stick and saying 'That is one metre', then this sample will manifestly enter into applications of the term 'one metre', provided I employ the metre-stick to measure objects. But not every ostensive definition involves a sample that is subsequently used as a standard of comparison. Would it not be absurd to maintain that some red scrap of paper once used to explain 'red' to a child and then incinerated 'enters into' his subsequent use of the word 'red'? Indeed, how can any *object* be involved in the application of a word if it is not employed as a standard of comparison? (This worry perhaps generates part of the pressure for locating samples in the mind,

---

[1] There are others too. PI §9 hints at one. Suppose I explain 'ten' by pointing in succession to each one of a group of ten marbles while counting aloud 'one, two, . . . ten'; have I thus given an ostensive definition of 'ten'?

for then it is not *obvious* that a sample used in explaining an expression is not always present whenever the explicandum is applied.) However these issues are resolved (cf. below), they are symptomatic of unclarity about the boundary separating explaining words from the mere history of their being taught and learnt (cf. PG 86).

Given his purpose of examining all forms of explanation that seem to establish connections between language and reality, it is appropriate for Wittgenstein to interpret the phrase 'ostensive definition' as generously as he does. None the less, one might object, conceding this point does not establish his conclusion that ostensive definitions are equipollent with other forms of explanation for a wide range of expressions. Are they not comparatively inadequate? In particular, though *correct*, are they not typically *incomplete*? Of course, it is correct, e.g., to explain 'circle' by pointing to a circular object and saying 'That is a circle', but does not a geometrical definition ('the locus of points equidistant from a given point') give a fuller, better understanding of 'circle'? Does a typical ostensive definition not give merely a partial understanding of what it explains?

This objection runs counter to Wittgenstein's account of explanation, involving misconceptions about correctness and completeness (cf. 'Explanation', pp. 38 ff.).

(i) It is far from trivial that ostensive definitions are so widely accepted as correct. This depends on a feature of our practice of explaining expressions, e.g. that we count as a correct *explanation* of 'red' any ostensive definition of 'red' using *any* red object as a sample. There is no *necessity* that we should treat all red objects as admissible for the purpose of explaining 'red'; hence the fact that we do so is a crucial aspect of the grammar of our language. Similarly, there is no *need* for us to incorporate any ostensive definitions in the practice of explaining 'circle'; the simple fact is that we *do*. It seems that since, e.g., my copy of the *Tractatus* has red covers, I *must* be able to use it in giving an ostensive definition of 'red' because I can, by pointing to it and saying 'This is red', correctly describe it as being red. It then seems wholly trivial that ostensive definitions are correct explanations. This is a residue of confusing explanations with applications (e.g. TLP 3.263), for it appears that we *must* acknowledge as a correct explanation of an expression any instance of its correct application. But an application is not an explanation, and nothing *forces* us to adopt given practices of explanation. We do accept ostensive explanations as legitimate, but this is not a trivial feature of our linguistic practice.

(ii) The possibility of misinterpreting an ostensive definition does not prove it to be incomplete. Nor, since *any* explanation can be misinterpreted, would this show ostensive definition not to be equipollent with other forms of explanation.

(iii) Consequently, the fact that ostensive definition presupposes stage-setting (especially knowledge of how to use the kind of expression to which the explicandum belongs) is not a proof of incompleteness.

(iv) Whether our explanation is complete is an aspect of its normative role in the application of the explained expression. This cannot be seen from close scrutiny of its form. Moreover, the fact that other explanations of an expression are treated as correct (or even as complete) does not demonstrate that a given explanation is not complete. Therefore, there is no general reason to condemn as incomplete any of the diverse ostensive definitions mentioned by Wittgenstein. Only detailed examination of individual cases could sustain such accusations.

(v) The illusion that ostensive definitions are incomplete is supported by an unclarity about concept-identity. We are inclined to acknowledge that a geometrical definition of 'circle' gives a fuller understanding than an ostensive definition and, similarly, that a zoological explanation of 'dog' is more complete than our everyday ostensive explanations. Perhaps a better response would be that the concepts explained in geometry and zoology are different from our ordinary ones, though closely akin to them.

Certainly, Wittgenstein's contention is that ostensive definitions are perfectly adequate, i.e. both correct and typically complete, for a much wider range of expressions and kinds of expressions than philosophers have commonly acknowledged. They do provide a part of the backing for the expressions in circulation in our language, but not in the privileged way depicted in the Augustinian picture.

3. The normativity of ostensive definition

In a context where an explanation is called for, pointing to a red object and saying 'That is red' is a criterion of understanding 'red'. More generally, giving an ostensive definition of an expression is a criterion of understanding it. But this does not suffice for a full characterization of ostensive definitions. In addition, it must be understood that ostensive definitions have a normative role in language. They guide linguistic behaviour by providing standards of correctness for applying the expressions whose meanings they explain. Wittgenstein insists that ostensive definitions are *rules* (BT 176; BB 12, 90); hence that they belong to 'grammar' (PR 78; PG 88; PLP 13 f.). In respect of normativity, they do not differ from lexical definitions (PLP 278).

This contention is indisputably present in Wittgenstein's work and crucial to much of what he says about ostensive definition. One can immediately raise two objections to it.

(i) Is it not a distortion of the concept of a rule to assert that 'tables,

ostensive definitions, and similar instruments . . . [are] rules' (BB 90)?
Are rules not abstract entities rather than concrete ones? Wittgenstein's
retort would be that the concept of a rule is a family resemblance
concept, explained by reference to similarities with members of some set
of paradigmatic examples (cf. PLP Ch. VII). Its boundaries are indeterminate (BT 67 ff., 246). For the purposes of clarifying the role of ostensive
definitions in our language, it is important to emphasize their similarities
with lexical definitions and hence advantageous to classify them together
as rules.

(ii) How is it possible to distinguish the case of following an ostensive
explanation (or an explanation by a table) from behaving in accordance
with it (PG 86)? How can such a rule guide behaviour? How can it enter
into the applications of the explained expression? Although this is a
general problem about clarifying the concept of applying rules, it seems
particularly intractable in the case of ostensive definitions. Wittgenstein
himself wrestled with it for some time, proposing a number of unsatisfactory solutions. One possibility is to claim that the function of an
ostensive definition is invariably to correlate a word with a *mental* sample
(e.g. the word 'leaf' with a mental image of the shape of a leaf (cf. PI
§73)) and that all applications of the word turn on comparisons with this
image (PG 90, cf. EBT 163). Secondly, one might assert that an ostensive
definition must enter into applications via a memory image; e.g. that
someone who follows the rule for using 'red' embodied in an ostensive
definition of 'red' must have the image of this definition before his mind
in applying 'red' (cf. PG 90). Thirdly, its entering into the application of a
word might be thought to consist in the fact that the ostensive definition
is rehearsed (or the table consulted) just prior to applying the word; it is
involved in the application if an expression of the rule forms part of the
process of applying the word (BB 12 ff.). Finally, the ostensive definition
might be deemed to enter into the application provided that it referred to
a sample that is used in the process of applying the defined word, e.g. as a
metre-stick is in metric measurement; in such cases the ostensive
definition furnishes a concrete standard of comparison. None of these
seems to give a correct general account of what it is to follow an
ostensive explanation in applying an expression. One is inclined to
object, 'Isn't it like this? First of all, people use an explanation, a chart, by
looking it up, later they as it were look it up in the head . . . and finally
they work without the chart . . .' (PG 85 f.). And is this not parallel to the
development of the way that the rules of chess typically enter into the
play of a chess-player as he gains experience (PLP 129 ff.)? This is correct,
and for this reason Wittgenstein came to reject all of these as general
accounts of how ostensive explanations enter into the application of
expressions. But he then denied that ostensive definitions were therefore
a matter of mere history (*contra* PG 86 f.). Their connection with the

applications of words is simply not made in the minds or the overt behaviour of speakers on each occasion of using these words, but in the *practice* of explaining (and applying) these words. They are analogous to the role of the standard metre in measuring; it is part of the *institution* of metric measurement. Provided that Wittgenstein's subsequent argument (PI §§185 ff.) undermines the general misconception that a person only follows a rule if he 'consults' it (in some sense), the special difficulty of conceiving of ostensive definitions as rules disappears.

Having set aside these two preliminary objections, one might wonder how it is possible for an ostensive definition to play the normative role essential to a rule. How can it function as a standard of correctness? How can applications be justified or criticized by reference to an ostensive definition? There seems to be no connection whatever between the ostensive definition of an expression and its subsequent applications. I point, e.g., to one red object and say '*This* is red', and then I apply the term to other objects, e.g. saying '*That* is red'. Surely since the objects are distinct, the correctness of what I say in the second case is a matter independent of anything uttered in the first case. This objection turns on a common misconception of ostensive definition: viz. that in saying '*This* is red' to explain 'red', I am simply describing a particular object as being red. If that were so, then what it is correct to say about another object would be independent of what is said in the ostensive definition. But the premise is false. The ostensive definition is not a description; rather, it explains what it is for any object to be red. That is why it is normatively related to applications of 'red' to objects. For, in saying in the second case '*That* is red', I mean that *that* is *this* colour (i.e. the colour of *this*, i.e. red). In this way we can see that ostensive definitions may be relevant to whether the applications of the explained expressions are correct.

None the less, it might be objected, it is still not visible *how* ostensive definitions provide standards of correctness. If I explain 'red' as the colour of *this* object, then of course something is red if and only if it is the colour of *this* object, but that is merely a tautology, viz. that something is red if and only if it is red. Moreover, nothing is said about how to decide whether an object is the colour of *this* object, and hence no provision is made for this sample of red to play any role in justifying or criticizing applications of 'red'. So what sense is left to the claim that ostensive definitions are rules constituting standards of correctness?

One possible account would be that the notion of resemblance mediates between ostensive definitions and applications of the explained expression. The ostensive explanation of 'red' is really elliptical: the full form would be to point at a red object and to say '*This* is red, and so is anything similar to *this* (in respect of colour)'. Then describing another object as red is justified by this rule provided that that object does resemble *this* one (in colour). This account rests on multiple confusions.

In particular, an ostensive definition of 'red' does not describe any object as being red; *a fortiori*, there is no such thing as ascribing to another object the same property that is ascribed to the sample in the explanation of 'red'. Moreover, even if there were, what it means to say that an object resembles a given red object in respect of colour is just that it is red; but its being red is not a justification for describing it as being red (cf. BB 130 ff.).

A better account involves treating an ostensive definition as a substitution-rule. We could, e.g., regard both the deictic gesture and the sample of red as symbols, and take the explanation '*This* [pointing at the sample] is red' as giving a complex and partly concrete symbol interchangeable with the word 'red'; in this case, that symbol would consist of the utterance of '*this*', the gesture of pointing at the sample, and the sample itself (BB 109). Instead of saying 'That pillar box is red', I could say, in the presence of the sample, 'That pillar box is *this* (colour) [pointing at the sample]', and vice versa. The ostensive definition thereby justifies saying 'That is red' by licensing its derivation from the utterance 'That is *this* (colour) [pointing at the sample]'; 'the ostensive definition may be regarded as a rule for translating from a gesture-language into a word-language' (PG 88). On the other hand, an ostensive definition (or a table) leading from a word to a sample is used differently from a translation-rule (or table) leading from a word to another expression (PG 91). In particular, although the word 'red' can always replace the complex symbol consisting of 'this', the gesture, and the sample, the converse replacement may be impossible because the sample is absent, lost, or destroyed. Should this be dismissed as an inconsequential deviation from the verbal substitution-rules? Another objection is that viewing ostensive definitions as substitution-rules makes a sham of their justificatory role in applying the expressions so explained. For, to say 'That tomato is *this* (colour) [pointing at the sample of red]' *is* simply to say 'That tomato is red', and hence it cannot be a justification for saying the latter. The real question seems to be what is the justification for saying that that *is* this colour, and appeal to the ostensive definition of 'red' seems irrelevant here. The proper reply to this objection is that such a judgement of colour is immediate. We do not assert of a tomato standing before us in good light that it is red because we have certain evidence. Our language does not acknowledge anything as grounds for such a judgement. There is, therefore, no such thing as checking this application of 'red' against the grammatical grounds for its application. Our judgement is groundless. Hence, in respect of its grounds, it cannot be said to be justified or unjustified. *A fortiori*, an ostensive definition interpreted as a substitution-rule does not furnish a standard for showing applications of 'red' to be justified or unjustified in this sense, and the sample of red is not compared with objects to decide whether or not they are red.

Once we note that judgements applying ostensively defined expressions may be groundless, the original puzzle simply evaporates. For the question how ostensive definitions provide standards of correctness was so framed that the answer had to have the form of exhibiting how they were implicated in the description of the grammatical grounds for applying the defined expressions. The presupposition of this question is false; viz. that any putative rule of grammar has a genuine normative role only if it is involved in specifying the grounds for applying some expression. An ostensive definition of 'red' does not explain how to *tell* if something is red, but what it is for something to *be* red. Its connection with the applications of 'red' is given merely in the *practice* of speaking the language. We do appeal to ostensive definitions in criticizing misapplications of 'red'; I might say, e.g., 'You described *that* as red, but *this* colour is red, and *that* is not *this* colour'. Speakers normally agree about which applications of 'red' are correct and which not; they agree on how to define 'red' ostensively; and, finally, they agree that correct uses of 'red' accord with these ostensive definitions. There is no mechanism connecting their ostensive definitions with correct applications of such words. The only connections are a contingent regularity and the grammatical convention according to which we treat both giving a correct ostensive definition and making correct applications of 'red' as criteria of understanding 'red'. This description of our practice is a complete description of the normative role of an ostensive definition of 'red'. (It is parallel to the normative role of any rule whose application is not mediated by an 'interpretation'.) It is therefore misleading to describe the sample used in explaining 'red' as a 'standard of comparison', since no *comparisons* with the sample take place.

The normativity of ostensive definitions is closely connected with some of Wittgenstein's most important arguments.

(i) An ostensive definition is a rule (PG 88), not a statement, proposition, assertion, or description. In this respect, it is similar to any explanation, e.g. to *Merkmal*-definitions. Although Wittgenstein had always insisted on the distinction of verbal definitions from propositions (TLP 3.343, 4.241), he had overlooked the parallel point for ostensive explanations (TLP 3.263; PR 54). The sentence 'This is red' may be used to describe an object picked out by the indexical 'this' together with a deictic gesture, or to explain the word 'red'. The crucial point is that it cannot be used simultaneously for both purposes. Its being used as an explanation is incompatible with its being used as a description. This is a particular application of a general observation about rules: no rule-formulation is a description or a statement of fact, although a sentence sometimes used to formulate a rule may on other occasions be used to state the fact that the rule is in force—and may occur as a proper part of a sentence used to state a fact, i.e. as a *Satzradikal* (BT 240 ff.; Vol. XI, 57 ff.;

PLP 142 ff.). Failure to appreciate that ostensive definitions are rules and belong to grammar is the source of most other fundamental misconceptions about them.

(ii) An ostensive definition stands to the uses of the expression that it explains in the same relation as a rule stands to its applications. Hence Wittgenstein's remarks about rule-following apply directly to ostensive definitions (and explanations by charts and tables). In particular, every ostensive definition can be misinterpreted (PI §§28, 86). Consequently, it can always be further interpreted. We may, e.g., explain an ostensive gesture by words (Vol. X, Um. 63; PG 90) or append to a table a rule for how to read it (PI §86; PLP 149 f.). Since the ostensive definition of 'red' does not by itself determine the network of 'internal relations' between red and other parallel determinates, we may supplement it with a formulation of the rules of colour-geometry. Similarly, since we cannot read off that 'red' is a colour-word from the object pointed at in ostensively defining 'red', we may supplement the ostensive definition with a specification of the category of red (e.g. by adding 'Red is a colour' or substituting 'This *colour* is red' for 'This is red') or with a description of the combinatorial possibilities of 'red' (as a colour-word). Rules can always be devised to guide the application of given rules, and in some circumstances various such supplementations may be required to avert or remove misinterpretations or misunderstandings. Hence we might say that any ostensive definition is only one rule among many that jointly guide the use of an expression (PG 61; PLP 61 ff., 200 ff.). Equally, we might claim that understanding an ostensive definition presupposes knowledge of the grammatical post at which the definiendum is stationed (PG 88; PI 29 ff.). But neither of these observations should be taken to imply that an ostensive definition by itself is not complete. A person may grasp how to use a word from its ostensive definition alone (PG 61 f.). If this is generally true and if the ostensive definition is acknowledged as a correct explanation within the linguistic community, then it is a complete explanation just as it stands. What bridges the logical gap between the ostensive definition and the use of the explicandum is a practice.

(iii) An ostensive definition should not be regarded as forging a 'connection between language and reality' (PG 89; PLP 277 ff.). That is linked with important misconceptions. First, it treats the ostensive definition of a word as an application of it and thereby conflates an explanation with a description. This amounts to confusing stepping outside word-language in framing an explanation with applying the explicandum to describe an object (Vol. X, Um. 59). Secondly, this conception fosters the idea that grammar reflects the essential natures of the objects correlated with expressions by ostensive definitions, as if combinatorial possibilities and internal relations flowed from the natures of these objects. Thirdly, it suggests that no ostensive definition can be further interpreted because, as it were, it reaches right up to the 'objective meaning' of the explicandum (cf. Vol. X, Um. 63). These implications are serious obstacles to a philosophical understanding of language. If ostensive definitions did connect language with reality, then they would provide the foundations of language. They would be the fundamental form of explanation, just as the Augustinian picture maintains. To overthrow that conception we should think of ostensive definitions not as connecting words with the world, but as explaining some symbols in terms of others and hence as remaining *within language*. We should conceive of the gesture of pointing as a symbol; this seems quite natural. More importantly, we should count the objects employed in ostensive definitions (and explanations by tables) as symbols, as parts of language, indeed as elements of grammar. 'It . . . causes least confusion to reckon the samples among the instruments of language' (PI §16). They belong to the 'means of representation' (PI §50). This is not a dogmatic claim, but rather the recommendation of a terminology for the purpose of facilitating attainment of an *Übersicht* of language (PLP 277 ff.). In particular, it promotes the insight that explanations explain only within language, and hence that language is 'self-contained and autonomous' (Vol. X, Um. 75; PG 97).

4. *Samples*

Ostensive definition is bound up with the use of objects as samples. Indeed, one might claim that to explain 'red' by pointing to something red and saying 'This is red' *is* to employ this object as a sample of the colour red. Although this situation seems typical, it is not true that every ostensive definition makes use of objects as samples, at least in Wittgenstein's view, because ostensive definitions of proper names do not. Conversely, it seems misleading to treat every case of explanation by means of a sample as an instance of ostensive definition, even under a generous interpretation of 'ostensive definition'; stretching the notion of pointing accommodates explanations by charts or tables and explanations by exemplification of tastes, sounds, or smells, but not even that allows inclusion of explanations by samples that are described or located (e.g., 'red is the colour of the stain on my carpet', 'Red is the colour of fresh blood', or 'One metre is the length of the standard metre in Paris'). It would be better to distinguish ostensive definitions by means of samples as a species within the genus of explanation by samples. Clarification of the notion of a sample is necessary for understanding Wittgenstein's account of the important class of explanations that are both ostensive definitions and explanations by reference to samples.

'Sample' is one out of a sizeable family of words closely related in meaning. Some others are 'type', 'specimen', 'pattern', 'model', 'example', 'paradigm', 'exemplar', 'archetype', 'standard', and 'prototype'. Although their uses are akin, they are subtly differentiated; e.g., a request to see specimens of Wilton broadloom carpets is quite different from a request to see samples of such carpets. Wittgenstein primarily uses the German term 'Muster', for which the best general translation is 'sample'. 'Sample' captures the idea that what is characterized as 'ein Muster' *represents* something and also captures the normative aura of 'Muster', i.e. being usable as a *'standard* of comparison'. 'Paradigm', 'exemplar', and sometimes 'pattern' or 'specimen' are other possible translations.

Instead of following up these subtleties, we might do better to treat 'sample' (i.e. 'Muster') as introducing a family resemblance concept. Central cases of its application are familiar: samples of cloth, colour-charts issued by paint manufacturers, samples of sodium chloride or of water from the Thames at London Bridge, museum specimens such as bird skins or fossils, patterns to be copied such as a spandrel from an antique clock, actions or activities used as precedents in common law decisions or enacted as authoritative examples to be followed by others, or species used to typify genera in a schema of biological classification. All of these are paradigmatic examples for explaining how to use the term 'Muster'.

There are four conspicuous features of what count as samples according to this explanation.

(i) The range of samples is very wide and heterogeneous. We may intelligibly employ almost any concrete object, action, event, or state of affairs as a sample in a suitable context. Moreover, it is doubtful that there could be any limits on what *can* be used as samples.

(ii) Samples enter into human activities and transactions in various different ways. If I want to order material of a particular colour, I might enclose a sample of this colour in a letter; the sample would be part of the order (PR 73). Similarly, oral orders might be accompanied by exhibiting appropriate samples, e.g. of colours (cf. PI §8) or sounds (PI §16). Somebody asked to fetch a bolt of cloth matching a sample in colour might take the sample with him and hold it against each bolt of cloth to judge match or mismatch, he might leave the sample behind and consult his memory image of it, or he might simply go off without the sample and come back with the correct material (BB 84 ff.). Museum specimens might be used to categorize dead animals, to examine the ability of students at zoological classification, or to standardize the terminology of classification. A sample of water from the Thames might be subjected to chemical analysis and used to formulate ecological policies. Such possibilities can be multiplied indefinitely. Where a sample plays a role in communication, it is natural to reckon it as a *sign*; hence Wittgenstein recommends calling it part of language (PR 73; PLP 108 f., 277 f.; PI §16; cf. Exg. §16). This description is, of course, only appropriate relative to that particular context; e.g. a piece of a wallpaper stripped from my wall, sent as a sample colour in ordering material, and then dumped on a rubbish heap would serve as a sign only transiently.

(iii) The status of something as a sample depends on how it is used. I might, e.g., take a sample of carpet from a sample-book in a shop and use it to carpet the floor of a doll's house; then it would no longer be a carpet sample.[2] Conversely, I might take a dinner service in use for many years and put it in a museum as a specimen of a particular type of china; it would then become a sample, although it had not been so before. Furthermore, a single object may have multiple uses as a sample. A particular swatch of cloth might be used one day as a sample for a colour, another day as a sample for a weave or kind of fabric. Alternatively, it might be used simultaneously, rather than successively, as a sample for several different things. To call something a sample is to characterize its role, not its 'intrinsic' features.

(iv) When used as samples, functional objects typically do not have their usual functions nor actions their standard roles. A sample set of china, e.g., sits unused in a shop window, and wallpaper samples are found in sample-books instead of being used to decorate a room. Similarly, a musician demonstrating how to play ornaments in Bach's Forty-eight is not playing a fugue, and a joiner showing how to cut a mortice may not be making a component of a piece of furniture.

Further clarification of the concept of a sample can be extracted from examining important threads of resemblance that bind together the various things classified as samples. On close scrutiny, each of them too seems to resolve itself into a family of concepts.

(i) A sample *represents* that of which it is a sample; i.e. an object in a context in which it functions as a sample is employed as a representative. Hence, it must belong to and be typical of the whole or kind which it represents. We may not use a class in a primary school as a sample of the British electorate, a stork as a sample of an elephant, nor a red object as a sample of green (cf. BT 49, PG 90 f.). A sample of red must be red (though a green object might be a symbol for red). Similarly, it must be clearly red, not a borderline case for the application of 'red'. Likewise, a sample set of electors used in an opinion poll, e.g., must be representative of the whole voting population in relevant respects (age, sex, occupations, etc.); or a sample of water from the Thames must be typical of the water in a given part of the river if it is to be useful for formulating policies of pollution control on the basis of its chemical analysis; or a specimen of a butterfly in a museum must be typical of the species to

[2] We owe this telling example to Dr W. Künne.

which it belongs if it is to serve as a basis for formulating a description useful for identifying members of the species. Conversely, something abnormal, deviant, or atypical may not legitimately be used as a sample; a deformed stork, e.g., cannot serve as a sample of a stork. These points are normative. A prediction of an opinion poll may be correct, but that does not entail that the survey group is representative of the electorate. Similarly, after taking a particular drug, we might all use a red object in a way similar to that in which we now use a sample of green, but that would not make it a sample of green. *De facto* success in the role normally discharged by a sample does not legitimate taking something to be a sample. What it is for something to be representative is not sharply circumscribed, and different standards are applied in different cases.

(ii) A sample can be *copied* or *reproduced*. We can, e.g., reproduce a colour sample by printing colour-charts, and we can copy it by painting a wall the same colour. Many different things, however, count as copying a sample, depending on our purposes, how we compare things with samples, and the context of the activity (PG 91 f.). The copy may, e.g., be on a bigger scale than the pattern (e.g. a Chippendale chair copied from the *Directory*), or on a smaller scale (e.g. a microcircuit in a calculator); it may be made by eye and without instruments (e.g. copying a pencil sketch) or in various ways with instruments or measurements (e.g. copying the construction of bisecting a line by straight-edge and compass or copying a particular angle with a protractor). Alternatively, it may imitate the sample (e.g. an action or activity), and this too in many different respects. Since copying is a characteristic use of samples and since objects are characterized as samples in respect of how they are used, it is tempting to conclude that the meaning of 'sample' ('Muster') varies systematically with differences in what counts as copying (Vol. X, Um. 66 = PG 91). The possibility of reproducing samples is equally important and complex. It is a feature of typical samples or specimens in natural science, of fair samples in statistical sampling, and of standards used in weighing and measuring. (It is one of the features emphasized in Wittgenstein's characterizing mathematical proofs as paradigms.) But what counts as reproducing samples depends on purpose and context. Moreover, the possibility of reproducing samples does not guarantee parity of esteem between the parent sample and its offspring; e.g. the standard metre may have metre-sticks as its ambassadors, but it is still prince.

(iii) A sample has a *normative* role; it might be characterized as a '*standard of comparison*' (though what counts as comparison is very variable (BB 85 ff.)). There is a risk in using this phrase, for we are apt to think that comparison must take one or the other of two forms: viz. *either* holding a sample of red or a sample of a leaf up against something to judge whether that object should be called 'red' or 'a leaf' as we measure an object with a metre-stick, *or* comparing an impression of something with a corresponding mental image to determine whether the term is applicable. In fact, the notion of 'standard of comparison' must be construed more liberally, even metaphorically.[3] The root idea is familiar: if I give a painter a colour sample to copy in decorating my kitchen wall, I will blame his work, not the sample, if I find that they do not match. The sample is, as it were, what measures, not what is measured. Samples typically function as standards of correctness and error; we appeal to them in justifying or criticizing acts of copying or reproducing them. We also use them as norms of representation; since, e.g., a museum specimen is representative of a species, it embodies what is normal and gives a foundation for describing what is deviant, atypical, or abnormal. The normative roles of the different things classed as samples themselves form a complex family. (The normative connotations of 'Muster' are stronger than those of 'sample' and are more akin to those of 'exemplar', 'paradigm', or 'archetype').

One focus of Wittgenstein's discussion of samples is their role in grammar (i.e. in the practices of explaining and applying expressions in language). But this does not exhaust his exploitation of samples for philosophical purposes. In particular, samples play a prominent part in his account of what it is to follow a rule or order. We are inclined to look for something common to all cases of rule-following in virtue of which they are cases of following rules, and we suppose that this must be something 'inner', i.e. some special experience or some mental process or act accompanying one's outward behaviour. This tendency is reinforced by the idea that rules are 'abstract entities'. Moreover, we conceive of the applications of a rule as somehow following from its content. This idea too is reinforced by taking rules to be abstract entities, for then they may be endowed with mysterious powers. Wittgenstein uses samples to attack both these misconceptions of rule-following. The subjective aspects are clarified by making rules concrete and hence external; we can, e.g., frame the rules for chess moves in pictures and diagrams, or we can use samples and gestures in issuing orders. This move externalizes the activities characteristic of rule-following; e.g. a person consults the rule by looking it up before making a move in chess or by comparing objects with samples for match or mismatch. This combats the illusion that some subtle inner process occurs in all cases of following rules or orders, for *any* such process can be externalized if the rule or order is made concrete. The same move also clarifies the objective aspects of following rules. A rule can be fully formulated in a diagram or chart, and there is little temptation to say that this *contains* its applications. Indeed, it is manifest that a rule so formulated does not literally contain its applica-

---

[3] Especially, e.g., in characterizing a mathematical proof as a paradigm.

tions. The use of samples in rules and orders is stressed in many of Wittgenstein's remarks. Since 'grammar' itself consists of rules, we could characterize his strategy as giving samples both first-order and second-order roles in the clarification of grammar—first-order in that they are part of many explanations of the meanings of expressions, and second-order in that they elucidate what it is to use an expression in accord with its explanation.

5. *Samples in grammar: Wittgenstein's position*

Any object used as a sample in communication should, in Wittgenstein's view, be counted as a sign relative to that particular context and accordingly should be reckoned as a part of language. This status of an object depends primarily on the whim of the speaker; it need not be permanent or generally accorded. By contrast, some samples have a more rigid, formalized role in communication. Their use is governed by standing principles widely acknowledged in the linguistic community and perhaps codified as a system of rules. They might be said to belong to the *grammar* of the language. Wittgenstein directs attention to this subclass of the class of samples.

The role of samples as parts of grammar is prominent in typical ostensive definitions and explanations by tables correlating words with samples. 'This colour is ultramarine', I might say, pointing to a scrap of coloured paper; this gives the sample a place in the explanation of 'ultramarine', and hence in the grammar of colour-words. This grammatical status of the sample has some permanence; as long as the sample is available, the explanation licenses the substitution of 'this colour' together with the gesture of pointing and the sample for the word 'ultramarine', and vice versa. It is also institutionalized, not because everyone uses the same scrap of paper to explain 'ultramarine', but because using this as a sample in an ostensive explanation is acknowledged as giving a correct explanation and treated as a criterion of understanding 'ultramarine'. Because the word is correlated with the sample in the ostensive explanation, there is no need for the sample to appear as part of an instruction for somebody to bring an object of that colour. The relation of the communication to the sample is forged by the explanation of 'ultramarine'. The sample is no longer a sign appearing as part of the instruction, but instead belongs to grammar.

There are samples used in explaining certain concepts which have a more conspicuously permanent and institutionalized status in grammar. The archetype of these samples is the standard metre. The unit length 'one metre' is explained as the length of the standard metre. So explaining the expression 'one metre' is itself a widespread practice, and this explanation has a certain primacy among all of the acceptable explanations of the expression. Careful preservation of the standard metre is intended to secure the permanent possibility of giving this explanation and hence of substituting a suitable reference to the sample for the words 'one metre'. Unlike a scrap of paper used as a colour sample in explaining a colour-word, the standard metre is not an ephemeral part of grammar, but it is a permanent 'means of representation' (PI §50).

Samples belonging to grammar are not confined to samples employed in explanations which can be regarded as substitution-rules. For samples may equally have a definite formal role in justifying or criticizing the applications of expressions. This role too is prominent in systems of measurement: metre-sticks, tape measures, etc., are used as samples of the length one metre for the purpose of determining, by juxtaposition with something, whether or not this object is one metre long. Since its grammar includes everything that plays a non-inductive part in justifying or criticizing the applications of an expression, metre-sticks must be counted as samples belonging to the grammar of 'one metre (long)' whether or not they are employed in giving correct explanations of the expression 'one metre'. The exact demarcation of inductive from non-inductive justifications is clearly open to dispute, but there is no reason why objects should not have a special institutionalized role in applying certain words. Though belonging to grammar, such samples are very different 'means of representation' or 'instruments of language' from the samples used in explaining expressions.

Even this addition does not exhaust the class of samples belonging to grammar. For we might also so classify any samples that have a relatively permanent and formalized role in communication. This possibility is exemplified by the colour samples used in the builders' language-game (PI §8). We might suppose that there was a definite set of colour samples containing just one sample for each colour; and hence, whenever a builder gives an instruction to fetch a stone of a certain colour, he must employ one particular object as the colour sample to be shown to the assistant. This would make the sample similar to a word; it would be part of a definite practice of communication, its use would be rule-governed, and it would have a permanent role in the language as one of the means of representation. Hence such a sample would itself have a place in the grammar of the language.

The set of samples belonging to grammar is extensive and heterogeneous; its members enter into the use of language in very different ways. For his philosophical purposes, Wittgenstein focuses almost exclusively on samples used in ostensive definitions and in explanations by charts or tables. Because of the vagueness of 'explanation', 'sample,' and 'ostensive definition', even this restricted subset has no sharp boundaries.

But sharpening up this notion does not seem necessary for his purposes.

The main thrust of Wittgenstein's contention that samples used in
explanations belong to grammar is to undermine one guiding idea of the
Augustinian picture of language, viz. that ostensive definitions connect
language with reality. That conception has dominated much of philosophy, ancient and modern, and it is as prevalent now as ever before. A
decisive repudiation of it would amount to an earthquake, having
repercussions throughout a wide range of philosophical reflection.
Wittgenstein's criticism of this conception has many facets. It can be
anatomized into the following contentions.

(i) Ostensive definitions are accepted as correct explanations for many
expressions of very diverse kinds. Their correctness is not impugned by
the possibility of correctly explaining these expressions in other ways,
e.g. by *Merkmal*–definitions (cf. pp. 84 ff.).

(ii) Although the sentence-forms used in giving ostensive definitions
can also be used for other purposes, in particular for giving descriptions,
a sentence used to explain an expression by reference to a sample is not
on that occasion used to describe anything. *A fortiori*, an ostensive
definition does not describe this sample, nor does it contain or entail such
a description (PLP 278). I can, e.g., use the sentence 'This is red' to
describe a book that I indicate by a gesture; in this use the sentence might
be paraphrased 'This book has the property of being red'. Equally, I
might use the same words in explaining 'red', and I might even use the
same book as a sample, indicating it by a gesture, but in doing so I would
not be describing this book as being red or asserting it to be red; rather, in
this use the sentence would best be paraphrased 'The colour of this book
(or, this colour) is the colour red' or 'This colour is called "red"'. (These
paraphrases need not be synonymous with the original sentences in their
particular uses; the important point is that giving one of them
as a sentence-explanation would count as a criterion of understanding
these particular uses of the sentence 'This is red'.) The ostensive
definition is a rule, not a statement of fact. It is part of the grammar of
language, unlike a description, which is an application of language (PG
88; PLP 13 f.). It determines the sense of an expression rather than
employing this sense (RFM 168).

(iii) Any ostensive definition, like any explanation of meaning, can be
misinterpreted (PI §28). Therefore, ostensive definitions do not secure
the foundations of language by providing explanations beyond the
possibility of misinterpretation (cf. PG 90) and hence beyond the sway of
Cartesian doubt. Moreover, someone's giving a correct ostensive definition is not a sufficient condition (but rather a criterion) of his understanding the explained expression; his applications may even show that he
misinterprets his own explanation.

(iv) The rules for correct use of an expression (i.e. its grammar) do not 'flow' from a correct ostensive definition of it (PLP 61f., 200). An ostensive definition has no magical powers, but functions only as part of a system of rules (PG 71). The grammar of a word cannot be extracted from contemplating the essential nature of the object correlated with it in an ostensive definition.

(v) Ostensive definitions are often correct and complete explanations of words (cf. PG 60 ff.). The fact that giving an ostensive definition is not a sufficient condition of understanding the explicandum does not prove that no ostensive definition can be complete, nor does the fact that understanding an ostensive definition presupposes stage-setting, i.e. knowing the category of the explicandum. This would be an over-reaction to the inadequacy of the conception of grammar as determined by meaning-bodies (cf. PLP 61 ff., 200 ff.). Whether an explanation is complete is an aspect of its normative role in the application of the explained expression, and this is not settled, positively or negatively, by the generalization that it is always possible to extend any explanation (cf. 'Explanation', pp. 39 ff.).

(vi) Ostensive definitions are rules of grammar. They have a norma-tive role parallel to that of analytical definitions or translation-rules. Indeed, they are best conceived as linking symbols. Like any genuine standard of correctness, ostensive definitions must be public for they must be capable of resolving disagreements.

(vii) An explanation of an expression by reference to a sample does not forge a link between language and reality. The sample itself is best conceived as a sign and hence as a part of grammar. Therefore, the explanation remains within language. There are rules for the correct use of a sample as a sample; hence the dictum that the meaning of a sign is its use in language can be applied to samples as well as to words and phrases. Consider the possibility of a gesture-language, i.e. a language consisting wholly of gestures and samples. A corollary of the contention that samples belong to language is the claim that this gesture-language would be no closer to reality than word-language; e.g. that no less of a gulf would separate the gesture-order to open the door from the act of opening the door than would separate this act from the order 'Open the door!' (BT 44). For the sample is a mere sign too. It is part of a complex sign (indexical, gesture, and sample) that can be substituted for the explained word. (To describe samples as belonging to language or to grammar is not to deny that the objects used as samples would appear on an inventory of the furniture of the world.)

(viii) Although both samples and words are signs, they differ from each other (PG 91); samples belonging to grammar must have the status of samples, whereas expressions used in verbal explanations need not. When I want to explain 'red', e.g., I do so by pointing at something red, thus using it as a sample of red (PI §429); by contrast, I could not use something green as a *sample* of red (BT 49 f.) and hence I could not explain 'red' ostensively by pointing to something green (cf. BT 52). There must be, as it were, a method of projection connecting something used as a sample with what it is used as a sample of (BT 50 f.). A sample of red, e.g., must *represent* the colour red; it must be representative of red things (cf. PG 89). Conversely, *copying* a sample of red must yield something red, not something green or something (e.g. middle-C) of which we do not predicate colours (BT 50 ff.; PG 91 f.). Although all signs are in a sense arbitrary (cf. BT 52f., PG 92), samples are subject to different constraints from words.

(ix) A sample in grammar must have one of the normative roles characteristic of samples, it must be capable of being employed as 'an object of comparison'. (This does not mean that all samples have exactly the same normative role; cf. pp. 100 f.) A sample in grammar belongs to the method of representation. An object when so used is not something described.

(x) 'Internal relations' among expressions explained by reference to samples consist in normative connections among the practices of explaining and applying these expressions, especially in the practice of using single objects simultaneously in explaining different expressions or of prohibiting such uses. Wittgenstein elaborates this conception with respect to the geometry of colour (RFM 75 f.) and principles for converting one system of measurement into another (cf. 'The standard metre', pp. 180 f.).

(xi) Although samples are signs, they not only differ from words but also might be characterized as '*primary* signs' in contrast with words, which are secondary signs (PLP 278, cf. BT 46 ff.). A metamorphosis of the Augustinian picture might yield this conception. Language does not rest on metaphysical foundations, but it may still seem to rest on samples which are used to assign meaning to the simple concept-words which are 'unanalysable'. Hence primary signs appear to be indispensable. We are inclined to ask 'whether it isn't the case that our language *has* to have primary signs while it could get by without the secondary ones' (PG 88). For primary signs appear to underpin every genuine explanation, since where analysis of complex concept-words ends, there lie the primary signs of language, samples which give the meanings of such terms as 'red', 'dark', 'sweet' (PI §87). Wittgenstein came to reject these implications of calling samples (and gestures) 'primary signs'. The thesis of indispensability strikes a false note in that it calls for an explanation of existing language instead of a mere description (BT 46; PG 88 f.). An honest description of language reveals that this *ersatz* foundations thesis is as dogmatic and misguided as its ancestral doctrine. Samples are essential to the use and explanation of just those words which we essentially explain and use by employing samples, just as words are essential to the use of words (BT 53 f.). But 'words are not essential to what we call "language", and neither are samples' (PG 93), nor are ostensive definitions (PLP 108). If there were no samples of 'sweet', 'sour', 'bitter', etc., our gustatory vocabulary would become defunct, but that would no more stop us talking about apples, loganberries, and almonds than it would stop us eating—even though *haute cuisine* would suffer. If there were language-users in a colourless world, they could not explain to each other (nor to themselves) what it would be for the world to be colourful. But the idea that samples underpin every explanation of any expression is illusory, a residue of the Augustinian conception of language and its attendant idea of analysis. A symptom of the deceptiveness of this view would be the embarrassment of a philosopher asked to replace a typical sentence by its translation into primitive signs (BT 54; PG 89). The crucial question is whether we acknowledge giving other explanations of word- and sentence-meaning than *Merkmal*-definition and explanation by samples, and the answer is obviously that we often do. Hence samples are not 'primary signs'.

The idea that samples used in explaining and applying words are signs or parts of language is the key to Wittgenstein's thoroughgoing criticism of the conception of word-meaning encapsulated in the Augustinian picture. In particular, it brings logical atomism down in ruins. Constructively it plays an equally important role in Wittgenstein's vindication of the thesis of the autonomy of grammar.

6. Samples in grammar: second-generation reflections

Thus far we have aimed at analysing the ingredients of Wittgenstein's conception that certain samples belong to grammar and at explaining what he takes to be the philosophical implications of this idea. His purposes in introducing the idea into the *Investigations* are predominantly negative; he elaborates it in connection with simple language-games that are intended to expose deficiencies in the Augustinian picture of language. Had his imaginary defender of this picture complained that his delineation of the roles of samples in these language-games was too schematic or unclear, Wittgenstein could have filled in the necessary details by stipulation, and provided that this could be done coherently, his criticisms would then be sustained. Nothing here hangs on an exact description of how samples are employed.

The situation is completely different if we seek to apply Wittgenstein's conception of samples to our own language. His conception seems to be pregnant with important implications since samples play a variety of roles in explaining and applying words. But extracting these implications presupposes giving an exact description of how we do employ such samples, and that seems very elusive. It is apt to appear as if the idea that samples may belong to grammar raises more problems than it could possibly solve. Reflecting on these leads one into waters that Wittgenstein did not clearly chart.

The beginning of wisdom is to enumerate the problems about the roles of ostensive definition and samples in language.

(i) It seems that ostensive definitions are superfluous in the description of what it is to have mastery of a language. Consider, e.g., the fact that we may use any red object (but only red ones) to explain 'red' ostensively. The ability to give an ostensive explanation of 'red' is parasitic on the ability to pick out red objects, i.e. on the ability to apply 'red' correctly, and having *that* ability is what understanding 'red' consists in. Therefore, the ability to explain 'red' either presupposes or collapses into the ability to apply 'red' correctly. Does this not make ostensive definitions of 'red' superfluous? Why should one presume that there are two distinct things involved in understanding 'red', viz. agreement in judgements and agreement in definitions (i.e. in choice of objects as samples for explaining 'red')? Is correct application not really the sole criterion for understanding any word explained ostensively?

(ii) It seems that the relation of concrete samples to the applications of words is typically a case of action at a distance and hence that samples are not part of the grammar of words. How, e.g., does the standard metre, used in explaining the expression 'one metre', enter into typical applications of this expression? Certainly not as an 'object of comparison', if that describes an instrument held up against a measured object. Similarly how is a red book which I now use to explain 'red' involved in subsequent applications of 'red', whether my own or the learner's? Must we conclude that either the real sample (object of comparison) is something mental or explanation by samples is relevant only to the genesis of understanding?

(iii) It seems that the employment of samples in either explaining or applying an expression makes this expression implicitly relational. If, e.g. 'red' is ostensively explained by pointing to a red book, does this not imply that an object is red if and only if it resembles this book in colour? Hence, in describing an apple as red, am I not saying that it resembles this book in colour and hence asserting a relation to hold between it and this sample? Similarly, if I use a metre-stick in measuring objects, is the statement that a table is one metre long not equivalent to the assertion that it has the same length as the metre-stick? Must we mortify our intuitions and recognize that such predicates really encapsulate resemblance-relations?

(iv) The idea that an explanation by reference to a sample is a substitution-rule seems problematic. The model for a substitution-rule is a lexical definition; this licenses the replacement of the definiendum by the definiens in any (extensional) context and vice versa, and it is taken to express a necessary truth. But suppose, e.g., that I define 'red' ostensively by pointing to a copy of the *Tractatus*. Can I replace 'red' in *every* extensional context by the demonstrative 'this', my copy of the *Tractatus*, and a gesture of pointing at it? Is it a necessary truth that the world includes this exemplar of the *Tractatus* or that this copy is bound within red covers? If not, does the explanation really have the status of a substitution-rule?

(v) If explanations by sample are treated as substitution-rules, and particularly if samples are indispensable for explaining some expressions, it seems that language gives hostages to fortune. The destruction of a sample or its appropriate alteration would have grammatical repercussions; e.g. loss of the standard metre or damage to it would transform the whole system of metric linear measurement. How can the presence of concrete samples in the grammar of our language be reconciled with the principle that the meaning of a sentence must be independent of the facts?

All of these problems arise from distortions and confusions that the *Investigations* was meant to extirpate. Although they are not explicitly discussed there, Wittgenstein's remarks do supply the raw materials for dissolving them. In most cases, the proper response is implicit in the ingredients of the preceding account of ostensive definition and the use of samples in grammar. In some cases, however, this requires supplementation by his account of rule-following and his conception of philosophy. Before outlining the responses to these problems, we will extend Wittgenstein's reflections by introducing some terminology to mark important distinctions among the ways that samples function in grammar.

(i) *Canonical samples*: sometimes an object has a unique role in our practice of explaining and applying a word; in the grammar of our language, it is irreplaceable. We call such a sample 'canonical'. Actual examples are prominent in systems of weights and measures: the standard metre and the standard kilogram in Paris, the Imperial Standard Bar at Greenwich, etc. We define the unit of length one metre as the length of the standard metre, the unit of mass one kilogram as the weight of the standard kilogram, etc. Imagined language-games might incorporate different ranges of canonical samples, e.g. colour samples (PI §§8, 46, 50f.), and they might not be homogeneous in function (e.g. there are no colour-words, and hence no explanations of colour-words, in the language-game of PI §8).

Because of their limited availability, canonical samples are not typically employed in ostensive definitions nor as instruments of comparison for determining the applicability of the defined expression. Rather, they are used in giving explanations by samples picked out by a definite description or proper name; e.g. 'one metre is the length of the standard metre'. An explanation by reference to a canonical sample may well not be the only explanation the giving of which is a criterion of understanding the explanandum; e.g. one may explain the phrase 'one metre' by pointing to a metre-stick and saying '*That* is one metre long'. None the less, the unique role of a canonical sample seems to give explanations by reference to it a certain primacy among admissible explanations. This reflects its typical function as a *pattern* for the production and calibration of objects used in giving alternative explanations and in settling the applicability of the definiendum. Standard weights and measures exemplify these functions of regulating the uses of instruments of measurement (e.g. metre-sticks and scales). Though we do not run to the standard metre to measure a bolt of cloth, persistent disagreement about its length not adjudicable by reference to ordinary metre-sticks could, in the last resort, lead to an appeal to the standard metre. This canonical sample serves as a final court of appeal to establish the propriety of metre-sticks made on its pattern, and hence indirectly it serves as the final arbiter of the correctness of metric measurement made by use of metre-sticks or tape measures. This normative role is important whether or not there are actual appeals to the canonical sample in settling disputes, indeed whether or not most of the participants in a system of measurement are even aware of the existence or role of the canonical sample in this institution (cf. 'The standard metre', pp. 175 f.).

Because canonical samples are unique, relatively inaccessible, and vulnerable to fortune, it seems advantageous to replace each of them by a definite set of equally authoritative samples or by a 'recipe' for producing indefinitely many such samples. Consequently, Parliament sanctioned several Imperial Bars for defining the length 'one yard', and the kilogram is commonly defined as the weight of one litre of pure water at maximum density.

(ii) *Standard samples*: in order to secure general agreement in judgements in conformity with our normal requirements of precision, we must judge the applicability of certain concepts by using certain objects as standards of comparison. The model for this procedure is measurement of length by a ruler. We cannot judge lengths without rulers accurately enough to serve most practical or theoretical purposes; we must make use of instruments of measurement, laying a measuring rod against the object to be measured and reading the length off from the calibrating marks. Metre rules, yardsticks, tape measures, etc., have this function; so too do kilogram weights, colour-charts, and tuning forks. We shall call objects so used 'standard samples', provided that their functioning in this way is laid down in the grammar of our language (and not merely justified by inductive argument). Their status as standard samples is independent of whether they are used in explanations (by reference to samples) of the expressions whose uses they govern. The characteristic function of a metre-stick as an object of comparison, e.g., is unaffected by whether or not we acknowledge as correct the ostensive explanation of 'one metre' by reference to an ordinary metre-stick.

Although standard samples are plentiful and accessible, measuring and weighing play important roles in our lives, so that small differences are often important. This makes it urgent to have a procedure for resolving disagreements in measurements, whereas the plurality of standard samples leaves open the possibility of chronic disagreement. One remedy is to adopt a canonical sample for each unit of measurement, e.g. the king's foot or the standard metre. Another is to fix a recipe or authoritative procedure for calibrating the standard samples, e.g. to use a litre of water at maximum density to calibrate metal kilogram weights. (Each of these strategies presupposes agreement on methods of matching the putative standard samples with the 'control', and these methods may vary according to our purposes.) The only antidote to the threat of chaos in applying concepts by reference to standard samples seems to be a movement in the direction of canonical samples or their equivalent (canonical recipes).

(iii) *Optional samples*: objects play a less institutionalized and permanent, but none the less important, role in the practice of explaining a wide range of expressions. This is particularly prominent in explanations of words for simple perceptual qualities, e.g. 'red', 'sweet', 'acrid', 'musty', 'rough', 'hard', 'cool'. We explain 'red', e.g., by pointing at some object clearly exemplifying the colour red and thus using this object in the context of this ostensive definition as a sample. Such a sample is not fixed permanently like a canonical sample. No object serves invariably in this explanatory role, nor does every explanation of 'red' employ the same object. Nor need the sample be employed as a standard of comparison in applying the explanandum; i.e. it need not be a standard sample. What is essential is its (transient) role in giving an explanation. We shall call such samples 'optional'. Relative to particular contexts of explanation, optional samples belong to grammar. They are used in the ostensive explanation of a very diverse range of expressions.

The status of an object as an optional sample is context-relative. What is now used as a sample for explaining 'red', e.g., may on another occasion be described as red. This dual role of an object, i.e. its now being an object described, now a sample, seems strange to the blinkered eye. We are inclined to forget that characterizing something as a sample does not turn on its intrinsic properties, but on how it is used. If we bear this in mind, the ephemeral status of optional samples is no more odd than the practice of a group of children who, wishing to play football in a field lacking goal-posts, use four among themselves to stand as post markers on the understanding that these will swap places with other players whenever a goal is scored. What the use of colour-words presupposes is agreement in definitions, i.e. an agreed practice in explaining them. This does not require permanently fixing some objects as samples, but only a substantial agreement on whether explanations by reference to particular samples are correct. Grammar contains a permanent set of rules for the use of colour-words, but even if every legitimate explanation of 'red' makes use of a sample, it does not follow that there must be some permanent *thing* of which every legitimate explanation makes use.

Calling something an optional sample characterizes only its role in the practice of explaining an expression. This is independent of whether it has in addition the role of a standard sample in applying the explanandum. An object, e.g. a particular metre-stick, may have both roles. On the other hand, many optional samples are not also employed as standard samples. This is characteristic of samples used to explain colour-words, such as 'blue', 'red', and 'green', perhaps even 'ultramarine' and 'scarlet'. Our recognitional and discriminatory abilities in respect of such colours fulfil our purposes far better than our corresponding abilities with respect to length or weight. For most purposes in most contexts, we do not place a sample of red alongside an object to judge whether it is red, but rather recognize (immediately) whether or not it is red. There are, however, contexts in which we do use standard samples of colours for specialized purposes. Colour-charts are used for the precise description or specification of shades of colour; in duplicating the paint on a wall we might hold a paint-card against the wall, comparing the patches of colour with the painted surface for match and mismatch, or we might use a colour-chart to label the product of a paint factory with the British Standard numbers (e.g. '06 C 18'). It is important to note that optional samples need not enter into the application of expressions in the way that standard samples do.

Armed with these distinctions, we can outline strategies for dealing with the problems that apparently beset an attempt to extend Wittgenstein's account of ostensive definition and samples in grammar from artificial language-games to the analysis of ordinary language.

(i) The suggestion that correct application is really the only criterion of understanding a word explained by optional samples, e.g. 'red', can be refuted by a pair of observations. First, giving an ostensive explanation by pointing to a red object is not to describe this thing as being red; it is not to apply the word 'red' to anything. Secondly, our linguistic practice does include treating an ostensive definition of 'red' as a criterion of understanding 'red' (PG 83); to deny this is to misdescribe the grammar of 'to understand "red"' or to propose a modification of this grammar, not to discover a hidden truth. The objection that only correct application of 'red' counts as a criterion of understanding is made plausible only by conflating ostensive explanations with applications of 'red' and by thinking that an object used as an optional sample must also have the function of a standard sample. The immediacy of colour judgements fosters the illusion that samples have no part in the grammar of colour-words. To counter the objection more persuasively, one might adduce arguments to support the thesis that the use of language presupposes agreement in definitions as well as agreement in judgements (cf. PI §242).

(ii) The idea that samples belong only to the genesis of understanding and hence do not belong to grammar is attractive primarily in the case of optional samples. It rests on an over-simple conception of what it is to follow an explanation in applying the explained word. By implication, it recognizes as part of the grammar of a word only samples serving the function of standard samples. Only these are deemed to enter into the application of the word; other samples are held to act only at a distance. This is too restrictive a conception of samples belonging to grammar, but it can be finally exploded only by a proper account of rule-following.

(iii) The conception that any expression explained or applied by reference to a sample must be implicitly relational springs from conflating explanations with applications of words. To say, e.g., that one object resembles another in respect of colour (or length) is to describe both objects as having the same colour (or length). But a sample, e.g. of red, used in an explanation is not described at all; *a fortiori*, to say of (another) object that it is red cannot be to describe it as having the same colour that the sample is said to have in the ostensive explanation of 'red'. Rather, to say that this other object is red is to describe it as having *this* colour [pointing at the sample] (cf. pp. 93 f. above). Similarly, a standard sample employed as an object of comparison in applying an expression is not something thereby described; e.g., in measuring a table with a metre-stick a person does not describe the metre-stick at all. *A fortiori*, in justifying the assertion that the table is one metre long by measuring it with the metre-stick he is not describing the table as having the same length that the metre-stick is said to have. To use a metre-stick as a standard sample is not to characterize it as being (really) a metre long, but to incorporate it in the method of representation. To say that a rod is one metre long because it coincides with the metre-stick asserts no more than that it is one metre long. The 'because' clause simply recapitulates an explanation of what it is for something to *be* one metre long. Consequently, an expression explained or applied by reference to a sample is not thereby rendered implicitly relational.

(iv) The objection to taking explanations by samples as substitution-rules flows from the tradition of identifying rules of grammar with necessary truths. The objection proceeds from the premise that no concrete object necessarily exists, infers that no explanation by reference to a sample can be the expression of a necessary truth, and concludes that no such explanation is a substitution-rule belonging to grammar. If this reasoning were sound, only necessary existents (if any) could qualify as samples belonging to grammar. This conclusion and the underlying argument are clearly contrary to Wittgenstein's conception of the matter, but exposition and defence of his reasoning involves a full account of his conception of grammar and of necessity.

(v) The objection that samples in grammar give hostages to fortune seems most compelling in the case of canonical samples, though it applies also to standard and optional samples. It too raises the issue of concept-identity. But it also conflates the empirical conditions in whose absence certain uses of language would cease to have any point with conditions logically necessary for the existence of language (cf. 'The standard metre', pp. 173 f.).

Our aim in these remarks has been programmatic. We have tried to extract from Wittgenstein's work the materials for dissolving the problems that appear to be serious obstacles to extending his insights about the function of samples in grammar to the clarification of actual language. If this is successful, then obviously there is much still to be learned from his discussions of samples and ostensive definition. The primary difficulty in exploiting these insights is the strong gravitational attraction of Platonism and idealism on reflections about concepts. It is extraordinarily hard to recognize that concrete objects used as samples in explaining or applying expressions belong to grammar or our method of representation. We are tempted to think that these objects are merely incidental, that the *real* samples are Platonistic or mental entities (e.g. the *length* of the standard metre, the *colour* of the patch on the chart, or the *image* of this colour in the mind of the perceiver). Wittgenstein warns against the temptations of Platonism:

In this case, too, you cannot say: 'A ruler does measure in spite of its corporeality; of course a ruler which only has length would be the Ideal, you might say the *pure* ruler.' No, if a body has length, there can be no length without a body—and although I realize that in a certain sense only the ruler's length measures, what I put in my pocket still remains the ruler, the body, and isn't the length. (PR 81)

The private language argument is a sustained attack on the idealist gambit. The obstacle to a correct conception of the role of samples in language seems to be the will: we do not want to acknowledge that samples are, as it were, partly concrete concepts.

7. Samples and simples

Wittgenstein's reflections on samples and ostensive definition provided a rich source of material for philosophical criticism. In particular, he put his novel ideas to use in striking ways in his repudiation of certain metaphysical doctrines of the *Tractatus*, especially its conception of simple objects.

The nature of 'objects' in the *Tractatus* is obscure. Some have argued that these are Platonic entities such as properties and relations; others that they are (mysterious) particulars which, somehow or other, generate properties and relations. But the very question is misconceived. Wittgenstein had no idea what objects were; all he knew was that there had to be entities satisfying his specifications if language was to be possible at all. Examples of objects would in due course be discovered by philosophical analysis. It seems clear that the demands laid upon objects are inconsistent; nothing could possibly satisfy them. The question that must be asked is not what exemplifies the *Tractatus's* concept of an object, but what in fact fulfils the needs which the *Tractatus's* objects were invented to satisfy. To the extent that these needs are genuine, the proper answer to this question is 'Samples'. Some important primary sources indicate that this was *his* answer too: the conception of the simples in the *Tractatus* stemmed from a distorted and ill-understood view of samples. In an early reconsideration of the matter, Wittgenstein calls the four primary colours 'objects' and characterizes them as elements of representation (WWK 43). So the question 'Are objects thing-like or property-like?' is meaningless. He proceeded gradually to develop this insight. What he had meant by 'objects' was whatever we can speak of without fear of non-existence (PR 72) and he cited as possible instances 'the four basic colours, space, time, and other data of the sort' (PR 169). Similarly, 'If you call the colour green an object, you must be saying that it is an object that occurs in the symbolism. Otherwise the sense of the symbolism, and thus its very existence as a symbolism, would not be guaranteed' (PG 209, cf. BB 31; PI §46). It is pointless to object that Wittgenstein later misinterpreted the *Tractatus,* since he had earlier insisted that colours were complex. The fact is that colours or shades of colours (LF) or basic colours (PR) are the nearest one can get to the objects of the *Tractatus.* (To add the atomicity requirement immediately renders the requirements self-contradictory by generating the incoherent demand for all entailments to be consequences of truth-functional combination.)

Wittgenstein's suggestion can be developed by systematically comparing the objects of the *Tractatus* with samples. This is illuminating, for it reveals the extent to which the former are distortions of the latter.

(i) Objects are simple (TLP 2.02). Samples too may be simple *relative* to a particular language-game (PI §48).

(ii) Objects are necessary existents, their existence being necessitated by logic, as a condition of the possibility of language (TLP 2.0211, 2.024, 2.026 ff.). This idea is encapsulated in the thesis that to imagine the

non-existent is to imagine non-existent combinations of existing elements (cf. Descartes: *Meditations* I). We are inclined to think that 'the
elements, individuals, must exist. If redness, roundness and sweetness did
not exist, we could not imagine them' (BB 31). This thesis seems
applicable to samples used in explaining words (PI §§55 ff.). But this is to
pitch the stakes far too high. If red samples did not exist, we would not
have our concept of red. If we lacked canonical samples of lengths and
weights, we would not have the system of measurement that we now
have. Samples are not necessary existents, but instruments in the
language-games we play. If we lacked certain samples or lost the ability
to use them correctly we would have lost certain instruments of language
and would not have the same uses for words hitherto explained by
reference to them. Language, far from resting on metaphysical foundations, is autonomous and self-contained.

(iii) Objects are constituents of states of affairs (TLP 2.0272). Indeed, a
state of affairs *is* a combination of objects (TLP 2.01). The objects which
are constitutive of a state of affairs stand together like the links of a chain;
no metaphysical glue in the form of a *relation* is necessary for the
combination of objects (TLP 2.03). It is easy to see the analogy with
samples. One can readily think of the fact that a given circle is red as a
combination of a circle and redness or of circularity and redness (PG
200). The 'object' red needs nothing extra to 'combine' with the 'object'
circularity to constitute the fact that this circle is red. Although this is
nothing but confusion and mystification (PG 199 ff.), the confusion
illuminates and is illuminated by reflection on the role of samples in
grammar.

(iv) It is of the nature of objects to combine together to constitute facts.
The combinatorial possibilities of objects are metaphysically predeter-
mined, and every possible combination is necessarily possible (TLP
2.012–2.0121). These metaphysical necessities are mirrored in the
logico-syntactical rules of language as a condition of sense. Later,
Wittgenstein criticized these alleged metaphysical necessities as mere
projections of grammar onto reality. Colours can 'combine' with shapes,
but not with sounds. But this is no law of ultra-physics, merely a
reflection of the fact that we do assign a sense to 'This circle is red' and do
not assign any sense to 'This note is red'. To know an object is to know
all its possible occurrences in states of affairs (TLP 2.0123). This amounts
to no more than the elementary truth that to know the meaning of a
word defined by reference to a sample is to know the rules for its use,
its combinatorial possibilities in grammar, and the conditions of its
application by reference to the standard provided by the sample (as used
by us).

(v) Objects stand in internal relations (TLP 4.123), which 'cannot be
said' in language, but only shown (TLP 4.122, 4.124). Significantly, the

only *analogical* example Wittgenstein gave was of the internal relation between light blue and dark blue (TLP 4.123). Equally significantly, the relations 'lighter than' and 'darker than' continued to fascinate Wittgenstein later. The two crucial points are: first, that the metaphysical necessity which seems to be expressed by the claim that dark blue is darker than light blue, is fully explained by reference to the use of samples (RFM 75); secondly, that even given this non-metaphysical explanation of colour-geometry, sentences such as 'White is lighter than black' are senseless; they have no use, unlike 'This object is lighter that that one' (since the object that is now lighter may darken later). The grammatical proposition 'White is lighter than black' is the metaphysical garb assumed by the linguistic remark that our conventions assign sense to speaking of two objects, the lighter one white, the other black, but not vice versa (RFM 48).

(vi) 'If two objects have the same logical form, the only distinction between them, apart from their external properties, is that they are different' (TLP 2.0233). Since colour (being coloured) is a form of visual objects (PT 2.0252), and arguably hardness a form of tangibilia, pitch a form of sounds (TLP 2.0131), this remark can be related to the subsequent view of samples. For two distinct colour samples (e.g. of red and blue) *seem*, when wrongly viewed, to be identical in all respects, apart from their irrelevant external properties such as shape or texture, i.e. identical in their 'logical form', except for the fact that one is red and the other blue, i.e. except for the fact that they differ. But the question 'What is the distinction between red and blue?' is meaningless, unless we take the object that has the colour to be a distinguishing mark of the colour (PG 208); which is itself absurd.

(vii) Objects can only be named, not described (TLP 3.221). If objects are samples 'seen through a glass darkly', one can see why this error should be so tempting. When we explain what 'red' means by giving an ostensive definition, it indeed appears that the 'object' in question (the colour) is named, and that nothing further can be said of it; it cannot be described, except by specification of its external properties, which are inessential features of the 'object'. But all that this amounts to is the lexical indefinability of a word like 'red' (PG 208). The red sample is not an object which lies beyond the descriptive powers of language, but is itself an instrument of language (cf. Exg. §§48 f.).

(viii) A name means an object, the object is its meaning (TLP 3.203). Names connect language with reality. This picture is at the root of the confusions embodied in the *Tractatus* (cf. WWK 209 f.). What is there construed as a connection between language and reality is a correlation in grammar between signs, viz. between name and sample. The sample is not the meaning of the name, but an instrument in the explanation of its meaning. The meaning of an expression is its use.

The conception of samples in grammar serves not only to provide an explanation of the meaning of 'indefinables' and a diagnosis of the conceptual hallucinations of the *Tractatus*, but other constructive and critical purposes. First, it explains a variety of internal relations, e.g. colour-exclusion and the geometry of colours (cf. pp. 83 f. above). Secondly, the conception of (public) samples is crucial in revealing the confusions surrounding the philosophical doctrine of the subjectivity of secondary qualities. Thirdly, the elaboration of the role of (public) samples in grammar is the background to the argument against the possibility of a private language; 'private samples' cannot fulfil the required role. Finally, samples are frequently invoked to dispel the illusion that mental representations are what give meanings to words; this illusion is fostered by the occult character of the mental, not by the representation, which can just as well be a physical sample (BB 4f.). These points will later be examined in detail.

VI

INDEXICALS

At various places Wittgenstein gives some attention to so-called indexical expressions. He normally concentrates upon 'this', but also touches on 'here', 'there', 'now', 'then', 'yesterday', 'a year ago', etc. Personal pronouns, especially 'I', are extensively discussed, the distorted picture of their use being the source of deep dialectical illusion (cf. Volume 2); the only pertinent point here is that 'I' is not the name of a person.

The term 'indexical', coined by Peirce, serves to emphasize the fact that in order to understand what is said by uttering some sentences containing words like 'this', 'here', 'now', etc., one must know such things as who uttered it, what he was pointing to, when and where he was when he spoke. Although others use different terminology, e.g. 'egocentric particulars' and 'token-reflexive words', we shall employ the term 'indexical' (without commitment to Peirce's analysis). In particular it must be emphasized that the uses of these pronouns or noun (or noun phrase) determiners and place- or time-relaters is manifold. It would be preferable to speak of their indexical use rather than to speak of them as indexicals.

The particular use of 'this' and 'that', 'these' and 'those' which has attracted philosophical attention is the deictic or ostensive use, in which the word is used as a demonstrative pronoun and is accompanied by a gesture of pointing. But other uses must be borne in mind. Discourse reference, whether anaphoric or cataphoric, is common ('That (this) is what I meant (mean)'). 'Here' and 'there' are similarly used as pro-forms for place adjuncts ('Look in the top drawer, you'll find it there'). The use of these expressions as noun or noun phrase determiners is common, as in 'this horse' or 'that old car'. Such determiners are often used to signify co-referentiality of two noun phrases, whether they have identical heads or not (e.g. 'He was given a bay mare for his fifteenth birthday. What a lot of fun he had with that mare.'; 'The boy with black hair is in our team. That lad is a good player.'). 'This' and 'that' can function as intensifiers premodifying an adjective '. . . this good', '. . . that empty', and may have anaphoric reference ('There are three hundred people in the Hall. I didn't expect it to be that full.'). 'This', 'these', 'that', 'those', together with such adjectives as 'very', 'same', 'identical' can be used to indicate identity of type of object rather than co-referentiality ('He bought a Jaguar XJ6. I bought that same car three years ago.'). 'Like' together with 'that' is even clearer: 'He reads the *News*. I wouldn't read a paper like that.' 'That which' often functions as a quantifier, as in 'That which glitters is not always gold'. Examples could be multiplied, but these suffice to discourage hasty generalization.

Though critical in intent, Wittgenstein's discussion of indexicals does not take the form of confronting philosophers' generalizations with a full list of indexical expressions and a complete tabulation of their multifarious uses. Hence no such detailed survey is necessary to follow his argument. He does not even cite mistaken theses about indexicals and subject them to careful examination. Although Russell is mentioned as an arch sinner, criticism is not so much targeted on him as directed at a very general position that is exemplified conspicuously in his writings.

Wittgenstein's central criticism is that even if we allow the syntactical concept of a name as generous a scope as is compatible with its retaining significant content, 'this', 'that', 'here', 'there', 'today', 'now', 'then', etc. are not names. His argument contrasts the uses of names with the uses of indexicals, and also the explanation of names with the explanation of indexicals.

Frege had little to say about indexical expressions or the indexical use of these expressions. He merely mentions them in noting that a context-dependent sentence does not express a complete thought (GA i. p. xvi f.; T 24). The use of such a sentence on appropriately different occasions expresses different thoughts, and what thought is expressed is a function not only of the sentence uttered but also of the context (including the speaker) of its use. Thus, the time of an utterance is *part of the expression of the thought* expressed by a sentence in which words such as 'today', or 'yesterday' occur, and similarly the place ('here'), the ostension ('there ↗ ') and the speaker ('I').

Pronominal indexicals would seem to count, on Frege's criteria, as degenerate proper names. They satisfy his superficial syntactical criteria of proper namehood. Their role is indeed that of a Fregean proper name, i.e. to single out a subject of discourse, a referent which is an 'object'. They are degenerate in that they cannot fufil this role without 'aid from outside', as it were. Their sense is incomplete, though incomplete in a rule-governed way. Each singles out a referent only by a systematic contextual supplementation. (If, like Frege, we claim that the place, time, speaker, object pointed at, etc., are part of the expression of the thought, then the indexical together with its counterpart is not, in any ordinary sense, a referring expression. 'There ↗ ' picks out a place, but 'There↗ ' together with the place does not pick out a place.)

It is noteworthy that Frege does not have any notion of meaning which would be suited to a discussion of these uses of expressions. For one clearly wants to say that 'this', 'today', 'here', etc., have constant meanings, even though their senses as conceived by Frege are incomplete, and when completed vary from occasion to occasion. This is not a wholly peripheral matter. Context-dependence is a pervasive feature of language.

To understand such expressions in language is to know how to use them, to grasp rules that govern their use, *inter alia* in making references. On Frege's account they do not have a sense (or, at any rate, a complete sense). But they are not meaningless. Their use can be explained and understood.

Unlike Frege, Russell had a lifelong preoccupation with indexicals ('egocentric particulars').[1] This was determined by his denotational conception of meaning and his quest for epistemologically guaranteed foundations for language (cf. 'Augustine's picture of language', pp. 20 ff.). Genuine proper names, according to Russell, are characterized by the following features: (i) they have meaning in isolation (are not incomplete symbols); (ii) they stand for particulars; (iii) the particular for which a name stands *is* its meaning; (iv) its meaning is a simple object logically independent of every other existent; (v) proper names are simple symbols; (vi) they cannot occur in sentences of the form 'ξ exists'. (Cf. 'Logically proper names', pp. 126 ff.) Indexicals seemed to fit this bill. 'This' appears to have, in its meaningful indexical use, a guaranteed reference (if it fails to refer, nothing with a meaning was uttered). It 'stands for' a particular (in its most common use), it is arguably a 'simple symbol', and 'This exists' makes dubious sense. It carries no descriptive load at all, and by its use one (normally) *means* such and such an object.

Russell's doctrine of logically proper names (unlike that of the *Tractatus*) demanded an epistemological guarantee that a name *does* refer. He wished to ensure *certainty* that a name has meaning. This is secured by the principle that only an object of acquaintance can be named. Acquaintance with a particular is both necessary and sufficient for understanding a name (LA 202 ff.). Russell eventually concluded that only actual objects of sense can be named.

That makes it very difficult to get any instance of a name at all in the proper strict logical sense of the word. The only words one does use as names in the logical sense are words like 'this' or 'that'. One can use 'this' as a name to stand for a particular with which one is acquainted at the moment. We say 'This is white'. If you agree that 'This is white', meaning the 'this' that you see, you are using 'this' as a proper name. But if you try to apprehend the proposition that I am expressing when I say 'This is white', you cannot do it. If you mean this piece of chalk as a physical object, then you are not using a proper name. It is only when you use 'this' quite strictly, to stand for an actual object of sense, that it is really a proper name. (LA 201.)

At this stage of his progress from darkness to darkness, Russell thus concluded that the only words used as proper names were the indexical

---

[1] For this terminology and Russell's final, bizarre, view, cf. Russell, *An Inquiry into Meaning and Truth,* Ch. 7.

pronouns 'this' and 'that'. From a Cartesian point of view, only one's use of 'this' is proof against a *malin génie*. These names were meaningful, but no one other than their user could know what they meant. Their meanings were conceived as essentially private. This did not disturb Russell at all:

> It would be absolutely fatal if people meant the same things by their words. It would make all intercourse impossible, and language the most hopeless and useless thing imaginable, because the meaning you attach to your words must depend on the nature of the objects you are acquainted with, and since different people are acquainted with different objects, they would not be able to talk to each other unless they attached quite different meanings to their words. (LA 195.)

Not only was the meaning of such a word incommunicable, but it was also conceived to be radically ambiguous, for 'it seldom means the same things two moments running'.

Although Russell ultimately repudiated these doctrines and replaced them by others (*Inquiry into Meaning and Truth; Human Knowledge, its Scope and Limits*) there is no need to pursue his confusions further since his later views post-date the criticisms of the *Investigations*.

Of the young Wittgenstein's views on indexicals little can be said. We must make what we can of the mysterious remark 'What seems to be given us *a priori* is the concept: *This*—identical with the concept of the *object*' (NB 61).

In his post-1929 writings Wittgenstein describes our use of indexical expressions, compares and contrasts their use with that of names, and reveals what similarities blind one to the deep differences between these fundamentally distinct kinds of expression. The issue is of general significance because it is a constant element in the illusory procedure of private ostensive definition, and hence in the private language argument, in solipsism and idealism, and in the doctrine of the subjectivity of perceptual qualities.

There are superficial similarities between names and 'this'. Both types of expression occur in an ostensive definition, where we point to an object. One can answer the question 'What colour is this?' by saying 'Yellow'; and answer 'What is yellow?' by pointing and saying 'This' (PI § 38). Furthermore, a name and 'this' can often (but not always) occupy the same position in a sentence, e.g. 'Jack is short' and 'This is short' (BB 109). This much is correct. There are also illusory similarities. If one thinks that a name *must* have a bearer, that it must be certain that it has a bearer, that the bearer is what the name means, one will also be tempted to think, as Russell did, that 'this' is a name, since it seems like a dart that cannot miss the bull's eye. Finally, since what the speaker means by 'this' is its referent, it is tempting, given the ambiguity of 'means', to think that the meaning of 'this' is its referent.

Yet all this is misleading: '. . . nothing is more unlike than the use of the words "this" and the use of a proper name—I mean *the games* played with these words, not the phrases in which they are used' (BB 109, cf. Vol. XII, 217). It is characteristic of names, according to Wittgenstein, that they can be explained ostensively—a procedure in which a sentence of the form 'This is A' is used. But it makes no sense to explain the use of 'this' by ostensive definition of the form 'This is this', nor that of 'here' by 'This is here'. Moreover, 'this', in its deictic use, is accompanied by an ostensive gesture, but the use of names is not. 'This' without the ostensive indication (or some alternative indication) is useless; names are not. Trivially, 'this' is deictically used only in the presence of the object pointed at, but names are frequently used in the absence of their bearers. The roles of the two types of expressions are fundamentally different. 'This' is no more the name of an object than 'now' is the name of a time, 'here' of a place, or 'I' of a person. An indexical expression does not differ from the *corresponding* name as a hammer from a mallet, but as a hammer from a nail (BB 108).

'Here' and 'now', in their indexical use are akin to the point of origin of a system of co-ordinates. They fix an 'index' by reference to which a host of related terms are employed, relative to that index, to pick out places and times, e.g. 'over there', 'n miles away', 'yesterday', 'tomorrow', 'last year', etc. They are not names of times or places, they do not designate a time or place in contrast to other times or locations, but are, rather, akin to the centre of one's visual field (BT 523 ff.). 'Today' is not a date, and one cannot informatively write at the head of a letter 'Here, now', although if one writes the place name and date at the head of the letter, one can begin the first sentence, 'Here, now, it is sunny and peaceful'. To master the system of indexicals is to grasp the determination of their 'point of origin' on any occasion of their (indexical) use, and the systematic relations that obtain between them.

Wittgenstein touches on the defects of the Fregean conception (BT 523 ff.; B i. §§705 ff.). It looks as if the meanings of indexicals are not determined in advance of their use (since on Frege's view they do not have a sense, or a complete sense, independently of their context; and together with such varying supplementation, their sense varies from occasion to occasion). But this is absurd. (i) 'Today' does not mean something different today from what it meant yesterday, 'here' does not have a different meaning here from what it means over there (B i. §705). This is not a case of ambiguity, as in 'Mr White turned white'. (ii) The meanings of indexicals *is* laid down in advance: one teaches and explains the use of *one* symbol, e.g. 'here', even though what one says by a sentence containing an indexical use of 'here' will vary according to place of utterance. (iii) The rules explaining the use of the various indexicals give their meanings. One understands the use of these expressions if one grasps these rules and the systematic truth links between the various indexicals (temporal, spatial, personal pronominal, etc.). (iv) Hence one must distinguish knowing how to use, e.g., 'this', and knowing what 'this ↗' is. So one must distinguish grasping the general principle governing the use of 'this' and grasping what is meant by a particular utterance 'Φ (this ↗)'. The fact that 'This ↗' (pointing to A) and 'This ↗' (pointing to B) can typically be replaced by 'A' and 'B' (respectively) does not show that the word 'This' means sometimes 'A', sometimes 'B'.

One can explain the general rules for the indexical use of these expressions, and one can likewise explain the meaning of an utterance which contains an indexical and hence is context-dependent. But one must not conceive the latter explanation as an explanation of the meaning of the indexical on that occasion of its use. Indexicals are not proper names, nor are they ambiguous. The relation between an indexical and what, on a particular occasion, it is used to pick out is not a paradigm of 'the name-relation'.

VII

LOGICALLY PROPER NAMES

1. *Introduction*

The notion of the logically proper name plays a central role in logical atomism. Russell introduces logically proper names in speaking of 'a name . . . in the proper strict logical sense of the word' (LA 201); Wittgenstein merely speaks of 'names' in the *Tractatus*. Despite some differences, the correlation of logically proper names with simple objects is the pillar on which logical atomism is supported.

In focusing here on the notion of logically proper names, we will set two issues aside. First, the nature of simples (cf. 'Ostensive definition and its ramifications', pp. 114 ff.). The account of logically proper names can be distinguished from the characterization of simples, even though these issues are not independent. The separability of the two issues is shown by the possibility of two different kinds of criticism of logical atomism. On one view, the fundamental error is semantic: the meaning of a name is never the object named, *a fortiori*, the meaning of a logically proper name is not a simple *object*. On the other view, the basic error is metaphysical: there are no simples, *a fortiori* the meaning of a logically proper name is not a *simple* object. Here we discuss only the semantic issue. Secondly, we aim to side-step here the issues of whether logically proper names exhaust the category of simple signs. The difficulty is to determine whether (some) properties and relations are objects, whether predicates can be logically proper names. Russell's official view seems to be that logically proper names are correlated only with particulars, not with relations (or properties) (LA 199). Predicates are correlated with properties or relations. If, however, a predicate is simple (e.g. 'red'), then Russell speaks of its meaning as being an object, so that grasp of its meaning depends on acquaintance with this object (LA 194 f.). Since such a predicate is both simple and construed as the name of an object, it seems to have the essential features of a logically proper name, apart from a 'superficial' difference of grammatical category. In interpreting the *Tractatus*, this difficulty is notorious. The thesis that all simple signs are names seems to conflict with Wittgenstein's explanation of his notation, and perhaps also with his account of the theory of types. On the other hand, it seems indispensable for making sense of his account of names and elementary sentences. Wittgenstein later interpreted the *Tractatus* in such a way that simple properties count among its objects (cf. Exg. §104). This controversy can be avoided by confining attention to logically proper names that function as simple names for particulars.

2. *Russell*

The concept of a logically proper name in Russell's theory of language belongs to the purified Augustinian picture that was made possible by his repudiation of the concept of denoting. The theory of descriptions removed the necessity of distinguishing meaning from denoting, and hence it licensed treating all expressions that survived analysis as names whose meanings consisted simply in the objects named.

The main features of logically proper names according to Russell are as follows.

(i) Logically proper names have meaning in isolation (PM i. 66). In this respect, they contrast with incomplete symbols, in particular with definite descriptions and class-names, for these have no meaning until they are supplied with appropriate contexts. Note (a) Russell assimilates this contention to the claim that incomplete symbols can be defined only in use, not in isolation from a context (PM i. 66). This wrongly suggests that the contrast between proper names and incomplete symbols coincides with the contrast between what can be explicitly defined and what can be defined only in context. This cannot be correct, however, because genuine proper names are indefinable (i.e. unanalysable) and also because incomplete symbols may well have an explicit definition (e.g. class-names can be defined by the schema: $\alpha = \{ x \mid \Phi x \}$). The intended contrast is between symbols that can be introduced by definitions, whether contextual or explicit, and those that cannot be so introduced, but can be explained only by ostensive definition. Such symbols (the indefinables) can be understood only by acquaintance with what they stand for, and this gives them meaning in isolation from any context (cf. PrM xv). (b) This thesis seems to be a reflection of a metaphysical doctrine, viz. that every particular 'stands entirely alone and is completely self-subsistent' (LA 201). Since the meaning of a name is what it stands for, the independence of particulars guarantees that a name has a meaning that is logically independent of any facts at all, *a fortiori* independent of how it is used in the context of sentences. In this way, its standing for a particular gives a name 'a meaning by itself, without the need for any context' (PM i. 66). (c) Finally, Russell's contrast between incomplete symbols and symbols with meaning in isolation from any context (proper names) has nothing to do with the valency of an expression. Any symbol that is not incomplete has a meaning by itself; in particular, simple (unanalysable) predicates have such a meaning (LA 194 f.). Consequently, simple names for particulars are not distinguished from other simple symbols by having meaning in isolation, even if they are to be distinguished by having no intrinsic valencies (unlike simple predicates).

(ii) The meaning of a logically proper name is the object named, its bearer. A logically proper name 'directly represents some object' (PM i. 66). It is a word for a particular, i.e. 'a word whose meaning is a particular' (LA 200 f.). Were identity indefinable, all sentences expressed with logically proper names on both sides of the sign for identity would be epistemologically trivial (PrM 64, cf. 451 f.). Whereas if identity can be defined in terms of second-order quantification, the triviality even of such identity-statements does not follow from identifying the meaning of a name with its bearer (cf. PM i. 168, OK 151).

(iii) To understand the meaning of a logically proper name is to be acquainted with its bearer. A logically proper name can be significantly used by a speaker only in application to a particular with which he is acquainted, since acquaintance with the particular named is just what his grasp of the meaning of the name consists in (LA 201). Indeed, this is a restriction of a more general thesis: understanding of any simple symbol depends on direct acquaintance with the 'object' which is its meaning (LA 194 f.), e.g. the word 'red' can be understood only by acquaintance with the colour red through seeing red objects; and terms of logic, e.g. 'particular', 'relation', 'universal', can be understood only by reference to 'logical expereience', i.e. 'acquaintance with logical objects' ('Theory of Knowledge', p. 181). Acquaintance with the object correlated with a simple symbol does not require any knowledge whatever of any of its properties, even if these properties are essential. Acquaintance with two shades of colour, e.g., in no way necessitates even the knowledge that they are different (OK 151), nor need acquaintance with two different colours, e.g. red and green, carry with it knowledge of their synthetic incompatibility (cf. PrM 233). That acquaintance is in this way independent of knowledge of truths seems to be a consequence of the independence of primitive propositions from indefinables in an axiomatized science. The identification of the minimum set of indefinables for a theory might well be agreed on independently of, and prior to, the identification of a minimal set of primitive propositions, even if, as in logic, the primitive propositions express *necessary* truths. It follows from the independence of acquaintance from 'knowledge about' that there can be no degrees of acquaintance with the object named by a simple sign and therefore no degrees of understanding of a logically proper name (OK 151).

(iv) The insertion of a logically proper name into the argument-place of the predicate 'ξ exists' yields a meaningless sentence, whereas the insertion there of an incomplete symbol (a definite description, a class-name, or a relation-name) is meaningful (IMP 178; 'Theory of Knowledge, p. 264). This cannot be used as a criterion for picking out logically proper names from other symbols. Rather, this thesis is the conclusion of a rather opaque argument whose major premise is that the meaning of a logically proper name is its bearer. A reconstruction of this argument requires two additional premises: (a) any sentence, in particular an existential sentence, has a meaning if and only if its negation has; (b) every existential statement has a peculiar property, perhaps that it cannot be a necessary truth, or that it cannot be known to be true *a priori* or that it cannot be immune from doubt, or even that it cannot be timelessly true. Russell's reconstructed argument must be that the sentence 'A exists' has meaning only if 'A does not exist' has meaning, and further that where 'A' is a logically proper name, 'A does not exist' would either be meaningless (if no particular were correlated with 'A' as its meaning) or false; moreover, it would be false in such a way that its positive counterpart must lack the property peculiar to existential statements. Therefore, on pain of absurdity, both 'A exists' and 'A does not exist' must be devoid of any meaning (cf. PM i. 66, PrM 449, IMP 178 f.).

The main probem about Russell's argument is the difficulty of identifying satisfactorily the property that he assumes every genuine existential statement to have. This is crucial for assessing the cogency of his reasoning (and for a correct characterization of particulars).

Russellian particulars are evidently not necessary existents (LA 200 f.). It is not even necessary that the universe should be non-empty (IMP 203, cf. 141). Hence the contingency of existential statements (a tenet of empiricism Russell accepted) cannot be the grounds for denying that a logically proper name can occur in 'ξ exists'. It is, however, clear that Russellian particulars are *certain* existents. If this contention is to be related to the claim that 'A exists' is meaningless if 'A' is a logically proper name, could it be that he thought that no existential statement can be known with certainty?

There is some support for this suggestion. Indeed, this is one way to interpret what appear to be statements that particulars are necessary existents. If epistemological possibility were meant instead of logical possibility, this would imply that these were in fact statements that particulars are certain existents. Consider, e.g., the argument that 'whenever the grammatical subject of a proposition *can be supposed not to exist* without rendering the proposition meaningless, it is plain that the grammatical subject is not a proper name . . . directly representing some object' (PM i. 66; our italics). This might well be taken to mean that the conclusion holds whenever it is compatible with the sentence having a meaning that there be *doubt* whether or not the grammatical subject exists, that it be possible for all we know that the grammatical subject does not exist. By contraposition, if 'A' is a logically proper name, it is impossible to doubt that A exists without rendering meaningless any sentence of which 'A' is the subject. In particular, this holds for the existential statement 'A exists'. Finally, it follows from a quite plausible assumption that any genuine existential statement must be open to the possibility of doubt. The necessary assumption is just the converse principle that if 'A' is not a logically proper name, it is possible to doubt that A exists without rendering meaningless any sentence of which 'A' is the subject. This principle tacitly underlies Russell's use of methodological doubt in epistemology.

There are two further supports for ascribing to Russell an epistemological characterization of logically proper names: the nature of particulars and the nature of acquaintance. First, Russell limited particulars to present sense data. It is only when a term is used 'to stand for an actual object of sense . . . that it is really a proper name' (LA 201). For this reason, particulars are both private and evanescent. What confines the range of logically proper names to present sense data is Cartesian doubt; in Russell's eyes, no particulars but sense data are immune from doubt as to whether they exist, and hence nothing else could be represented by a logically proper name. Earlier Russell had been slightly more liberal: 'a particular with which we are acquainted is either a sense-datum, or a datum of immediate memory, or an image' ('Theory of Knowledge', p. 337). None the less, acquaintance does not extend 'beyond the narrow range of the immediate past', and hence any name will soon have to be replaced by a description ('Theory of Knowledge', p. 325). Secondly, the meaning of a logically proper name is grasped by acquaintance with the particular named. Russell characterizes acquaintance as the converse of the relation of presentation and hence its hallmark is immunity from the possibility of doubt. If an object X is directly presented to a person A, then A cannot doubt the existence of X. By the definition of 'acquaintance', this conclusion holds too if A is acquainted with X. On the assumption that A is acquainted with X if he cannot doubt the existence of X, logically proper names are names of objects whose existence is not open to possible doubt. For both these reasons, Russell appears to subscribe to the thesis that an expression is a logically proper name if and only if it names an object whose existence is *certain*.

A noteworthy consequence of this is the penetration of epistemology into logic. The determination of the logical form of a sentence rests on the outcome of an epistemological investigation. It is epistemology that yields the conclusion that a sentence about another's mental states cannot be logically of subject/predicate form, since 'there seems no reason to believe that we are ever acquainted with other people's minds, seeing that these are not directly perceived'.[1] In particular, it is the consequence of an epistemological argument that no ordinary proper name is a logically proper name (LA 200, cf. PP 54 f.). Without appeal to the possibility of doubting the existence of physical objects and persons, it would not be possible to show that ordinary proper names are incomplete symbols

[1] 'On Denoting', in *Logic and Knowledge,* ed. R. C. Marsh (Allen and Unwin, London, 1956), p. 42.

(LA 200 f.). (That they are disguised definite descriptions is a further and independent assumption.) The paradox that no ordinary names are logically proper names gives the measure of the intrusion of epistemology into Russell's logic.

(v) The relation of a logically proper name to the particular named is both external and opaque.

Words are objects (or at least classes of objects). This makes relations between logically proper names and particulars genuine relations between objects (or between classes of objects and objects). Given Russell's Platonist conception of universals, relations between any simple symbols and what they stand for are real relations between objects. He speaks of such relations as relations of meaning, e.g. the relation of meaning expressed in the statement that 'Napoleon' *means* Napoleon (AM 188). Russell contends that there is a unique relation in which each logically proper name stands to the particular named by it. This may be designated by Carnap's phrase 'the name-relation'. Russell treats this relation as the prototype for the relations between all simple symbols and what they stand for, e.g. the relation between 'white' and the property of being white. Indeed, it is only the theory of types that prevents his saying that there is a unique relation in which every simple symbol stands to the 'object' that corresponds to it. Only this prevents his claiming that the relation of 'Napoleon' to Napoleon is the relation of meaning (*simpliciter*). This claim, in his view, captures the spirit of the matter, but must be qualified by the rider that the relation of meaning is systematically ambiguous, i.e. that strictly speaking there are as many different relations of meaning as there are *types* of things (LA 268 f.).

The name-relation, since it is a relation between self-subsistent objects, is contingent and external. That 'N' means N is not a necessary truth and cannot be established *a priori*. Instead, the truth of this claim rests on the existence of a correlation between the word 'N' and a certain particular. Russell's doctrine of acquaintance restricts particulars to mental entities (sense data, and sometimes 'memory data'). Therefore, that 'N' means (i.e. names) N depends on the existence of a psychological correlation (e.g. private ostensive definition) between a logically proper name and an object (of acquaintance).

In 'The Philosophy of Logical Atomism', Russell surprisingly contends that the name-relation is also opaque, i.e. it is never certain or self-evident that 'N', an apparent name, stands in the name-relation to anything at all. This seems inconsistent with the epistemological characterization of logically proper names. But Russell calls it merely an article of faith that there are any simples at all (LA 202) and hence that there are any logically proper names.[2] He cannot prove that analysis does not

---

[2] Similarly, he earlier argued that one cannot *prove* that the class-names are incomplete symbols (PM i. 72).

continue *ad infinitum*. Accordingly it can be no more than an hypothesis that actual objects of sense are particulars.[3]

(vi) Logically proper names, as a species of simple signs, resist analysis. They would have a function in a 'logically perfect language' (LA 197 f.), and so stand in contrast to incomplete symbols. These latter disappear altogether on analysis. The model for this is definite descriptions as treated by the theory of descriptions. The categories of simple symbols (or proper names 'in a generalized sense') and incomplete symbols are jointly exhaustive and mutually exclusive (at least until Russell, under Wittgenstein's influence, distinguished logical operators as an altogether different kind of symbol). Every expression either directly represents some object or else any sentence in which it occurs must be capable of being so analysed that it shall disappear (PM i. 66).

On Russell's view, the thesis that simples cannot be analysed does not entail the thesis that simples have no essential properties. There may well be necessary truths about simples (PrM 233). What there cannot be are *self-evident* truths about simples. Understanding of a logically proper name, e.g., is logically independent of recognizing the truth of any statements about the particular named (knowledge by acquaintance is independent of knowledge of truths). Simples may have logical but not epistemological essences.

Simple symbols cannot be analysed and hence cannot be defined by analysis, e.g. by *Merkmal*-definitions. They can only be '*explained*' by means of descriptions intended to point out . . . what is meant' (PM i. 91). Perhaps the most important form of such explanation would be ostensive definition (cf. LA 200 f.). Russell conceives of 'explanations' as propositions incorporating the simple symbol which are intended to bring it about that a person becomes aware of which object of acquaintance it is meant to designate.

(vii) Logically proper names are simple symbols. Russell characterizes as a simple symbol 'a symbol whose parts are not symbols' (LA 194; IMP 173). This is probably an incorrect formulation of the point that simple symbols resist analysis, that they are incapable of being defined or analysed. The simple symbol 'this' does contain parts which are symbols, e.g. 'his' and 'is'. But, unlike 'the author of Waverley', the meaning of the expression 'this' is not determined by reference to the meanings of its parts.

(viii) What is symbolized by a logically proper name can *only* be symbolized by a logically proper name. This follows from Russell's distinction between simple and complex objects: 'those objects which it is impossible to symbolize otherwise than by simple symbols may be called "simple", while those which can by symbolized by a combination

---

[3] The opacity and externality of the name–relation are even more prominent in Russell's later causal theory of meaning (cf. AM 197 f. 227).

of symbols may be called "complex"' (LA 194). Since definite descriptions are not simple symbols, it appears to follow that what can be named cannot be described, and that what can be described cannot be referred to by a logically proper name. Although it might provide for the mutual exclusion of knowledge by acquaintance and knowledge by description, this consequence seems outrageous. Instead of christening a present sense datum 'John', I could refer to it as 'the sense datum I am now having'; in doing this I would be describing what can be named, and I would be introducing an item with which I have acquaintance by means of a definite description.

In fact, Russell does not intend this dictum to be so understood. In stating that simple objects can be symbolized only by simple symbols he means 'symbolized' to be synonymous with 'named'. He considers defining 'red' as 'the colour with the greatest wavelength'. This, however, is not a *definition* of 'red', but rather a true description of the colour red. The point is that 'red' cannot be defined or analysed, though of course red can be described (LA 194 f.). This presupposes that 'the colour with the greatest wavelength' does not *symbolize* red, though it describes red. On this account, Russell's dictum is a perhaps misleading recapitulation of the thesis that simples cannot be analysed, or its linguistic counterpart, that simple symbols cannot be defined. So understood, this thesis is compatible with what appears to be its contradictory, viz. that if we want to speak of particulars, 'we have to do it by means of some elaborate phrase, such as "the visual sensation which occupied the centre of my visual field at noon on January 1, 1919"' (AM 193). In so far as actual language lacks logically proper names, particulars can only be referred to by means of definite descriptions, though they cannot be analysed.

(ix) Logically proper names are distinct from ordinary proper names. Indeed, no ordinary proper name of a person, place or thing is a logically proper name; every one of them is an incomplete symbol (LA 200; PP 54 f.). Russell treats them as disguised definite descriptions, holding that each of them is an abbreviation for some definite description (perhaps very complex). This thesis is, however, not a necessary concomitant of the claim that ordinary names are incomplete symbols, for they might be incomplete symbols of a new kind (*sui generis*). (Both class-names and propositions are actually treated as incomplete symbols distinct in kind from definite descriptions (PM i. 44, 187; 'Theory of Knowledge', p. 200).)

(x) Demonstratives ('this' and 'that') when used to refer to actual objects of sensation are logically proper names, indeed the only examples of logically proper names that Russell can find.[4] (He does not consider such spatial or temporal indexicals as 'now', 'then', 'here', 'there'.) Of

---

[4] Earlier he had thought the personal pronoun 'I' was a logically proper name (pp 50 f., but cf. OK 81 f.).

course, demonstratives are not typically used as logically proper names. 'It is only when you use "this" quite strictly to stand for an actual object of sense, that it is really a proper name' (LA 202). (Russell later retreated from this view, distinguishing all 'egocentric particulars' from names.)

3. *The* Tractatus

The concept of a logically proper name in the *Tractatus* is another development of the Augustinian *Urbild*. In part it is probably a revolt against Russell's conception. Wittgenstein's concept is purely logical; epistemological considerations are excluded from any role in its explanation. In spite of this difference in motivation, there is a striking degree of agreement with Russell's characterization of logically proper names, though not with his account of particulars. (We will follow Wittgenstein's terminology here and speak merely of 'names'.)

(i) Names do not have meaning in isolation. 'Only in the context of a sentence does a name have meaning' (TLP 3.3, cf. 2.0122). Hence names cannot be contrasted in this respect with definite descriptions or, more generally, with incomplete symbols.

Although what Wittgenstein means by this principle is not transparent (cf. 'A word has a meaning only in the context of a sentence', pp. 151 f.), it is correlated with a rejection of part of Russell's metaphysics. Russell's principle that every particular 'stands entirely alone and is completely self-subsistent' carries two implications. First, any particular can exist independently of being a constituent of any fact whatever. Secondly, no particular belongs to every possible world, so that the set of particulars common to every possible world is empty. Wittgenstein rejects both these contentions. 'It is essential to things (objects) that they should be possible constituents of states of affairs' (TLP 2.01). He takes this to exclude the possibility that an object could exist entirely on its own (TLP 2.0121). The second thesis is repudiated in characterizing objects as the substance of the world (TLP 2.021, cf. 2.027–2.0272). 'If objects are given, then at the same time we are given all objects' (TLP 5.524).

(ii) 'A name means an object. The object is its meaning' (TLP 3.203). Wittgenstein accepts the obvious corollary that any sentence with names flanking the identity-sign on both sides is logically trivial. Indeed, this is an essential part of his proof that the identity-sign can be excluded from a proper conceptual notation (TLP 5.533).

Although this thesis looks unambiguous, there is a problem about interpreting it. In the claim that the *Bedeutung* (meaning) of a name is the object named, what is meant by 'Bedeutung'? If the term were used as it is by Frege, then this would be a truism. Hence it would be immune from

later criticism as a mistake (PI §40). But clearly Wittgenstein either does
not follow Frege's terminology or disagrees with Frege about a substantive thesis, for the *Tractatus* asserts that the sense of a sentence is a
function of the meaning (*Bedeutung*) of its constituents and its form (TLP
3.318, 4.024–4.027).

This doctrine suggests an alternative interpretation of the term
'Bedeutung': viz. that it means what Frege meant by 'Sinn', though
Wittgenstein calls this 'Bedeutung' because he collapses together *Sinn* and
Bedeutung for names. His later criticism of the view that the *Bedeutung* of a
name is its bearer is to be read as a repudiation of this identification for
names, i.e. a repudiation of the doctrine that the bearer of a name is, or
uniquely determines, the *Sinn*. (It is noteworthy that Wittgenstein then
apparently introduces an account of the *Bedeutung* of names that is
generally treated as a variant of Frege's explanation of *Sinn* for names
(Exg. § 79).) According to this interpretation, names are a peculiar kind
of symbol, peculiar in that *Sinn* collapses into *Bedeutung*. Since objects are
necessary existents and identity-statements are meaningless, Frege's
original reasons for maintaining any distinction disappear in the case of
names, viz. the possibility of *Sinn* without *Bedeutung* and the non-
triviality of some identities of the form 'A = B'.

A variant of this interpretation would deny the identification of *Sinn*
with *Bedeutung* even for names, but would identify the *Sinn* of a name as
degenerate or trivial. To understand a referring expression is to know to
what individual, if any, it refers in every possible world. Names are
peculiar in that they have a referent in every possible world, and also in
that each name has a constant referent in every possible world. Names
are, as it were, constant functions from the set of all possible worlds to
objects. They are thus degenerate functions of this type. Conflating a
constant function with its value would lead to identifying the sense of a
name with its bearer.

But, tempting as they are, neither of these interpretations is a correct
account of the *Tractatus*. Both presuppose that names are marked out as a
special case, as expressions for which (exceptionally) *Sinn* and *Bedeutung*
are identical or for which (exceptionally) *Sinn* is degenerate. According
to Wittgenstein, however, there is no possibility of contrast. There are no
expressions other than simple expressions in fully analysed sentences
(apart from logical constants) and hence no expressions that have *Sinn*
distinct from *Bedeutung* or that have non-degenerate *Sinn*. The *Tractatus*
leaves no room for Frege's notion of *Sinn* for the constituents of
sentences. To assign *Bedeutung* to every simple symbol is to determine
the *Sinn* of every possible sentence. This is an almost pure example of the
Augustinian conception of language. Wittgenstein aims at the total
exclusion of Frege's contrast between *Sinn* and *Bedeutung*, not at
piecemeal modification of Frege's doctrine. This is what he means by

identifying the *Bedeutung* of a name with the object named. A partial collapse of *Sinn* and *Bedeutung*, or the recognition that some expressions have degenerate *Sinn*, is a much weaker claim than that made in the *Tractatus* (though all three views might find themselves simultaneously under fire from later criticisms).

(iii) What it is to understand the meaning of a name is a psychological problem. Therefore it is not discussed in the *Tractatus*. None the less Wittgenstein subscribed to one of Russell's major theses, viz. that understanding of a name is independent of knowledge of any true statements about the object named. He explicitly accepts that I need not know its external properties if I know an object (TLP 2.01231). This also follows from the general principle that a person can grasp the sense of a sentence (i.e. understand it on the basis of understanding the constituent expressions) without knowing whether it is true (TLP 4.024). Since this holds for any significant sentence, no ascription of an external property to an object needs to be known to be true to understand the meaning of a name for that object. The internal properties, by contrast, must be known, but they cannot be stated, only shown (TLP 2.0123–2.0141).

(iv) The insertion of a name into the argument-place of the grammatical predicate 'ξ exists' yields nonsense (*Unsinn*). There are various routes that converge on this conclusion. One sets out from the demand that propositions be bipolar, one from the conception of the existential quantifier as a logical operator, and the third from the eliminability of the sign of identity from language.

Wittgenstein demands that every sentence with sense be bipolar: i.e. it must be possible for it to be true, and possible for it to be false. This eliminates the possibility of sentences expressing necessary truths except where they can be exhibited as being constructed by logical operations on constituent sentences that are bipolar. Every 'necessary truth' is either a tautology or a nonsensical pseudo-proposition; i.e. either senseless (*sinnlos*) or nonsense (*unsinnig*). Given Wittgenstein's conception of objects as necessary existents common to every possible world, this precludes the possibility that a significant sentence can express the existence of an object. A *fortiori*, the sentence 'A exists', where 'A' is a name, cannot have sense if it is so used. Since it cannot be exhibited as a tautology, it must be nonsense (*unsinnig*). It violates the conditions of significant language by attempting to say what can only be shown (in this case by the use of 'A' as a name), thereby misusing the (grammatical) predicate 'ξ exists'.

The grammatical predicate 'ξ exists' is correctly used as a logical operator, not as a concept-word (not even as a second-level concept-word standing for a property of concepts). In a proper logical notation, it should be represented not by a predicate-letter, but by the existential quantifier (cf. PT 4.00151). (One application of the slogan 'existence is not a predicate'.) Any proposition containing a logical operator is a truth-function of a certain set of elementary propositions. In particular, the sentence '$(\exists x)\, \varPhi(x)$' is analysed as a disjunction (perhaps infinitary) of all propositions of the form '$\varPhi(x)$' (TLP 5.52–5.521). It is immediately obvious that a sentence of the form 'A exists', where 'A' is a name of a particular, does not have this logical form. Since 'A' is not a predicate, it does not define a class of proposition suitable for the introduction of the existential quantifier as a truth-function. Therefore, 'A exists' must be meaningless (*unsinnig*), since no provision has been made for assigning any sense to this combination of signs (cf. TLP 5.4733).

A possible line of defence against the argument that 'A exists' is meaningless takes the form of identifying the sense of 'A exists' with that of the formula '$(\exists x)\ x = A$'. Identity of sense seems plausible in virtue of the necessary identity in the truth-values of these sentences. The property of being identical with A does define a set of propositions which is suitable for the introduction of quantifiers as certain truth-functions of its members. Therefore, this interpretation of 'A exists' saves it from condemnation as nonsensical. This line of argument presupposes that identity-statements have a sense. Wittgenstein, however, rejects this thesis. Every sentence of the form 'A = B', where 'A' and 'B' are names of particulars, is either necessarily true or necessarily false. Since no such sentence is molecular, it cannot be a tautology. Therefore, by the requirements of bipolarity, it must be nonsense (*unsinnig*) (TLP 5.534). (It tries to say what can only be shown by identity of signs (cf. TLP 5.53).) It follows that every truth-function of such sentences is nonsense; in particular, that '$(\exists x)\ x = A$' is nonsense (TLP 5.534). So even if this were what it meant, 'A exists' would none the less be nonsense.

(v) There is a genuine relation between names and objects, and it is both external and opaque.

Words are things. They can stand in genuine relations to other things. To assign meaning to names is to establish correlations between things, viz. between names and objects. (If the objects of the *Tractatus* were type-homogeneous, then there would be a unique relation that held between a name and the object named. Otherwise there are as many relations of names to objects as there are types of names.)

The relation of a name to the object named, or the correlation of a name with its meaning, is merely 'psychological' (NB 99). This entails that it is not a logical relation, not an internal relation but an external one. Meaning is a matter of establishing mental correlations with the intention of always using a name to stand for the same object. What gives language its life are mental acts (cf. BB 4). (Cf. NB 129: it is a 'matter of psychology to find out' what kind of relation holds between the elements of a thought and the elements of a fact.)

The name-relation is also opaque. It is not self-evident what the objects are, hence not self-evident whether any given expression is a name. Wittgenstein later saw himself as committed by the *Tractatus* to the view that future analysis will reveal what the objects and atomic propositions are and thereby reveal the real meaning of our language (WWK 182 f.). All this is subject to discovery (TLP 5.55, cf. NB 95 f; LF 163 f., 171). What alone is self-evident is that there must be names (and objects).

(vi) Names are primitive signs: they resist analysis (TLP 3.26, 3.261). In this respect they contrast with 'sentence-constitutents that signify complexes'. These latter must either be (definite) descriptions of a complex or abbreviations of such descriptions, and hence in either case such symbols will disappear in the course of analysis (TLP 3.241).

Whether a symbol can be broken down by analysis has nothing to do with epistemology; it is not a matter of immunity to Cartesian doubt nor of whether it is *certain* that what it denotes exists. It is a purely logical issue. What can be analysed can be defined. The definition states the essence of the complex. Under Wittgenstein's presumption that all necessity is logical necessity (TLP 6.37, 6.375), if something has a statable essence, then the symbol standing for it can be defined, i.e. analysed. Therefore the indefinability of names is the expression of the thesis that the essence or form of an object cannot be stated, only shown; that internal properties are ineffable (cf. TLP 2.0233, 2.02331). If simple objects could have essential properties that could be stated, then there would be necessarily true propositions that were not tautologies.

(vii) Names need not be simple signs, but they are simple symbols (cf. TLP 3.32 ff.). Any complexity of the sign for a name is an accidental, not an essential, feature of the sign. The real name of an object would be what all symbols that signified it had in common. Hence it would be simple, since one by one all kinds of composition would prove inessential to it (TLP 3.3411). This simplicity of nature would require that names, in a proper logical notation, should be represented by simple signs. (Since names *could* be simple signs, they *should* be.)

(viii) According to the *Tractatus*, what is symbolized by a name can be symbolized only by a name. 'Objects can only be *named*' (TLP 3.221). Wittegenstein thought that Russell was not rigorous enough in his adherences to this doctrine and its converse, that what can be described cannot be named. Facts can be described; hence they cannot be named. In particular, sentences are not names of facts (NB 93). (The same conclusion can be reached from the premise that facts are not objects (cf. TLP 1.1). 'Situations can be described but not *given names*' (TLP 3.144).) Conversely, objects can only be named; they cannot be described. This does not mean that they cannot have external properties. But it does mean that their internal properties cannot be stated, hence that an object is not correctly symbolized by any definite description.

4. *Wittgenstein's criticism*

The *Investigations* criticizes the concept of a logically proper name. Most of the atomists' theses about names are explicitly repudiated. In the few remaining cases, apparent verbal agreement hides radical underlying disagreement, so that negative verdicts on the atomist interpretation of these theses emerge clearly in the course of the argument.

Wittgenstein's criticisms do not merely find fault with details in the formulation of the atomist theses. Instead he attacks the presuppositions that underlie the atomists' concern with logically proper names. Though these differ in Russell's atomism and in the *Tractatus*, they are severally undermined. Russell's search for logically proper names is motivated by the goal of giving secure foundations to empirical knowledge. In seeking to identify the particulars that are the meanings of logically proper names, Russell is pursuing a traditional epistemological inquiry, but describing it in novel terminology. In advocating that particulars are presently experienced sense data, he is giving a familiar solution to this problem. The *Investigations* elaborates criticisms of the search for foundations of knowledge. It explicitly repudiates the Cartesian foundations that Russell advocates: both the private language argument and the doctrine of avowals are incompatible with treating reports of immediate experience as incorrigible truths. The logical motivation of the *Tractatus's* commitment to logically proper names is likewise assailed. Names (and simple objects) were required as guarantors that the sense of every sentence be completely determinate. The *Investigations* repudiates the very notion of determinacy of sense and the associated preconceptions (cf. 'Vagueness and determinacy of sense', pp. 221 ff.). Once the *Tractatus's* demand for determinacy of sense is cast away, the postulation of names and simples is pointless.

Furthermore, Wittgenstein's criticisms of logically proper names are interwoven with his remarks on ordinary proper names, since the mistakes of atomism about logically proper names originate at least in part in total misconception about ordinary proper names. Their meaning is assumed at the outset to be their denotation in accord with the Augustinian *Urbild*. Difficulties that arise from this presumption are met by relegating most ordinary names to the category of incomplete symbols (e.g. disguised definite descriptions). This launches a search for 'real' names. This quest for the logically proper name is rooted in a picture. The only effective means for demonstrating its futility is to shatter the illusion on which it rests. The idea that the meaning of a proper name is the object named is not grounded in observation of how ordinary proper names actually behave. It is a preconception that philosophers bring to the analysis of language before they set to work.

This is manifested in their reluctance to give it up in spite of the accumulation of adverse 'evidence'. Instead of throwing it away, they justify its failure to throw light on everyday language by claiming that the phenomena are opaque; that these must be seen through in order to recognize its truth; and that one will then discover that ordinary proper names are recalcitrant to this analysis precisely because they are not names at all, but rather incomplete symbols masquerading as names. One therapy for this disease of the understanding is a simple, prosaic account of how ordinary proper names function in language. A correct account of proper names will itself constitute a criticism of the concept of logically proper names. Indeed, the two projects are inseparable. If the first is done convincingly, the second can be left to take care of itself.

In surveying Wittgenstein's criticisms of the notion of a logically proper name, it is important to bear in mind that they are made within the framework of his own conception of ordinary proper names. He equates explaining who N is with explaining the meaning of N's name 'N'. This commits him to a number of substantial claims which are problematic. We shall here elaborate his cricitisms without questioning their framework.

(i) A word has meaning (*Bedeutung*) only in the context of a sentence (PI §49). This contradicts Russell's thesis about logically proper names. It is in *apparent* agreement with the *Tractatus*, which also cites Frege's slogan with approval. But Wittgenstein's interpretation of the slogan is different in these two contexts. This difference runs deep. Indeed, the interpretation of this slogan in the *Tractatus* cannot consistently be carried over into the *Investigations*, nor is the gloss given it in the *Investigations* consistent with its significance in either the *Tractatus* or Frege's writings. (See 'A word has meaning only in the context of a sentence', pp. 152 ff.)

(ii) The meaning (*Bedeutung*) of a proper name is not its bearer, the object named (PI §§40 ff.). In this context Wittgenstein recommended thinking of the meaning of a word as its use in language. He advances two arguments to support the thesis that the meaning of a proper name is never its bearer. First, loss or destruction of the bearer of a name 'N' does not deprive 'N' of meaning. When a person dies, his name soldiers on (PI §40) and when a tool is broken a name for it may well continue to have meaning (use) (PI §41). Secondly, a name 'N' which has never had a bearer may have a use or meaning (PI §42). We might add that it may be perfectly clear that a name has a use even though we cannot determine whether it *has* a bearer (e.g. 'Homer') and also that it has a use when we know it has *no* bearer, e.g. 'Vulcan' (the supposed intra-Mercurian planet).

In addition to these counter-arguments, Wittgenstein gives a diagnosis of the philosophers' mistake of identifying the meaning of a name with its bearer. It results from a misconception about the nature of ostensive definition. Even though who N is may sometimes be explained by pointing to the bearer of 'N', this does not show that the meaning of 'N' is the person or thing pointed at (cf. PI §43, PG 63 f.).

(iii) Grasping the use of a proper name need not involve acquaintance with the bearer (or the relevant bearer, if the name has more than one bearer). Even if it does involve such acquaintance (as in being introduced to Mr N.) it does not consist in acquaintance with the bearer.

To understand an utterance incorporating the name 'N' does not require knowing N, but rather knowing who (or what) N is. There are various criteria for knowing who (in a given context) N is (see 'Proper names', pp. 242 f.).

The related atomist thesis that understanding of a proper name is independent of the knowledge of any truths about its bearer conflates various claims, some true and some false. If read as the claim that giving a description of N never constitutes a criterion for knowing who N is, it is false. There is a grammatical connection between giving appropriate descriptions and knowing who N is (who is referred to an utterance 'ΦN'). On the other hand, this connection is not an entailment. Therefore, if the atomists' thesis is read as the denial that giving any description of N entails that the speaker knows who N is, it is true. Finally, if read as a version of the logical thesis that the satisfaction of a definite description is never either logically necessary or logically sufficient for being the bearer of a proper name, then it may be acceptable. For it seems at least compatible with the proposition that giving a description of N is a criterion for knowing who N is that there is no grammatical connection between satisfying this description and being N.

(iv) The insertion of an ordinary proper name in the argument-place of the predicate 'ξ exists' or its negation does not typically yield a meaningless sentence, although in some contexts it is a needlessly obscure way of making perfectly clear statements. The sentence 'Moses did not exist' is perfectly in order (PI §79), and people have carried on serious arguments about whether Homer existed, whether Jehovah exists, and whether Vulcan exists. Not only are such sentences in order, but also, in Wittgenstein's view, they may mean different things (PI §79) and be explained in different ways. Neither 'N exists' nor its negation makes a statement that is necessarily true.

There are three roots of the atomist thesis that a sentence of the form 'N exists' is meaningless where 'N' is a genuine proper name. The first is the mistake of identifying the meaning of a name with its bearer. The second is a misconception about ostensive explanation of names. If a name 'N' could only be explained ostensively, then it might appear to follow from the nonsensicality of 'This exists' (except in very special circumstances) that sentences of the form 'N exists' are also nonsensical. But even if that is correct, it is quite wrong to think that names are always explained ostensively. If someone does not know who N is, there are numerous different ways of explaining this; ostensive explanation occupies no privileged position. The third is the mistake of projecting the form of representation of the predicate calculus on to ordinary language. Dummy names cannot occur as arguments of second-level functions such as the existential quantifier. But to infer from this that one cannot legitimately say that Vulcan does not exist would be erroneous.

(v) There is no such thing as the name-relation. Rather, there are many different relations of names to objects (PI §37; BB 172 f.). Even if there were a single relation of naming, it would be neither external nor opaque. That 'N' is the name of (or 'stands for') N is not a truth of psychology (BB 3), but a truth of grammar. It may be understood in two ways. First, it may be interpreted simply as an instance of the schematic formula ' "x" is the name of x'. The schema expresses a grammatical truth. Every substitution-instance of it is true in virtue of the conventions for the use and mention of names and of the meaning of 'is the name of'. Consequently, a substitution-instance of it will be recognized as a grammatical truth even by a person who does not know the meaning of 'N', at least if he knows that 'N' is a proper name. Secondly, ' "N" is the name of N' may be interpreted as an expression of the rule of grammar that explains the use of the name 'N'. If a person knows who N is, then the meaning of 'N' can be explained to him by the rule ' "N" is the name of N' (or, more accurately, by a rule such as ' "N" is the name of *that* person (viz. N)'). On either interpretation the sentence ' "N" is the name of N' (or even ' "N" refers to N') expresses an internal relation between a name and an object.

The name-relation (if we countenance such talk) is also transparent. First, it can be established with certainty whether or not an expression is a proper name. Whether it is or not depends merely on how we use, explain, and understand it, not on any kind of research, whether scientific or philosophical, into what it refers to. There is no such thing as discovering, contrary to our previous opinion, that what we all thought to be a proper name is in fact not a proper name at all. No mystery enshrouds the notion of a proper name; there are no deep problems to be solved in deciding which expressions are proper names, which not, although there are borderline cases. Secondly, there is no distinction between what speakers of a language take 'N' to refer to and what 'N' (really) refers to. There are no transcendent questions about references, although of course we may remain ignorant about Homer's or King Arthur's existence. Wittgenstein's reinterpretation of his earlier distinction between logic and psychology is in part intended to show that such a transcendent distinction makes no sense.

(vi) The atomist thesis that names cannot be analysed is approximately correct in one respect. Typically, there are no conditions logically necessary and sufficient for an object's being N (or being identical with N), where 'N' is a proper name. Consequently, typical proper names cannot be analysed as abbreviations of definite descriptions even where they are explained by descriptions. Their explanations also take other forms.

On the other hand, it is not a consequence of this thesis that there are no criteria for correctly understanding or grasping the use of a proper name. In particular, it does not follow from the fact that a typical name 'N' is not logically equivalent to any definite description that giving a description which in its context individuates N is not a correct explanation of who N is and hence a criterion for understanding 'N'. Denial that names can be analysed is independent of denial that they can be explained.

(vii) Whatever limited truth there is in the claim that proper names are simple symbols (see 'Proper names', pp. 248 f.), this alleged simplicity does not entail either that such names cannot be defined (explained) or that there are no criteria for their correct understanding. Or better: it does not entail that there are no criteria for correct understanding of utterances in which names occur.

(viii) The atomist thesis that what is symbolized by a name can be symbolized only by a name seems primarily intended as an alternative formulation of the thesis that names cannot be analysed. It just asserts that the role of names cannot be taken over by definite descriptions. *This* is true, but it does not have the dramatic implications the atomists took it to have. In particular, it does not justify the absurd claim that what is named cannot be described. This is absurd because it presupposes that naming and describing stand 'on the same level', so that they might compete with each other. Whereas, in fact, naming, far from excluding description, should be seen as 'a preparation for description' (PI §49).

(ix) The distinction between ordinary proper names and logically proper names is completely misguided. It is not possible by the method of restriction to make the atomist ideal of a proper name fit any set of expressions. The class of logically proper names is empty, and hence the logic characteristic of logically proper names is literally a logic for a vacuum. The counterpart thesis that most ordinary proper names are incomplete symbols is false. For ordinary names there are criteria of understanding, there is a distinction between meaning and bearer, and there is a possibility of their being significantly used as arguments for the predicate 'ξ exists'. But it does not follow that they can be analysed, that they are logically equivalent to definite descriptions. Distinguishing ordinary proper names from logically proper names is doubly mistaken. It mischaracterizes ordinary proper names in claiming that they can be analysed, and it misleads by suggesting that the set of logically proper names is not empty.

(x) Demonstratives are quite distinct from proper names. To assimilate them to proper names is to ignore the important logical differences between them. (See 'Indexicals', pp. 123 f.)

We noted at the outset that the criticisms are made from a vantage point involving a number of questionable commitments. Explaining who N is is equated with explaining the meaning of N's name 'N'. Hence proper names are individuated by their bearers. Hence many kinds of names (e.g. 'John Smith') suffer from radical ambiguity. That a name has a meaning that is explained in saying who its bearer is is a claim that is never questioned. So an ostensive explanation of who N is is equated with an ostensive definition of N's name 'N'. All these claims will be subjected to critical scrutiny (cf. 'Proper names', pp. 251 ff.). However, it is important to note that criticizing Wittgenstein's criticisms does not resuscitate their target. His criticisms retain their force and are unaffected by the transformations in their formulation (some already tacitly undertaken) which are necessary if their framework is altered.

'A WORD HAS A MEANING ONLY IN THE CONTEXT OF A SENTENCE'

1. *Introduction*

Semantic atomism dominates the psychologistic conception of language derived from Descartes and Locke. This doctrine conceived of the meaning of a word as typically consisting in an idea (commonly, but not uniformly, taken to be a psychological entity) for which the word stands. The relation of word-meaning to sentence-meaning was barely considered and, by omission, the role of structure in determining sentence-meaning was minimized. Accordingly, either knowing the meanings of words is independent of knowing how to construct sentences from words, or a sentence is a mere list of names. If understanding words is independent of understanding sentences, and understanding sentences is not a trivial consequence of understanding their constituents, then a linguistic competence consists of two distinct abilities: knowledge of word-meanings and knowledge of how to combine words to yield meaningful sentences. Alternatively, semantic atomism must argue that once the meanings of words are understood the grasp of sentence-meanings follows as a trivial consequence. This conception of language and understanding is a classical version of the Augustinian picture of meaning.

The thinker to whom modern philosophy is most indebted for destroying the grip of semantic atomism is Frege. It is to him above all that the contemporary emphasis upon form or structure in philosophical semantics is due. It was he who first formulated the dictum 'a word has a meaning only in the context of a sentence'. On the assumption that 'meaning', which is here equivalent to Frege's technical notion of content, converges on our intuitive idea of meaning, this dictum is commonly thought to embody one of Frege's most important insights. We shall call it 'the contextual dictum' and call the cluster of doctrines associated with this dictum 'contextualism'. *In vacuo* the contextual dictum is obscure. Not only is it not self-evident, but it is not even obviously true, nor in accord with Frege's practice. For surely we can say what a given word means independently of its sentential occurrence; that is just what formal definitions do and what dictionaries are primarily concerned with. Moreover, there are numerous meaningful uses of words other than in sentences, e.g. names on labels, numerals on houses, pages, licences, etc., book-titles on books. What the import of the dictum is depends upon the use to which it is put in the context of a general account of meaning. Frege propounds the dictum, and so does Wittgenstein, both in the *Tractatus* and in his later writings. This immediately generates two puzzles. For whatever should be understood by the contextual dictum, it evidently stands in contrast to semantic atomism, itself a version of the Augustinian picture. But Frege's semantics, we have argued, consists of a baroque structure elaborated to preserve intact the fundamental commitments of an Augustinian picture (cf. 'Augustine's picture of language', pp. 15 ff.). If so, what is the role and importance of the contextual dictum in Frege's elaborate *defence*, not of semantic atomism, but of the Augustinian conception of language? Secondly, if the dictum is fundamental to Frege's enterprise, what can be the justification and point of Wittgenstein's *reasserting* it in the context of a prolonged attack on the Augustinian picture? The answer to both puzzles will become clear when we see how different Frege's affirmation of the contextual dictum is from the later Wittgenstein's.

In this essay we shall first survey Frege's contextualism in order to grasp the meaning and rationale of the various contextual principles which he expresses by the contextual dictum. By isolating the rationale of Frege's contextualism (and the rather different variant in the *Tractatus*), we shall show how these foundations are undermined by Wittgenstein's later criticisms. But detaching the contextual dictum from Frege's calculus model of language leaves it bereft of any clear justification. It therefore stands in need of a different rationale and distinct interpretation. Starting afresh, we shall examine the significance commonly attributed to the contextualism in general accounts of meaning and corresponding accounts of understanding which are pursued in the spirit of Frege's calculus conception of language but without commitment to Frege's specific rationale for contextualism. This requires close scrutiny of its alleged explanatory power in accounting for our ability to understand new sentences constructed out of known constituents. For it is this explanatory role that is commonly taken as a main ground of the indisputable acceptability of contextualism. Finally, we shall suggest a justification for the dictum which is independent of a calculus or quasi-calculus model of language, yet nevertheless prevents us from falling back into the manifest errors of semantic atomism. This account of the dictum will be consistent with Wittgenstein's later remarks on explaining and understanding sentences, even though the central tenets of a contextual theory of meaning are undermined.

2. *Frege's contextualism.*

To grasp correctly the use Frege makes of the contextual dictum it must be seen in relation to four overarching principles that dominate his philosophy. First, the content (later, the sense) of a sentence is limited to inference-relevant aspects of its meaning. This is naturally understood as identifying its content or sense with its truth-conditions. Secondly, the content of a subsentential expression is some correlated entity (object, concept, or function). The sense/reference distinction modifies, but does not abandon, this Augustinian conception. Thirdly, the use in logic of the grammatical analysis of sentences into subject and predicate is replaced by extending the mathematical notion of a function to the articulation of sentences and their contents. A sentence is analysable into argument-expression and function-name, and its content decomposes into argument and function. (The thought is later conceived as decomposing into the sense of an argument-expression and the sense of a function-name.) Fourthly, a function is completely determined by specification of its value for every admissible argument. This is held to ensure content for a function-name.

These principles collectively represent language as a kind of calculus. The point of contact between them is the idea of treating concepts as functions and hence concept-words as function-names. Concepts are functions whose values are truth-values. A logically adequate language must ensure that every concept-word corresponds to a fully defined function. The idea of articulating a sentence into function-name and argument-expression stands in sharp contrast to the semantic atomists' conception of the sentence as composed of words signifying homogeneous, independently existing ideas. Frege's conception of sentence and content of judgement alike give unprecedented prominence to the notion of *logical structure*.

In *The Foundations of Arithmetic* the contextual dictum is repeated four times and given prominence in Frege's methodological remarks as well as in his own account of number. It provides a focal point for the above cited principles and corollaries. However, it is important to realize that the contextual dictum does not express a single sharply circumscribed thesis in the *Foundations*. Rather, a set of interconnected ideas cluster around it. This is evident from a survey of its occurrences. In the first, it expresses a heuristic maxim: 'Never to *ask* for the meaning of a word in isolation, but only in the context of a sentence' (FA p. x). In its second occurence (FA §60), it is also linked with a sufficiency condition: 'That we can form no idea of its content is therefore no reason for denying all meaning to a word. . . . . . It is enough if the sentence taken as a whole has a sense; it is this that confers on its parts also their content.'

All that is necessary for a subsentential expression to have meaning (stand for something) is that it play a non-trivial part in expressing a judgement and thus in determining inferences that may be drawn from the sentence. It is noteworthy that the converse of this sufficiency condition is a compositional principle of content or meaning. Since the contents of the

logical constituents of a sentence are derived from the decomposition of
the judgeable content expressed, the content of such a sentence is trivially
composed of the contents of its constituents. The dictum is also here
associated with a restrictive condition: '. . . we ought always to keep
before our eyes a complete sentence. Only in a sentence have the words
really a meaning' (FA §60). Only a sentence expresses a judgement and
hence only in a sentence can a subsentential expression have a meaning or
content, i.e. contribute to determination of valid inferences. In its third
occurrence (FA §62), the dictum expresses both the sufficiency and the
restrictive condition. The restrictive principle is required to justify our
limiting attention to *sentences* containing numerals when we try to specify
the content of number-words. The sufficiency principle is needed to
justify taking specification of the content of a sentence containing a numeral
as sufficient for assigning content to that number-word. Thus via these
two conditions Frege justifies contextual definition. In its final occurrence
(FA §106), the dictum recapitulates four of these five points.

    This does not exhaust its use and significance. The contextual dictum
interlocks with Frege's other two methodological principles in the *Foundations*. The first is 'always to separate the psychological from the logical'.
Frege recurrently warns that only by observing the contextual dictum can
one avoid psychologism (FA p. x, §60, §106). He gives no argument in
support of this claim, but the history of post-Cartesian philosophy suggests that there is at least a contingent connection between psychologism
and failure to comply with the heuristic and sufficiency principles.
Nevertheless, it is surely false that psychologism or semantic atomism are
virtually unavoidable unless the heuristic maxim is observed. The second
connected principle is 'never to lose sight of the distinction between
concept and object'. In arguing against formalism (FA §§96 ff.), Frege
links this principle by implication with the contextual dictum. The connection is by means of the idea that what kind of entity (object or concept) an
expression in natural language stands for depends upon its logical type,
and its logical type depends upon its role in a sentence. Many ordinary
expressions can occur in more than one logical role; hence what content
such an expression has depends upon what role it fulfils in a particular
sentential context.

    It should be emphasized that whatever the cogency of these various
contextual principles for Frege's conception of content or meaning, they
do not obviously apply to our ordinary notion of meaning. We can and do
'ask for the meanings of words' in isolation, and dictionary definitions
(and other explanations too) give us the meanings of words outside the
context of any particular sentence. While it is only in a sentence that a word
contributes to determination of valid inferences, it is not true that words
have no meaning when used extra-sententially.

    In the *Foundations*, 'Sinn', 'Bedeutung', and 'Inhalt' are used interchangeably. Later, however, he differentiates content into sense and reference. It has been argued that with the introduction of the sense/reference distinction Frege tacitly repudiates the contextual dictum. The reason for this is held to be the explicit assimilation of sentences to proper names of truth-values, thus denying the distinctive role of the sentence which was stressed by the dictum. Frege allegedly argues that words have meanings only in the context of sentences because sentences are the minimal units of communication, i.e. the smallest expressions with which to 'make a move in the language game' (PI §49). This insight has to be abandoned once sentences are treated as complex proper names, and this explains Frege's failure to repeat the dictum in his later works.

This misinterprets Frege's contextualism. These ideas do not rest on the internal nexus of sentence and assertion. Even before explicitly assimilating sentences to names Frege acknowledged only a weak, external connection between the bearers of truth-values and assertion, and there is no evidence that the primacy he attributed to the sentence turned on recognition that it is the basic unit of speech and communication. The foundations of his contextualism consist in the ideas that sentences express judgeable contents (later, thoughts) that are the basic units of inference and bearers of truth-values, that these are articulated into function and argument, and that whether a function-name has a content depends only on whether it is assigned a value for every admissible argument. These ideas are integral to the *Basic Laws* as well as to the *Foundations*.

The continuity of Frege's contextualism must be sought for in the *Basic Laws* by splitting each of the earlier contextual principles into two, one for sense and one for reference, and seeing whether the result is embodied in the later work. We shall not go through this exercise in detail, but merely pick out those principles of *sense* which after 1892 can be seen as heirs of earlier contextual principles. Both the sufficiency condition and its complement, the compositional principle (cf. CO 54), are reaffirmed for senses in the following crucial passage: 'The names . . ., of which the name of a truth-value consists, contribute to the expression of the thought, and this contribution of the individual [component] is its sense. If a name is part of the name of a truth-value, then the sense of the former name is part of the thought expressed by the latter name '(BLA i. §32). The restrictive principle, though not explicitly reaffirmed, is implicit in Frege's claim that what belongs to the thought is only what determines validity of inferences and in his restricting the senses of subsentential expressions to their contributions to thoughts. Although Frege repudiates contextual definition of number-words, he continues to employ contextual definitions (as long as they are not piecemeal). Frege's contextualism is not abandoned after the *Foundations* but transformed into principles stating the interdependence of sense between sentences and subsentential parts of speech.

Partial confirmation of this interpretation can be found in Frege's polemics against Hilbert in 1903–6 (cf. FG 8, 23 n., 53, 67, 70 ff.). Frege here insists that expressions that have no sense determining a reference (e.g. letters in algebraic notation) must have their contribution to the expression of the thought fixed. Of these he says, 'it is only in the context of a sentence that they have a task to fulfil, that they contribute to the expression of the thought. But outside this context they say nothing' (FG 67). Of expressions in a sentence that do have sense and reference, Frege demands that their sense (and reference) likewise be fixed. But to settle the sense of a subsentential expression *is* to settle its contribution to the sense of a sentence in which it occurs. So the core of his contextual principles soldiers on in the form of theses about the relations of subsentential expressions and the sense of sentences.

The heart of contextualism in the *Basic Laws* is a strong compositional principle of sense. According to this principle the construction of a sentence out of components which have a sense generates a thought, provided the components are combined according to the rules of logical syntax. However Frege's contextualism continued to evolve after the *Basic Laws*. In an unpublished paper written in 1914 (NS 243), Frege connected this compositional conception of sentence-sense with a corresponding account of understanding sentences. A sentence expresses a thought that is composed of the sense of its subsentential constituents, and we understand a sentence in virtue of compounding our understanding of its constituents and our grasp of its structure. Our understanding of a sentence is therefore something that results from our calculating or deriving its sense from the senses of its constituents and their mode of combination. This may be called 'a generative theory of understanding', and although never developed by Frege, it occurs in the *Tractatus*[1] as an integral part of the theory of meaning there elaborated.

Concurrently with his generative theory of understanding, Frege introduced, and immediately resolved to his satisfaction, the so-called problem of the 'creativity of language', encapsulated in the simple question 'How it is possible for us to understand sentences we have never heard before?' Frege answered this by means of his generative account of understanding:

The achievements of language are wonderful. By means of a few sounds and connections of sounds it is capable of expressing a vast number of thoughts, including even such as have never before been grasped or expressed by anyone. How are these achievements possible? It is in virtue of the fact that thoughts are built up out of thought-building-blocks. These building blocks correspond to groups of sounds from which the sentence is constructed, so that the construction of the sentence from sentence-components corresponds to the construction of the

---

[1] It is difficult to accord priority here and impossible to disentangle the causal influences. The idea occurs in Frege's *Nachlass* in 'Logik in der Mathematik' (1914), but only appears in print in his 'Gedankengefüge' (1923) i.e. after publication of the *Tractatus*. The same idea occurs explicitly in Wittgenstein's 'Notes on Logic' of 1913 (NB 94).

thought from thought-components. One can call the thought-components the sense of the corresponding sentence-components, just as one conceives of the thought as the sense of the sentence (NS 243).

This picture has exercised a powerful fascination upon the philosophical imagination. Language is represented by Frege as a kind of calculus. Meaningful sentences are conceived as flowing from the operation of its rules. Meaning and understanding sentences are conceived of as acts or processes that result from operating this calculus of language. This powerful combination of a calculus theory of meaning and a generative theory of understanding make Frege's late contextualism the forerunner of much contemporary theorizing in philosophy of language and linguistics despite great differences in detail. It also makes Frege's grand strategy one of Wittgenstein's primary targets in the *Investigations* (cf. PI §81). The conception of language as a calculus is deeply mistaken, the idea of understanding as a mental process of operating rules is an illusion, and the problem of the creativity of language is, by implication, bogus.

3. *Contextualism in the* Tractatus

Wittgenstein invokes the contextual dictum in the *Tractatus* (3.3 and 3.314). The differences between the two philosophers over the analysis of language in terms of sense and reference are profound. So too are their disagreements about the nature of logical form. But important features of their respective versions of contextualism are similar. In the *Tractatus* the dictum is invoked as an integral part of the picture theory with its bizarre theory of isomorphism. The syntactical form of a name mirrors the logical form of an object. Just as a name has a *Bedeutung* only in the context of a proposition, so too objects (which are the *Bedeutungen* of names) exist only when concatenated in facts. The sole rationale for the dictum is a rather obscure passage (PT 2.0122). Wittgenstein's thought appears to be guided by the notions of logical form (given by syntax), sense of a sentence (given by truth-conditions), and meaning of names (determined by some method of projection (given that form is fixed)). The sense of an elementary sentence is a function of the *Bedeutungen* of its constituent names. The role of a name in a sentence is to contribute to determination of its truth-conditions. Outside the context of a sentence it has no such role. So it can no more be said to have a meaning outside a sentence than an ink bottle can be said to have a meaning, even though the fact that the ink bottle is on the table might be used to signify that I am at home. It is only in use that a sign is a symbol (TLP 3.326–3.327).

Prominent in the *Tractatus* is Wittgenstein's *explicit* invocation of the principle to *explain* the so-called creative powers of language (TLP

4.02–4.03).[2] To understand a proposition is to know its truth-conditions, and it is understood if one understands its form and its constituents, i.e. knows their meanings. It is of the essence of a proposition that it can convey a new sense by a structure utilizing old expressions. The meanings (hence also the forms) of the (elementary) constituents must be explained to us, but, once they are grasped, the sense of sentences constructed from them will be understood without further ado. The ability acquired when the meanings of names are grasped is not distinct from the ability to construct, out of those names, sentences with a new sense. Understanding a language, according to the *Tractatus*, consists in tacit (concealed) knowledge of its primitive expressions and of the combinatorial rules of the language. How this is effected is a matter for psychological investigation into thought–constituents.

It is only in the post-1929 writings that Wittgenstein undermines the rationale for the contextual principles as understood by Frege and the *Tractatus*. The dictum is not repudiated, but its interpretation changes. As Wittgenstein shifts emphasis from form (structure) to use, its importance diminishes, since it emphasizes form and is indifferent to the variety of uses which words and sentences of the same form have. Similarly, as the multiplicity of kinds of explanation of meaning of words and sentences is recognized, and *pari passu* the diversity of criteria of understanding clarified, the defects of contextualism as part of a 'theory of understanding' are made manifest. Finally, the repudiation of *explanation* in philosophy forces drastic reconsideration of reliance on contextualism to explain the 'creative powers of language'.

4. *Wittgenstein: undermining the Fregean foundations*

Wittgenstein quotes the contextual dictum with approval in many post-1929 writings (PR 59; M 261; BT 1; PI §49). But his explicit criticisms of Frege undermine the original justifications for the principles, and his thoroughgoing criticisms of calculus conceptions of meaning force a substantial reconsideration of the justification and interpretation of the dictum.

We have already noted that there is a strong link between an underlying Augustinian picture of language and the sophisticated abstract structures of Frege's semantics. *Sinn* is in effect a tier which Frege superimposes upon what is at root an Augustinian conception of language. Every significant expression (barring, e.g., the assertion–sign and variable letters) stands for something, but only in the context of a

---

[2] As noted, Frege too sketched out such an answer, similarly invoking a generative theory of understanding. But he neither developed the idea nor integrated it into his theory of sense.

sentence. What type of entity an expression stands for depends on its logical form: a proper name stands for an object, a first-level concept-word stands for a concept, etc. But the logical form of an expression is determined by logical syntax, itself a quasi-mathematical structure of argument and function. An expression which stands for an ordinary object (e.g. 'Napoleon') in a simple subject/predicate sentence stands for a sense in an oblique context. 'Vienna' in 'Vienna is the capital of Austria' stands for Vienna, but in 'Budapest is no Vienna' it is part of an expression that stands for a concept. 'Cicero' in 'Cicero was a great orator' stands for Tully, but in 'Tully is identical with Cicero' it is part of the function-name 'is identical with Cicero', which stands for a concept. 'Horse' in 'Black Beauty was a horse' stands for a concept, but in 'The concept horse . . .' it is part of the name of an object. Since sense is the 'route' to reference, and grasping the sense is grasping a mode of presenting this reference, and since reference depends, *inter alia*, on logical form as determined by syntax, the sense of an expression cannot be read off or grasped independently of its logico-syntactical role in a sentence. Hence, if these logico-mathematical principles of syntax are unsound, contextualism will need a new rationale.

In the 1930s Wittgenstein explicitly criticizes Frege. First, the argument/function structure, which Frege claimed to be 'founded deep in the nature of things' (FC 41), is a *sublimation* of the subject/predicate form in grammar, as the notion of a point-mass in physics is of a material object (PR 119 ff.; PG 202 ff.). The distinction between object and concept *is* the distinction, duly refined, between subject and predicate. Secondly, the subject/predicate form is a norm of representation, our manner of mapping reality on to language, a mould into which we squeeze the proposition. It conceals countless different logical forms; the uniformity of mode of representation conceals the diversity of methods of projection. It is analogous to the case of projecting different geometrical figures from one plane to another, with the convention that only circles should occur on the second plane. In this case it is the diversity of the methods of projection which will illuminate the nature of the figures on the first plane, not the circularity of the figures on to which they are mapped. The 'part of speech' which characterizes an expression is determined by *all* the rules for its use, of which the ability to occur in the subject position is only one. Hence Frege's 'concept' and 'object' are not discoveries, not results of 'analysis', but a projection of grammatical moulds. Thirdly, the Fregean use of 'object' is aberrant. To say that the simultaneous occurrence of an eclipse of the moon and a court case is an *object* is misguided (PR 137). Fourthly, Frege construes a concept as a sort of property, but it is unnatural to construe sortal nouns as names of properties of a substratum and erroneous to take everything that he calls an object as a bearer of properties (PR 120). Fifthly, the Fregean and

Tractatus conception of the sentence as *necessarily* complex is repudiated. There are imaginary language-games in which symbols satisfy the criteria for word and sentence alike (PI §§19 ff.), and a non-complex symbol may be a name, yet sometimes used as a description—a proposition (PI §49).

These brief criticisms can readily be developed. Many further grounds for objecting to Frege's model can be extracted from Wittgenstein's writings. But it suffices for our purpose to have established that Frege's contextualism was rooted in his functional theory of language, and that Wittgenstein repudiated the functional theory (and not merely in the Platonistic form it assumes in Frege). Indeed, he rejected other more general calculus conceptions of language, yet continued to propound the contextual dictum. Since he never later associates the dictum with the doctrine of the functional structure of the sentence, he must have thought that it has a quite different rationale. Conceivably, its rationale may be less arcane and more down to earth than that propounded in the mysteries of Frege's Platonistic vision.

5. Beating about the bush: meaning and understanding

Rather than pursuing a rationale for the contextual dictum directly, it may be worthwhile beating about the bush a little. In particular, we should look at the role played by contextualism, explicitly or implicitly, in the calculus model inherited from Frege by contemporary philosophical semantics. This may make the quarry easier to pin down.

A Fregean theory of language has two aspects: it elaborates a theory of meaning and also a theory of understanding (the latter subordinate to the former). The theory of meaning displays the logical structure of language, purporting to show how complex expressions, including sentences of varying degrees of complexity, are built up from simpler expressions by a series of determinate operations. This calculus of language, once brought to light, will show how the meanings of any complex expressions are derived from the meanings of simpler constituents. Hence, given the primitives of a language, the formation and transformation rules will provide a method for deriving, and specifying, all meaningful compound expressions in the language.

Side by side with this programme of a theory of meaning for a language lies a correlative theory of understanding. This will show what is involved in grasping the meaning (sense) of any expression. Neo-Fregean contextualism, applied to the theory of understanding, amounts to the claim that we understand sentences in virtue of understanding their constituents and forms. This claim can be taken in various ways. The most extreme contention would follow Frege himself in arguing that we *derive* our understanding of a sentence from our knowledge of the meaning and structure of its constituents. Since prior to Frege's invention of his *Begriffsschrift* no one knew ('explicitly') the logical structure of sentences, this would imply tacit or unconscious knowledge of logical syntax (perhaps akin to Chomsky's claims that we have innate knowledge of the deep structure of transformational grammar). A much more modest and humble contention would be that if we understand a sentence we must understand its structure and the meanings of its constituents.

Contextualism, in this familiar modern form, is only marginally connected with the contextual *dictum*, but crucially connected with the contextual principle of composition and the correlative conception of understanding. Two classes of objection to it may be propounded. The first consists of identifying problematic areas for the theory, both with respect to a calculus of meaning-rules and with respect to the understanding of complex expressions. The second consists of objections of principle to the general enterprise.

A few problematic areas are worth displaying. The difficulties listed concern, in the first instance, a calculus model of meaning and only derivatively the correlative conception of understanding.

(i) *Word clusters and analogical relations*: language is rife with analogical extension. We speak of animals running, taps running, rivers running, paint running, stains running, routes running (from X to Z via Y), and of politicians running for office.[3] We distinguish a bachelor from a bachelor of arts, a knight-bachelor from a bachelor seal. We talk of a person's foot, the foot of a mountain, the foot of a page, and of the measure one foot. In cases such as these we have something akin to a word cluster, a network of interrelated terms woven together by different patterns of analogy. The expressions in each cluster are related, but it is not obvious that the meaning of a given expression within a cluster can always be represented as derived by a set operation from another. In particular, the analogies involved are not evidently regular and predictable. It will avail little to attempt to account for members of a given field by embedding an 'analogy operator' in the analysis, e.g. 'Φ*b' = 'b doing-something-similar-to-what-a-does when Φa'. First, it is not evident that there always is a 'central case'. Secondly, there is no way of circumscribing similarity. We talk of bachelor seals, but not of bachelor dogs. We talk of the foot of a mountain, but of its foothills, not its feet. Although rivers run, winds do not. Though the engine of a car may run (idle), the car does not run (although it may be running in, or running well (i.e. engine functioning well) and an owner can be said to run a car). No theory will tell us which analogy will give rise to a significant combination of words.

---

[3] In America they run; in England they just stand!

(ii) *Figurative meaning*: our language, including that of science, is run through with verbal 'pictures' (Benthamite archetypes). Perhaps these begin their life as metaphors. But they rapidly become fossilized, cease to be metaphors, and become part of the regular currency of language. This is especially obvious in discourse concerning the mind. Our language concerning intellection, volition, and affection is largely composed of figurative expressions. Ideas strike, impress, or shake us. Our memories are engraved upon our mind, things are dimly or vividly recollected. We have flashes of insight, sparks of wit, flights of fancy. Our spirits sink low, we drown in sorrow or plunge into an abyss of grief. Our attitudes are stiff, our passions blind, our will steely. Considering the centrality of such discourse to our lives, it would be absurd to dismiss this feature of language as unimportant for a 'theory of language', as derivative or poetic. The phenomenon of figurative meaning is ubiquitous, and it is not obvious that there are general principles (as opposed to *ad hoc* enumeration of cases) that will display a set of generative rules which will show how such-and-such combinations of words are generated from such-and-such elements, and others debarred. To exhibit our understanding of such expressions as derived from our understanding of their constituent words and our knowledge of combinatorial rules is not obviously a promising strategy to pursue.

(iii) *Metaphor*: philosophers who purport to be giving a purified account of language for 'truly scientific purposes' are prone to brush metaphor aside as being 'merely poetic' and as involving 'secondary or derivative meaning'. This is doubly misleading. First, large areas of scientific research progress by means of fruitful metaphor or analogy, e.g. the hydrodynamical model for electrical theory. Secondly, it is not generally true that metaphor involves different word-meanings. 'Life is a tale told by an idiot' does not employ any word in a different *meaning* from its customary one. Metaphor is not standardly explained by explaining the meanings of constituent words and their mode of combination. Schelling's remark 'Architecture is frozen music' would not be thus explained, but it resonates powerfully and is readily grasped. If it had to be explained, the explanation would be analogical, and if someone did not understand it he would be exhibiting a kind of 'meaning-blindness'.

(iv) *Category restrictions*: Wittgenstein repudiated the idea that categories are in general sharply defined (cf. Exg. §§29, 97). The test of substitutability *salva significatione* is futile. If a theory of meaning is to demonstrate the derivability of every meaningful expression from defined primitives by means of various operations, it must surely also ensure that the calculus will not produce meaningless expressions. If a theory of understanding is to explain what our grasp of language consists of in terms of understanding constituents and forms, it must show, in these terms, why we do not understand categorial nonsense. 'The cow ate the cabbage' is meaningful, and *prima facie* has the same form as 'The cabbage ate the cow'. But is the latter meaningful? If the calculus theorist argues that it is meaningful but false, then the onus is upon him to explain what it would be for it to be true. And here it is no use saying 'You know what "cabbage" means, and you know what "ate" means and you know what "cow" means, so you must know what "the cabbage ate the cow" means.' For that uses as a premise the conclusion which is yet to be established. If the theorist agrees that it is meaningless, he must show that it violates combinatorial rules. He might do so (e.g. in 'ξ eats' only the name of an animate creature can occupy the argument-place). But it is none too easy (what of 'Acid eats metal'?). Moreover, it is only possible on the assumption that categories are sharply circumscribed. But there is no available test which will satisfactorily display consistent category membership (given that substitutability *salva significatione* will not do the trick).

These four objections indicate *some* of the difficulties facing any form of calculus theory, difficulties that have to be tackled simultaneously on two fronts, i.e. meaning and understanding. But we have only sketched in the very first move in the struggle. Conceivably, with sufficient ingenuity and a sufficiently high-minded attitude to ordinary intuitions and common concepts, the calculus theorist may at least appear to surmount the difficulties. A vastly complex theory, together with a bold degree of regimentation, may seem a strategy worth pursuing. To be sure, there will be a high price to pay. Our intuitions about what constitutes a meaningful expression may be rejected. Explanations of meaning in the model may obliterate the subtle networks of ramifying analogies that give the soul of our language. Metaphor may be pushed aside as derivative and unimportant. Categorial nonsense may be ruled to be sensible. Some will be willing to pay the price in the name of scientific progress.

But we need not, for our purpose, follow through the tactical manoeuvres of each side in this conflict. Quite apart from the difficulties mentioned, there are different objections of principle to the enterprise. First, the explanations of meaning of compound expressions by generative rules will, for the most part, be divorced from our common explanations. For although we sometimes explain the meaning of a sentence in terms of its structure and the meanings of its constituents, we do not always do so. In many cases such an explanation would be illegitimate and useless. Numerous other kinds of explanation (by paraphrase, by analogy, by exemplification, etc.) are legitimate and useful. If the explanations given by the model are divorced from our ordinary explanations, what is the point of the theory? If it shows that our linguistic practices can be mapped on to a calculus, does that show that we have been operating a calculus? (If one can map a game of chess on to Zulu war dances, does that show that chess-players are dancers?) Secondly, if the defender of the enterprise is willing to meet all difficulties by countenancing, at least in principle, exceedingly complicated rules to budget (by epicycle within epicycle) for analogy, metaphor, figurative language, idioms, and the varied range of 'semantic irregularities', what guarantee is there that the theory will not divorce its explanations, not only from our *actual* explanations, but also from any *possible* explanation usable by us? For there is no *a priori* guarantee that the projected rules and transformations will be surveyable or learnable by us. They may simply be too complicated (like a proof in the notation of *Principia Mathematica* that $25^2 = 625$).

These two objections of principle are not trivial. For what is the role of a general account of meaning if it is severed from a corresponding account of understanding? Explanations of meaning have a dual role: they explain what it is that we understand when we understand an expression, and they are the content of activities (giving explanations) that constitute criteria of understanding. But if the explanations given by a calculus model are divorced from our actual and possible explanations, it is difficult to see what their point is. They have neither normative nor evidential role with respect to justification of our application of language or to our understanding. Nor do they, in any acceptable sense, replace our common-or-garden explanations.

Further objections of principle can be brought against this application of contextual principles. What has been conspicuously missing from the discussion thus far is any attempt to lay bare the internal relations that obtain between meaning, use, and understanding. If the structure (in some fairly weighty sense) and meanings of constituents jointly determine the meaning of a sentence, it should follow that sentences with the same structure and same constituents have the same meaning. It should also follow that structural difference should always yield difference in meaning (unless some operations cancel out). Finally, structural similarity should imply that any differences in sentence-meaning are wholly attributable to differences in constituent-meaning. But what, in this conception of the matter, is the role of the use of a sentence? Are differences of use irrelevant to meaning? Can one be said to understand what someone has said if one does not grasp what use he made of the sentence he uttered?

Context-dependent sentences show that sentences with the same structure and constituents are not necessarily used to propound the same thing. Indexicals (temporal or spatial) or pronouns do not have a different meaning from one occasion of use to another. The differences in the statements made by 'This is red', 'He is ill', 'Today is my birthday', etc., are not attributable to differences of structure or meanings of constituents, but to context (time, place, person) and use (e.g. the contrast between using 'This is red' to explain what 'red' means and using it to describe an object, and the contrast between using the same sentence to describe A, or B, or C).[4] That a person understands the meaning of the constituents and the structure of the sentence does not show that he grasps what was propounded. A similar negative verdict is delivered by consideration of differences of meaning not captured by structure and content that are independent of indexicals. Thus, e.g., 'Brutus is an honourable man' said by Cassius does not have the same meaning as when said by Anthony. Again, 'I do' said in response to 'Who plays tennis?' as opposed to 'Do you take . . . as your wedded wife?' differs, not merely because of context and speaker, but because of the difference between 'performative' and 'non-performative' *use*.

It is false that structural difference always yields difference in meaning. Different grammatical moods can be used identically. Interrogative sentences, by any ordinary notion of structure, have a different structure from declarative sentences. But a rhetorical question means the same as the corresponding declarative sentence. Here the interrogative form is *used* to make an assertion. 'I would like to know whether p' is a declarative sentence, but it is typically used, like 'p?', to ask a question. Whether 'You will Φ' is a prediction or an order depends on its use, not on its structure. 'p', 'That p is true', 'It is true that p' appear different in structure (like 'p', 'That p is exciting', 'It is notorious that p'), but they typically have the same use.

It is not true that given structural similarity any differences in the meaning of utterances must be attributable to the constituents of the uttered sentence. The form of so-called 'performative utterances' does not differ from that of 'declarative' ones (in the first-person present tense). They differ in use. More controversially, the differences between first- and third-person psychological sentences (upon which Wittgenstein lavished so much attention) is most implausibly attributable to differences in meaning between 'I' and 'he'.

These objections of principle become even weightier when we shift our attention to the account of understanding. The application of the contextual principles in the framework of a neo-Fregean or calculus model of language demands that in some sense our understanding of a complex expression (e.g. a sentence) is derived from our understanding of its constituents and its structure. In the absence of a particular account of structure, the requirement is nebulous. In view of the kinds of

---

[4] In MS. 131, 141 f., Wittgenstein remarks 'Man hat die Idee, es sei der Sinn des Satzes zusammengesetzt aus den Bedeutungen seiner Wörter. Wie ist z.B. der Sinn von "Ich habe ihn noch immer nicht gesehen" aus den Bedeutungen der Wörter zusammengesetzt?' ('One has the idea that the sense of a sentence is composed of the meanings of its words. How, e.g., is the sense of "I still haven't seen him" composed of the meanings of the words?')

objections we have already considered, it is highly dubious. The contention may take various forms. The most extreme will be the claim that we actually derive our understanding of a sentence from our knowledge of the meanings of its constituents and our grasp of its structure. But we do not, in general, perform such calculation (except, perhaps, in translating a sentence from another language in which we are not fluent). Indeed, in the requisite sense of 'structure', i.e. logical syntax, we do not even know the structure. Understanding is not a process, but akin to an ability (cf. 'Understanding and ability', pp. 331 ff.), an ability to use an expression correctly and to explain what it means. If a person uses a sentence correctly we have adequate grounds for ascribing to him a grasp of its meaning. Does it follow that he grasps its logico-syntactical structure? Do ordinary English speakers understand the logical syntax of *Begriffsschrift* or of some as yet undiscovered calculus of language? Is this relevant to whether they understand English sentences? To be sure, we sometimes attribute lack of understanding to misunderstanding of structure. But the sense of 'structure' we employ is more down to earth than that of logical syntax. And such explanations of lack of understanding do not commit us to explaining understanding by reference to derivation from structure and constituent meaning. We similarly attribute understanding to a person if he correctly explains what a sentence means. But not all explanation of sentence-meaning is in terms of structure and constituents. A common form is paraphrase, and there is no reason to suppose that the paraphrase will be identical in structure to the explanandum. In general, the judgement that A understands 'p' does not rest on the evidence that he grasps its structure.

In view of previous considerations it is evident that knowledge of structure is not sufficient (together with knowledge of the meaning of constituents) for grasp of meaning. For the same structures may have wholly different uses and different structures the same uses. Idiomatic, figurative, and metaphorical uses of language cannot uniformly be explained in terms of the meanings of constituent expressions and their modes of combination. No doubt there is some fairly loose sense of 'structure' according to which failure to grasp the structure of a complex expression leads to misunderstanding. But it is not clear that this truism gives any foothold for ascending to the heights of a calculus theory of understanding. Just as the application of contextual principles as understood by the calculus theorist exaggerated the contribution of structure to sentence-meaning and wholly neglected use, so too their application to an account of understanding misconstrues the role of grasping structure in understanding sentences.

6. Understanding new sentences

The *Tractatus* employed contextual principles in order to explain the so-called 'creative' powers of language. The question of how it is possible for us to understand sentences we have never heard before has been thought to be particularly profound (it has, after all, a sonorous Kantian ring about it). Contextualism, propounded in the framework of a calculus model of language, seems to provide the only possible answer to this deep question. We can understand new sentences *because* we understand their structure and the meanings of their constituents. Yet previous considerations have cast doubt on the cogency of this accepted understanding of contextualism. Does this not render intolerably mysterious our remarkable ability to understand new sentences? Does not the explanatory power of contextualism with respect to the creativity of language suffice to justify it in the face of any criticism?

Philosophers who are impressed by our ability to use and understand novel sentences invoke contextual principles to explain this apparently mysterious ability. Our linguistic understanding appears to reach out to infinity, for there is no limit to the sentences we can understand. We can, it seems, do things we have never learnt, and this, it is argued, must be explained. The key to the explanation obviously seems to be contextualism. A word has a meaning only in the context of a sentence, and its meaning consists in its contribution to the meaning (truth-conditions) of any well-formed sentence in which it may occur. What a competent speaker knows is the meanings of the words of the language and the general structural principles of formation and transformation for the generation of compound expressions. This knowledge enables a speaker to *derive* the meanings of all well-formed compound expressions in the language. The task of the theorist of language is to articulate explicitly the general form of such generative rules which will display how, given the axioms of the theory of language (the word-meanings), the meanings of all meaningful sentences are generated.

This ambitious programme and its attendant explanation of our understanding are not without difficulties, quite apart from those already cited. The system of rules in question, which, it is argued, we all tacitly know (since this knowledge is what explains our infinite understanding), is not *explicitly* known by *anyone*, let alone the average native speaker. The rules await discovery by the linguistic theorist, and to that extent they are hypotheses. There is no guarantee that the average native speaker could understand any acceptable statement of these generative rules, for their correct statement may be too complex and theory-laden for common understanding. Even if a speaker could, after due explanation and tuition, be brought to understand these rules, his ability to understand the theorist's statement of the rules he has 'discovered' presupposes just that mastery of language which the alleged implicit knowledge of the rules was meant to explain.

The hypothetical rules which the theorist seeks to uncover are no less mysterious than the phenomena they are intended to elucidate. For the institution of their use is lacking. If they had any role, it would indeed be that of 'action at a distance'. Since these rules are not explicitly known, citing such rules is not, for us, a criterion of understanding expressions allegedly derived from their application, and failure to cite them is not a criterion of failing to understand such expressions. Similarly, the ordinary speaker does not appeal to any such rules in his own common-or-garden explanations of the meanings of sentences he utters. Hence these rules lack any normative role in our linguistic practices. Lacking any normative role, they also lack any genuine explanatory one.

Any sequence of behaviour can be mapped on to more than one rule. Hence there can be no guarantee that there will be one unique system of rules in terms of which to represent the generation of sentences in the language. If the rules were sought after merely for purposes of elegant systematization or for future pedagogic purposes, this would not matter. We could choose between different systems of such rules on 'aesthetic' grounds or on grounds of ready surveyability by learners. If the rules were sought after merely in order to predict which sentential structures are likely to be accepted as meaningful by a native speaker and in order to specify their meanings, it would not matter either (although the enterprise would be singularly pointless). The theorist's system of rules would have the explanatory weight of a hypothetico-deductive theory in science, and one would choose between different sets of possible rules according to predictive accuracy and calculative convenience. But the theorist intends the rules he discovers to *explain* our linguistic behaviour in a much weightier sense. First, the rules are meant to *explain* how we can understand novel sentences, not merely to predict which strings of words we will accept as legitimate. Secondly, the theorist insists that we possess tacit knowledge of these rules, and this insistence only makes sense if that tacit knowledge explains our behaviour and our ability to understand new sentences in some weightier sense than the mere fact that the various discovered systems of rules enable the theorist to derive the meanings of all well-formed sentences of the language. Hence there must be some criteria to choose, from among the various systems of possible rules, that set of rules which we actually tacitly know. But it is unclear what these can possibly be.

What is here forgotten is that any ordinary speaker of a language does follow a multitude of humdrum and familiar rules. They are evident in the explanations of utterances that he gives when asked, that he acknowledges in others as criteria of understanding, that he appeals to when required to justify a given use. It is such normative phenomena that reveal that it is these rules which he *follows*. That there may be indefinitely many hypothetical rules in accord with which he unknowingly acts is irrelevant to his behaviour and to its explanation. So if the theorist does produce some very general rule for generation of the meanings of a given sentence-type (classified according to the requirements of his theory) from given types of constituents (also so classified), what will show that a speaker tacitly knows, and follows, *that* rule, in addition to whatever rules are embedded in the various explanations he actually gives when asked to explain the meaning of certain sentences? The mere fact that the application of the theorist's general rule yields the same 'output' certainly does not do so (any more than the fact that a child correctly spells 'conceive' and 'frieze' shows that he tacitly knows and follows the rule of English spelling[5] concerning 'e' before 'i'). The institution of the *use* of these hypothetical rules is lacking. We forget here that rules do not settle their own application independently of our practices of applying them, our criteria of accord or lack of accord with given rules and our appeal to rules as justifications. Rules which await discovery are hypothetical, possible rules, not actual ones. (This critically important theme will be examined in Volume 2.)

The notion of tacit knowledge is neither unknown nor in principle illegitimate, although it needs to be explained and its limits circumscribed. Nevertheless, there must, in this case, be something that will reveal the difference between tacit knowledge of these rules and ignorance of them, something *other* than the mere fact of the speaker's correct discourse. If his correct discourse is *all* that shows his tacit knowledge and incorrect discourse is *all* that shows ignorance, then the hypothesis that he can produce and understand new sentences because of such tacit knowledge is both untestable and vacuous, and the very claim that he possesses tacit knowledge is empty. The mere (theoretic) possibility of concocting a set of rules the product of whose application coincides with a fragment of our speech does not show that we tacitly know these rules (any more than the additions and subtractions of an ancient Roman show that he tacitly knew the Peano axioms).

If these qualms are justified, it becomes evident that appeal to contextual principles as part of an explanation of our ability to understand new sentences is highly questionable. The very possibility of producing a theory of meaning of the type in question is doubtful. But even if it is possible, and were successfully executed, that theory and this version of contextualism which is part of it, would not have the explanatory power demanded of it. For the 'tacit knowledge' of as yet undiscovered,

---

[5] It is unobjectionable to claim that there is such a rule, for many people can cite it and do appeal to it. It is only objectionable to claim that everyone who can spell correctly tacitly knows and follows it irrespective of whether he can cite it or does appeal to it.

hypothesized rules, the statement of which may or may not be intelligible to an ordinary speaker of a language, does not, in any sense, explain our current ability to speak or understand sentences, whether new or old.

Does this, however, not leave wholly unexplained something which stands in need of explanation? Before jumping to this conclusion we should re-examine the question 'How is it possible for us to understand new sentences?' The question is obscure. First, what exactly is the phenomenon, i.e. understanding, which calls out for explanation, and what would count as an explanation of it? Secondly, what kind of possibility is in question? Thirdly, in what way is the novelty of the object of understanding relevant?

Understanding is not an act, process or state. If it is to be classified in such categorial terms, we may say that it resembles an ability in important and distinctive ways. A person understands sentences to the extent that he reacts appropriately to their utterance, uses them correctly, and explains them cogently. So the question of how it is possible for a person to understand new sentences boils down to the question of how it is possible for a person to be able to do those things of which that ability consists, namely to react to, use, and explain new sentences.

A question of the form 'How is it possible to Φ?', where Φing is a complex act, is most naturally taken to be a question about the methods, means, or techniques of Φing, or about the conditions or circumstances of Φing. 'How is it possible?' amounts to 'How does one do it?' But this is not a question one can ask about an ability. Hence 'How is it possible to understand a new sentence?', if construed as 'How does one do it?', is misplaced. The contention that our understanding of new sentences is explained by reference to our deriving their meaning from knowledge of their constituents and form implicitly takes understanding to be an act, assumes that the question of its possibility requires specification of a means of performing it, and contends that this understanding is achieved by means of a method of calculation or derivation. But understanding is not an act at all (although the phenomenon of sudden understanding makes it appear like one (cf. PI §§143 ff.)), and one does not typically understand a new or old sentence any *how*; either one understands it or one does not.

Given that understanding is akin to an ability, how should one understand the question as to its possibility? Is it a question about empirical causes and psychological or neurological underpinnings of our linguistic ability?[6] We can construe the question in various ways. It may

---

[6] If so, then invoking contextualism as part of the explanation of this ability gives it the status of an empirical hypothesis which must be verified or refuted. This in turn implies that there is *no* internal relation between understanding sentences and knowledge of structure—it is merely an empirical matter and only experiment will tell.

be a question about the structure of the *vehicle* of our linguistic ability; or it may be about the prerequisites for the possession of the ability.

Explanations of powers and abilities are characteristically given, in the advanced sciences, by specification of the physical structure of the vehicle of the ability (e.g. the brittleness of glass is explained by reference to (but not reduced to) its molecular structure). The vehicle of a person's understanding is the person's brain. Neurophysiology may, one day, give a specification of the neural structure of the cerebral cortex which will, in one sense, explain our ability to master language. But that kind of explanation is not the goal of the linguistic theorist, nor part of the task of philosophy.

If the question of how it is possible to understand new sentences is concerned with cognitive prerequisites, it may be psychological or logical. As a psychological question, it can be understood as a question about the mode of acquisition of the ability and the psychological or pedagogical prerequisites for its possession. This is philosophically irrelevant. If it is a logical question, it boils down to 'What are the general conceptual conditions for understanding new sentences?' This can be taken to be a question about what a person must typically know in order to understand new sentences. The general form of the answer to *this* is neither mysterious nor startling: one must know whatever is requisite to satisfy the criteria for understanding new sentences. For how else can it be shown that one *must* know a given item in order to understand an arbitrary sentence unless it can be shown that the manifestation of understanding is internally related to possession of such knowledge? But now, it seems, the question of the novelty of sentences is irrelevant. For the criteria for A's understanding 'p' are not different when 'p' is a new sentence from what they are when 'p' is familiar to A. (Indeed, we commonly do not know, when we judge that A understands 'p', whether it is novel or familiar.) However, there is no unique thing that a person must know in order to satisfy the criteria for understanding an arbitrary sentence. He must, indeed, use it correctly, react to it appropriately, explain it cogently. But there is no general mechanism for 'derivation' of correct use which is pertinent to the criteria of understanding, and there is no unique, privileged, form of explanation which requires any special knowledge in order that a person satisfy the criteria of understanding. In particular, no reason at all has ever been given why it is necessary that a person who understands well-formed sentences of a language should possess tacit knowledge of a theory of meaning for a language which, when 'discovered', will generate the meanings of all well-formed sentences from axioms and rules. We explain sentences, like words, in many different, but equally acceptable, ways. Structural explanation, in a very modest and thoroughly familiar sense, is only one form of explanation among others. It has no special privileges, and in many cases derivation from structure and constituents would not show understanding at all.

If contextualism, as commonly interpreted, is meant to be a profound insight into 'the possibility of understanding new sentences', it is evident that its role is grossly exaggerated and that the possibility it is meant to explain is but little understood.

Paradoxically, thus invoking contextual principles to explain the so-called 'generative' or 'creative' powers of language, and to explain how we can understand new sentences, diminishes the creativity of language and language-users. For the underlying picture is of a calculus of meaning-rules which, given an array of primitives, will churn out a potentially infinite set of meaningful sentences quite independently of us. It is as if our role is to set up the initial mechanism of definitions and rules, and thenceforth our creation soldiers on independently of us. We may not have anticipated twenty-seven-term relations, but the calculus of language will decide the matter for us. Evidently this picture is diametrically opposed to Wittgenstein's conception of the matter. Rules are not bits of invisible machinery whirring away in an ethereal medium. Our creative role does not terminate with the creation of rules and assignment of meaning to primitives. Nothing follows from a rule independently of our (collective) decision that such-and-such is in compliance with the rule, that *this* is to count as accord. Our rules do not create new meanings, our conventions do not dictate to us what has sense and what has not. We create new meanings, determine the limits of sense by what we do with our language. Grammar is a free creation of the human mind. It may seem to force our hand. But in fact nothing forces our hand except our own determination.

7. Wittgenstein's later affirmation of the contextual dictum

Beating about the bush suggests that our quarry is less significant than it first seemed. Wittgenstein's later affirmations of the dictum do not allude to its explanatory role *vis-à-vis* the 'creativity of language', nor do they connect the dictum with any notion of logical syntax. The claims made for the contextual dictum are important, but much more modest. The restatement of the dictum in the *Investigations* §49 clearly connects it with the notion of a minimal move in a language-game. Putting a chess piece on the board is not a move in chess. So too naming an object is not describing it, nor using the name to say anything.

Wittgenstein's point is surely similar to Bentham's:

By anything less than an entire proposition, no communication can have place. In language therefore the integer to be looked for is an entire proposition—that which logicians mean by the term logical proposition. Of this integer no one part of speech, not even that which is most significant, is anything more than a fragment; and in this respect, in the many worded appellative, part of speech, the word part is instructive. By it an intimation to look out for the integer of which it is a part may be considered as conveyed.[7]

Wittgenstein's later remarks here rest on a similar insight. The dictum is not repudiated, although exceptions to it are acknowledged. But it rests on quite different foundations from Frege's and ramifies in quite novel directions.

A sentence is, in general, the minimal unit by which a move is made in the language-game. It is only with sentences that we actually *say* anything. Understanding a sentence is knowing what it *says*, and understanding begins with the whole sentence (PG 44). There are no 'half propositions' (*Sätze*) — half a sentence (*Satz*), like a word, has a meaning only in the context of a whole sentence (BT 1). Half a proposition does not stand to a proposition as half a bread roll to a whole one, but as 'half a knight's move' to a knight's move.

A sentence is akin to a move in chess, and a move is only a move in the context of a game. So even a sentence has no meaning in isolation. Understanding a language is the background against which a sentence acquires meaning, as understanding chess is for a move. A sentence is a position in the 'game of language' (PG 172), hence to understand a sentence is to understand a language (BB 5, PI §199).[8] Thus interpreted, the contextual dictum is directly connected with *use*. It is connected with structure only in so far as structure reflects use, or alternatively only in so far as understanding, mastery of the use of a sentence, is shown in explanation of meaning by reference to structure. And that too is merely one form among others of explanations which constitute criteria of understanding sentences.

It is by using sentences that we perform acts of speech. If, by using a single word, we do make a move in the language-game, then that word thus used constitutes a sentence. What we said or did can be reported in indirect speech employing, e.g., a propositional clause (there are, to be sure, exceptions here, e.g. 'Hurrah!', 'Ow!'). Since we combine words to form many-worded sentences, mastery of the use of words is the very same as ability to use them in sentences. Both Frege and Wittgenstein use the contextual dictum to stress the internal relation between these abilities. But Wittgenstein's employment of the dictum differs from Frege's both in its rationale and in the consequences that can be drawn from it. What

---

[7] J. Bentham, *Works*, ed. Bowring (Tait, Edinburgh, 1843), Vol. VIII, p. 188.

[8] Wittgenstein is not committed to the absurd view that one cannot understand any part of language unless one understands every part. Language must be segmentable, otherwise neither learning nor teaching would be possible, the criteria for understanding any part of a language would coincide with the criteria for understanding the whole language, and the ability of which mastery of a language consists would not admit of gradation.

use a sentence has cannot be uniformly displayed as a function of the meanings of its constituent words and its structure. Hence, too, what sense, if any, a sentence has is not simply determined in this way.

> 'How do I know that the colour red can't be cut into bits?' That isn't a question either.
> I would like to say: 'I must *begin* with the distinction between sense and nonsense. Nothing is possible prior to that. I can't give it a foundation.'

> . . . if what gives a proposition sense is its agreement with grammatical rules then let's make just this rule, to permit the sentence 'red and green are both at this point at the same time'. Very well: but that doesn't fix the grammar of the expression. Further stipulations have yet to be made about how such a sentence is to be used; e.g. how it is to be verified. (PG 126 f.)

Many syntactically permissible structures are senseless because they lack any acceptable use. Nothing has been stipulated about the conditions under which it is correct to apply them. 'I feel the visual image to be two inches behind the bridge of my nose' or 'I feel in my hand that the water is three feet underground' (BB 9) are not syntactically awry. Is their nonsensicality attributable to the meanings of constituent words, i.e. that they do not *fit together* to yield a meaningful sentence? Such a claim invokes a mythical 'meaning-body' underpinning words (cf. Exg. §138), or is just a misleading way of saying that sentences lack sense.

This interpretation of Wittgenstein's later use of the dictum reveals how misleading it is to say that the meaning of a word consists in its contribution to the meaning of sentences in which it occurs and hence that knowing its meaning consists in knowing this contribution. It is easy to see why Fregeans think this. For the fundamental form of explanation of word-meaning, for Frege, is a specification of necessary and sufficient conditions for application. This is simply a relativization to words of a specification of the sense of sentences by means of truth-conditions. Hence, in Frege's view, explanation of word-meaning is explanation of the contribution of a word to determination of the truth-conditions of any sentence in which it may occur. But meaning is what is given by an explanation of meaning. Explanations of meaning are diverse, and explanation by necessary and sufficient conditions of application is only one kind. Many types of correct and, indeed, complete explanations do not consists of application rules and do not specify necessary and sufficient conditions. In what sense can we say of such explanations that they give the meaning of an expression by specifying its contribution to determination of truth-conditions of sentences? In what sense does 'This ↗ is red' do so? Similar considerations hold for explanations by example, by drawing an object, exemplifying an action, making an appropriate gesture, giving a locative explanation, etc. These explanations do give the meanings of their explicanda, but not by specifying any sentential role.

It might seem that this forces us back to the semantic atomist view that word-meaning is wholly independent of sentential role and hence that understanding a word has nothing to do with grasping its role in sentences, either because there is nothing else to grasp (if sentences are conceived as mere lists of names) or because there is something else *in addition* to its meaning to grasp. This is illusory. We must bear in mind the duality of criteria of understanding. It is here that understanding the meaning of a word and knowing its sentential role make contact. One kind of criterion of understanding is giving a correct explanation, the other is using the expression correctly. Since the sentence is the fundamental unit of *speech*, using a word correctly is typically using it in (or as) a sentence. Meaning is given by explanations of meaning; giving an explanation of meaning is a criterion of understanding, but so is correct use *in sentences*. Someone who understands the meaning of a word *can explain* it correctly and *can use* it correctly in sentences. For of a person who cannot do one or the other it would, *ceteris paribus*, be correct to say that he does not understand the word. Fregean contextualism is not the only alternative to semantic atomism.

This non–Fregean interpretation of the dictum makes it possible to budget for the many meaningful extra-sentential uses of words. Words are used to label, number, paginate, etc. But writing a number on the garden gate is not to use a sentence. Similarly, words used extra-sententially in greetings and farewells, in oaths and expletives, in expressions of joy ('Hurrah!') or contempt ('Boo!'). Yet, on the whole, such uses of words are not independent of their use in sentences. 'Sodium Chloride' on a container labels the contents, whereas 'Shake Well' does not. Numerals are used on pages, licences, houses, but these uses are not independent of their use in sentences. The dictum 'A word has a meaning only in the context of a sentence' must not be understood to imply that words thus used are meaningless because they are not sentences. But it is only with sentences (one- or many-worded) that we say anything, and the different extra-sentential uses of words to label or paginate or signify a place or indicate a name are related to differences in the corresponding sentential uses of the same words.

In Frege's philosophy, the contextual dictum was the focal point of various key principles in his theory of meaning. In theories of language that have been developed on Fregean foundations some of these principles (although not the dictum) have occupied the centre of the stage in calculus models of language. Contextualism thus conceived is the keystone of modern theories of meaning and understanding. Wittgenstein's criticisms of such pictures of language (only a small part of which have so far been examined) undermine contextualism as a general programme for an account of language, meaning and understanding. The contextual dictum, dethroned from its original august position, has a much more humble role in Wittgenstein's later philosophy of language. As in the calculus theories, the dictum emphasizes the internal relations between word-meaning and sentence-meaning, and between understanding words and understanding sentences. Yet unlike the calculus theories, Wittgenstein accounts for these internal relations not as consequences of structure, but in terms of use and the practices of a linguistic community.

IX

THE STANDARD METRE

1. *Introduction*

Although the standard metre is mentioned only in an analogy in the *Investigations* §50, an understanding of Wittgenstein's conception of linear measurement and the role of canonical samples in the practice of measurement is vitally important for various reasons.

(i) Samples used to define units of measurement have a definite, formalized role in our lives. This is extensively discussed by scientists and is roughly familiar to the well-educated. Consequently, such canonical samples provide illuminating comparisons in analysing the role of samples in less institutionalized practices.

(ii) Measurement is a family resemblance concept that raises philosophical problems. Wittgenstein stresses two: (a) Augustine's question 'How is it possible to measure time?'; (b) Einstein's question (and answer) 'How is it possible, given the Lorenz equations, to measure simultaneity of distant events?' (PLP 11 ff.). The dissolution of such problems provides, in Wittgenstein's view, a paradigm for the proper method of philosophizing, but it presupposes a grasp of the concept of measurement.

(iii) Measurement (especially linear) is one of Wittgenstein's favourite sources of analogies, but these illuminate only if measuring is correctly understood. (a) He compares the relation of measure to measured with the relation of proposition and what makes it true to dispel the illusion of an intermediary between proposition and fact (WWK 185). (b) The notion of a *Satzsystem*, and the associated explanation of colour exclusion rests on an analogy with rulers (WWK 63 f., 74; PR 75 ff., 110 ff.; PLP 57 ff.). (c) He likens a 'truth of mathematics' to a ruler and to a principle of conversion of different linear metrics, and its proof to the standard metre itself (RFM 167 f., 355 ff.).

(iv) In general, methods of measurement provide a fruitful special case to illuminate the thesis of the autonomy of grammar (BT 240 f.).

This essay aims to clarify some important aspects of the uses of samples in measurement.

2. *The rudiments of measurement*

Measuring things is a pervasive feature of our life. Learning to measure and weigh is part of elementary education. Measuring more recondite properties or measuring these properties more accurately is part of scientific evolution. The familiarity of the basic forms of measuring and the theory-laden subtleties of the advanced forms both make a surview of measurement difficult. We fail to notice the over-familiar and we wrongly extrapolate from the over-sophisticated.

We shall start by considering the most rudimentary form of linear measurement (we can think of it as a primitive language-game). The simplest case would be using an uncalibrated stick (let us call it a 'metre-stick') to decide whether or not something was exactly one metre long according to whether or not its ends coincide with those of the stick. If asked to explain what 'metre' meant, each person would simply point at his own stick and say 'That is one metre' (hence there may be many distinct concepts of length as stick-owners, although a Guiding Hand may make all the sticks coincide). Introduction of calibrating marks and standardization of samples are natural developments from this primitive game.

Wittgenstein notes important features of measuring that are present even in this rudimentary game.

(i) Measuring and calculating are distinct. Measuring the length of a pole is a simple experiment whose result would be formulated in a sentence (e.g. 'This is one metre long') that could be used as a paradigm of an empirical proposition. But someone could use the same sentence to say that his stick was one metre long. His ground for *this*, however, would not be an experiment, for he cannot lay his metre-stick beside itself to see if it is the same length as itself. His 'ground' would simply be that this object is his metre-stick, i.e. his standard of measurement. 'This is one metre long' thus used has a different meaning from its use to formulate the result of a measurement (experiment). Definition and experiment, *a fortiori* calculation and measurement, are mutually exclusive (LFM 104).[1]

(ii) The measure (metre-stick) has a normative role. It has a uniform use as a standard of comparison for other objects. In our imaginary language-game no provision is made for measuring (or calibrating) my metre-stick. It is always what measures, never what is measured; always what judges, never what is judged. Even in our more complex practice of measurement this normative role is apparent. The crucial point is that if A is being used to measure B, B cannot at the same time be used to measure A (RFM 199), i.e. that nothing can simultaneously both measure and be measured against the same thing. (The normative role of instruments of measurements is built into the etymology of our general normative vocabulary: 'norm', 'rule', 'canon', 'regulation'.)

---

[1] In complex measurements the distinction is less obvious. Measurement often includes calculation (e.g. conversion of yards into inches); we may weigh on scales or calculate weight from measuring volume; whether a procedure is a calculation or experiment is often context-dependent (RFM 95, 172).

(iii) Description of a practice of measurement must not only define the units of measurement and the instrument but also include specification of admissible methods of *comparing* objects with instruments of measurement. Even in our primitive case we must stipulate that an object is a metre long if its ends coincide with the ends of the metre-stick when the two are juxtaposed. In more complex cases the background understanding is more obviously necessary. The method of juxtaposition does not explain what it means to measure the distance between two stars ('If we imagine a series of rulers extending from one star to the other . . .' (RFM 146 f; LFM 273 f.) is a bogus explanation). For refined linear measurement even the method of juxtaposition must be qualified to take account of thermal expansion and gravitational distortion.

A caveat is necessary. To say that A is n metres long is not to describe it as having been measured in any special way. Neither statements of length nor definitions of units of measurement entail specifications of methods of comparison. But both presuppose a general practice of measuring. Indeed, no concept of length is independent of some practice of measuring length. Length, tautologically, is what is measured in measuring length. More perspicuously, knowing what it is to measure length is not a matter of knowing what length is and what it is to measure something (PI p. 225). Indeed, that misconception underlies Augustine's puzzle about time—as if measuring a time-interval must involve juxtaposition.

(iv) In our simple language-game each person's metre-stick has a dual role, as a sample to explain his unit of measurement, and as an object of comparison for measuring lengths. These two roles could be severed. We might, e.g., alter the grammar of 'one metre long' by laying down the transitivity of spatial coincidence, and then use any rod measured to be a metre long as a standard sample of the length one metre. (Now we would be using our metre-stick as a 'private' canonical sample for generating standard samples. So in addition to conventions for methods of measuring objects we would need conventions for comparing our metre-stick with our standard samples. These conventions need not coincide (e.g. in respect of thermal conditions).) If a unit of measurement is defined by such a (canonical) sample, this sample need not be used as a standard sample for applying the defined expression. Conversely, if something is used as a standard sample in applying an expression it *need* not also be used as a sample in defining the unit of measurement. (That depends on the *practice* of explaining the system.)

(v) A system of measurement exemplifies the autonomy of grammar. Samples (or recipes) used to define units of measurement can be characterized as useful or useless, but there is no question of truth or falsity in their choice and no possibility of getting into conflict with the truth by adopting a particular definition (LFM 55 f.; RFM 38 ff.). Using

the metre bar to define 'one metre' does not depend on the fact that the
bar is *really*, *ideally*, one metre long. The usefulness of a choice of unit (or
conversion principle, e.g. '60 seconds = 1 minute') does not depend on
the intrinsic nature of the sample, but on our purposes and the circumstances of its use. In altered conditions what we now consider useless (e.g.
rulers which are elastic or have a high coefficient of thermal expansion)
might prove useful (LFM 83; RFM 38 ff., 91) and vice versa (RFM 355 f.,
381 ff.).

Though the grammar of a method of measurement is 'grounded' in a
technique of measurement and also in the facts that make it possible and
useful, such 'grammatical propositions' reflecting the rules of this
grammar do not entail descriptions of this technique and these facts
(RFM 355). The definitions of units of measurement and principles for
conversion of units have the role of rules. This is liable to be overlooked.
First, many of the same sentences generally used to express rules can be
used also to make predictions. Secondly, empirical connections may
motivate adopting a rule, and the fact that cessation of certain regularities
would undermine the point of having a rule may be conflated with the
idea that the sentence expressing the rule asserts that these regularities
hold (LFM 292). Illusions pile up most strongly around 'external'
conversion principles, e.g. rules for translating metric measurements into
the imperial system ('1m = 39.37 in.', etc.). These seem to be synthetic *a
priori* truths, expressing real relations among the samples used to define
units in unrelated systems. Properly conceived, however, these principles
too are rules of grammar. They may originate in experiments, but using
them as conversion principles transforms the result of an experiment into
a rule (LFM 117 f.; RFM 6, 194). It is best conceived as the simultaneous
use of samples in different ways, e.g. the use of the standard metre also as
a sample of the length 39.37 in. (cf. LFM 118 f., RFM 30 f.).

3. The standard metre and canonical samples

The simple language-game of measuring we have described is seriously
defective. Each participant has his own standard, defines his concept of
metre by reference to it alone, and measures only by applying his
standard to the objects measured. The game is, as it were, 'atomistic'.
Even if an Invisible Hand had cut all measuring rods to the same
measure, assiduous tampering (like clipping of coinage) could disrupt the
pre-established harmony. For the game to have a serious point in a
complex society it must be standardized and institutionalized.

The obvious remedy is to establish an object (e.g. the monarch's rod)
as the authoritative (canonical) sample of a metre length. This was the
role of the standard metre in the Louvre (or imperial bar at Greenwich).

Introducing a canonical sample typically will not affect players' use of their rods both to measure and to define 'one metre'. But it will, in our game, render 'one metre' a shared, public concept. It will establish a criterion of correctness for ostensive definitions given by players by reference to their rods. No longer is each person's rod something he never measures but always uses to measure; now he may measure his rod against the canonical sample to judge its correctness as a standard sample. Now his ostensive definition by reference to his rod is correct only if his rod coincides in length with the canonical sample. Equally, his judgement that A is a metre long turns not only on A's coincidence in length with his measuring rod, but also on whether his rod coincides in length with the canonical metre. Thus canonical samples standardize common measuring instruments and provide a court of final appeal for resolving disagreements in definition and judgement. The canonical metre, however, is never something measured, but always what measures (typically, but not necessarily, it measures—calibrates—standard rods in general use).

It is important neither to exaggerate nor to underestimate the function of a canonical sample like the standard metre. We are prone to exaggerate its role if we think that 'One metre = Df. the length of the standard metre' is the only adequate definition of the term (superseding ostensive definitions). This is an illusion. Giving this definition is one *criterion* of understanding the term. Giving an ostensive definition is another, equally defeasible. Giving the verbal definition no more guarantees understanding than giving the latter. Both kinds of definition may fail to establish understanding if the person does not know how to apply the expression correctly. This illustrates three important points. First, a quite general feature of explanations (cf. 'Explanation', pp. 37 ff.): There may be multiple correct explanations for a given term. Secondly, equally generally, explanations do not apply themselves, hence giving a correct explanation does not guarantee ability to apply the defined term correctly; hence it is only a criterion, not a sufficient condition of understanding. Thirdly, to understand a unit of measurement one must have a general grasp of the practice of measuring things and the role of the canonical sample in the institution (RFM 167 f.). We might summarize these points by saying that knowing that one metre is the length of the standard metre is but one aspect of understanding the expression 'one metre long'.

We may equally underestimate the significance of the standard (canonical) metre. Most people who participate in the practice of metric measurements are ignorant of the role of the standard metre, and yet may correctly measure quite unproblematically. This makes it appear as if the function of the standard metre is an instance of 'action at a distance', i.e. something that drops out of a description of what is understood in understanding the metric system. This is illusory: the *practice* includes aspects of which the ordinary man is ignorant, e.g. procedures for calibrating metre-sticks. If asked whether his metre-stick was accurate he could not give a correct answer, i.e. the answer that is part of the practice. He has only an incomplete grasp of the normative role of ordinary metre-sticks, and hence only a partial understanding of the whole practice of metric measurement (although sufficient for most of his purposes). By speaking of degrees of understanding we can do justice to the idea that the standard metre does have a role in a (full) understanding of 'one metre'.

4. *At the mercy of samples*

If samples, which are objects with a special use, belong to our method of representation, then does not their vulnerability to fortune place logic at the mercy of the facts? While introducing canonical samples enables us to check the standard samples used in applying the term for which they are samples, it seems to put all our eggs in one basket. Would damage or destruction of the standard metre affect our practices of measurement?

There are two actual remedies to this threat. (i) We might multiply authoritative samples, giving each equal status, and preserve them in different places. (ii) More sophisticatedly, we may replace canonical samples by canonical recipes for generating samples (e.g. '1 metre = Df. 1,553, 164.13 wavelengths of the light in a particular line in the spectrum of cadmium', '1 kilogram = Df. the weight of one litre of pure water at maximum density'). This increases the accessibility of authoritative samples and seems to protect the system of measurement from annihilation, since a canonical recipe cannot be blown up. But both remedies undermine what they were designed to save. The (vulnerable) canonical sample was introduced to maximize harmony in a practice of measurement. Reducing the consequent vulnerability of the practice opens up fresh possibilities of disruption, since the multiplicity of authoritative samples or samples manufactured by recipe may well reintroduce disagreement in definition and judgement. So we remain at the mercy of samples.

This impasse results from misconceiving the uses of samples.

(1) *Any* system of measurement must be at the mercy of samples. In the simple language-game with metre-sticks each person is at the mercy of his own measuring rod. Introducing canonical samples or recipes does not change vulnerability to general facts of nature. Unless every definition of the length one metre were subject to a yet higher court of appeal, the system of metric measurement must at some point be at the mercy of fate. But, in a qualified sense, our fate is in our hands (see below).

(2) 'One metre = Df. the length of the standard metre' can be taken in two ways. (a) One metre is the length of the standard metre *whatever that may be*. This is absurd, since we would then have to surrender to whatever we found in Paris (which, if stretched, might be the length of a telephone pole). (b) One metre is the length which, as a matter of fact, the standard metre now has. But now we are not at the mercy of the sample at all. If the standard metre were stretched it would not *then* have the length it *now* has. More perspicuously, we *now* use the standard metre as a canonical sample, but we could cease to do so (physicists have!). The illusion of being at the mercy of samples is best exposed if we focus on the facts of how we *use* objects as samples rather than on reformulations of these facts in the guise of definitional equivalences.

(3) The meaning of 'one metre' depends on how we *do* use samples, not on how we might (or might not) use them in different conditions. Using the standard metre as a canonical sample constitutes one aspect of the use (meaning) of the expression 'one metre'. (Other rules for its use determine methods of comparing objects with samples in measuring.) However, if the definition 'one metre = the length of the standard metre' is correct, then it must, like any adequate definition, express a necessary truth or internal relation. But, unless the sentence is wrongly read as 'one metre = the length of the standard metre whatever it may be', it cannot express a necessary truth, because damaging the standard metre may alter its length. One might, therefore, conclude that neither the verbal nor the ostensive definition of 'one metre' by reference to the standard metre determines even a part of the meaning of 'one metre' or establishes an internal relation between the standard metre and the length one metre. All they do, it seems, is to 'fix the reference' of the expression 'one metre' by indicating an object (the standard metre) that contingently has the property of being one metre long.

There are two tactics in response to this challenge. (a) We may accept that definitions express necessary truths, but deny that the definition 'one metre = Df. the length which, as a matter of fact, the standard metre now has' fails to express a necessary truth. Surely the length of the standard metre would not be the length that it is if it were not *that* length (i.e. one metre)! This tautology, however, hardly disperses the metaphysical fog. (b) We may by-pass necessary truth and internal relations, and focus upon our use of samples in explanations.[2] We *do* explain 'one metre' by

---

[2] There are independent reasons for so doing. (i) The concept of necessity is philosophically contentious. (ii) What are the putative bearers of necessary truth? If sentence-types, then many are unclassifiable as necessary or contingent because their tokens may be used grammatically or descriptively (e.g. 'This is one metre long'). Is it then the statements expressed by sentence-tokens? This too is unclear. On one view of statement-identity the two sentences 'The litre of water in this beaker weighs one kilogram' and 'The water in this beaker [which happens to contain exactly one litre] weighs one kilogram', if uttered in the appropriate circumstances about the same water, express the same statement. But then the

means of samples, and we *do* acknowledge as correct its definition by reference to the standard metre. Such explanations have a role parallel to that of paradigmatic analytical definitions. Nothing constrains us to use any particular object as a sample for explaining 'one metre', nor can anything prevent us from so using it. Rather, no changes in the object or in its surroundings can prevent us from continuing to use it for this purpose, though, trivially, if it ceased to exist we could no longer use it as a paradigm (PI §50). If the standard metre were bent or compressed and we continued to define 'one metre' by reference to it, we would not get into conflict with 'the truth' (RFM 38), although we would get into conflict with our previous judgements and this explanation by reference to the altered paradigm would be far from useful given the uses to which we put measurement. On the other hand, if we were to cease to acknowledge explanations of 'one metre' by reference to the standard metre as being correct—*for whatever reason*—this expression would no longer have the meaning that it now has. (Note: meaning is what is explained in explanations of meaning.) The possibility of so altering the use we make of the standard metre no more demonstrates that 'one metre' cannot be defined by reference to this sample than the possibility that we might alter the meaning of 'three' shows that 'triangle' cannot be defined as a three-sided plane figure. The meaning of any term defined by reference to a sample depends only on the actual practice of using the sample. That homespun truth is rendered misleading and opaque if dressed up in metaphysical garb, e.g. as the statement that ostensive definition does not establish an internal relation between an expression and an object.

(4) Similarly, if we now use a canonical recipe to specify the unit length one metre, then our using samples generated by this recipe as authoritative standards confers on the expression 'one metre' part of its meaning. There is a similar objection to this position, viz. that it is not a necessary truth that correctly following the recipe always produces a uniform result. The proper response to this objection is exactly parallel with that to the previous one. The fact is simply that we do treat the products of a canonical recipe alike in using them as samples; that we cannot get into conflict with 'the truth' by doing so; and that, if we ceased to do so, for whatever reason, the meaning of the expression 'one metre' would differ from what it now is. The meaning of any term defined by reference to a

contrast between the grammatical use of the first and the non-grammatical use of the second cannot be accounted for by the claim that these sentences are used to make different statements, one necessary and one contingent.

It would be a serious misunderstanding to think that Wittgenstein denies that one can say that the standard metre is a metre long on the grounds that *that* is a necessary truth, and necessary truths are ineffable. Rather, he simply describes our practice without the mediation of philosophical dogmas.

canonical recipe depends only on the actual practice of using the recipe and the samples generated by it. Once again a metaphysical formulation of this point would be opaque and confusing, e.g. the statement that definition by a canonical recipe fails to establish an internal relation between an expression and each of a set of samples because it fails to guarantee the necessary identity of the generated samples in respect of the defined property.

Once these misconceptions are cleared away, it is apparent that we are not at the mercy of what we use as samples in explaining and applying expressions. Indeed, it would be better to say that objects are used as samples only on our sufferance, i.e. that their status as samples is at our mercy. Through no fault of its own, we may change the use of a sample or cease to use it as a sample at all. (This change might be motivated by a shift in our purposes or a refinement in methods for comparing objects with samples.) The standard metre, e.g., has been demoted from its former status as the canonical sample of the length one metre (and replaced by a canonical recipe), but not because it has suffered any damage. Samples are, in a sense, creatures of our will.

5. *Uses of samples and uses of sentences*

Wittgenstein notes various fallacies generated by the use of a sample, especially evident in the case of a canonical one; e.g. that it necessarily exists, that it necessarily has the property it is used to define, that these necessities are ineffable (cf. Exg. §§50, 58). What is misrepresented by these metaphysical claims is the fact that samples belong to the means of representation (cf. 'Ostensive definition and its ramifications', pp. 97 ff.). Wittgenstein agrees that the standard metre cannot be said to be or not to be one metre long, but interprets this as merely marking the special role of the standard metre in the institution of measurement (PI §50). Two separate issues are encapsulated here: the use of a sample and the use of a sentence ('The standard metre is a metre long'). To use sentences such as 'This is one metre', 'This length is one metre', 'This rod is one metre long', 'The length of this rod is one metre', to explain the term 'one metre' is not to describe the rod. This 'grammatical' use[3] of these sentences as ostensive definitions involves using the ostended rod *on that occasion* as a sample, not as something described; but it is independent of whether the sample is canonical, standard, or optional. A piece of string one metre long can, on one occasion, be used as a sample in an ostensive

---

[3] Wittgenstein sometimes talks of grammatical propositions (*Sätze*) and distinguishes them from genuine propositions (which must be bipolar). It is the *use* of sentences that determines whether they are 'grammatical' or genuine propositions, and different tokens of the same type-sentence may be differently used.

explanation, but on another it can be *described* by the (genuine) proposition 'This is one metre long'. In this respect the uses of samples and the
uses of sentences seem independent of each other. (Note the parallel with
explanation and ascription of colour predicates.)

Dependence, however, emerges when we consider canonical samples
in a general practice. In our primitive measuring game each participant
defined 'one metre' solely by reference to his own rod, i.e. it was *the*
sample for explaining *his* unit of measurement. Here the use of 'This is
one metre long' said when pointing at one's own stick cannot but be
grammatical. Hence, in this language-game, there is, relative to each
player, *one* thing of which *he* cannot say that it is, or is not, one metre
long. But relative to the whole group, there is nothing with this
privileged status, since nothing is used as a community-wide sample for a
shared concept of a metre. This indicates how to relate our use of the
standard metre as a canonical sample with uniformity in the use of the
sentence 'The standard metre is a metre long'. Our standard (canonical)
metre plays a role relative to everyone that parallels the role played in the
primitive game by each person's rod relative to himself alone. Hence in
our practice there is indeed *one* thing that cannot be said (described) to be
or not to be one metre long, viz. the standard metre. Just as the standard
(canonical) metre has a uniform use in that it is never something
measured but always used as a device to measure and calibrate other
things, so too the sentence 'The standard metre is a metre long' has a
uniform use as a 'grammatical' sentence. (Likewise 'That is one metre',
'The length of that is one metre', etc., uttered when pointing at the
standard metre could not but be grammatical, i.e. ostensive explanations.) This makes clear that claiming that the standard metre cannot be
described as being or not being one metre long is not to attribute to it an
extraordinary metaphysical property, but simply expresses the special
role that a certain platinum-iridium bar has in the institution of linear
metric measurement. Nothing prevents our modifying this institution by
altering the role of this object and giving the sentence 'The standard
metre is a metre long' a use as a description. The only impossibility lies in
simultaneously using the standard metre as a canonical sample and
describing it as measuring one metre in length. There is no such thing as
something which always measures and is never measured, but which is
also sometimes measured and found to be one metre long.

This correlation between uses of samples and of sentences does not
exhaust the possibilities. An object may have multiple uses as a sample
(e.g. samples of white and black used also to explain 'lighter (darker)
than'). The standard metre may be used as a canonical sample both for 'a
metre' and for '39.37 inches'. Such multiple uses of samples are correlated
with uniform uses of certain sentences as grammatical truths. In particular, the grammatical status of a conversion principle, e.g. '1 metre = 39.37

inches', reflects a double use of the standard metre as a canonical sample.

Given the canonical role of the standard metre, the sentence 'The standard metre is one metre long' has only a grammatical use. It functions (*inter alia*) as a rule 'justifying' the inference from 'X is the same length as (i.e. coincides in length with) the standard metre' to 'X is one metre long'. Consider the following pattern of argument:

> Y is the same length as X
> The length of X is one metre
> .˙. the length of Y is one metre

If 'X' is replaced by 'the standard metre', then the second premise drops out, and the inference is immediate.

The idea that we cannot say of the standard metre that it is or is not one metre long seems to generate a paradox. For, if this is correct, then we cannot say of it that it has a length. Surely it could not have a length that is neither the same as nor different from one metre! On the other hand, this consequence looks absurd. First, *every* rod has a length; *a fortiori*, the standard metre has a length. Secondly, if it had no length, then nothing could be described as being (or not being) one metre long because to say that X is one metre long is to say that the length of X is the same as the length of the standard metre. Thirdly, we might measure the standard metre with a trusty foot-rule and discover its length to be 39.37 inches; since it can be said to have a non-metric length, it can be said to have a length *tout court*. In this way we seem to face the Antinomy of the Standard Metre.

This paradox arises from our looking slightly askew at the use of samples and the use of the sentence incorporating the predicate 'has a length'. First, the sentence 'Every rod has a length' typically has a grammatical use (PI §251). This is obvious from considering how it would be verified, what grounds there are for asserting it, and how it might be used in arguments. It is not grounded in measuring objects, nor would it be refuted by any conceivable measurement of a rod. Secondly, the argument that nothing would have the length one metre unless the standard metre has a length rests on a mistaken conception of what it means to say that something is one metre long. If X and Y are each one metre long, then they have the same length, i.e. the length of X is identical with the length of Y. But it does not follow that to say that X and Y have the same length is to say that there is some length that they share, i.e. that the analysis of this statement must introduce quantification over lengths. Rather, to say that they have the same length can be represented by a primitive dyadic relation, viz. that X coincides with Y (when both are juxtaposed). Consequently, all that is required for concluding that X is one metre long is that X coincides with the standard metre. The inference is immediate, and hence does not depend on the 'premise' that the standard metre has a length. Thirdly, we are invited to think of a sentence of the form 'X has a length' as a logical consequence of our assertion of the form 'X is n metres long' or 'X is m inches long', i.e. as derived from a specification of a particular length by existential generalization. On this view, the form of 'X has a length' will depend on what constitutes a specification of the length of X; in particular, there will be as many logical forms disguised in the sentence-form 'X has a length' as there are logically different ways for answering the question 'What length?' Experiment (i.e. measuring) is the means for determining the correct specification of the length of a typical rod (e.g. a lid-prop for a harpsichord). But, in the case of the standard metre, the specification of its length as one metre is not arrived at by experiment, but by calculation (definition). Consequently, to say of the standard metre that it has a length is not to say of it what one says of a lid-prop in *saying* that *it* has a length. This reasoning could be circumvented only if it were possible to *measure* the standard metre. Whether this is so depends on whether there is any system of linear measurement in which it does not play the role of a canonical sample. If so, it could then be said to have a (non-metric) length, but not a metric one. Clarity would be better served, however, by simply describing the different role of the object in the two systems of measurement.

We do ask such questions as 'How long is the standard metre?' or 'What is the length of the standard metre?' These are used as requests for explanations of the expression 'one metre', and typical answers would be '39.37 inches long' or 'A bit more than a yard long' or 'This long' (pointing at a suitable object). Is thus specifying the length of the standard metre conceding that it has a length? How we answer this question does not matter as long as we acknowledge that in explaining the expression 'one metre' in these ways we are not *describing* the standard metre and hence not saying that it has a particular length.

6. *Conclusion*

The question of whether or not the standard metre can be said to be a metre long seems scarcely to merit a lengthy discussion. Wittgenstein's comment in §50 seems merely an aside. This appearance is deceptive. Philosophical illusions surround ostensive definition and the uses of samples in explaining and applying expressions. These cluster most densely around the use of canonical samples in systems of measurement. Consequently, Wittgenstein's remarks about the standard metre are a test-case for one's grasp of his conception of the role of samples. If one cannot bring sharply into focus his understanding of the sentence 'The standard metre is one metre long', one has missed the point of his important remarks on ostensive definitions and the uses of samples. And if these are correct, a misconception about the standard metre condenses into a drop of grammar a whole cloud of confusion.

X

FAMILY RESEMBLANCE

1. *Introduction*

The notion of family resemblance is both one of the ideas most commonly associated with Wittgenstein and one of the most widely used tools of contemporary philosophers. It is put to work in ways undreamt of by its creator and for purposes which he would probably have criticized. It is important to see it aright in the context of the *Investigations*.

The celebrity of family resemblance is itself surprising. The idea that some words are applied on the basis of overlapping resemblances, not of common properties, is already present in the writings of familiar philosophers (e.g. Whewell, Mill, Nietzsche, and James). Is Wittgenstein's exposition simply more arresting? Some of these earlier discussions occur in the context of a general consideration of using words to classify things and hence imply generalizations about explaining and applying general words. By contrast, the ostensible purpose of Wittgenstein's discussion is negative; it is to criticize the dogma that every general term *must* be applied on the basis of properties common to everything that falls under it. Although this dogma is a cornerstone of the conception of analysis in the *Tractatus* and hence one of the cardinal sins of his youth, why should Wittgenstein's later criticism of it exercise such a general fascination?

The answer to these puzzles is, perhaps, that the metaphor of family resemblance applied to concepts is a forceful challenge to one of the main ingredients of the pervasive Augustinian picture, and that its significance is a measure of unconscious commitment to this *Urbild*. But the danger of separating Wittgenstein's account from the context of an explicit criticism of the Augustinian picture is that one may replace the venerable idol of *Merkmal*-definition by the new idol of explanation by overlapping similarities among paradigms; one might think that here is the foundation for constructing a 'new theory of universals'.

2. *Background*

There is a long tradition of conceiving definitions as analyses. They dissolve concepts into their constituents; they have the role of solvents in the chemistry of concepts. This idea is so venerable and widespread that it is aptly called the classical or orthodox conception of definition (EMD 211; CO 32). The conception is so ingrained in our thinking that it does not even strike us as metaphorical. 'A definition breaks down a complex idea into its constituents, i.e. the ideas that are parts of and together make up the defined idea'—this seems a literal description of something familiar.

According to this conception, definitions have only a heuristic role. They are the verbal counterparts of analyses or syntheses of ideas, perhaps useful in teaching language, in exposing hidden implications, or in compressing complicated thoughts. They are, however, *logically* superfluous. They introduce abbreviations for complex ideas. In principle, these can always be eliminated. Any sentence is logically equivalent to some sentence which is derived from it by substitution of definientia for definienda.

This dovetails with the Augustinian picture of language. Just as any physical object is compounded out of chemical substances, so any thought is put together out of simpler ideas. This is made visible in the analysis of the sentence expressing it, but is typically hidden in its usual verbal formulations. It is natural to limit the application of the Augustinian picture to analysed sentences.

The analogy between definition and chemical analysis can be, and often is, extended in various directions.

(i) Chemical analysis comes to an end in atoms or elements that cannot be further decomposed (at least chemically). It is natural to think that the analysis of concepts must similarly terminate in simple ideas, in what is unanalysable and hence indefinable, i.e., the atoms or elements of thought and language. Every sentence has a unique complete analysis, i.e. a sentence logically equivalent to it which is derived from it by successive substitution of definientia for definienda until every expression stands for a simple idea. The fully analysed sentence would strictly conform to the Augustinian picture.

(ii) Given a familiar object, we know that it must be compounded out of the familiar chemical elements; or at least this is an accepted working assumption. The parallel idea is familiar, e.g. in British empiricism. We are thought typically to have the full range of simple ideas, and we know in advance of carrying out an analysis of any given idea that it must be compounded somehow out of these basic building blocks. Any failure to analyse our idea into its simple constituents must be ascribed to limitations of our abilities.

(iii) Chemical analysis yields the elements out of which any substance or stuff (e.g. water) is compounded, but equally those out of which any particular object (e.g. a metal bar) is compounded. It seems to be simultaneously an analysis of individual things and of kinds of stuff (conflated with kinds of things). The analysis of concepts is often conceived to be parallel. It reveals both the constituents of concepts or ideas and the ingredients of particulars or individuals; the property of rigidity is both a logical part of the concept of a beam and ingredient of any object that is a beam. According to this conception, the search for definitions is the search for those ingredients of everything falling under a concept that makes things fall under this concept. We can in thought (viz. by abstraction) isolate the pure substance that is common to whatever falls under a concept and then analyse this into its constituent elements. Concept-words name such pure substances, themselves readily conceived of as ideal particulars perfectly (i.e. without adulteration) exemplifying the properties that they embody.

Many philosophers have adhered to the conception of analysis and regarded this conceptual chemistry as the primary business of philosophy. Indeed, philosophy is often considered to be nothing but conceptual analysis. Wittgenstein notes and criticizes this conception in Plato's dialogues: to know what justice is is identified with being able to give a definition of justice, analysing the concept into its essential parts, while every other form of explanation is rejected as worthless (PPI §67; PG 120 f.; BB 20; TS. 302, 14). But most important, Frege, Russell, and the author of the *Tractatus* were all imbued with the idea that explanation of concepts must take the form of analysis. This is the essential background of Wittgenstein's criticisms (PI §§65 ff.).

Frege demanded of the definition of a concept-word that it specify conditions necessary and sufficient for its correct application. He focused upon *Merkmal*-definitions, although he recognized other ways of meeting this demand.[1] Since nothing turns on this distinction for present purposes, we, like Wittgenstein, disregard this complication. Definition is logical analysis (*logische Zerlegung* (FC 32)) into *Merkmale* that are the logical constituents (*logische Teile* (FG 35)) together making up the defined concept (FA §53). Just as chemistry analyses all substances into unanalysable elements, so logical analysis, if pursued, ends in what is logically simple and hence indefinable (CO 42 f.; FC 32), i.e. in the ultimate building-blocks of thought (FG 143). No definition of a name for what is logically simple is possible; such a term can be given only an explanation (*Erklärung*) or elucidation (*Erläuterung*) which hints at what is meant (FC 32; CO 42 f.), but which, unlike a definition, is not part of a scientific language (e.g. a formalization of geometry). Frege distinguishes sharply between the logical constituents of a concept (*Merkmale*) and its properties (*Eigenschaften*) (CO 51; FA §53; FG 4); although the properties of a concept may sometimes be inferred from *Merkmale* just as the durability of a building may be inferred from the type of stone used, its properties are not ingredients of it (FA §53). Unless a concept is one of the ultimate building-blocks of thought, it must be analysable into its *Merkmale*.

[1] E.g. for analyzing 'prime number', 'continuity', etc., although he often conceived of these too as analyses into *Merkmale* (cf. FA §§49, 53, 104; CO 51).

Russell conceived logical analysis to be the essence of philosophy.[2] He aimed to give the greatest possible analysis of ideas into their constituent ideas and so to reduce to a minimum the number of simple, unanalysable, 'primitive' ideas necessary in giving a logical reconstruction of what we know (PrM 27; PM i. 1). Analysis has the form of definitions; these give symbolic abbreviations for complex ideas constructed out of the primitive ideas and therefore are theoretically superfluous (PrM 429). Where analysis comes to an end, its residue is 'indefinables' or logical atoms (PrM xv; LA 179). Although no definition of these is possible, they can be *explained* by descriptions pointing out what is meant (PM i. 91). But these will be successful only for somebody who has direct apprehension of the relevant simple ideas by being acquainted with them (PrM xv). Russell subscribed to the empiricist doctrine that experience is the foundation of understanding. Hence he thought that 'logical experience' was presupposed in grasping the indefinables of logic.

Although the *Tractatus* did not discuss *Merkmal*-analysis, it clearly regarded this as a primary means for carrying out the complete analysis of a proposition into a truth-function of elementary propositions each of which contained only names. Names, and their metaphysical counterparts the simple objects, are the necessary residue of analysis, like Russell's logical atoms. Names cannot be defined, yet they can be explained (*erklärt*) by means of elucidations (*Erläuterungen*) (TLP 3.263). But these can be understood only if the meanings of the names (i.e. the objects named (TLP 3.203)) are already known (TLP 3.263). This seems very close to Russell's conception that acquaintance is necessary to understanding indefinables. Wittgenstein later accused himself of having held in the *Tractatus* that properties are ingredients of the objects that have them; e.g. that a red circle is composed of redness and circularity (PG 200 f.; cf. BB 17).

Although Frege, Russell, and the early Wittgenstein all conceived of definition as analysis and subscribed to correlative doctrines about indefinables and the distinction of definitions from explanations, there is a certain ambiguity about their attitudes towards the doctrine that everything falling under any particular concept shares common properties. Is the thesis that everything to which any single concept-word is applicable *must* have common properties? Or is it rather that everything *does*? Or that everything *should* (e.g. in a language fit for scientific purposes)?

The thesis that everything to which a concept-word applies *must* have common properties seems very naïve. First, it is not compatible with simple ambiguity. (This might be avoided by distinguishing among different senses of concept-words (or different concepts) and relativizing

[2] Russell, 'Theory of Knowledge', p. 188. His conception is close to Moore's; cf. Moore, *Principia Ethica*, §§7–10.

the thesis to them.) Secondly, it is not necessary for understanding a concept-word to be able to give a *Merkmal*-definition of it; hence it *seems* unnecessary to know the common properties of things in its extension in order to know its meaning. (This might be circumvented by asserting that understanding transcends explanations or by attributing knowledge of common properties simply on the grounds of the ability to recognize to what objects a concept-word can be applied.) Thirdly, it is unclear why there must be common properties. Would the concept-word otherwise be useless? Would it be useless if it were explained otherwise than by a *Merkmal*-definition? Although naïve, this thesis can plausibly be attributed to Plato, as Wittgenstein seems to do (C 8, 75; PPI §67). There is, in addition, a more sophisticated version of it that he later claimed underlay the concept of analysis in the *Tractatus* (BT 253; PI §81). This makes use of the notion that understanding or meaning something by an expression must consist of using it according to a definite rule. Hence, whether or not I can explain an expression, the fact that I mean to say something definite by using it proves that there is some general rule according to which I am using it, and this in turn presupposes that there is a general characterization of the objects to which a concept-word is applicable when it is used as I mean it, i.e. that these objects must have something in common. My explanations of a concept-word need not mention such common properties, but that merely shows that my understanding transcends my ability to explain. At the deep level of what I mean and understand by expressions, everything that falls under a concept-word as I understand it on a particular occasion must have common properties. (This strategy is developed and criticized in PI §§75–88.)

We might retreat from this position by conceding that what falls under a concept-word *need not* and often *does not* show common properties. Many words are in fact used without definite fixed meanings, and hence search for a *Merkmal*-definition of them is doomed to failure. However, such a language seems unfit for rigorous thought. What a given concept-word applies to *should* have common properties, and if these objects do not, then using this concept-word is an abuse of language. This conception is characteristic of the British empiricists and of Frege; it is quite explicit in the writings of Mill[3] and Russell.[4] A very few philosophers have gone even further and challenged the idea that everything falling under a concept-word *should* have common properties

---

[3] Mill emphasizes that language grows, as it were, organically. He particularly notes the importance of resemblances in the gradual widening of a term's extension, and he cites an analysis given by Dugald Stewart of ordinary concepts whose extensions are connected by different overlapping similarities via a series of intermediate links. Cf. J. S. Mill, *A System of Logic*, I,i,5, I,vii.7, IV,iv.2, IV,iv.5.

[4] Cf. PP 7, OK 208 ff.

if the term is fit for scientific purposes. One is William James.[5] He argues that a serious study of religion or government is more apt to be impeded and distorted than assisted by an initial search for a definition to exhibit the essence of the phenomena. That strategy promotes oversimplification and dogmatism. The legitimate use of definitions in such cases is simply to demarcate the scope of a particular inquiry. Whewell[6] earlier gave a much fuller elaboration of similar ideas in discussing the use of classifications in science. He emphasized that classifications in natural history depend on our purposes, especially on that of framing fruitful generalizations. It is fallacious to suppose that scientific purposes demand that natural classes be defined by essential characteristics. Indeed, examination of developed branches of natural history reveals the successful use of classes determined by resemblance to paradigms ('types'). These serve the purpose of generalization; indeed, they may do so better than terms introduced by stipulating defining characteristics.

Against this background, Wittgenstein's account of family resemblance would stand out only to the extent that it criticized the demand for *Merkmal*-definitions of concept-words deployed in a language fit for 'scientific' purposes. Although this is an element of his account, it hardly seems the dominant one. Much more apparent is his hostility to the idea that there *must* be properties common to whatever a concept-word applies to—both in its naïve Platonic form (PI §66; PPI §67; TS. 302, 14) and in its sophisticated form (PI §81; BT 253). Surprisingly, he shows no special eagerness to combat the idea that *Merkmal*-definitions are necessary in science (PLP 93 f., 183).

3. *Family resemblance: a minimalist interpretation*

The *locus classicus* of the elucidation of the notion of family resemblance is the *Investigations* §§65–71. The notion is introduced and clarified primarily with reference to the concept of a game. (In virtue of the analogy between language and games, this tactic provides indirect support for the thesis that the concept of language is a family resemblance concept (§65).) The salient points of Wittgenstein's account are well known.

(i) The activities called 'games' have no common properties in virtue of which we apply the same word to them all (§65). If we look carefully at various games, we see that the dogma is false that they *must* have something in common (§66).

(ii) Consequently, there is no correct *Merkmal*-definition of 'game' (cf.

---

[5] W. James, *The Varieties of Religious Experience* (Longman, London, 1902), Ch. II *ab init.*
[6] W. Whewell, *The Philosophy of the Inductive Sciences*, 2nd edition (Parker, London, 1847), Vol. I., pp. 466–99.

§§68–9). Any suggested definition would agree only in part with the actual use of 'game' (PLP 180).

(iii) Consequently, too, the ability to give a *Merkmal*-definition of a word is not a necessary condition of understanding it (§70; PPI §67). If games have no common properties, it is impossible so to define 'game' and hence nobody has the ability so to define it (TS. 302, 14); but it does not follow that nobody can understand or explain 'game' (cf. §§69, 75).

(iv) What makes the various activities called 'games' into games is a complicated network of similarities, a large number of relationships between these different activities (§66). Such a concept resembles a long rope twisted together out of many shorter fibres (§67). It is held together by the overlapping of many similarities, similarities 'in the large' and 'in the small' (cf. Exg. §66).

(v) The expression 'family resemblance',[7] when applied to such concepts, invokes a metaphor (§67). The network of overlapping similarities constituting the concept of a game is compared with the various resemblances that hold between members of a family. These may be of very different kinds: resemblance in build, facial features, colour of eyes or hair, gait, temperament, manner of speaking, attitude, or manners. In specifying respects of resemblance between people recognizably of the same family, we do speak of such things as the Churchillian manner or Hapsburg chin. Although we can make such respects of resemblance precise, it is not in virtue of their all having some set of common properties that we group together members of an extended family; no property is sufficient for membership in the group, nor is any one necessary. This is what makes the metaphor of family resemblance so illuminating when applied to such concepts as that of a game.

(vi) The explanation of what a game is primarily consists of giving examples (§71), i.e. of describing games (§69). To these examples there *may* be coupled a similarity-clause: 'These and similar things are called "games"' (§69). Or, perhaps, a discussion of how other sorts of games can be constructed on analogy with these, or a specification of certain activities that would not be included among games (§75). The crucial point is that the examples used to explain 'game' are meant to be taken and used in a particular way, viz. as paradigmatic examples (§71). They are, as it were, 'centres of variation' (EPB 190). Somebody, e.g., who took them as an exhaustive list of (possible) games would not understand the explanation correctly. *Multiplicity* of examples seems an important feature of explaining such a concept.

(vii) Consequently, 'game' can be *explained* though it cannot be given a

Merkmal-definition (cf. §75). It is a fallacy to think that an indefinable expression cannot be explained.

(viii) The adducing of relevant similarities justifies applications of 'game', since it is on account of the relationships among games, especially on account of those between activities and the paradigmatic examples of games, that we correctly call games 'games' (cf. §65). Presence of similarities justifies us in using the same word for all these activities; we call something 'a game' because it is very similar to other activities that are properly called 'games' (cf. §67).

(ix) Games from a *single* family (§67). What holds them together and gives them a unity is the overlapping of the many similarities among games. In view of this unity, it is appropriate to speak of *the* concept of a game, *the* concept of number, etc. (§§68, 70).

(x) The concept of a game has no sharp boundaries (§§69, 71, cf. §68). Since it is not explained by a *Merkmal*-definition, there is no rigid, precise circumscription of its extension. Instead, the explanation is by paradigms; and even if it includes a similarity-clause, it does not specify the range or degree of similarities with the paradigms required for an activity to fall under the concept of a game (cf. BT 68, PG 117). Explanations by examples are comparable to indicating a place by pointing, not to demarcating it by drawing a boundary (§71; PG 118).

(xi) For special purposes we can draw boundaries around the concept of a game (§§68 f.). But whether we should draw it here or there depends only on what facilitates achieving these purposes.

From the text it is obvious that the main thrust of this whole discussion is negative or critical. Wittgenstein's aim is to dethrone a prevalent picture shaping philosophical reflection on the meaning of concept-words. His quarry is the dogma that there must be something common to everything to which any concept-word is applicable. We are, he thinks, so much in the grip of this dogma that we must repeatedly be exhorted to look and see for ourselves whether it correctly describes what we know about the use and explanation of concept-words. The demand for *Merkmal*-definitions, and the associated denigration of other forms of explanation, have no justification. The utility of a concept-word in no way depends on the possibility of so defining it.

Although predominantly negative, the remarks on family resemblance might be thought not to be purely negative and anti-dogmatic. Does Wittgenstein not propose some new dogmas in place of the old?

(i) He affirms that games have *no* common properties, even suggesting that we can *see* that they have none (§§65 f.). But how could we prove this, let alone see it? Wittgenstein here advances an unnecessarily strong statement: to disprove the assertion that there *must* be common properties, it is sufficient to establish that here *need not* be any, and that is a weaker claim than that there *are* none. Most parallel passages are more circumspect, arguing for this weaker thesis (BB 86 f.; IMT 237; PG 75 f.; PLP 180 ff.; but cf. TS. 302, 14). The essential points are that we know of no properties common to all games; that we do not explain 'game' by enumerating *Merkmale* of games; and that even if we were to discover a property common to all games, it would not reveal part of our concept of a game because it would not belong to our (present) practice of explaining 'game'.

(ii) He implies that the similarities among games justify calling games 'games' and that the absence of relevant similarities would justify refusing to call an activity 'a game'. But must there always be grounds for applying or witholding the term 'game'? Even if there are, must these always be similarities? One might (erroneously) think that different blue things have nothing in common with each other, but that the whole range of blue things is connected by similarities; could this conception not be combined with the (correct) idea that there are no grounds for calling an object 'blue'? Further, the metaphor of family resemblance itself suggests that grounds for witholding a family resemblance concept may be something other than absence of similarities; although most of the characteristic features of a particular family may be present in a marked degree in a particular person, he may none the less not be a member of the family, and that judgement rests simply on his lineage. These matters require fuller scrutiny. But nothing would seem to be lost if Wittgenstein were simply to retreat to the negative thesis that games (languages, numbers, etc.) have no one thing in common in virtue of which we use the same word for all (§65).

(iii) The alleged unity of a family resemblance concept seems equally precarious. What are the criteria of identity for a 'family'? What does it mean to affirm that games form *one* family, not several? And how could judgement about the unity of the concept be affected by possible multiplicity of explanations of 'game', e.g. by different sets of para-digms? Wittgenstein's purposes would be equally well served and these awkward questions avoided if he were simply to claim that the fact that 'game' is explained by paradigms is itself not a cogent reason for arguing that there is not a single concept of a game.

(iv) Wittgenstein asserts that family resemblance concepts have no sharp boundaries. Does this mean that there must be borderline cases or disputes about their applicability? Does peace among mathematicians about applying 'number' disprove that numbers form a family? These conclusions would not be warranted. Wittgenstein does not argue that family resemblance concepts are in any way less useful than ones introduced by *Merkmal*-definitions; in particular, he does not think them to be vague or 'essentially contested'. Their lack of sharp boundaries is nothing other than a reflection of their not having *Merkmal*-definitions. Terms defined by *Merkmale* are not proof against disputed applications

(PLP 180, cf. PI §87), nor are terms otherwise explained especially susceptible to them.

Even when given the most minimal interpretation, the remarks on family resemblance are a sweeping challenge to the orthodox conception of definition as analysis. In addition, they criticize the associated conceptions of what it is to explain concept-words, to justify or criticize their applications, and to understand them. In particular, Wittgenstein implies the following points.

(i) Different explanations of a single concept-word may be legitimate; a single concept may correspond to explanations by different sets of paradigms.

(ii) The justifications for subsuming different objects under a single concept need not be uniform; different similarities or similarities with different paradigms may be appealed to in justifying different applications of 'game', 'number', etc.

(iii) Assigning meanings to concept-words, hence the classification of things as falling under concepts, can be justified or criticized only in respect of usefulness in facilitating achievement of the purposes for which we use these words. Things are not given to us ranged into natural kinds whose boundaries are fixed by congeries of metaphysically simple properties. Hence our classifications cannot get into conflict with the truth, though they may be more or less expedient.

4. Sapping the defences of orthodoxy

Various strategies in defence of orthodoxy can be deployed. Wittgenstein surveys and undermines these in §§65–88.

The first strategy is straightforward: it assumes that a parallelism exists between the properties of concepts and our explanations and understanding of them, and then it challenges the cogency of Wittgenstein's criticisms. This may take a number of forms.

(i) Games (numbers, etc.) do share common properties, but these have the peculiarity of being disjunctive (§67(c)).

(ii) Such a concept is legitimate because it is a truth-function (e.g. a logical sum) of sub-concepts each of which has a *Merkmal*-analysis (§68). (This involves a slight liberalization of the dogma that whatever falls under a concept-word must share common properties.)

(iii) 'Game' is ambiguous; there is no single concept of a game, but rather a number of different closely related concepts each of which is determined by a *Merkmal*-definition (cf. §§67(a), 69, 77).

(iv) The concept of a game is itself a simple concept. Games have in common the property of being games, just as blue things share the common property of being blue. What §66 shows is that they have nothing *else* in common, i.e. that the property of being a game is unanalysable (cf. §72, PG 118).

(v) There is no such thing as the concept of a game, i.e. no such thing as a concept without a *Merkmal*-analysis (without sharp boundaries) (§71). The word 'game' is useless or has no agreed use.

(vi) The concept of a game is a 'cluster concept'. There is a complex definition of 'game'. The full explanation of 'game' by reference to paradigms must specify not only a set of paradigms, but also a set of respects of resemblance, perhaps differentially weighted, which are relevant for determining whether an activity is a game. Accordingly, the predicate 'ξ is a game' may be defined by stipulating that it is true of X provided that the sum of the weights of the respects in which it resembles some one (or perhaps any) of the paradigms exceeds a particular threshold-value.

Wittgenstein's moves against these positions are mostly obvious in the text, except for (iv) and (vi). Clearly he would argue that (iv), like (i), distorts the concept of a common property. The objection to (vi) would be simply that such a calculus of thresholds and weights is *not* part of our explanation of 'game', and hence not a part of what we understand given the assumption of parallelism between explanation and understanding.

The second line of defence is constructed on a repudiation of this assumption of parallelism: our understanding of a concept-word may go somewhat beyond our explanations of it, and therefore inability to define it does not prove that the objects falling under it do not share common properties. This too may take several forms.

(i) An explanation of 'game' by examples is an indirect means or a vehicle for conveying to another knowledge of the common properties that make activities into games. These properties are not expressed or put into words, but someone who understands 'game' as a result of the explanation must see what the examples have in common (§§71 f.).

(ii) An explanation by examples is successful only if the learner acquires from it a mental image of what is common to all the examples; only if he has such a 'sample in his mind' can he apply the concept-word to fresh instances (§73).

(iii) An explanation by examples succeeds only if the learner sees the examples in a particular way: e.g. only if he sees the paradigmatic games as examples of games, and therefore can employ them as standards for determining whether other activities are games. A particular experience in conjuction with the examples is essential to achieve understanding from an explanation by examples (§74, cf. §§34 f.).

Each of these arguments treats explanations by examples as the basis for understanding, but each in a different way supplements the explanations to arrive at the content of our understanding. Wittgenstein's objections are explicit in §§71–4.

The outermost line of defence drops the assumption that there is any relation between explanations and the content of understanding. An explanation of 'game' by examples has nothing to do with knowing what a game is. Understanding 'game' consists in using the word according to certain definite rules hidden away in the medium of the mind, and there is no reason to suppose that these must be related in any way to what we say when asked to explain what 'game' means. Indeed, divergence is shown by the fact that what we mean and understand by 'game' is something definite, whereas what we say in explaining 'game' gives the concept no sharp boundaries. The system of hidden meaning–rules operated unbeknownst to us by our minds must be *rules*, i.e. perfectly general specifications of the circumstances in which words are to be used. Within this limitation, the rules may have a variety of forms: the specification of *Merkmale* of concepts, the construction of the concept out of sub-concepts by means of truth-functions, or the calculus of weighted degrees of resemblance and thresholds distinctive of 'cluster concepts'. The crucial point is that mental operations are essential to meaning and they conform to the orthodox conception of the meaning of concept-words. Explanations do not so conform, but that merely shows the gap separating them from the content of understanding.

Wittgenstein's immediate moves against this position (which he sees as characteristic of the *Tractatus* (BT 253)) are developed in §§75–87. They are, however, only provisional (§81). A definitive response would presuppose a correct conception of what it is to understand or mean something, and, in particular, of how understanding is related to explanation. There are only hints about this (especially in §§69, 75), to be developed later (§§143 ff.). (Cf. 'Explanation', pp. 42 ff., and 'Meaning and understanding', pp. 361 ff.)

There are still two lines of retreat open to the defenders of orthodoxy. The first would be to drop the assumption that existence or non-existence of common properties among things falling under a concept-word is any way related to what it is to understand such a word. Could one not concede that understanding 'game' does not presuppose that games have something in common, but that none the less games *must* have something in common? Why should that issue turn solely on what is involved in understanding 'game' (let alone on how 'game' is explained)? The second retreat would be to object that a concept-word not susceptible to a *Merkmal*-definition is not fit for use in science or other serious inquiries into truth. Could one not call it 'inexact' or even 'defective'?

In Wittgenstein's view, the first retreat is futile. Whether the objects falling under a concept share common properties is only of any philosophical interest on the assumption that this question bears on our understanding of concept-words. Once that assumption is dropped, there is nothing worth discussing. The second line of retreat Wittgenstein cuts off in a coda (§88). He criticizes its notion of what is perfect or ideal as very primitive and incapable of coherent elaboration (cf. Exg. §§88, 130).

Though usually regarded as a scattering of aperçus, §§65–88 set out an argument which is both complex and systematic. Wittgenstein's campaign is designed to make surrender the only viable option with respect to the picture of definition as analysis.

5. *Problems about family resemblance concepts*

If the concept of family resemblance is seen as a new tool of philosophical analysis, there are many questions that arise about how to employ it. Philosophers have been quick to raise them, and most have found Wittgenstein's answers either non-existent or inadequate. But since the concept is introduced for a purely negative purpose, and since all of Wittgenstein's own applications of it are particularizations of a general critical argument, there is no need for him to give a general account of how to use the concept and no fault in his having failed to do so. The questions traditionally raised about his account arise only once the notion is used for purposes different from his. None the less, much can be learned from clarifying why these issues do not arise from his point of view.

(i) *Bounds*: how are the lines of demarcation to be drawn between family resemblance concepts and other kinds? What feature is it that makes a concept into a family resemblance concept? Wittgenstein leaves these matters unclarified.

Family resemblance concepts are associated with a characteristic form of explanation of meaning: the specification of a set of paradigms. But even the boundaries of this form of explanation are unclear. Wittgenstein's explanations of 'game' and 'number' specify *types* of entity as paradigms; e.g. type-activities like 'chess' and 'football' or types of numbers like rationals or reals. But what if the paradigms were particular or concrete? We might explain 'game' by pointing to a number of token-activities (particular games of chess, football, patience, etc.), perhaps adding that things like these are called 'games'; or we might explain 'number' by citing paradigms such as 2, -1, $\sqrt{2}$, $2+i$, and $\sqrt{2}+3i-j-2k$. Would these count as explanations of the same form? If so, this form of explanation would overlap with explanations by sample and ostensive definitions. Or again, what of a species-name explained by reference to a single museum specimen? Or a genus-name explained by reference to a single typical species? And what if we supplemented an explanation of either kind with a specification of relevant respects of resemblance? Should multiplicity of paradigms be treated as a necessary

condition for our explanation to have the form exemplified by explanations of family resemblance concepts? Or as a sufficient condition? Does
an explanation of 'red' by multiple samples or an explanation of natural
number by saying '0, 1, 2, 3 and so on are natural numbers' have the same
form as the explanation by multiple paradigms? It would seem better to
treat explanations by paradigms as themselves constituting a family. In the
absence of some special purpose, there is no point in drawing a sharp
boundary around them, and Wittgenstein certainly does not do so.

Even if there were not this unclarity, there would still be uncertainty
about the bounds of family resemblance concepts. How is the categorization of concepts related to the classification of explanations? One
possibility would be that we characterize as a family resemblance concept
any expression whose explanation *may* take the form of an explanation
by paradigms. This would make the class *very* wide. Moreover, it would
block Wittgenstein's negative use of the notion; e.g., the fact that I
can correctly explain 'circle' by a series of ostensions does not show that
circles have nothing in common, i.e. that we do not also acknowledge a
Merkmal-definition of 'circle' as correct. The antithetical possibility
would be to characterize as a family resemblance concept any expression
whose complete explanation *must* take the form of an explanation by
paradigms in order to conform to our practice of explanation. This
would make the class very narrow; indeed, it would appear to restrict the
range primarily to traditional *summa genera* (e.g. 'plant', 'number', 'colour'). For, although many sortals may be explained by paradigms and resemblance, they may also be explained by definitions *per genus et differentiam.*
The fact that we may explain a concept by examples is compatible with
its not being a family resemblance concept. Refinements of this criterion
of classification might be necessary to exclude concepts of simple
perceptual qualities (e.g. redness and sourness) from the class of family
resemblance concepts. There is considerable latitude in classifying concepts on the basis of a categorization of explanations. How this should be
exploited depends on the purposes of making the classification.

(ii) *Coherence*: is any family concept coherent? If it is explained by
reference to overlapping similarities through a chain of intermediate links
with some paradigms, then it must be essentially unbounded (cf. PG 76).
Everything whatever will, in accord with this explanation, be subsum-
able under the concept. For everything resembles everything else in some
respects, and given any two things we can construct a chain of
intermediate cases in which each neighbouring pair is linked by *many*
similarities. Hence, since nothing could fail to fall under any concept so
explained, any family resemblance concept is vacuous.

This argument can be countered in a variety of misguided ways. Each
starts from the assumption that giving a set of paradigms cannot be a
correct explanation of a family resemblance concept, but only a fragment

of a correct explanation. There are different strategies for specifying the required supplementation. First, one could demand a precise catalogue of the respects of resemblance relevant for determining whether something falls under the concept. Secondly, one could instead require direct resemblance with a paradigm, rather than resemblance via a chain of intermediate cases. Thirdly, one could demand the indication of negative paradigms, i.e. an explanation by examples of what does not fall under the concept.

These formalistic responses to the challenge are muddled. The important facts are that we do not explain 'game' by giving a *Merkmal*-definition; that we do have a tolerably definite practice of using the word; that we do not apply it to everything whatever; and that we do generally accept (as correct) explanations that enumerate varied examples of games. It is not the proper business of philosophy to construct an explanation for how all this is possible. Rather, one must show what is wrong with the philosophical argument that it is impossible. That is a matter of directing attention away from the form of the explanations by examples of 'game' to the *use* that is made of these explanations. 'A rule that can be applied in practice is always in order' (PG 282).

(iii) *Applications*: is there necessarily a possibility of justifying and criticizing applications of family resemblance concepts? And, if so, are the only relevant grounds similarities and dissimilarities? Wittgenstein suggests a positive answer to both questions in saying that it is because of the relationships between the phenomena called 'language' that we call them 'language' (§65).

That we can always justify or criticize applications of family resemblance concepts seems a natural generalization from intuitions about Wittgenstein's examples. There seems to be something to discuss about whether shooting is a sport or whether gladiatorial combat is a game. 'Why do you call it a sport?' seems a legitimate question, and the retorts 'Just look at it!' or 'Can't you see?' seem outrageous.

On the other hand, must justification and criticism be limited to appeals to degrees of resemblance and dissimilarity with paradigms? Must that alone be relevant in an argument about whether blood sports are really games? One might think that distinguishing between games and rituals, between games and theatrical performances, or between games and forms of warfare is not just a matter of totting up the numbers and degrees of resemblances between activities and paradigmatic games. Reaching a verdict on this issue is made difficult by the unclarity of Wittgenstein's notion of 'similarities in the large' (cf. Exg. §66). The sorts of consideration that would be adduced in denying that mid-eighteenth-century continental battles were games (e.g. the socio-political consequences of their outcomes and the loss of life attendant on them) might well be subsumed under 'dissimilarities in the large'. (As it were, the difference between similarities in the small and in the large is whether they are noted by looking *at* or *around* the phenomena.) Only a lot of stipulative sharpening of the concept of similarities in the large would make possible a decision on whether all justifications and criticisms of 'game' turn on similarities and dissimilarities. This is quite unnecessary if the concept of family resemblance is used only for Wittgenstein's purposes.

There are two mistakes readily slipped into from the idea that there are justifications and criticisms of applications of family resemblance concepts. First, justifications appealing to a few similarities out of a sizeable set of relevant respects of resemblance are typically defeasible; e.g. there is a considerable range of striking similarities between certain kinds of warfare and many paradigmatic games (competition, winning and losing, sets of rules), but these are 'overbalanced' by other striking dissimilarities. Wittgenstein seems to suggest that *any* justification by appeal to similarities with paradigms is defeasible (cf. PG 119 f., BB 145 f.). One reaction to this defeasibility is to insist that a correct explanation of a family resemblance concept must assign weights, both positive and negative, to respects of resemblance with and difference from paradigms, thereby revealing the calculation settling whether or not something falls under the concept. Secondly, the possibility of justifying or criticizing applications of such a concept is easily thought to presuppose that an explanation by examples is incorrect unless it is explicitly supplemented by a similarity-clause (e.g. 'these and similar things are games'). How else could the explanation by examples make contact with applications of the concept and hence enter into justification or criticism of these applications? Both inferences are unwarranted. Once again the fallacy is to assume that how an explanation is used must be packed into its form. The crucial matter is how the paradigmatic examples are used, not the form of the explanation in which they are enumerated.

(iv) *Unity*: the unity of a family resemblance concept seems precarious. What binds together the complex pattern of using 'game' into a single family of cases? What licenses speaking of *the* concept of a game?

Further reflection seems to aggravate the problem. The justification for applying 'game' to activities varies from case to case; different respects of resemblance to different paradigms may be adduced. But does the unity of a concept not lie in uniformity of the means for determining what falls under it? Similarly, there are presumably different correct explanations of 'game'; different lists of paradigms may be used, and it is far from obvious that any two correct explanations must use even overlapping lists; and some explanations may include a similarity-clause, while others do not. How is assigning a single invariant meaning to 'game' compatible with variability in explanations of the term? What is the criterion for concept-identity? Can one introduce some sort of equivalence-relation on explanations of 'game' such that any explanation chosen from a well-defined equivalence-class constitutes a correct explanation of 'game'? How would this equivalence-relation be defined? How would its use be justified? These questions seem to demand urgent attention if meaning is tied closely to explanations of meaning.

These worries and any theory of concept-identity in reply to them rest on confusions. First, both the worries and any solutions to them rest on connecting the form of explanations too closely with their use. What seems puzzling is that difference in lists of paradigms is not correlated with difference in use, and a solution is constructed by showing that explanations apparently different share a form defined by an equivalence-relation and therefore can have the same use. But surely the matter to focus on is simply the fact about our practice of explaining a term such as 'game' that we accept as correct different explanations. That, not a hypothetical equivalence-relation, is the bedrock of unity of the concept of a game. Secondly, the proper task of philosphy is not to explain how it is possible for there to be a single concept introduced by varying explanations by examples, but rather to show what is mistaken about the argument that there is any difficulty or impossibility here. The basic points are that we do give and accept as correct varying explanations by example of 'game'; that we do give and accept variable justifications and criticisms of applications of 'game'; that we do not take 'game' to be ambiguous (in contrast to 'light' or 'bank'); and that we do wish to apply 'game' to all these phenomena (cf. PI §532). This is paradoxical only from the standpoint encapsulated in the demand that every explanation of a concept-word must take the form of a *Merkmal*-definition. That is precisely the framework of thought called into question by Wittgenstein, and hence there is nothing special to discuss about the unity of family resemblance concepts.

(v) *Range*: what is the range of family resemblance concepts? What concepts fall within this class? More important, are there any kinds of concept all of which or none of which fall within it? If so, what are the implications of this fact?

One might suggest that a concept-word introduces a family resemblance concept only if it is not possible (i.e. not part of our practice) to give it a *Merkmal*-definition. In this sense, a family resemblance concept is 'unanalysable'. Many philosophers have taken unanalysability to be a deep and significant property of a concept. It has often been thought to reveal something profound about the nature, the metaphysical structure, of reality. Wittgenstein's conception of the autonomy of grammar repudiates this reason for assigning profound significance to the analysability of concept-words. Indefinability (like indescribability (cf. Exg. §78)) is a feature of a concept-word within a given form of representation and relative to its norms of explanation. That we might, with sufficient ingenuity, concoct a *Merkmal*-definition of a concept-word does not show that, contrary to our previous beliefs, it really is analysable. Analysability is neither discovered nor concealed, but stipulated. What determines the analysability of a concept-word is whether any such definition is currently employed as a criterion for understanding the word, i.e. whether the practice of explaining it includes giving *Merkmal*-definitions.

Nevertheless, it may be of philosophical importance to note that certain kinds of concept are unanalysable relative to certain systems of other concepts, and it may in addition contribute to an *Übersicht* of our language to characterize some such classes of unanalysable concepts as consisting wholly of family resemblance concepts. The importance of the negative observation turns on the inclination to misconstrue concepts of certain kinds as being *Merkmal*-definable even though giving such definitions is no part of our practice. For, in certain cases, we readily construct a mythology to explain away the appearance of unanalysability. Wittgenstein concentrates on two such cases: formal concepts (e.g. the concepts of *Satz*, proof, language, name, object, number, property) and psychological concepts (e.g. the concepts of thinking, meaning something, understanding, intending, believing, willing). In nearly every case, concepts that he asserts to be family resemblance concepts fall into one or the other of these two classes. That is because philosophers are particularly liable to obscure their vision with myths and then to fall into dogmatism. In the first case, the temptation is to suppose that formal concepts are ineffable; i.e. that all the things falling under a formal concept share an essence, but that we cannot say what this is. In the second case, the temptation is to compensate for the absence of behaviour or mental phenomena common to all the things falling under a psychological concept by postulating a hidden shared spiritual activity (TS. 302, 13 ff.; PG 74 f.; PI §36). Wittgenstein seems to invoke the notion of family resemblance primarily as an antidote to these two forms of philosophical superstition.

6. *Psychological concepts*

For a certain period the notion of family resemblance had prominence in Wittgenstein's discussions of psychological concepts (i.e. expressions which seem to stand for certain mental activities, states, or processes or whose use is connected with such mental phenomena). It crops up in his account of such verbs as 'think', 'expect', 'know', 'intend', 'wish', 'mean', 'understand', 'read', 'calculate', 'derive', 'believe', and 'observe', and also in his analyses of such expressions as 'knowing what I want to say but being unable to say it', 'comparing from memory', 'being guided', 'trying to copy', 'alluding to N', 'trying to do something', and 'motive' (TS. 302, 14, 25 f.; PG 74 f., 141; BB 19 f., 32 f., 86, 115, 119, 124 f., 144 f., 152; PI §236; Z §26; PLP 183 ff., 354 f.). Wittgenstein emphasizes that each of these expressions is applied to a family of cases having complex kinship with each other. His purpose in many cases is overtly negative; viz. to release us from a too primitive conception of language that stands in the way of careful scrutiny of the various instances in which concepts are applied (TS. 302, 13 f.; PG 74 f.; BB 17 ff.; PLP 183 ff.).

There is a characteristic first/third-person asymmetry in the use of such psychological concepts. Wittgenstein initially invoked the notion of family resemblance to clarify both first- and third-person applications. It is natural to construe an utterance beginning 'I mean that . . .', 'I intend to . . .', 'I know that . . .', 'I believe that . . .', etc., as a description of an inner state or process, i.e. as parallel to a description of the speaker's immediate experience, such as 'I have a toothache'. But that is mistaken. If intending, believing, meaning something, etc., are characterized as mental states, then they are hypothetical mental states, not something known to us as a part of what we experience (TS. 302, 1). For when I scrutinize my experiences in reading or listening to a conversation, I see nothing common to all of them that is the process of understanding; instead, what I note is a whole set of experiences, characteristic of different cases of understanding and variously related to each other. Such experiences are the mental accompaniments of understanding, but not the putative process of understanding. Consequently, one must recognize that 'I understand . . .' (and, similarly, 'I intend that . . .', 'I believe that . . .', etc.) is a description of a family of mental states, processes, and activities (together with accompanying behaviour), not a description of some single experience which is the common ingredient of all cases of understanding (cf. BB 20, 32 f., 86 f., PLP 183 ff.).

The corresponding second- and third-person utterances (e.g. 'He believes that . . .') are patently not descriptions of the speaker's immediate experience. They can be supported or criticized only by reference to descriptions of the behaviour of the person referred to, including his verbal behaviour (e.g. his saying 'I believe that . . .'). It is tempting to construe statements as hypotheses made more or less probable, but never conclusively verified, by descriptions of behaviour. Wittgenstein seems to have viewed them in this way for a brief period; then he criticized and repudiated this idea in the *Blue Book*, thereafter continuing to maintain that there must be behavioural criteria for attributing inner states to others. Here too he applied the notion of family resemblance. For we are tempted to think that there is some one peculiar mental activity, process, or state which is as it were hidden behind the behaviour characteristic, e.g., of expecting someone, but which manifests itself in this behaviour; we are inclined to suppose that there must be a particular state of affairs which a sentence such as 'He is expecting someone' refers to—a state of affairs, as it were, on a plane above that on which the special behavioural manifestations of his expecting take place (cf. BB 113 ff.). What we should acknowledge is that there is a great variety of patterns of behaviour which we call 'expecting' (or 'believing', 'understanding', etc.) and that these are connected by a family resemblance (cf. BB 33, 114 f., 124 f., 144 f., 152). There is no particular behaviour common to all cases of expecting someone, nor is the sentence 'He is expecting someone' identical in meaning with any description of that person's behaviour which is a criterion for asserting it (cf. BB 115).

It is striking that the application of family resemblance to both these aspects of the use of psychological concepts later diminished and is virtually absent from the *Investigations*. Indeed, it completely disappears from the analysis of first-person utterances. An utterance such as 'Now I understand' is not a description at all, *a fortiori* not a description of a family of mental states, processes, and activities. On the other hand, the earlier account has an heir: viz. the contention that meaning something, understanding, expecting, intending, believing, thinking, etc., do not stand for mental processes, states, or activities that *accompany* behaviour (especially the use of language). What happens *while* one reads, means, or remembers something is not what reading, meaning, or remembering consist in (PI §§33 f., 152 f., 321 f., 332 f., pp. 217 ff., 231). In the case of second- and third-person utterances, the notion of family resemblance is applied only once (PI §164): Wittgenstein concludes a description of various cases in which a person is said to read by remarking '. . . we . . . use the word "to read" for a family of cases'. (That remark from EPB is perhaps anachronistic.) Since the purpose of introducing family resemblance was primarily negative, this eclipse of the notion in the *Investigations* is hardly surprising, since Wittgenstein there elaborates a positive account of the meaning of the relevant second- and third-person utterances based on the notion of criteria.

There is, however, a residual worry. Wittgenstein sometimes appears to give accounts of third-person utterances simultaneously applying the notion of family resemblance and the notion of behavioural criteria for inner states (BB 144 f.; PI §164). Are these two accounts compatible? Criteria are defeasible, and hence the application of psychological concepts according to behavioural criteria is, as Wittgenstein insists, not a form of behaviourism (PI §307). But treating 'He believes what he says' as an application of a family resemblance concept seems to put this sentence on the same level as descriptions of the person's behaviour; it invites the comment that under appropriate circumstances 'He believes what he says' means that he speaks in a certain tone of voice (cf. BB 115); and hence it looks like a form of behaviourism, i.e. it looks as if 'He believes what he says' is a description of someone's behaviour. This argument is, however, problematic. At no time after the emergence of the concept of family resemblance did Wittgenstein subscribe to behaviourism. He may first have treated sentences such as 'He believes what he says' as hypotheses, but, if so, the justification of such an assertion by reference to behaviour would be defeasible. Not only is defeasibility a hallmark of criteria, but it is also emphasized in his application of the notion of family resemblance to psychological concepts (BB 145 f., PLP 141). This suggests that the appearance of a conflict in his thinking is the product of misunderstanding. It is a result of reading more into his account of family resemblance than he intended to convey. The crucial point is negative: that we do not give (or accept) *Merkmal*-definitions of these concepts (e.g. of 'believe', 'understand', 'intend', 'expect', 'mean', 'think'). *That* is surely compatible with explaining them in terms of behavioural criteria. The only other clear point in Wittgenstein's account is that family resemblance concepts are explained by example. That too is unproblematic. We do give and accept explanations by example as correct explanations of such expressions. Any further extension of the account of family resemblance concepts is speculative. If it conflicts with Wittgenstein's analysis of expressions by reference to criteria, then this is a reason against attributing these ideas to him, not a reason for blaming him for an inconsistency. According to his conception, such terms as 'believe', 'intend', 'understand', 'mean', 'think', do stand for family resemblance concepts, but that is only the beginning of wisdom. The idea that inner states have outward criteria is a further, more important step in achieving an *Übersicht* of language.

7. *Formal concepts*

In the *Investigations* the primary application of the notion of family resemblance is to what Wittgenstein had earlier characterized as formal concepts. It appears in his explanations of 'language', 'number', and 'sentence' or 'proposition' (*Satz*) (PI §§65, 67 f., 108, 135, 179), and implicitly in his discussion of 'name' (§38). Elsewhere it occurs in his accounts of the diverse logical forms represented in Russell's notation by '(x) $\Phi(x)$' and '($\exists$x) $\Phi(x)$', of the concepts of proof, mathematics, and applications of a calculus, and of the ways in which mathematics forms concepts (LFM 270; RFM 138, 155, 180, 186). Waismann considerably extends such applications of family resemblance, including 'ostensive definition', 'sign', 'rule', 'arithmetic', 'rule of grammar', and 'geometrical point' in addition to 'name', 'number', and 'Satz' (PLP 66 f., 78 f., 104 ff., 108 ff., 137 ff., 185 ff., 298 f., 374; IMT 235 ff.).

It is remarkable that in earlier texts, the notion of family resemblance is not applied to formal concepts even though the idea of such an application seems very close to Wittgenstein's thought. He emphasizes that such expressions as 'Satz', 'number', 'rule', and 'word' are explained by examples; that such concepts go as far as similarities with such examples; and that they have blurred boundaries (BT 60, 70; PG 112 ff.). He also suggests that we do not call things 'rules' because there is something common to them all, but rather because there are many analogies between them (cf. BT 68, PG 117). But he refrains from invoking family resemblance here.

The explicit application of family resemblance in the explanation of 'language', 'Satz', 'number', etc., marks development from this earlier conception of formal concepts. It emphasizes that these words, if used intelligibly at all, must have their everyday meanings; this must be true of them even if they appeared in a philosophical grammar. The things called 'Satz' or 'language' are families of structures related to each other in complicated ways; they have neither the formal unity nor the formal equivalence that Wittgenstein had once imagined (PI §§96, 108). Such words must be brought back from their philosophical to their everyday use (PI §116).

There are four important aspects of treating formal concepts as family resemblance concepts.

(i) We do not explain such words as 'word', 'Satz', 'name', 'concept', 'object', 'number', 'language', 'explanation', or 'rule' by giving *Merkmal*-definitions, but rather by giving examples to which they apply. Consequently, there is no such thing as the essence of *Sätze*, the general form of propositions, to be revealed by *analysis* of the concept of a *Satz*. Nor any such thing as the essence of numbers or of languages. (This preserves one of the ingredients of Wittgenstein's earlier claim that these words expressed formal concepts.)

(ii) This absence of *Merkmal*-definitions must not be explained by claiming that the essential characteristics of formal concepts are mysterious, transcendent, and ineffable (PLP 165), that they cannot be *stated* but only *shown* in the use of what falls under these concepts. Expressions such as 'word', 'Satz', and 'number' are part of everyday language and have a determinate use. These concepts are what the philosopher must clarify, not some other ethereal concepts that we do not in fact deploy (PLP 82 ff.). The danger lies in thinking that these concepts are too coarse and material, i.e. that we should be investigating something much more subtle, abstract, and sophisticated.

(iii) Resemblance with paradigms is a matter of degree; it leaves us generally free to decide whether or not to apply a concept explained by examples to a particular case. Our understanding of formal concepts does not settle in advance how they should be applied to new instances, and it even licenses revisions of previous classifications. This point is emphasized with respect to formal concepts: we are at liberty to widen or narrow such concepts as that of *Satz* (PLP Ch XIV; PG 117), ostensive definition (PLP 106 ff.), number (IMT 235 ff.), rule of 'grammar' (PLP 58 ff.), etc. Our freedom is not, as it were, one of movement within a given logical space, but rather the freedom to extend or alter this space itself (BT 61; cf. PG 115). This lack of sharp boundaries of formal concepts is one (inessential) support of the autonomy of grammar (PLP 78 ff.), hence one of the reasons why there is no scope for metaphilosophy (BT 67; PG 116; cf. PI §121).

(iv) Formal concepts explained by paradigmatic examples have a unity; or, at least, the fact that different *Merkmal*-definitions mesh with only parts of the legitimate applications of such a concept-word is not a reason for declaring it to be ambiguous. In this respect, Wittgenstein's thought runs counter to advanced 'scientific' philosophy. We are impressed with the idea that categorial terms stand for abstract entities required for the construction of explanatory theories of meaning, that we need to clarify them by laying down precise criteria of identity, and that different criteria of identity determine different concepts. Hence sophisticated English-speaking philosophers distinguish (not always in the same way) type- and token-sentences, eternal sentences, statements, inscriptions, propositions, assumptions, descriptive contents, and assertions within the set of phenomena that Wittgenstein characterizes simply as *Sätze*. Accordingly, they accuse him of failing to make (or to make clear) an important and necessary set of distinctions. (This generates a correlative 'problem': how to translate *Satz* when it occurs in his remarks.) But he would surely not welcome this 'advance' in contemporary philosophy. It answers to spurious needs and generates the appearance of gulfs separating what are closely related phenomena. There are many similarities among the different things called *Sätze* and many differences. This is what must be clarified. We must not assimilate sentences such as '2 + 2 = 4', 'I have a headache', and 'He has brown hair', nor overlook differences in how they are used; but neither must we be blind to their similarities. If both similarities and differences are acknowledged, it will be of no importance which utterances are classified as *Sätze* and which are not.

To neglect aspects of *Sätze* that are highlighted differently by the terms 'proposition', 'sentence', 'statement', and 'assertion' would be a defect in our understanding. To mark these aspects by using different technical expressions is a legitimate procedure. It does, however, carry the risk of obscuring the many respects of resemblance between what fall under different concepts. More importantly, it promotes quasi-scientific theory-building. After aeons of unclarity, we are at last in a position to identify the true bearers of truth-values or the vehicles of meaning! Statements, e.g., are proclaimed to be what are really true or false, while assertions, thoughts, sentence-tokens, propositions, etc., can only derivatively be characterized as having truth-values. Similarly, type-sentences are what have or lack meaning, while inscriptions, sentence-tokens, utterances, assertions, etc., can only derivatively (if at all) be ascribed meanings. Only choice of the appropriate abstract entity supplies the building-blocks for theories of truth, reference, or sense. In Wittgenstein's view, this development is both ridiculous and pernicious. It is as ridiculous as the claim that mathematical sophistication reveals at last that only rational numbers, but not irrationals, can be used in specifying the measurements of objects. And it is pernicious because it encourages the growth of explanations in philosophy at the expense of a more detailed description of the phenomena that generate perplexity. We are under the illusion that the difficulty of philosophy lies in describing extreme subtleties (PI §106), whereas the real difficulty consists in bringing into sharp focus the familiar and mundane.

XI

VAGUENESS AND DETERMINACY OF SENSE

1. Introduction

The contrast between the *Investigations* and the *Tractatus* is nowhere more obvious, nor more commonly remarked on, than in their attitudes towards determinacy of sense. It is a fundamental thesis of the *Tractatus* that sense is completely determinate; that there is no such thing as indeterminate sense. Its metaphysics is explicitly constructed to satisfy this constraint. The demand for simple objects is the demand that sense be determinate (TLP 3.23). Any modification of this requirement would undermine the rationale for the metaphysics of the *Tractatus* and shatter the mirroring relation between language and the world. The stance of the *Investigations* is the diametrical opposite. The demand for determinacy of sense is a striking example of philosophical dogmatism. It is not a description of how language actually works based on simple observation. It is imposed as part of a misguided attempt to demonstrate that language and communication are really possible. But for this purpose it is both unnecessary and unjustified. Concepts with indeterminate boundaries are not useless; many are perfectly serviceable (PI §§69, 71, cf. 79). The *Investigations*, by simply describing the explanations and uses of expressions, exposes the demand for determinacy of sense as a prejudice obstructing philosophical understanding of language.

This account is correct. The criticism in the *Investigations* of the demand for determinacy of sense is important and closely related to the other criticisms of the Augustinian picture of language and logical atomism. But it is easy to obscure this insight by giving a positive reformulation of Wittgenstein's criticism. This is commonly done. He is taken to have demonstrated that *vagueness* is an *essential* feature of language and that, far from making communication impossible, vagueness may be *advantageous*. However close they may seem, these ideas are in fact remote from Wittgenstein's own. More important, they are very misleading. At the grand strategic level, this interpretation of the *Investigations* contributes to underestimating the radical nature of the criticism of the *Tractatus*. Wittgenstein's aim is a total reorientation of philosophical thought about meaning, whereas, on this view, the only correction necessary is to drop an optional extra (the demand for determinacy of sense) from the conception of meaning in the *Tractatus*. At the strategic level, the positive reformulation dissipates the close connection between remarks on 'vagueness' and the systematic criticism of the Augustinian picture and logical atomism. Finally, at the tactical level, this interpretation promotes one or the other of two inappropriate responses. One is to tinker with the details of a Fregean theory of meaning, to modify the system of semantic rules to accommodate vague expressions and so to construct a semantics or logic of vagueness. Recognition that vagueness is a pervasive feature of language renders the task of constructing a theory of meaning more challenging and therefore more alluring. The second response is to restrict attention to 'primary' or 'central' applications in analysing the uses of expressions. Citing the fact that ordinary language is infinitely complex, vague, flexible, and subtle, many philosophers bargain away the rigour of their investigations, legitimating this procedure by Wittgenstein's charisma. But both of these responses conflict with his conception of philosophy. What is important for obtaining an *Übersicht* of problematic points of language is an *exact description* of how expressions are explained and used, not a theory more sophisticated than that of the *Tractatus* nor an impressionistic account of some arbitrarily selected uses of expressions.

2. *Determinancy of sense in Frege and the* Tractatus

Although there are important differences in their treatment of the issue, there is a striking underlying resemblance between Frege's and Wittgenstein's conceptions of what it is for sense to be determinate and considerable agreement on how this is achieved. Here we sketch these two conceptions. Later we explore some deeper links (cf. §5).

(A) FREGE Determinacy of sense is, for Frege, an ideal. It is only imperfectly realized in natural languages. But it is a requirement for the construction of a systematic language adequate for scientific purposes. Frege demands of the explanation of any concept-word 'Φ' in such a language that it alone determine for every object whether or not this object falls under the concept Φ, whatever facts may obtain (GA ii. §56).

What motivated Frege to identify this feature of a constructed language as an ideal? And why did he take this ideal to have any bearing on everyday language?

A very fundamental reason is a presumption underlying his enterprise of demonstrating the analyticity of arithmetic. Any cogent proof of this thesis presupposes that the fundamental concepts can be sufficiently sharply defined that appeal to their definitions will objectively settle the truth of all statements of arithmetic which are recognized to be true. Unless definitions had consequences in making other statements true, and unless the definitions were determinate enough for these consequences to be well defined, the project of proving that arithmetic consists of analytic truths would be hopeless. The more nearly a language approximates to Frege's ideal, the clearer will be the interconnections, if any, between the content of its sentences. The question of the analyticity of arithmetic can only be settled if the relations of logical consequence among arithmetical sentences are sharply circumscribed, and this presupposes at least a complete systematic characterization of the truth-conditions of every arithmetical sentence. Bereft of a good measure of determinacy of sense, Frege would be left with nothing to discuss.

Another deep motivation is related to his conviction that the possibility of communication of thoughts presupposes that the sense of expressions is something objective. The sense of 'x' is as objective as the reference of 'x'. It is the mode of presentation of this reference. Vagueness threatens the very idea of sense. How can we speak of '*the* sense' of a proper name, e.g., if the name is not associated by different speakers with a principle sharply determining its reference? If it is not linked with a single determinate criterion of identity, how can it have a single sense? Without that must we not conclude that sense, far from being necessary to guarantee the possibility of communication, is either inessential for or an impediment to communication? Banishing vagueness from a scientific language guarantees the possibility of applying to it the concept of sense. The vagueness of expressions in everyday language is a measure of how far these systems of communication deviate from the ideal.

There are some more immediate sources of the demand for determinacy of sense. One is the conviction that the principle of bivalence is crucial to the construction of any systematic theory of meaning. Every sentence should be determinately true or false in any possible world. (Frege actually frames this requirement differently, using the Law of Excluded Middle instead of the principle of bivalence (GA ii. §56).) Believing that any theory of meaning must have the form of a two-valued semantics, and recognizing that the semantics of a language containing vague expressions cannot be a straightforward two-valued one, Frege was driven to exclude vague expressions from any language to which his theory of meaning was directly applicable.

A second source is the functional analogy. The sense of any complex expression is derived from the senses of its constituents and its structure, and similarly, its reference is a function of the references of its parts. This conception has two different aspects, run together in the principle of completeness of definitions. First, just as a function is defined only when its value is stipulated for every admissible argument, so a predicate, conceived as a function from objects to truth-values, is well defined only when its value is stipulated for every argument, i.e. every object. Secondly, should an expression lack reference, then so too does every complex expression in which it occurs. This makes vagueness highly contagious. To the extent that the sense of any expression is vague, so too is the sense of *every* expression of which it is a part. In particular, its vagueness will infect the truth-conditions of any sentence in which it occurs. Frege's strict adherence to the functional principles for sense and reference demands the total exclusion of indeterminacy of sense.

Frege satisfied all of these desiderata by imposing on the construction of a truly scientific language the requirement that definitions be complete. This is stated for the definition of concept-words of first level (GA ii. §56). It makes three separable demands on a definition: (i) that the definition alone, unsupplemented by extraneous considerations, determine, together with the facts, all applications of the defined word; (ii) that it determine for *any* object whatever whether it falls under the concept; and (iii) that this be determined *whatever* the facts may be. Frege thus demands complete generality in two respects. Parallel demands are made for proper names and concept-words of higher level. A definition meeting the requirement of completeness will determine once and for all every possible application of the defined expression. Therefore, grasping it will provide someone with a complete knowledge of how to use the expression.

Ordinary language falls far short of this ideal. Most of its explanations do not satisfy the requirement of completeness of definition. They often leave some applications of expressions in dispute, and they typically lack the requisite generality. Frege just brushes aside the problems raised by this fact. Vagueness (and lack of generality) is treated as a measure of the imperfection of natural languages for the purposes of science. In particular, for the purpose of proving that arithmetic is analytic, it is enough that we can compare our actual arithmetical practice with the output of applying laws of logic to a system of definitions.

(B) THE TRACTATUS Wittgenstein purports to describe the conditions for any possible language in the *Tractatus*. One is the requirement that sense be determinate. This is not an ideal to which actual languages approximate, nor a constraint on the construction of an 'ideal' language (as Russell wrongly thought). Rather, the sense of any sentence in any language must be completely determinate. There is no such thing as indeterminate sense.

Of course, vagueness is an apparent feature of everyday language. Wittgenstein's strategy in the *Tractatus* is to argue that this is an illusion: There is much more in our thoughts than is represented in their outward verbal clothing (TLP 4.002), and this must be added to their expression to determine what is meant. Our thoughts or what we mean to convey are quite definite; they are always completely determinate pictures of possible states of affairs. Thoughts are themselves symbols with sense. In the inner language of thought there is no such thing as indeterminacy of sense. Since the outer language of words is backed by thoughts, the apparent vagueness there is not real.

What motivated Wittgenstein in demanding determinacy of sense is parallel to what underlay Frege's ideal of completeness of definition. He too aimed to prove that arithmetic rested on logic (not that it consisted of tautologies, but that equations were systematically related to logical truths). An acceptable definition of logical operators must provide for their iteration, and the definition of numbers involves only the iteration of logical operators. But, in the *Tractatus*, the 'truths' of arithmetic are derived from the rules assigning meaning to logical operators in our actual language (as well as every possible language), not from definitions of numerals that are not dictated by our actual practice of using them. The validation of our arithmetic must proceed within our language.

Wittgenstein's other deep motivation was the initial insight that language is in order as it is (TLP 5.5563). It takes care of itself (NB 2, cf. 107; TLP 5.473 f.). It is in perfect logical order already; what we have to do is simply to describe what this is (NB 11). Logical order is to be discovered within language, not imposed from outside. Given an unshakable commitment to two-valued semantics, the contention that language is in order as it is forces the conclusion that there is no vagueness in it.

Two more proximate motivations are similar to Frege's. First, a commitment to the principle of bivalence. Every proposition must divide logical space. Reality, however constituted, must make it true or make if false (TLP 4.025). This is a crucial component of the picture theory of meaning. Secondly, Wittgenstein too embraces the functional analogy (though in a modified form). The sense of every sentence is a function of the meanings of its constituents and its logical structure (TLP 3.318). This too is crucial for the picture theory. It shows how it is possible to grasp the sense of an unfamiliar sentence through understanding its component expressions (TLP 4.024 ff.). This constraint of functionality means that toleration of vagueness in the meaning of any expression would infect with vagueness the sense of *every* sentence in which this expression occurs non-vacuously.

There is a third proximate motivation. Like Frege, Wittgenstein takes the sense of a sentence to be the content of the thought that it expresses, what is understood in understanding it and what is meant in uttering it. The senses of sentences are the contents of beliefs, understanding, intention, meaning, and other propositional attitudes. But he takes it as obvious that what is meant, what is understood, what is believed, etc., must be absolutely clear and definite. There can be no vagueness in what I mean when I say 'The watch is on the table'. Indeed, 'what we MEAN must always be "sharp"' (NB 68).

In the *Tractatus* there are two ingredients necessary for determinacy of sense. The first is the uniqueness of analysis. Any sentence can be broken down in only one way into its simple constituents; it is a truth-function of elementary propositions. Secondly, the postulation of simple objects is taken to guarantee determinacy of sense for elementary propositions. The meaning of each name in such a proposition is the object named, and the concatenation of these names depicts precisely a unique state of affairs. This pair of theses secures all that is intelligible in Frege's conception of completeness of definition.

Wittgenstein's position on determinacy of sense is notorious. Though we allegedly know that the sense of any token-sentence is completely determinate, we are unable to show what it is. We do not know how to analyse a single sentence of any language, to exhibit it as a truth-function of elementary sentences. We cannot even give an instance of an elementary proposition or a logically proper name. Actual language is as far removed as possible from being logically transparent. We know what structure it must have, but this structure is deeply buried and as yet quite unknown except in general outline. Analysis will one day reveal the means by which a particular language in fact satisfies the requirement of determinacy of sense. Though not an ideal, the requirement is similar to one in that it is not *visible* in a description of what it is to speak a language. Its satisfaction is known only as the outcome of *a priori* deduction.

3. *Wittgenstein's Copernican revolution?*

There is a readily accessible outlook from which the *Investigations* appears to be the diametrical opposite of the *Tractatus* in its attitude towards vagueness. There Wittgenstein argued that there is no such thing as indeterminate sense even if it should seem that there is. Here he seems to argue that there is no such thing as completely determinate sense even if it should seem that there is.

We can, apparently, extract from his remarks the argument that all language is more or less vague. The meaning of an ordinary proper name like 'Moses' is typically somewhat indeterminate (§79), and there is no way even in principle to eliminate this indeterminacy. The best we could do would be to define 'Moses' by tying the use of the name to a single description of a person. 'Moses' means 'the man who led the Israelites out of Egypt'. But this would leave room for disputed applications of 'Moses' because doubts might arise about the words of this explanation. If we proceeded to define them, doubts would still be possible about the applicability of such unanalysable expressions as 'red', 'dark', 'sweet' (PI §87). Therefore, it seems, no explanation of a name can completely determine its use.

This reasoning can be extended to other kinds of expression (BT 253; PI §80). No word can be explained so thoroughly that every possible question about its applicability is settled once and for all. This pervasive feature of explanations backs the sweeping claim that it is impossible to exaggerate the importance of vagueness in a philosophical account of language (PLP 72).

It might seem that we could identify in Wittgenstein's work an argument for Russell's thesis that all symbols are infected with some degree of vagueness. Both envisage that verbal explanations of meaning will come to an end with certain 'indefinables' such as 'red', 'dark', 'sweet'. These will presumably be explained ostensively. But Wittgenstein apparently holds that any ostensively defined expression is vague since an 'ostensive definition can be variously interpreted in every case' (PI §28). Since he too apparently takes all explanations to terminate in ostensive definitions, he seems committed to the idea that every expression inherits some degree of vagueness from unanalysable expressions.

Wittgenstein also seems to undermine the hope that the language of the exact sciences is free from vagueness. This hope is based on a misconception. Whatever may be the justification for calling them 'exact', the exact sciences do not remove all possibility of disputes about the applicability of their basic terms. On the contrary, they allow uncommonly large scope for *possible* disputes precisely because there are comparatively seldom actual disputes about the application of these terms. Though it passes unnoticed, a fluctuation between criteria and symptoms is typical of the concepts of science (PI §79; Z §438). Therefore, construction of a language adequate for the purposes of science offers no salvation from pervasive vagueness.

Given this outlook, Wittgenstein's revolution seems even more radical. He shows not just that all language is vague, but that we should not deplore this fact. Vagueness is not necessarily a defect of language. His most minimal claim is that it is not always an obstacle to communication. By saying to somebody 'Stand roughly there', we may get him to do just what we intended him to do (PI §71). Hence an order containing a vague expression is not always of diminished utility. Similarly, we succeed in making ourselves understood by the use of proper names that have no 'fixed meaning' (PI §79) or by the use of sortals that are not governed by explanations settling every possible application (PI §§69, 80). Our ability to deploy family resemblance concepts is concrete proof that vagueness does not make concepts useless.

Wittgenstein apparently advances some yet more ambitious theses. First, precision and exactitude are not absolute, but relative. There is no single standard of exactitude that governs explanations of meaning, no single ideal of precision. What is appropriate as a standard depends on circumstances and our purposes (cf. PI §88). Secondly, vagueness is not contagious. A word whose meaning is partially indeterminate need not infect with vagueness the sense of every sentence in which it may occur. My description 'The ground was covered with plants' may be quite clear even if I cannot give a precise definition of 'plant' (BT 248, cf. PI §70). Analogies show up the absurdity of the contagion-thesis. If the boundary of a country is partly in dispute, does it follow that nobody can definitely be said to be a citizen of this country (Z §556)? Or, if legislation on prices leaves out of account certain products commonly traded, does this mean that it fails to fix prices at all (cf. BT 250; Vol. XI, 43 f.)? Reacting to vagueness with panic is not warranted. Thirdly, we should adopt a more pragmatic attitude towards explanations. The important issue is whether they serve to establish an agreed practice in the use of the defined expressions, not whether there are conceivable circumstances, different from the actual ones, in which they might fail to do so (cf. Z §114 ff.). An explanation is in order if it works in practice, just like a signpost (PI §87). No *improvement* is made by adding something to a signpost that removes a possible misunderstanding that nobody has. The adequacy of explanations is to be judged by everyday practical standards, not by some arcane theoretical ones. It is absence of agreement in a practice that is a defect of language, not the mere possibility that there might be irresolvable disagreements which never in fact arise.

Wittgenstein seems to push the bidding even higher: that vagueness is impossible to eliminate even in principle and is indispensable to the efficient use of language for communication. One might even complain that Wittgenstein does not do justice to our intuitive conviction that vagueness is a defect of language.

Even now we have not delineated the full extent of what many consider to be his revolution. His remarks on vagueness contain hints capable of development into a semantic theory for expressions whose meanings are more or less vague. He certainly sparked off much of the contemporary interest in vagueness and many of the attempts to construct 'logics of vagueness'.[1]

We could round off this caricature of the *Investigations* by noting the centrality of vagueness in Wittgenstein's repudiation of the *Tractatus*. He systematically criticizes and dismantles the theory that he had erected to secure determinacy of sense. There is no such thing as a logically proper name. Analysis is not conceptual chemistry. It is superstition to suppose that every sentence must have a unique analysis. The harmony between language, thought, and the world is trivial since the metaphysics and psychology of the *Tractatus* were constructed simply to secure it. The

---

[1] Cf. M. Black, 'Vagueness: an Exercise in Logical Analysis', *Phil. of Science*, Vol. 4 (1937), and S. Körner, *Conceptual Thinking* (Cambridge University Press, Cambridge, 1955) and *Experience and Theory* (Routledge and Kegan Paul, London, 1966). Suggestive texts include PR 263 ff., PI §§77 ff., PG 236 ff.

heart of his later criticism of the *Tractatus* is the demolition of the pillars supporting determinacy of sense. Therefore, the centre of gravity of the *Investigations* must be a vindication of vagueness in language. *Here* it is that Wittgenstein has turned around our whole investigation of meaning by rotating it about the axis of our real need (PI §108). Previously he had argued that the possibility of saying anything presupposed determinacy of sense and hence that the fact that language somehow meets this requirement is what accounts for our communicating by means of it. Now, it appears, Wittgenstein stands this reasoning on its head: our language is in order provided that we can use it successfully to communicate, and hence the fact that expressions not satisfying the requirements for determinacy of sense are useful proves that these requirements are unnecessary.

4. *Preliminary objections*

Although the preceding interpretation of the *Investigations* is radically misconceived, it has a double importance. First, it develops a line of thinking about Wittgenstein that is widespread, even if it is not customarily so fully elaborated. Secondly, it is a form of error that contains a lot of truth. It is, so to speak, tangential to the correct interpretation because an account of vagueness is parasitic on an account of meaning. Therefore, clarifying the mistakes of this interpretation contributes to understanding Wittgenstein's conception of meaning.

There are a number of preliminary objections to this interpretation of the *Investigations*.

(i) The idea that all language is more or less vague is the outcome of reflection on what is involved in giving explanations of meaning. It is a necessary truth established *a priori*. The fundamental point is that no explanation *can* settle every possible doubt about how an expression is to be used. The conclusion is that every expression is *necessarily* vague to some degree. There is no sense in speaking of its having a completely determinate sense. But then it follows that it makes no sense to speak of its having a sense that is *not* completely determinate. If all language is *necessarily* more or less vague, then the term 'vague' is deprived of meaning. There would be no point in characterizing any expression as 'vague'.

(ii) The term 'vague', like the term 'inexact', is pejorative. To call a statement or an explanation vague is a reproach. A vague explanation is defective just in that it serves the goal of establishing an agreed practice in using an expression less perfectly than a more precise explanation (cf. PI §88). Consequently, it would make no more sense to say that every expression is vague than it would to say that every expression is defective.

(iii) Let us call a term vague if there is, in the practice of its application, significant disagreement about what uses of it are correct. This is a matter of there being actual disagreements in judgements about its applicability in conformity with what are recognized as correct explanations of it. Such disagreements, irresolvable within the practice of explaining the term, may produce a general agreement that there are borderline cases of its application. Here the term can be said to be definitely vague. This is a matter of recognition that the practice of applying an expression in accord with accepted explanations neither legitimates nor invalidates its application to certain types of actual cases. But a term might be vague without being definitely vague. Its lacking determinacy of sense is something quite different: this is the *possibility* of there being irresolvable disagreements in judgement about its applicability. Accordingly, determinacy of sense is the impossibility of vagueness; and its opposite not vagueness, but the mere *possibility* of vagueness (what Waismann christened 'open texture'). The crucial point is that an expression may be indeterminate in sense and yet not be vague; i.e. that 'open texture' is compatible with agreement in judgements. If the *Investigations* is addressed to the *Tractatus*, it need not vidicate vagueness, but it must vindicate the use of expressions whose explanations leave open the possibility of vagueness. Failure to make this distinction between vagueness and indeterminacy of sense makes intelligible the usual interpretation of the *Investigations*. To say that an expression does not display determinacy of sense need not be a reproach, just as a doctor is not blameworthy in virtue of the fact that he has the ability to poison people if he should wish to do so. An explanation is not defective in virtue of the fact that it might prove unhelpful in certain bizarre circumstances.

(iv) Someone who does not know what it is for an expression to have a meaning (or sense) cannot have a full grasp of what it is for an expression to be vague or open-textured. If we are in the dark about Wittgenstein's whole conception of meaning, how can we use his conception of vagueness as a candle to find our way about? Philosophers must be *at least* as confused about vagueness as they are about meaning!

5. *The centrality of determinacy of sense*

Faced with these difficulties of making sense of the alleged necessary truths that all language is vague or that it is possibly vague (or open-textured), we might take the opposite side, asserting that the discussion of vagueness is of no real interest to philosophy and taking this to be Wittgenstein's point. Surely the argument of §71 is just that Frege's requirement of completeness of definition, embodied in his comparison of a concept with a line enclosing an area, is a gratuitous assumption. Should we not see the parallel demand for determinacy of sense in the *Tractatus* as a blunder? Why need a concept without sharp boundaries be useless? Once we break the fascination exerted by the idea of determinacy of sense, there is nothing left to discuss. With appropriate liberalization, we can easily extend the theory of meaning to analyse vague expressions. Wittgenstein merely pleads for tolerance and his work has been superseded by subsequent investigations showing how to tame vagueness within systematic theories of meaning.

This reaction is equally misguided. It misses the central position of the demand for determinacy of sense in Frege's work and in the *Tractatus*. This demand is fundamental, not optional; and it is compound, not simple. The means for securing it accomplish not just one thing, but many. Adherence to Frege's principle of completeness of definition, e.g., secures the principle of bivalence, the generalized Law of Excluded Middle, and the thesis that the sense of an expression is the content of the shared understanding of it. If we disentangled these strands, we would discover that in some respects the demand for determinacy could be treated as something optional, but in other respects as something fundamental.

The idea that the demand for determinacy of sense is a simple blunder fails to do justice to an intuitive feeling that vagueness is a defect of language. This is the truism of which Frege and the *Tractatus* made too much. Therefore, clarifying its roots should help to establish the respects in which the demand for determinacy was central to their work and also to point the way to a correct account of Wittgenstein's later criticisms.

One deep root of the idea that vagueness is a defect is the notion that the meaning of a sentence is derived from the meanings of its constituents and its structure. Although we know that everyday language does conform to this conception, how it does so is opaque. One task of philosophy is to show clearly how it does so conform. The obvious means is to compare everyday language with a precise formal language that visibly fulfils this requirement. Such a language will be a sort of calculus: from the explanation of its terms and of its structures we will be able systematically to calculate the meanings of its sentences. Indeed, these calculations might even take the form of formal derivations within an axiomatic system. Such a language would embody the ideal of being in perfect logical order: its workings would be transparent. Whether or not actual languages can be shown to be equivalent to such systems, it is appropriate to investigate them by means of this comparison. Frege and the *Tractatus* treat language from this perspective of investigating a calculus. Both implicitly accept one corollary: that there must be some ideal form of explanation which will not only be definitive, but also bridge the 'gap' between meaning and application. By this standard many actual explanations of meaning are defective, and must be replaced by something better.

This conception gives one rationale for treating vagueness as a defect of language. Any uncertainty about the meaning of a word will spill over into uncertainty about the meaning of any sentence in which it occurs (especially into indeterminacy in the truth-conditions of assertions). The functional principle concerning the sense of a sentence guarantees, it seems, that vagueness will be contagious. Understanding of a sentence must be at least as indeterminate as the understanding of its vaguest constituent. If lack of a firm understanding of sentences is detrimental to the use of language, then vagueness is a serious defect.

The other deep root of this idea is a pervasive conception of what it is to understand an expression. The model for understanding a concept-word is knowing a *Merkmal*-definition of it. Generalized, this gives a conception of understanding an expression as knowing a set of conditions necessary and sufficient for its application. (This does not require the ability to *state* these conditions.) This conception of understanding gives a rationale for assimilating the various phenomena called 'vagueness' and treating them as defects of language. Inconsistency in applying an expression is a sufficient condition for not correlating it with a determinate set of conditions necessary and sufficient for applying it; hence, it betokens a defective understanding. Equally defective would be understanding of an expression in whose explanation there was vacillation; moreover, such inconsistency must be reflected in discrepant application of the expression over part of its range. Finally, the mere *possibility* of either inconsistency of application or inconsistency of explanation is a sufficient condition for not having a definite understanding of an expression. The *possibility* of vagueness is as much a defect of language as *actual* vagueness in the form of disagreements about explanations or applications.

Both of these underlying ideas seem to leave no alternative to a form of demand for determinacy of sense. The sense of a sentence can be calculated from its constituents only if the latter have a determinate sense. Similarly, there seems to be no such thing as an expression's having an indefinite meaning if whatever meaning it has must consist in conditions necessary and sufficient for its application. An indeterminate meaning is no meaning at all. Of course, it is not necessary that there be no undetermined applications of the expression; e.g. it is not necessary that the principle of bivalence holds for the ascription of *any* property to any object. What is necessary, however, is that the undetermined case be determinately undetermined (cf. Z §441 f.). Or, more generally, it would suffice that it be determinate whether a case was undetermined or whether it was undetermined whether it was undetermined or . . ., etc. (Sometimes it is said that we can dispense with bivalence, but that we must have some analogue for it.) The functional principle concerning the sense of a sentence and the conception of understanding as knowing conditions of application seem crucial in distinguishing the essential from the optional components of the notion of determinacy of sense. Together these considerations emphasize the centrality of this notion in Frege and the *Tractatus*.

Reading the *Investigations* as merely arguing that bivalence is an optional feature of language is correct, but superficial. This interpretation neglects the fact that Wittgenstein there attacks these roots of the demand for determinacy of sense. He argues against treating language as a calculus, and he gives a more sophisticated and fuller account of what it is to understand an expression.

6. *Rejection of the demand for determinacy of sense*

Wittgenstein's method in examining the demand for determinacy of sense is characteristic. On the one hand, he scrutinizes the various purposes explicitly backing the demand as well as the different components of it. On the other hand, he addresses himself to considerations that shape this explicit thinking, the pictures that guide philosophers of a particular genre. Consequently, his criticisms of the demand for determinacy can be separated into three levels: the criticism of unacknowledged assumptions, that of conscious desiderata, and that of the ingredients of this demand. His campaign is extensive and exhaustive.

At the deepest level, Wittgenstein strikes at both the root assumptions supporting determinacy of sense.

(i) He criticizes various facets of the idea that the sense of a sentence is determined by the meanings of its parts and its structure. There is a grain of truth here: explaining the sense of a sentence may, sometimes does, take the form of explaining its constituents (and, if necessary, its structure). But it does not follow that the sense of every sentence can be derived or calculated from explanations of its constituents and its form. First, the sense of a sentence is its *use*, and there is no way of making intelligible the idea that this follows from its form together with explanations of its constituents (see 'The uses of sentences', pp. 73 ff.). Secondly, the functional thesis confuses an account of the mechanism of understanding with an account of what it means to say of someone that he understands a sentence. The psychological thesis is false, viz. that we work out the meaning of every sentence from the meanings of its constituents. What is correct is that one acceptable criterion for understanding some sentences is explaining constituents and structure (cf. 'A word has a meaning only in the context of a sentence', p. 160). Thirdly, explanations of words even of one logical type are not homogeneous in kind, and there are typically multiple correct explanations, even of different kinds, of a single expression. Hence it would be unclear how to reconcile this diversity with a uniform method for calculating the sense of a sentence from the meanings of its parts (i.e. from what is explained in explaining its parts). Finally, there are other ways of manifesting understanding of a sentence than by explaining its constituents and its structure.

(ii) He criticizes various aspects of the idea that understanding an expression amounts to knowing conditions necessary and sufficient for its application. Acceptable explanations of expressions may take forms other than statements of such conditions (cf. 'Explanation', pp. 37 f.). Understanding may be manifested in ways other than explaining an expression by stating such conditions, viz. by giving another kind of explanation or by using it correctly. The idea that understanding consists in knowing a set of necessary and sufficient conditions of application is vacuous unless there are clear criteria for whether or not a person has such knowledge. Otherwise, we have only a form of representation for redescribing understanding: someone's understanding might consist in 'implicit' knowledge of ineffable necessary and sufficient conditions (cf. Exg. §75 ff.).

Wittgenstein also scrutinizes an underlying assumption of this view. In thinking of understanding as consisting in knowing a rule for applying an expression, we take for granted that the rule, at least if it has the favoured form of stating necessary and sufficient conditions, already 'contains' its applications. Because these 'flow' from the rule, our applying the expression correctly 'flows' from our knowing the rule. Wittgenstein criticizes this idea at length (cf. Volume 2). No sense can be given to the notion that a rule 'contains' its applications. Consequently, even if understanding consisted in being able to state necessary and sufficient conditions for applying a term, this would not be the end of a full understanding of language, but the starting point for further philosophical investigation.

Supplementing these fundamental sources for the demand for determinacy of sense are criticisms of the more specific grounds for it which are explicit in Frege and the *Tractatus*.

(i) Justification of arithmetic: as noted, Frege's programme of proving that arithmetical statements are analytic presupposes the idea that one grammatical truth may generate others as its consequences. So too does the account of arithmetic in the *Tractatus*. Against this conception now stand Wittgenstein's arguments in support of the autonomy of grammar. Arithmetic has no foundations.

(ii) Objectivity of sense and understanding: this was conceived of as resting on the possibility of comparing the applications made of any expression as calculated from the conditions necessary and sufficient for its use with the use actually made of it by any speaker of the language. This depends on a misconception of the relation between rules and their applications. It would also presuppose the possibility of formulating for every expression necessary and sufficient conditions for its application if the required calculation were to be one that might be carried out. A correct conception of the objectivity of understanding depends on a grasp of criteria of understanding.

(iii) Language being in order as it is: although the *Tractatus* defended this view, it argued that this order was not apparent in the actual explanation and use of expression, but hidden beneath these practices. Wittgenstein now argues that there is nothing more to the meaning of an expression than what is perspicuous in the actual practice of using and explaining it. Hence, in particular, the fact that language is in order is not to be identified with the idea that the use of words coincides with the output of some calculus of rules for using these words, but rather with the fact that there is agreement in judgements and in definitions.

(iv) Bivalence: Frege and the *Tractatus* argued that securing bivalence requires imposing restrictions on the structure of a language, especially the exclusion from it of vague expressions. Wittgenstein now argues that the principle that every proposition is true or false needs no foundations. It is simply a part of the explanation of the concept of a proposition (*Satz*). Its validity is compatible with admitting vague expressions into language. (We could say, e.g., that applying a vague predicate 'Φ' to a borderline case named 'a' yields a sentence 'Φa' not expressing a proposition.) The principle of bivalence is an autonomous rule of grammar.

(v) Determinacy of thought: Wittgenstein earlier thought that what we mean or understand by any sentence must be completely sharp or definite even if what we say is vague. This presupposed a conception of the relation between mental states and their expressions which he now attacks. Thoughts are not things that we apprehend by introspection and then describe more or less precisely. Rather, the expression of a thought is internally related to its content. A person's expressing a particular thought is a criterion for his having *that* thought (and not some other one). There is no possibility, therefore, of a general contrast between what we think and what we say, *a fortiori*, no such general contrast in respect of degree of vagueness.

Finally, Wittgenstein complements these criticisms of the origins of the demand for determinacy of sense with criticism of the means for satisfying it.

(i) *Merkmal*-definitions: this is treated as the norm for the explanation of concept-words. To the extent that an explanation deviates from the norm, it is commonly thought to be defective, and the meaning of the defined expression to be vague. Wittgenstein now repudiates this conception. Many expressions are explained otherwise than by giving necessary and sufficient conditions. There is no sense in the claim that all such explanations are defective. In particular, there is no need for deviation from the norm of *Merkmal*-definition to be accompanied by disagreement about applications of expressions. (Nor, conversely, is conformity to the norm a sufficient condition for agreement in applications.)

(ii) Names as disguised descriptions: the analogue for proper names of *Merkmal*-definitions of concept-words is explanation of a name by a logically equivalent definite description. Wittgenstein advances parallel objections in both cases (cf. Exg. PI §§43, 79; 'Proper names', pp. 234 ff.).

(iii) Meaning and bearer: in the *Tractatus*, determinacy of sense is secured ultimately by names whose meanings are the objects named. Wittgenstein now rejects this conception. For proper names it never makes sense to identify its meaning with its bearer (PI §§40 ff.), nor does it make sense to treat the identity of objects as transcendent (cf. PI §377). For unanalysable concept-words, it is wrong to treat what is pointed at in an ostensive definition as the meaning of the word; rather, it is a sample and is best considered as an instrument of language (cf. PI §16 and 'Ostensive definition and its ramifications', p. 97).

(iv) Self-sufficiency of definitions: Frege requires that an adequate explanation *alone* suffice to settle whether or not the defined expression is applicable; e.g. that a proper definition of 'number' must tell us that Julius Caesar is not a number. Wittgenstein criticizes this idea. A practice of explaining meaning is adequate provided that it serves to establish an agreed pattern of applying the defined expression. Consequently, an explanation will typically delineate how to use an expression only in those respects in which there is a serious risk of misuse. If we have no inclination to apply the term 'rule' to stone walls, clouds, cabbages, or numbers it is no defect of an explanation of 'rule' that it draws a boundary only between rules and descriptions, expressions of desires, reports of regularities, etc. (cf. BT 60, 69). An explanation does not merit our thanks merely for ruling out absurdities which no one would dream of including.

(v) Universal range of definitions: Frege's principle of completeness of defnition is incoherent in requiring of an explanation of a concept-word that it determine for *every* object whether it fall under the defined concept. Wittgenstein would criticize even the qualified version where this is required only for every object of an appropriate type. One reason is the fluid and purpose-relative character of classification of words into types (cf. Exg. §17). Another is the point that explanations are adequate provided they avert misunderstandings.

(vi) Universal competence of definitions: another ingredient of Frege's principle of completeness of definition is that an adequate explanation must fix the application of an expression in all possible circumstances.

Wittgenstein rejects this contention too. An explanation is adequate provided it establishes an agreed pattern of application given prevailing circumstances. The term 'person', e.g., has a 'composite use': its use would disintegrate if there were a cessation of the regularities that are presupposed in the use of our multiple criteria for personal identity (BB 62). An explanation is in order if under normal circumstances it fulfils its purpose. There is no such thing as an explanation that removes every *possible* doubt about how to apply an expression (PI §87).

Examination of these ingredients reveals that the demand for determinacy of sense is composite and its underlying assumptions complex. Under this heading are included a range of distinct demands on explanations of meaning. Some may be satisfied by some expressions, others by others, and yet others not at all. The only proper response to the question 'Is sense determinate?' is the counter-question 'What does it mean for sense to be determinate?' If, e.g., this means that every concept-word must be explained by stating a *Merkmal*-definition and every proper name by formulating an equivalent definite description, then determinacy of sense is not a feature of actual languages nor even of any possible language.

Although the demand for determinacy of sense is composite and the means for satisfying it diverse, there seems to be an underlying unifying idea. This is the conception that a *complete* explanation of meaning would in principle remove *every possible* doubt about how to apply the defined expression correctly and that explanations are imperfect to the extent that they diverge from this norm. The sense of an expression would be determinate only if there were such a complete explanation of it. This concept of determinacy of sense is incoherent. There is no such thing as an explanation that is complete in this sense of 'complete' (PI §87). Therefore, there is no such thing as determinacy of sense correlative to such complete explanations. No expression, not even a concept-word given a *Merkmal*-definition, could have a determinate sense.

If this is the conception of what it is for sense to be determinate, then Wittgenstein's conclusion is not that every expression is more or less vague, nor even that every expression has open texture.[2] For if there is no such thing as determinacy of sense, there is no such thing as absence of it. Since no expression could be determinate in sense, it makes no sense to ascribe to any expression the property of not having this 'property'. Instead, we should rest content with saying that there is no such thing as an explanation that forestalls every possible doubt about how to apply an expression.

---

[2] Waismann's concept of open texture is doubly incoherent according to the outlook of the *Investigations*. It is internally related to the concept of hypothesis (*Hypothese*), being the correlate of the thesis that an hypothesis can be made only more or less *probable* by any relevant evidence (cf. Exg. §80).

7. *Vagueness and meaning*

Although there is no such thing as determinacy of sense according to the important interpretation of this phrase, there is such a thing as vagueness. Some expressions can be characterized as vague. Vagueness must not be confused with absence of determinacy of sense. Nor should Wittgenstein's attitude towards the latter be confused with his attitude towards the former. Was then one of his purposes in the *Investigations* the vindication of vagueness?

The most important fact about vagueness is that its characterization is relative to an account of the meaning of expressions. Vagueness is an aspect of meaning and hence cannot be understood independently of a correct general account of meaning. Hence it cannot be characterized independently of an understanding of what it is for an explanation to be complete and exact, and how explanations are related to the use of the expressions explained. These matters, together with a general account of meaning, are clearly central concerns of the *Investigations*.

Once the background is clear, there will probably be little to discuss about vagueness. One desideratum might be a delineation of the different kinds of vagueness; another a clarification of the relations between them and such concepts as imprecision, generality, inexactness,[3] indefiniteness, unclarity, ambiguity, and indistinctness. In general, what is necessary is a clarification of the criteria for calling an expression vague: that it is vague, e.g., if its explanation contains such qualifications as 'roughly' or 'approximately' (Vol. XI, 42).

The apparent philosophical significance of vagueness simply evaporates once we abandon the preconception that any adequate explanation of meaning must specify conditions necessary and sufficient for its application. Vagueness is treated as *the* measure of how far the explanation of an expression departs from this norm. It is *the* obstacle to applying a Fregean theory of meaning to actual languages. Consequently, a criticism of the Fregean conception of meaning is easily confused with an emphasis on the vagueness of language. But this would be a correct characterization *only from the Fregean viewpoint*. If we retain the perspective of Frege and the *Tractatus* then many of the remarks of the *Investigations* amount to a vindication of vagueness.

The moral is clear: to the extent that an interpretation of the *Investigations* attaches importance to the idea that language is vague, it embodies an outlook on meaning which it was Wittgenstein's primary task to criticize and eradicate. To the extent that we learn from him the pervasive significance of vagueness we have learned nothing of what he

---

[3] It is noteworthy that the Fregean ideal of exactness is bogus (cf. Exg. §88).

most wanted to teach. It is the final irony, the acme of incomprehension, to take his remarks as stimuli to constructing logics of vagueness or semantics admitting vague expressions, since such pseudo-scientific forms of philosophy were what he was most eager to stamp out.

XII

PROPER NAMES

1. *Introduction*

Proper names have been a central topic of philosophical debate for the last century. Together with definite descriptions, they have monopolized attention in the philosophy of language. At first sight, this seems inexplicable. For surely they are merely one kind out of a host of equally interesting and problematic kinds of expressions. On further reflection, however, their pre-eminence seems intelligible. The whole Augustinian picture of language appears to be a generalization of an intuitive picture of proper names. For of a *proper* name it seems a truism that its meaning is the object named by it. Therefore the claim that every word is a name whose meaning is what it stands for is tantamount to the thesis that all words function exactly as proper names are thought to; i.e. that the relation of 'Napoleon' to Napoleon is the archetype of what it is for a word to have meaning (cf. AM 188). Since the whole Augustinian picture rests on this foundation, it seems natural that philosophers should devote exceptional energy to the scrutiny of proper names.

Though attractive, this explanation fails to fit the facts. Controversy about proper names is not treated as a dispute about the acceptability of the Augustinian picture as a framework for investigating meaning, but rather as a disagreement within the framework of this *Urbild*. The issue is not whether *any* entity is the meaning of a proper name, but rather *which* entity is; in particular whether its meaning is simply its bearer or some other thing (its sense). In conformity with the Augustinian picture, attention is limited to the contribution of proper names to descriptions (to the truth-conditions of declarative sentences). They are thus construed as one species of singular referring expression.

There is something paradoxical, perhaps even incoherent, in such a study. Everyday proper names are the paradigm used to explain the concept of meaning within the Augustinian picture. How then can it be an open question within this framework whether proper names really fit the 'Fido'-Fido model of meaning? How is it intelligible to argue, as Russell does, that no everyday proper name fits this model? Is this not a case of sawing off the branch on which one is sitting? The search for a *locus sedendi* is the futile quest for the logically proper name.

If this initial incoherence can be circumvented, the investigation of proper names within the Augustinian framework takes the predictable course of comparing them with other singular referring expressions. Proper names are to be located on the spectrum whose end-points are

definite descriptions and demonstratives. This produces the familiar polarization of no-sense theories assimilating them to demonstratives and
disguised description theories assimilating them to definite descriptions.
This grouping carries with it two dangers. First, although proper names
are, *inter alia*, devices for singular reference, they have many other uses and
differ in crucial ways from both demonstratives and descriptions. This is
likely to be under-emphasized if the subject is approached from this
perspective. Secondly, elaborating affinities with demonstratives and
descriptions is only fruitful to the extent that one is clear about the nature
of these expressions, but this clarity has been conspicuously absent.

Concentration upon the referential role of names, particularly in the
framework of a philosophical semantics, has led to gross distortion of the
nature of proper names. Philosophers have focused upon the contribution names make to the truth-conditions of declarative sentences, upon
the 'mechanism' of reference, upon devices to cope with names which
lack reference or have ambiguous reference. From a 'logical point of
view' names seem nothing but arbitrary marks for distinguishing objects
(by some means). The desideratum *unum nomen, unum nominatum* would
be secured if there were as many distinct names as there are objects to be
distinguished. For such philosophers reference numbers would be the
ideal names.

It is worth bearing in mind from the outset some of the consequent
distortions (to be discussed in detail later).

(i) Philosophers commonly treat proper names as ambiguous. There
are, accordingly, as many distinct names typographically represented by
'N' as there are objects named 'N', i.e. identity of bearer is a necessary
condition for identity of name. This misrepresents and distorts the fact
that many names are generated out of a limited stock and that many
people, places, etc., have the same name.

(ii) Philosophers contrast names with descriptions and demonstratives
by attributing to them context-invariant reference, a principle upheld by
the 'convention' making identity of reference a necessary condition of
identity of name, since this guarantees that a name cannot assume a
different reference in a different context. But this is clearly false, e.g., for
most Christian names. Another 'convention' is necessary to ensure
permanency of reference, i.e. any name that has a referent always refers
to that self-same object (the 'name-relation' is timeless). This too is
clearly false: Abram became Abraham and ceased to be Abram, while
after his conversion Paul was no longer Saul.

(iii) The referential function of names in declarative sentences is the
philosophical centre of gravity. But to neglect the multifarious uses of
names is perilous because many aspects of non-referential uses of names
may turn out to be inconsistent with features attributed to proper names
by a philosophical theory of reference. Bear in mind that names are used

in greeting others, addressing them in discourse, directing messages to them, calling them, introducing them. Proper names are employed as labels, place-holders at dinner parties, marks of ownership; they have a role as signatures, autographs, in religious rituals, in oaths and curses. It is cavalier to assume that all this is mere anthropology and beneath consideration, or else that it can all *somehow* be exhibited as systematically related to the 'primary' referential role.

(iv) Names, in contrast to descriptions, are commonly held to be semantically simple, i.e. a name has no significant parts, or else, if it does, its reference is not determined by them (and we do not understand what it names in virtue of understanding its parts). This is to ignore the apparent complexity of, e.g., 'John D. Rockefeller III', 'Oxford Road', 'Harold Godwinson'. Alternatively, philosophers introduce a new criterion of simplicity: a referring expression is simple if it is *possible* for the reference assigned to it to diverge from the reference that would be assigned to it according to its composition out of its constituents.

(v) Many names, indeed many *kinds* of names, appear to lack reference. This is an embarrassment if they are conceived as paradigmatic devices for singular reference and also (unlike descriptions) to be context-invariant. The embarrassment is reflected in two ways. First, the tendency to treat all kinds of 'empty' names as similar, thus masking differences between names of people and places in fiction (e.g. 'Mr Pickwick', 'Xanadu'), in religion (e.g. 'Zeus', 'Baal'), in myth (e.g. 'Pegasus', 'Hercules'); also names of imaginary individuals (e.g. 'Kilroy'), imaginary individuals in fiction (e.g. 'Mrs Harris' in *Martin Chuzzlewit*) and even names in science (e.g. 'Vulcan' (the supposed planet)). An apparent common feature of greatly disparate language-games is taken to justify uniform treatment. Secondly, philosophers have devised numerous strategies to explain away empty names, e.g. invoking realms of 'subsistence', 'extending ontology' to 'fictional universes of discourse'; or, rather differently, arguing that these are not really names but abbreviated descriptions; or that in fiction names are not used to refer, but only to 'pretend' to refer, or that 'empty names' are not actual but only potential names. These different strategies share a common unease about the claim that 'N' is a proper name yet lacks reference, and also a common tendency neither to distinguish the different kinds of empty names nor to describe the differences by reference to the different linguistic and other activities in which these expressions are at home.

Although many other features of proper names are similarly neglected, these considerations suffice to show that philosophers filter proper names through a set of conventions and preconceptions which threatens to strip them of their distinctive features and customary roles. Moreover, the names they thus filter are taken from far too narrow and unrepresentative a range of examples of proper names. The explanation, not surprisingly, lies in Frege's semantics with its root in the Augustinian *Urbild*. The Augustinian picture conceives of the essence of words (in general) as *naming*, and the essence of sentences as describing. It is but one small step to conceive of the simple subject/predicate sentence as describing a state of affairs by means of a proper name whose role is to pick out, refer to, an object and a predicate name which names a property attribution of which to the object constitutes a description. This naïve picture is built up into a sophisticated 'theory of language' in Frege's influential semantics.

2. *Frege: the general principles*

Since Frege it has seemed a truism that language has a systematic structure. Also, it has seemed an insight of great magnitude that the meaning of a sentence is derived from the meanings of its constituents and its structure, and that we understand a sentence in virtue of knowing its structure and the meaning of its constituents (cf. 'A word has a meaning only in the context of a sentence', pp. 145 ff.). The structure of a sentence splits up into argument-expression and function-name. The sense of a sentence is said to be *composed* of the senses of its constituents and to be its truth-conditions. The reference of a sentence is argued to be its truth-value, and this is a function of the references of its constituents. The very term 'semantics' attests to the grip of the idea that matters of reference and truth-value alone are what belong to the essence of language and communication. This is the background rationale for excluding from philosophical consideration all aspects of uses of names not directly related to their contribution to the truth-conditions of declarative sentences, i.e. whatever is irrelevant to determining their reference. It also provides an immediate argument for the claim that proper names have a meaning. For 'ΦA' and 'ΦB' (where A ≠ B) clearly differ in meaning. Since the only difference between them consists in the occurrence of the distinct names 'A' and 'B', and since the meaning of a sentence is composed of the meanings (senses) of its constituents, it must be the difference in the meanings of the proper names which explains the difference in the respective sentence-meanings. Within this framework of thought the question of whether it is correct to attribute meaning to proper names in the first place is simply foolish.

The analysis of names is the gateway to the construction of a systematic theory of meaning, given the assumption that the meaning of an expression is its contribution to the truth-conditions of declarative sentences in which it occurs. We must, as it were, break into the sense of a sentence in order to analyse it. Frege did so at the point of singular referring expressions (which he called 'proper names', and of which proper names are a special case). By 'subtracting' the senses of proper

names from the truth-conditions (sense) of sentences we can arrive at the
senses of other sentence-constituents (incomplete expressions of various
types). Hence, for Frege, the success of the whole enterprise of constructing a philosophical semantics hangs on producing a satisfactory account of
singular referring expressions.

We have already noted Frege's functional principle that the truth-value
(reference) of a sentence is a function of the references of its constituents
(so two names standing for the same thing are intersubstitutable *salva
veritate*). Another fundamental assumption is the objectivitity of truth
(GA i. xv ff.). Combining these two assumptions yields the principle of
objectivity of reference. What a referring expression stands for is settled
by the facts quite independently of what we take its reference to be.

The principle of objectivity of reference has three important aspects.

(i) Generality: for *every* referring expression our judgement that it
stands for a particular object does not guarantee that it does.

(ii) The mechanism of referring: if it always makes sense to contrast
what 'x' refers to with what we take it to refer to, we need an account of
what it is for 'x' really, objectively, to refer to a particular. The questions
'How does "x" secure its reference?', 'What *is* it for "x" to refer to an
object?' have dominated discussions ever since. There must, given
Frege's conception, be associated with every referring expression some
way of determining its reference (which must appeal only to facts
independent of our judgements). Only thus, it seems, will the reference
of 'x' be settled independently of us by the relevant facts and the mode of
reference-determination. Since the meaning of 'x' consists in its role in
determining what 'x' refers to, Frege in effect identifies the necessary
way of determining the reference of a proper name with its meaning
(or, more accurately, its sense). The sense of 'x' is objective; it determines, together with the facts, whether 'x' refers to anything, and if so,
to what.

(iii) Knowledge of reference: the grounds of any justified judgement
about the reference of 'x' must be the sense of 'x' and the relevant facts.
Hence knowledge of reference must be derivative, not immediate. So
'How do you know that "x" stands for this?' is *always* in order. (It is
therefore not surprising that scepticism about reference, worries about
undetected reference-failure or unknown ambiguous reference play so
large a role in post-Fregean discussions.)

Frege introduces the notion of sense not only as the mechanism of
securing reference but also to resolve problems concerning the possibility
of mutual understanding. Successful communication requires shared
understanding: the content of understanding must be objective (not
identity-dependent on persons, like mental images). Frege invokes the
notion of sense to account for what it is that is mutually understood in
discourse. (He takes it to be obvious that we cannot explain the notion of

the content of understanding in terms of reference: two people can both understand a proposition without knowing its truth-value, a definite description without knowing its reference, a name in fiction that has no reference, a true contingent identity statement without knowing it to be true.) Frege's elegant solution is to take the means for determining the reference of a referring expression (its sense) as being also what is understood in understanding a referring expression. Sense, being objective and existing independently of us, is the intersubjective content of communication.

What then *is* the sense of a particular expression? The obvious answer is that it is what is given by an explanation of the principle determining its reference. The sense of a proper name is given by an explanation of the objective means of determination of its bearer, i.e. what is expressed by an application rule. This application rule, according to Frege, must contain a *criterion of identity*: 'If we are to use a symbol *a* to signify an object, we must have a criterion for deciding in all cases whether *b* is the same as *a*, even if it is not always in our power to apply this criterion' (FA § 62). It is clear that a criterion of identity[1] which is contained in the sense of '*a*' must consist of conditions necessary and sufficient for identification of its referent (and 'a means of recognizing it again as the same').

3. *Frege and Russell: simple abbreviation theories*

On the grounds of a footnote (SR 58) it is common to attribute to Frege an abbreviation theory of ordinary proper names. He argues that the sense of a proper name, e.g. 'Aristotle', may differ from person to person; e.g. one person may take the sense of 'Aristotle' to be given by the description 'the pupil of Plato and teacher of Alexander the Great', while another will understand its sense as 'the teacher of Alexander the Great who was born in Stagira'. One should note, however, that Frege never explicitly states that proper names are disguised (abbreviated) definite descriptions, and elsewhere in his writings he intimates that different ways of recognizing an object as the referent of two different names suffices to attribute different senses to the names, without committing himself to the doctrine that the sense of a name is always equivalent to a definite description.

It is crucial to note that Frege, and many of his successors, take wholly for granted a vital assumption. This is that an explanation of who N is, or at least a definitive explanation which provides a means of unique

---

[1] It is crucial to notice that this conception of a criterion is totally different from Wittgenstein's; the contrast is between necessary and sufficient conditions and *a priori*, but defeasible, evidence.

identification, is itself tantamount to an explanation of the meaning or sense of the name 'N'. Frege does not apparently notice that this assumption commits him to individuating names by their bearers (or, worse, by their possible bearers!). He does notice, as the cited example shows, the variability of explanations of a given name (individuated by its bearer). However, his admission that different explanations betoken different senses is not trivial. For it threatens the assumption that it is shared sense that makes communication possible. Frege's response was to treat the variability of explanations of names as a defect of ordinary language to be eliminated in an ideal language. N's name has a multitude of distinct senses, but this is tolerable since they all determine the same reference, and our primary interest is the truth-value of statements, not the identity of the thought expressed. This is inadequate—for one of the points of introducing the notion of sense was to explain shared under-standing in terms of identity of sense. But, by Frege's admission, ordinary names are a counter-example to this thesis; yet successful communication does occur. Moreover, since he admits that fictional names, e.g. 'Odysseus' (SR 62 f.), have sense but no reference, he cannot even brush aside differences of sense as an impediment to understanding on the grounds of identity of reference.

Whether Frege was or was not an 'abbreviation theorist' is debatable. But Russell's position is unequivocal: 'The names that we commonly use, like "Socrates", are really abbreviations for descriptions' (LA 200). Accordingly, he denies that ordinary names are really names at all (cf. 'Logically proper names', p. 132).

We shall briefly summarize some of the points in favour of an abbreviation (disguised description) account of proper names. (i) Uni-quely identifying descriptions provide a means of identifying the referent of a name, which is one task for which the notion of sense or meaning of names was introduced. (ii) Descriptions, if substitutable for names, provide *one* possible strategy for avoiding paradoxes arising out of sentences of the form 'x exists' (a strategy adopted by Russell). (iii) The cognitive non-triviality of non-trivial identity-statements is rendered perspicuous on the assumption that the two co-referential names have distinct senses given by different descriptions. (iv) It explains how a sentence containing a name without a reference nevertheless has a sense. (v) One way of explaining who N is to give an identifying description. (vi) It explains how a name, which is the name of more than one individual, can be used to refer to only one of them on a given occasion.

Against this simple abbreviation account weighty arguments can be mustered. (i) Contrast proper names with definite descriptions. (a) The question 'Who was the victor of Austerlitz?' typically requires the answer 'Napoleon', not 'The husband of Josephine'. (b) The victor of Austerlitz was *named*, *christened*, *called* 'Napoleon' (or 'Napoleone'), but is correctly *described* as the victor of Austerlitz. He became, and then ceased to be, the Emperor of France, but did not change his name, nor, arguably, did his name change its sense. (c) One uses names as signatures or autographs—not descriptions. (d) People are given, have, and sometimes change their names; descriptions apply or fail to apply to them. A husband gives his wife his name, but that is not the same as giving her his description. (e) The question 'What does "the man who broke the bank at Monte Carlo" mean?' is a request for an explanation of meaning of the description, and is incorrectly answered by 'N'. The latter answer would only be appropriate for the question 'Who broke the bank at Monte Carlo?' (ii) Who N is is often *not* explained by description but by ostension, introduction or self-introduction. Although a description can be milked out of the ostensive explanation, or introduction, is it obvious that the name has not been understood until a definite description has been squeezed out? (iii) If N's name 'N' (disregarding all others named 'N') is equivalent in meaning to a description, *which* description? As Napoleon progressed from cradle to grave, did the sense of his name continually change? When he won Austerlitz, did he also unknowingly change the meaning of his name? Saying that a name abbreviates a description *at a time* is of no avail, for surely the meaning of 'Napoleon' in 1769 was not 'The victor of Austerlitz in 1805'? (iv) Conversely, people change their names (e.g. popes, women on marriage), but do they keep its meaning? If John Smith walks into a registry office, and comes out Jack Jones, has he kept the meaning of his original name?

We now turn to Wittgenstein's objections to Russell's claim (cf. Exg. §79), leaving aside for the moment any consideration of the legitimacy of ascribing meaning or sense to names in the first place and of identifying explaining who N is with explaining what 'N' means. (i) If a name is defined by a description, and different people give different descriptions (or the same person gives different 'definitions' on different occasions), then, it seems, that name is ambiguous, and so is every sentence in which it occurs (this was Frege's predicament). (ii) In fact, no one would give such a Russellian equivalence. For if it turned out that the given description of N rendered one's statement 'ΦN' false, one would normally simply give an alternative description. No definition of 'N', whether by a single description or by a conjunction of descriptions, need be acknowledged as expressing what I mean and understand by 'N'.

4. *Cluster theories of proper names*

Given some of the difficulties that arise out of the simple abbreviation theory, it was entirely natural that Frege's insights should be preserved by modification within the over-all framework. Hence the growth of cluster theories. They took their original inspiration from the *Investigations* §79. Since this involved a misinterpretation of that passage (cf. Exg. §79), we shall ignore it in this discussion.

The core of cluster theories consists in the claim that the meaning of a proper name 'N' is given by a cluster of uniquely identifying descriptions, such that if most (or a weighted proportion) are satisfied by X, then 'N' refers to X (i.e. X is identical with N). This strategy seems to save part of the spirit of a Fregean approach by relaxing the demand for strict determinacy of sense, contending that mutual understanding admits of degrees, and admitting that particular explanations may be incomplete.

It is noteworthy that variants of the cluster theory can be constructed exploiting at least two degrees of freedom. (i) It may take a social or 'anthropological' form; i.e. the cluster associated with the name 'N' may be the set of (overlapping) descriptions in terms of which the speakers in a community cash 'N'. Alternatively, it may take an individualistic form; i.e. a cluster will be defined relative to each speaker, consisting of the alternative descriptions which he uses on various occasions (or is disposed to use) in explaining 'N'. (ii) It may introduce the cluster of descriptions for each name 'N' in a highly regimented form appropriate to a calculus; e.g. assigning a weight to each member of the cluster and specifying precise values of the sum of the weights of the descriptions satisfied by X to function as thresholds for settling whether X is N and whether X is not N. Alternatively, it may take a much looser and weaker form; i.e. it may demand only that there be *some* internal connection between each name 'N' and *some* set of descriptions, since otherwise it would be unintelligible that demonstrated misapplications of 'N' could be treated as criteria for not knowing who N is.

The advantages of the cluster theory, viewed from the Fregean perspective, are patent. Variability in the explanations of a name among speakers or, over time, with one speaker, does not entail that this name has multiple senses. Communication does rest on shared understanding whose extent is determined by reference to the sense of the expression (i.e. the degree of overlap of clusters of descriptions). The sense of a name 'N' is associated with a complex means for determining its reference, since satisfying a certain proportion of the descriptions of the cluster is a condition for being N. Hence the cluster theory shows how to extend Frege's conception of sense to singular referring expressions whose sense appears more or less indeterminate. (There is a parallel extension for concept-words exploiting the notion of cluster concepts, cf. 'Family resemblance', p. 195.)

The defects of the cluster theory are perhaps not so apparent, but none the less real and important.

(i) It is too restrictive in several respects. First, explaining who N is need not take the form of describing N; it might be done by pointing to N or to a picture of N. Unless such explanations are somehow transformed into descriptions, the cluster theory cannot be a complete account of knowing who N is. Secondly, explaining who N is need not consist of giving a true description of N; e.g., someone's explanation of who Christopher Columbus was might be a false description, and in spite of that he might be asserting something about Columbus or asking a question about him. What is crucial is that his giving this description is treated as a criterion for knowing who N is. Thirdly, explaining who N is need not consist in giving a uniquely identifying description of N; e.g., in suitable circumstances an acceptable answer to 'Who was Plato?' might be 'A great Greek philosopher'. What is required to establish knowing who N is may vary with circumstances; what is accepted as a criterion here may be giving a description that falls far short of being uniquely identifying. Fourthly, explaining who N is by pointing to N or by giving a description of N is in many cases treated as a complete explanation of who N is and as a criterion for full knowledge of who N is. This is inconsistent with the guiding idea that the content of the cluster goes far beyond what is explicit in particular explanations of who N is. On that view, giving any particular explanation (at least short of a conjunction of all the descriptions in the cluster for N) could at best be good inductive evidence for full knowledge of who N is.

(ii) The cluster theory does not establish that there is shared understanding of names because it does not succeed in showing that there is anything in common between two people each of whom knows 'the meaning of "N"'. According to the anthropological version, only the investigator who has collected the data really knows the meaning of 'N', and the claim of common understanding is as empty as the thesis that a community has communal property because each member of it owns his own plot. According to the individualist version the meaning of 'N' is something hypothetical, transcending particular explanations of who N is. Severing the meaning from these explanations leaves no clear means for determining what the meaning of 'N' is and hence no basis for shared understanding.

(iii) Conceived as outlining an account of the meaning of proper names, the cluster theory divorces understanding from explanation and thereby contravenes the principle that what is understood in understanding an expression is just what is explained in explaining how to use it (i.e. that understanding is the 'correlate' of explanation). In the calculus version, this is obvious. Explanations of who N is (conceived as explanations of what 'N' means) do not take the form of specifying a large cluster of definite descriptions together with a set of weightings and threshold values for being and for not being the referent of N. We *do not* so explain names (though of course we might do so). The same divorce of understanding and explanation holds for a weak cluster theory. This account concedes that explanations of who N is may take many forms, including pointing at N or at a portrait of N; but it insists that these explanations, whatever their surface form, must set up some internal connection between something's being N and its satisfying certain definite descriptions, since otherwise misapplications of 'N' could not be treated as criteria for not knowing who N is (for not understanding 'N'). Of course, I may explain to someone who N is by pointing him out in a crowd; and if the learner later misidentifies N, I might criticize him by saying 'That's not N; his hair is straight, but N's is curly'. But does this imply that I meant to convey by my ostensive explanation that N has curly hair and that the learner understands my explanation only if he gathers this information from it? According to the weak version, whether or not we suppose that this explanation by description is hidden in the ostensive explanation, there is a logical gap between what is understood by 'N' and what is contained overtly in explanations of 'N'.

(iv) Every version of the cluster theory presupposes that there is an internal connection between something's being N and its satisfying (a certain proportion of) certain definite descriptions. This has two props, each of which is shaky. First, a fallacious inference from the fact that giving certain descriptions characterizing N is a criterion for knowing who N is: this expresses a 'grammatical' relationship between explaining who N is and knowing who N is, and it is assumed that this presupposes a parallel 'internal connection' between the descriptions given in the explanation of who N is and the property of being identical with N. This supposition is quite gratuitous (cf. 'Meaning and understanding', pp. 361 ff.). Secondly, there is a fallacious inference from the facts that correct identifications of a person as N can often be justified by citing features of the identified person and that misidentifications of N can be criticized by citing features of the mistaken person. This does not prove that knowing that N either has or lacks this relevant feature is part of knowing who N is; still less that a complete explanation of who N is must mention this point or that there is an internal connection between having or lacking this feature and being N. This line of reasoning makes the same gratuitous assumption as the previous one, but compounds the error with a defective conception of completeness of explanation and an unsupported attribution of implicit knowledge. The cluster theory assumes that there must be some internal relation between uniquely satisfying certain descriptions and being N and tinkers with its details, whereas there is no need for this presumption to be satisfied.

These criticisms of the cluster theory are not definitive. What they establish, however, is that the cluster theory has deep implications concerning the relations of meaning to understanding and of understanding to explanation. This suggests the absurdity of pursuing controversies about the cluster theory in isolation from much wider considerations having no special bearing on proper names. It shifts the focus of controversy to deeper and more general issues. It also opens up the possibility of making a fresh start on the discussion of proper names by building up from some of the general principles gleaned from the *Investigations* rather than setting out from current 'theories of proper names'.

5. *Wittgenstein: the general principles*

In previous discussions we have started to establish a case for some fundamental principles in Wittgenstein's philosophy of language. Meaning is what is given by explanations of meaning. Giving a correct explanation of meaning is a criterion of understanding. Understanding is an objective matter, establishable by reference to a person's behaviour; but since that behaviour does not *entail* understanding, its being true that a person understands an expression never collapses into our taking him to understand it, even though satisfaction of the criteria of understanding renders it certain, *ceteris paribus*, that he understands. The objectivity of understanding is thus established without reference to the objectivity of reference and truth.

Consequently, the Fregean conception of objectivity of reference is erroneous. That the reference of 'x' is objective does not require that there be some means for identifying its reference which, together with the facts, determines independently of us what 'x' refers to. It requires only that what someone takes 'x' to refer to be a distinct question from what 'x' refers to. This distinction obtains if there is an established *practice* of using referring expressions against which a particular person's applications of 'x' can be checked. The basis of objectivity of reference is the practice of using referring expressions; no transcendent viewpoint is presupposed. On the other hand, absence of a transcendent viewpoint does not reduce us to scepticism. The defeasibility of a person's claim that 'x' refers to such-and-such does not entail that it cannot be established with certainty, nor that he cannot be said to know it. There is no incompatibility between objectivity of reference, rightly conceived, and the possibility of certainty in determining the reference of an expression.

The key to a surview of proper names lies in the different aspects of understanding names and of understanding different sentences in which they occur. Wittgenstein never elaborated this point, but it is surely in harmony with his conception of meaning, understanding, and explanation. The method we shall adopt to exhibit the complexity of these matters is to consider different forms of manifesting lack of understanding of names in sentences in which they occur.

(i) Understanding a token of 'x' as a name: someone might not construe a token of 'x' as a name, even though it is one (e.g. one might wrongly take a use of 'the Rocky Mountains' to be a description, not realize that 'If' is the name of Kipling's poem, fail to recognize mention of a book title for what it is); similarly, one may misconstrue a token of 'x' as a name even though it is not one (e.g. taking 'Moreover' in 'Moreover, the dog licked his wounds' as the dog's name). Understanding a name presupposes recognizing it as a name. That in turn requires knowledge of the rich and varied conventions concerning what is named and what stock of names is drawn upon for given types of objects in a particular language.

(ii) Understanding the type-name 'x': someone might not know what the name 'Peter' means (viz. 'rock'), that the second component of 'Leif Ericson' is a patronymic, that 'Vanya' is a diminutive of 'Ivan', or that 'Mathilda' is a woman's name. For many names there are such possibilities of failures in comprehension, some of which bear on knowing the use of the name (e.g. patronymic, diminutive) and others which do not (e.g. the meaning of 'Peter'). Titles of many books, plays, operas, poems, etc., occupy a rather curious position, for many such names are not, *qua* type-expressions, generally employed as names (e.g. 'War and Peace', 'Wuthering Heights'). Understanding, here, is complex. One must grasp the expression as the name of such a work of art, grasp the meaning of the title, and perhaps also understand the rationale of the name (read *Much Ado about Nothing*, then you will understand the title).

(iii) Understanding how names are used: someone might not understand the practice of using names to address messages, to call persons, as signatures to assume legal obligations, to commemorate people, etc. (Names of people, in this respect, are very different from place names, let alone names of books.) Part of understanding a name is grasping at least the important elements in the institutions of name-using characteristic of the community to whose language the name belongs.

(iv) Understanding who or what a token-name is used to refer to: a person might not know, or might misidentify, which S (where 'S' is a sortal) 'N' is used to refer to. Doubtless the question 'Who is N?' or 'Which N do you mean?' are the most common questions that arise with respect to proper names. Because of our general command of all the facets of how to use names (in our society), our understanding of an utterance incorporating a particular name is commonly fixed up to this last point: knowing who or what 'N' stands for.

The beginning of wisdom is recognition of the multiple aspects of what is called 'understanding names'. The second step is to note the complexity of the criteria severally linked with each of the aspects of understanding. This alone opens up the possibility of a critical, but nevertheless conservative, reaction to the Fregean tradition. This conservative reaction is indeed closest to Wittgenstein's remarks about proper names. It leaves undisturbed three interrelated fundamental assumptions: (i) that names have meanings (Wittgenstein never hesitates on this issue); (ii) that explaining who N is is explaining the meaning of 'N'; hence, (iii) that names are typically ambiguous inasmuch as indefinitely many people may bear the same name. Nevertheless, the conservative reaction stresses three significant points missing from the traditional account. (i) There are diverse aspects, quite distinct from reference, to understanding names and sentences in which they occur. (ii) There are diverse *criteria* for knowing who N is which are compatible with mutual understanding. Equally, there are diverse criteria for understanding different practices and institutions of using names. (iii) There is the possibility of a constant fluctuation between symptoms and criteria of 'understanding names', in particular in knowing who N is.

Leaving aside for the moment the first three, less familiar, aspects of understanding names, and the relations between them, we turn to the question of the criteria for understanding to which S 'N' (in a given utterance) refers. If we restrict 'N' to a person's name, this is the question of the criteria for knowing who N is. The forms of explanation of who N is, and the criteria for knowing to whom 'N' refers, are diverse.

There are radically different kinds of explanation of who N is. (i) Ostensive explanation. (ii) Locative explanation. (iii) Explanation by description: we give a description of N *sufficient in a particular context* to identify N and distinguish him from others with whom he might be confused. Different descriptions may be appropriate in the same context, some descriptions may be useless in some contexts (e.g. a description of someone's career will not help to identify him in a crowd (EBT 494)), and what is sufficient in one context may be insufficient or excessive in another. (iv) Explanation by another proper name. (v) Explanation by anaphoric pronoun (important in fiction). (vi) Explanation by introduction and self-introduction. (vi) Explanation by photographs and portraits.

There is equal diversity in the criteria for understanding who N is, namely giving a correct explanation (the possible diversity of which has just been noted) and using 'N' correctly. The internal diversity of the criterion of correct use is evident too, e.g. using 'N' to call N, address him, make statements about him, to give directions for finding him, to make a list of people who . . ., etc.

Like the duality of criteria for understanding an expression in general, the duality of criteria for knowing who N is has important corollaries. Potential conflict of criteria for knowing who N is can be avoided only by the assumption that correct application of a rule (explanation) flows from knowing it. Wittgenstein argues at length against this picture. In the case of two kinds of criteria for knowing who N is, this is tantamount to claiming a logical connection between them: viz. that giving a correct explanation of who N is entails applying 'N' correctly. But the criteria for knowing who N is are logically independent of each other. It is important to our use of names that a person who correctly explains who N is generally goes on to use 'N' correctly. But it is a contingent regularity, and it is noteworthy that one may be able to explain who N is, yet be unable to recognize, identify, him.

Giving a correct explanation of 'N' is a *criterion* for knowing who N is. Hence *any* explanation of who N is will be open to revision in the event of defeating evidence. The indefinitely extendable possibility of revising such explanations is prominent in Wittgenstein's account (PI §§79, 82, 87). Moreover, in certain circumstances a person's giving an explanation of who N is that would be incorrect if taken as an application rule may none the less count as a criterion for his knowing who N is (e.g. a schoolboy who explains that Columbus was the Spaniard who was the first European to land in North America).

Although defeasible, satisfaction of criteria for knowing who N is establishes with certainty, *ceteris paribus*, that a person knows who N is. The *possibility* of defeat by additional evidence does not demonstrate that the explanation is inadequate and needs completion (PI §87). No extension would purchase immunity to revision and hence none would constitute an improvement on the original explanation in the absence of defeating evidence.

6. *Wittgenstein: some critical consequences*

The strategy delineated has important bearing on traditional approaches to the issue which are conducted under the same set of general assumptions.

(i) No-sense theories, e.g. those of Mill and Kripke, fail to make provision for criteria of understanding. A person's making any number of correct statements about N is accordingly compatible with his not knowing who N is. At best, whether someone knows who N is can be a more or less probable hypothesis. The same conclusion holds, *ex hypothesi*, for whether he understands 'N'. Nor is any provision made for aspects of understanding names that do not pertain to knowing the reference of a name (conceived as individuated by bearer). (Our criticisms of archetypal no-sense theories is to be found in 'Logically proper names', pp. 138 ff.)

(ii) Both abbreviation and cluster theories identify knowing who N is with knowing a rule stating necessary and sufficient conditions for someone to be N. This confuses a defeasible criterion of knowing who N is with a sufficient condition for being N.

(iii) The independence of the two kinds of criteria for knowing who N is reveals another misconception: that a person's knowing who N is, where not manifested in his ability to explain necessary and sufficient conditions for someone to be N, must consist in his implicit knowledge of such a rule. It is assumed that someone's identifications of N must flow from something; if not from a principle that he can state, then from one that he knows implicitly but cannot formulate. But the *only* ground for attributing such implicit knowledge is that the person applies 'N' correctly, and this is already a criterion for his knowing who N is. So the manoeuvre is redundant unless the reservoir picture of knowledge is correct.

(iv) The variability of explanations of who N is seems tantamount to radical ambiguity of 'N' (Frege), unless these explanations are selections from a single, highly complex, hypothesized application rule (cluster theories). The horns of this dilemma are avoidable if giving any one of various explanations is viewed as a criterion of knowing who N is. This applies to names the conclusion that the multiplicity of criteria for understanding an expression does not entail multiplicity in what is understood (cf. 'Meaning and understanding', pp. 361 ff.).

(v) Knowing who N is may be described as knowing how to identify N. This platitude may mislead. 'Knowing how to identify N' seems to legitimate the request for a justification of *any* identification of N. No doubt we can sometimes justify taking a person to be N. But if someone introduces himself by saying 'I am N', does it make sense to ask how he knows? Of someone with whom I live (wife, husband, parent, child), does it make sense to ask how I know who this person is? Must I always have a justification for saying 'That is N'? That there are criteria for a person's knowing who N is, indeed that a person can and does explain who N is, does not entail that his knowledge of who N is must be derivative knowledge.

(vi) Recognition of the non-triviality of contingent identity-statements does not force us to embrace a Fregean theory. Giving *some* correct explanation of who A is is a criterion for knowing who A is. Whether not knowing that 'B' is one correct answer to 'Who is A?' manifests ignorance of who A is depends on what we deploy or count as criteria for not knowing who A is. But typically we do not treat ignorance of this kind as such a criterion. Hence there is no inconsistency in attributing to someone knowledge of who A is and knowledge of who B is yet denying that he knows that A is the same person as B (see p. 253 below).

(vii) Similarly, the intelligibility of sentences incorporating 'empty names' does not entail the truth of Frege's account. All that is required is that there be criteria for someone's understanding a sentence of the form 'ΦA', that involve neither his standing in some relation (e.g. acquaintance) with A nor his specifying conditions under which something *would* be identical with A. This requirement is fulfilled. An explanation of who Sherlock Holmes is would not be ostensive, nor would it stipulate conditions necessary and sufficient for a person to be Sherlock Holmes which happen not to be satisfied (see p. 250 below).

Even the most conservative reaction to traditional 'theories of proper names' along lines intimated by Wittgenstein would be revolutionary. In particular, it suggests that the traditional battle-lines between no-sense and disguised-description theories are indefensible. That in turn suggests that we may be well advised to begin afresh, to try to look with an unprejudiced eye at the practices of using proper names.

7. *The significance of proper names*

Philosophers since Frege have examined proper names almost exclusively as part of a 'theory of singular reference' within the framework of an endeavour to construct a 'philosophical semantics'. Our investigation suggests that giving an account of proper names boils down to elucidating criteria for understanding names and sentences in which names occur, and that such understanding has many aspects each of which may give rise to misunderstandings of various types. Hence a proper investigation of *proper names* requires one to cast one's net wider than philosophers customarily do.

(i) Possession of a name: 'Why should it not be possible that a man's own name be sacred to him? Surely it is both the most important instrument given to him and also something like a piece of jewellery hung around his neck at birth' (GB 32). Wittgenstein here stresses a point wholly disregarded in philosophical debate: the enormous significance in most cultures of having a name, and the importance we attribute to our name. Names, for us, are not mere referring devices, replaceable, in principle, by numerals. One could not say of prisoners' numbers what Goethe said of persons' names[2] (MS. 131, 141). We speak of bringing glory to our name, of making a name for ourselves in the world, of dishonouring our name or besmirching it, of having our name dragged through the mud. Christians have held possession of a name (through baptism) necessary for salvation, hence the importance of christening infants immediately after birth or even before (e.g. 'Vitalis'), lest they die

---

[2] Goethe's remark from *Dichtung und Wahrheit* is quoted in Exg. §171. Cf. also Jean Valjean's striking remark in Victor Hugo's *Les Misérables* V, vii, 1:
'Fauchelevent may have lent me his name, but I have no right to use it. A name is an identity . . . To make use of a borrowed name is an act of dishonesty, as much a theft as to steal a purse or a watch. I cannot cheat decent people in that way—never, never, never! Better to suffer the tortures of the damned! And that is why I have told you all this." He sighed and added a last word: "Once I stole a loaf of bread to stay alive; but now I cannot steal a name in order to go on living.'

nameless. The corollary of attaching importance to having a name is dread of losing it. Hence a severe form of punishment is deprivation of one's name (e.g. outlawing some clan names in eighteenth-century Scotland). Referring to a person (e.g. a prisoner) by a numeral rather than his name is a form of degradation. Enforced allocation of new names from a select stock, as was common with respect to slaves in the eighteenth century, reflects the attitude held towards the slaves. Even 'harmless' punning on a person's name (as Herder on 'Goethe') is commonly felt to be peculiarly insulting and hurtful. In all these cases the 'significance' of a name extends far beyond its role as a singular referring expression. Somebody who did not understand this would betray at least a partial failure to understand names and their uses. For these features are not mere anthropological curiosities. They interlock with the form of life of a culture and involve features of the correct use of proper names.

(ii) Uses of names: Wittgenstein's correlating meaning and use should promote a closer examination of the use of names. They have a wide variety of roles apart from their referential function. Criteria of under-standing allow direct consideration of their uses in non-declarative sentences: vocatively, in questions, and in commands. It may be that in these cases the traditional appeal of the notion that names function primarily as singular referring expressions whose significance is exhausted by how they stand for individuals will still dominate. Hence one will try, e.g., to explain their vocative role by reference to their 'primary' referential role. But there are many familiar uses of names for which this move seems far-fetched, cases where the wider 'significance' of a name, though obvious, is screened out by viewing it primarily as a referring device. A symptom of this is the fact that there are uses of a name where it cannot be replaced by any other expression, not even by a definite description conceded to have the same reference. A name may be irreplaceable. This is so in certain oaths, in the ceremony of swearing by one's name, in signing a legal document, in staking a claim to a piece of property, in a marriage ceremony, etc. Another symptom concerns the prohibitions or restrictions on the use of a name by certain persons in certain circumstances, e.g. the use of pet-names, nicknames, forename or surname, name with or without title, etc., or the impermissibility in some societies of mentioning or using the name of a deceased person for a given length of time, or of A's using B's name if A stands in a certain kinship-relation to B. It is not obvious that this very wide range of features, only a few of which are here mentioned, should be dismissed as 'mere pragmatics'.

In certain circumstances a name is not only irreplaceable, but also has, as it were, a life of its own. The closest approximation to immortality is fame. A person 'lives on' after his death provided his *name* survives, enshrined in the hearts and minds of men. This seems very much a part of our conception of names, not just a ridiculous superstition.

Names are used to label property (clothes), on door-bells, on tomb-stones and memorials, on signposts to show directions, on maps, and in numerous other ways. Knowing the use of a name involves far more (and in some ways far less) than knowing an unerring means for identifying its bearer on a given occasion of its use.

(iii) Ubiquity: most names are drawn from a relatively limited common stock; indeed, from common stocks—for there are different stocks of names for different kinds of things (e.g. Christian names of males, of females, names of different kinds of pedigree animals, names of battleships). Naming, Wittgenstein noted, is rather like attaching a label to an object, perhaps like hanging the label 'PORT' on a decanter. In our linguistic cupboard, as it were, we have a store of names appropriate for different kinds of things. Allocating a name to the correct stock is part of understanding it, misallocating it a form of misunderstanding. 'Mathilda' is a woman's name, not a man's; 'Fido' is a dog's name, not a person's; and 'Moreover' is not a name at all. Taking 'Mathilda' as a man's name is a criterion for failing to understand this name. (It has nothing to do with the ability to answer the question, 'Who is Mathilda?') This connotative aspect of proper names may be more or less rigid. Nothing prevents a person today from calling his son 'Mathilda'. Name-giving not in accord with the 'connotation' of a name typically, with us, results merely in eccentricity. But it would have been impossible to christen a child 'Beelzebub' or 'Judas' in medieval England.

(iv) Etymology: the derivation of a proper name might seem of mere antiquarian interest—not a contribution, except by coincidence, to clarifying its meaning. But in the case of proper names this conclusion is mildly perverse. The question 'What does "Peter" mean?' has one (and only one) quite ordinary use, and the answer to it would be 'rock' (from Greek '$\pi\acute{\epsilon}\tau\rho o\varsigma$'). Hence what philosophers dismiss from consideration is the only admissible answer to their question as ordinarily used and understood. (Other kinds of answer to 'What does "N" mean?' may be appropriate for other kinds of names, e.g. the seventeenth-century Christian name 'Original', the book-title *Principia Mathematica* or the play-title *Back to Methuselah*.)

(v) Name-giving: philosophers treat name-giving as a species of stipulative definition. Baptism is likened to the ostensive definition of a new symbol. This means that bestowing a name is not a use of the name at all. Hence it cannot be a misuse. Every act of name-giving is an autonomous linguistic activity, a preparation for the real business of using a name to refer to its bearer. This conception ignores the fact that proper names are typically chosen from a common stock. More impor-tantly, it ignores the fact that there are principles restricting or necessitating certain choices. Principles of restriction are obvious. At the least stringent end of the spectrum is our segregation of forenames into male and female names, or a ban on giving the same forenames to different living children of the same parents. More restrictive would be the practice of choosing a child's name from among the forenames of deceased ancestors, or limiting certain names to the eldest child (e.g. 'Original') or to twins. Even more restrictive would be the practice of selecting names from a limited stock with the proviso that the chosen name must not already be owned by a living member of the society. Here, if the stock were meagre, a child might have to wait for a name, perhaps without any right to refuse the first vacated name offered. Here principles of restriction collapse into principles of necessitation. These too are familiar. In a name system incorporating patryonymics, nobody can choose his or another's patronymic. The father's death may pre-ordain the name ('Posthumus' or 'Posthuma'). In certain systems of necronyms or technonyms a person's name, or part of it, is predeter-mined by principles for allocation (and change) of name. The more prominent, institutionalized, and stringent the principles governing the selection of names, the more name-giving resembles a *use* of a name; equally, the more relevant to understanding the name will be its connotative aspects. In a name system where each person has a forename, middle name and surname, each restricted or perhaps necessitated by different conventions, there is much to understand in bestowing names upon a child, and much to be understood from the mere name of an adult. Deviant (attempted) name-giving may be a criterion of misunder-standing the name. Equally, failure to realize that a person's middle name signifies his father's or mother's lineage, his totem or tribe, his relation-ship to a significant object or person, etc., will also show a form of misunderstanding. This may be reflected in many ways, e.g., asking closed questions, or what amount to self-contradictory questions.

(vi) Complexity: names are held to be unanalysable or simple; they are not understood in virtue of understanding their parts (if any). Apparent counter-examples are circumvented by appeal to a counterfactual, e.g. that this road (person) might still be called 'Oxford Road' ('Harold Godwinson') even if it were impassable to traffic and no longer led to Oxford (even if he were not Godwin's son). Hence it is inferred that the constituents of a name are (a) irrelevant to understanding it, and (b) do not determine (or have a role in determining) its referent, because there are possible circumstances in which they would not do so. This conclusion is unwarranted (and, incidentally, embodies a pattern of reasoning against which Wittgenstein argues extensively). That some things *might* not, in changed circumstances, fulfil a certain role (e.g. samples, methods of measurement and calculation) does not prove that they *do* not.

This mistaken traditional reasoning rests on two assumptions about names. First, only questions concerning reference-determination are relevant to understanding a name. Hence knowing how to determine its reference amounts to complete understanding. Would someone lacking knowledge of the system of Roman nomenclature, who was told 'That / is Marcus Tullius Cicero' have a full understanding of this name, know its use (e.g. how to address its bearer)? Anglo-Saxons commonly find Russian novels bewildering because they do not understand the Russian name system of patronymics, diminutives, etc. As noted above, in many name systems the complexity is genuine; different constituents are governed by different principles of selection and make distinctive contributions to the name—and hence involve distinct criteria of understanding. Secondly, it is assumed that the content of understanding a name must be given by a *Merkmal*-application rule. This is what gives room for the counterfactual argument: e.g. being Godwin's son is not a logically necessary condition of being Harold Godwinson, hence not part of what is understood in understanding the name. This assumption is attacked in relating meaning to criteria of understanding. For there are criteria for understanding a name, even though there are no principles specifying necessary and sufficient conditions for its application.

(vii) Secondary reference: there is a strong temptation to speak of multiple reference in the case of allusive use of proper names. It is a product of too limited a conception of understanding names and sentences in which they occur. An account in terms of different degrees or depth of understanding is preferable. There is no simple answer to the question whether 'Mozart' in Mörike's novella refers to the composer. But clearly one would not fully understand this work if one knew nothing about the composer or failed to relate one's knowledge to the central figure in *Mozart's Journey to Prague*. Discussion of such allusions calls for sensitive judgement. The question 'What is the reference of "N"?' is an inappropriate vehicle for such discussion, whereas 'What is involved in correct understanding of particular sentences incorporating "N"?' is more fruitful.

(viii) Empty names: in connection with names, philosophers suffer from a *horror vacui*. It results, again, from conceiving of names exclusively as referring devices and of understanding them as being exhausted by knowing the means of reference-determination. But names are derived from recognized stocks, often by systematic rules, and there is nothing odd in there being unallocated names. Wittgenstein emphasizes this in the analogy between names and labels, for a label might not be hung on anything (EBT 577). The multiple forms of so-called reference failure must be examined separately, for they are severally distinctive. But none of the forms of emptiness (fiction, fable, myth, jokes, pagan deities, as well as 'unallocated' names, etc.) threatens treating an expression as a genuine proper name. What advantage can be derived from making the classification of an expression as a proper name depend on the factual question of whether it has a reference?

One important aspect of distortion concerns knowing who N is in a variety of cases of so-called 'empty names'. One strategy (Frege's) equates knowing who N is with knowing the meaning of 'N', i.e. knowing a means of identifying N. What is known and understood is the sense of 'N', and this, together with the facts, will secure reference for 'N'. In the case of empty names what we know is what *would* have to be the case for 'N' to secure reference, and hence for any sentence containing 'N' to be true. But what would 'have to be the case' for 'Zeus' to 'secure reference', or 'Pegasus', 'Sherlock Holmes', or 'Kilroy'? Surely the answer is that *no* set of facts would establish that someone was Zeus or Sherlock Holmes, or that some horse was Pegasus. Yet any reader of Conan Doyle can say who Sherlock Holmes is! A different temptation is to equate knowing who N is with knowing the reference of 'N', and to conceive of the latter as involving a relation between the speaker and the reference. At the Russellian limit this relation may be conceived as acquaintance; less extreme versions may be satisfied with, e.g., a putative causal link. Both strategies err. One knows who N is if one can satisfactorily explain who N is, and what counts as an explanation depends upon the context of the language-game in which the name is at home. To know who David Copperfield is one need neither possess a means of identifying a person which together with the facts will determine an object as being David Copperfield, nor need one, *per impossibile*, stand in some relationship to David Copperfield. But one must know something about the practice of story-telling, and possess some minimal knowledge of Dickens's novel. Knowing who N is in such cases does not require that N 'exist', nor does it in general necessitate knowing what would have to be true for N to exist. It involves using 'N' correctly, in relevant contexts of discourse about novels, pagan religion, myth, etc., and explaining who N is correctly by reference to such contexts.

(ix) Timelessness of reference: the practical adoption of this allegedly anodyne 'convention' by a person would manifest a form of misunderstanding of names and their use. After Miss Smith has married Mr Jones, she is Mrs Jones, not Miss Smith. Nor need her previous name remain 'vacated'. In eighteenth-century England 'Miss Smith' would be used to designate the eldest unmarried daughter of the Smith family, so that a younger sister would assume this name as soon as the next older one 'vacated' it. To persist in using 'Miss Smith' to refer to Mrs Jones would be a mistake or an insult. This is even more obvious and incontrovertible in name systems involving necronyms or technonyms. So too in cases of religious conversion (e.g. Paul and Abraham), adoption, or the medieval practice of allocating a new name on confirmation in special cases (Archbishop Peckham's ruling: the person's name before God and in law is (thenceforth) that conferred at confirmation in such cases).

All these aspects of the 'significance' of proper names have been ignored by philosophers. Looking at names from the viewpoint of criteria of understanding can remedy this defect. It might lead us to appreciate how different proper names are from arbitrary signs or index numbers. A community whose language contained no expressions comparable to proper names in their ramifying 'significance' would have a way of life and thought very different from ours.

8. Proper names and meaning

Thus far we have skirted gingerly around the elementary question 'Do names have a meaning at all?' It is time to face this question head on.

Frege had at least five reasons for ascribing meaning or sense to names: (i) to explain how a sentence of the form 'ΦA' has a sense; (ii) to explain the difference in sense between 'ΦA' and 'ΦB'; (iii) to explain the informativeness of non-trivial identity-statements; (iv) to explain how we can understand a sentence containing an empty name; (v) to provide a 'mechanism of reference' (a means of identifying a reference) that will simultaneously explain the contribution of a name to the meaning of a sentence and provide the content of understanding when names (and sentences containing them) are understood.

Wittgenstein speaks freely of the meanings of proper names. He distinguishes the meaning of a name from its bearer (PI §§40–3) and points out that the meaning of a name is sometimes explained ostensively (PI §43). In PI §79 he speaks of defining the name 'N'. We have not yet attempted to clarify whether, and to what extent, our application of some of Wittgenstein's principles to the matter of explaining and understanding proper names commits one to attributing meaning to names over and above the innocuous sense in which 'Peter' means 'rock' or 'Moses' means 'drawn out of water'.

We shall start with some common-or-garden hestitations. The *only* use we give to such questions as 'What does "John" mean?' or 'What does "Carter" mean?' is as requests for explanations of the etymology or derivation of these names. (Further refinements are necessary for other kinds of names, e.g. place names and titles of books, songs, plays, etc.) We do not ask 'What does "Napoleon" mean?' (except in the above sense) but rather 'Who was Napoleon?' Still less do we ask when we do not know who is being talked about, 'What does *the name* "John" mean?', but rather 'Who is John?' or 'Which John do you mean?' or even 'John who?' (answered by, e.g., 'John Smith' or 'John, the plumber'). We do not treat such answers as explanations of the meaning of 'John', although they may be partial explanations of what was meant in saying 'John called this morning'. We speak of different persons bearing the same name, but would be bewildered if told that in 1899 there were two Winston Churchills (one a statesman, the other an American novelist)[3] but each one's name had a quite different meaning from the other's. If we do not understand an assertion 'ΦN' because we do not know who N is, *that* is what we would say, not 'I don't know the meaning of "N"' or 'I don't understand the name "N"'. Are these mere matters of idiom?

These humble considerations may, however, be reinforced by examining some of the consequences of philosophers' attributions of meaning or sense to individuals' names. Frege must embrace the thesis that there are as many senses of the expression 'John Smith' as there are people called 'John Smith', because, in his view, the sense of a name determines what it stands for. (In fact, he is committed to even more radical ambiguity, since each John Smith's name has, or may have, different senses attached to it by different speakers.) Wittgenstein would be forced to the same conclusion if knowing who N is constitutes any part of what it is to understand 'N'. For then there must be as many distinct things understood by 'N' as there are bearers of the name 'N'. Bestowal of a name 'N' on somebody would be comparable to a stipulative definition. It would introduce a new symbol into language, either a new sign or an old symbol (e.g. 'John Smith') with a new meaning.

This ambiguity thesis is a distortion of the familiar fact that many people, places, pets, etc., share the same name. It also distorts the very notion of ambiguity. Ambiguity of words is a local, language-specific feature, not commonly preserved in translation into a different language,[4] never in translations into numerous other languages. So names are not, in any ordinary sense, ambiguous. It is an important datum that people may share the same name, and absurd to conceive of N.N. *père* saying to N.N. *fils* 'I have given you my name, but not its meaning'. 'Mr White is white' *is* a case of ambiguity (compare translations of it); 'Mr White the plumber and Mr White the joiner both . . .' is not.

Do we need to attribute meaning to a particular person's name even for Frege's purposes?

(i) One can explain that a sentence 'ΦA' has meaning without attributing meaning to 'A'. It is the misguided commitment to Fregean contextualism, i.e. to the idea that the meaning of a sentence is composed

---

[3] For the amusing exchange of letters see W. S. Churchill, *My Early Life* (Fontana, London, 1959), pp. 223 ff.

[4] However, names do belong to a language; 'Peter' is an English name, 'Pierre' a French one. But Giuseppe Verdi isn't Joe Green. Nevertheless, Jerusalem *is* Yerushalayim and Rome *is* Roma. Is this translation? Or should one rather say that 'Jerusalem' and 'Rome' are the English *versions* of the Hebrew and Italian names?

of the meanings of its constituents, that makes this conclusion compelling. For then it seems that denying meaning to 'A' would deprive of meaning any sentence of the form 'ΦA'. This inference is gratuitous. What is required for 'ΦA' to have meaning is that there be criteria for understanding this sentence and acceptable ways of explaining its meaning, but this does not imply that someone who understands 'ΦA' either knows or can explain the meaning of 'A' (cf. 'A word has meaning only in the context of a sentence', pp. 168 ff.).

(ii) One can explain the difference in meaning between 'ΦA' and 'ΦB' without attributing it to the different meanings of 'A' and 'B'. That 'ΦA' differs in meaning from 'ΦB' is manifest in the explanations of these two sentences (in a given context) which are accepted as correct. Admissible explanations are diverse. They may include explanations of who (in that context) A and B are. No explanation of 'ΦA' or 'ΦB' or of the difference in their meanings need be interpreted as involving an explanation of the meanings of 'A' and 'B'.

(iii) The informativeness of non-trivial identity-statements does not require assigning different senses to 'A' and 'B' (where A = B), as long as it is intelligible that one knows who A is and knows who B is without knowing that A is the same person as B. And this surely is perfectly intelligible. To know who A is is manifested by giving some appropriate answer to the question 'Who is A?', but does not require knowing *every* correct answer to it.

(iv) The intelligibility of a sentence containing an empty name is likewise unproblematic, as long as there is a correct answer to the question 'Who is N?' It is perfectly possible to answer questions such as 'Who is David Copperfield (Zeus, Kilroy, Odysseus)?' even though, in one sense, these names are 'empty' or 'lack a bearer'. Indeed, it is nonsense to assume that sentences containing them are uniformly truth-valueless. This stems from applying the standards of one language-game to another rather different one.

(v) There is no *mechanism* of reference. There is rather a practice of using names in various contexts, *inter alia* to refer to people, and a practice of explaining who, in a given context, is referred to by a particular name. Objectivity of reference is ensured because the existence of a practice of explaining who was referred to by 'N' in a particular utterance 'ΦN' ensures a distinction between believing that 'N' refers to so-and-so (e.g. to that ↗person) and the fact that 'N', in a given context, does refer to him. Appropriate answers to the question 'Who is N?' vary from context to context. What is appropriate in a classroom ('Who was Aristotle?') would be inappropriate at a sherry party ('Who is N?'—'There he is, over there ↗' (a uniquely individuating *curriculum vitae* would be useless here)). What may be appropriate in a history lesson may be wholly misleading in a literature lesson. None of this, however, forces us to admit that names, individuated by their bearers, have meanings which consist in means of uniquely identifying their bearers.

The argument thus far opens up the possibility of a much more radical criticism of traditional accounts of proper names than that so far considered. We do not need to assume that names have meanings, and traditional accounts of their meaning have unwelcome consequences. So we can now jettison the three dogmas left undisturbed by the conservative reaction, i.e. that names have meaning (in the preferred sense), that explaining who N is is explaining the meaning of 'N', and therefore that names are typically ambiguous.

If we jettison the assumption that names have meanings (as conceived by the dominant philosophical tradition), then there can be no such thing as explaining their meaning. What is described as 'an ostensive definition' of the name 'N' is typically an ostensive explanation of who N is, relative to a particular utterance. The name 'N' may be uttered as a one-word sentence (vocatively, assertorically, or interrogatively). This utterance can be explained. But an explanation of the meaning of a one-word token-sentence is not typically an explanation of the meaning (if any) of its constituent. Nor is an explanation of who N is an explanation of 'N!' or 'N?' The possibility of explaining the meaning of the one-word sentence-token does not entail that the name 'N' has a meaning, nor does denying meaning to the name imply that the sentence is meaningless. Moreover, although in N's presence one can replace 'N' in 'N is tall' by 'He ↗ is tall', it does not follow that 'N' therefore has a meaning, but only that the two statements have the same meaning. The converse view would commit us to the synonymity of different names of the same person (his forenames, surname, nickname, diminutive, etc.) as well as to the ambiguity of common proper names.

One and the same name may, but need not, have many bearers. This truism does not imply that names are ambiguous, unless one has already decided that a name has a meaning which consists in a means of reference-determination. All it implies is that one must know who (which N) is being referred to in an utterance 'ΦN' in order to understand what statement is made.

The analogies and disanalogies between proper names and indexicals are instructive here. In both cases there *is* something to understand, namely a grasp of the conventions concerning the type-expression. In the case of indexicals (e.g. 'this'), if one understands the general conventions concerning the use of 'this' and one knows the context of an assertion 'Φ (this ↗)', then one is in a position to explain the meaning of the assertion and what object is referred to by this use of the indexical. Knowledge of the conventions for the use of 'this', together with relevant knowledge of the context of its use in an utterance suffices for knowing what that token of 'this' refers to and hence its contribution to the truth-conditions of that assertion.

As with such context-dependent expressions, so too with proper names we must distinguish the general rules concerning the use of the expression from knowing who or what is referred to in a particular utterance incorporating the expression. That I do not understand what statement is made by an utterance 'Φ (John)' because I do not know who, in this utterance, is meant, does not imply that I do not understand the conventions governing the use of the type-name 'John' (that, e.g., it is an English male forename). An explanation of who is meant is no contribution to my grasp of the use of the name in general, but merely part of an explanation of the particular utterance—namely who is being referred to. A fortiori, my ignorance of who else bears this name is not ignorance of other meanings of the name.

Unlike indexicals, however, proper names are not context-dependent. An aspect of grasping the use of indexicals is knowing how their reference in an utterance is determined by the context of the utterance (time, place, speaker, etc.); i.e., if one knows the relevant aspects of context yet does not know what 'this' or 'yesterday' refers to in a given utterance, then one satisfies a criterion for not understanding these words. Not so with proper names: there is no general systematic relation with the context of utterance such that one can determine from the general conventions concerning the type-name together with the context what the reference of 'A' is in an utterance 'ΦA'. What one needs to know is simply which A is being spoken of, or who A is, or who is meant. And this one must know, whether 'A' has many bearers or only one. Even if the system of nomenclature and name bestowal and the internal complexity of a given proper name together are such that an explanation of the type-name suffices uniquely to determine its bearer (e.g. that only the eldest son of X.X. can be named 'N.N.'), giving this explanation of the name may not count as giving an explanation of who N is and hence may fail to qualify as a criterion for knowing who is spoken of. Although it is true that John D. Rockefeller III is the son of John D. Rockefeller Jr, such a statement is typically not an acceptable answer to 'Who is . . .?', although it manifests understanding of an aspect of a naming system.

The central point to grasp here is that the multiple features of understanding names hitherto elaborated do not satisfy the requirements which the Fregean tradition demands of the sense or meaning of a proper name, viz. a means of reference-determination, a content of shared understanding which will display the contribution of the name to the determination of the truth-conditions of any assertion in which it occurs.

Nevertheless, there is much to understand about names apart from knowing what a token-name refers to. Should not these different dimensions of understanding names lead us to the conclusion that names (considered as types) have a meaning? Such an inclination is reinforced by invoking the principle that an explanation of the use of an expression is an explanation of its meaning, that understanding the use of an expression is understanding its meaning, and that using an expression correctly is a criterion for knowing its meaning. Speaking of the meaning of names in this sense has advantages and disadvantages. Certainly, there are complex rules governing the bestowal, change, and significance of names, and very complicated practices involving the use of names. If names are to be correctly used, then these rules and practices must be understood. It seems natural to extend the notion of meaning to include these aspects of the use of an important type of expression in the language. If, in this sense, one knows the meaning of a name, then one will understand a sentence in which it occurs in a sense somewhat analogous to that in which one understands a sentence containing an indexical whose context one does not know.

On the other hand, this notion of meaning of names is decidedly stipulative and unorthodox (although no more so than Frege's notion *was*). Since knowing the meaning of a name, in this sense, will not ensure that one knows the contribution of the name to the truth-conditions of any utterance of the form 'ΦN', this notion of meaning has no role in a semantic theory (a dubious disadvantage perhaps). Moreover, where the connotative aspects of type-names are minimal, e.g. with male or female English forenames today, we will presumably have to admit that many different names have the same meaning. But, of course, sameness of meaning (i.e. being an English male forename) does not imply intersubstitutability *salva veritate*, still less that every identity-statement of the form 'John = Peter' is an analytic truth, nor does it imply indifference in selection of names for bestowal (e.g. both 'Richard' and 'Thomas' are English male forenames, but there may be numerous conventions of bestowal restricting or compelling choice between them). In this respect using this notion of meaning clashes with philosophical parlance as well as ordinary idiom.

The immediate consequence of these considerations is to force us to re-examine the relationship between understanding names and understanding sentences in which they occur. (This is a special case of a general question concerning attributing meaning to certain kinds of expression, e.g. applicatives, prepositions, pronouns, particles, auxiliaries; cf. 'Explanation', pp. 40 f.) Understanding sentences incorporating names commonly involves grasping various facets of the practice of using names, i.e. understanding their 'significance'. Failure to understand these aspects of name-use leads to incorrect uses of names, improprieties, incorrect explanations of, inappropriate utterances of, or improper reactions to sentences incorporating names. These constitute criteria for misunderstanding or not understanding such *sentences*. But only a misguided commitment to Fregean contextualism seems to force the conclusion that proper names have a meaning of which these various dimensions of 'significance' are a part.

We do not speak of the meaning of token-names, and only rarely do we speak of the meaning of type-names. Generalizing and 'regimenting' the idea of the meaning of a type-name breeds further confusion, not clarity. Within the limited domain in which we do speak of the meaning of type-names, we understand perfectly well what we are speaking of, what phenomena we are explaining. Outside these narrow confines we flounder in a morass of pseudo-theories. But there is *no need* for this. There are various rule-governed practices of name-use. These can be explained. There are criteria for understanding sentences incorporating names, criteria which sometimes involve reference to the background practices of using names. These criteria can be described. Once this is done, is there anything left that has not been explained? Is there any significant feature about the use of names and the explanation and understanding of sentences incorporating them that has not been mentioned? Only the insistent demands of a dogmatic *theory*. Then it is *this* that must be subjected to criticism, *this* which needs extirpating.

XIII

THE NATURE OF PHILOSOPHY

1. *Russell's conception of philosophy*

Among intellectual disciplines, philosophy occupies a unique and peculiar position. There is a wide-spread disagreement about what activities it is legitimate for philosophy to pursue. At first glance, this seems nothing deep—just an everyday demarcation dispute. Yet it is of fundamental significance and reaches down to the essence of the subject. In philosophy not merely the answers but also the questions themselves and the methods appropriate for investigating them are called into question. Characterization of the nature of philosophy is itself a philosophical issue. Many controversies can be traced back to radical disagreements about this.

The most obvious way to clarify the nature of any discipline is to compare it with other familiar and relatively unproblematic ones. Applied to philosophy, this method seems to many to yield the conclusion that philosophy has a unique status relative to all of the special sciences and humanistic studies. Unlike them it seems to lack any sharply delimited subject-matter and to have no distinctive methods. Yet even agreement about this does not terminate chronic disagreement, for it leaves open alternative conceptions of the nature of this subject.

According to one conception, philosophy is extra-ordinary in that it adjudicates the bounds of sense. It clarifies which questions are intelligible and which investigations are in principle relevant or irrelevant for answering them. This view Wittgenstein held and argued for throughout his career. It is in this sense that he thought of philosophy as the activity of clarifying thoughts (TLP 4.112) or as striving for a deeper understanding of language (PR 7). The sciences are totally different in nature and pursued for very different purposes. Consequently, science is irrelevant for philosophy. At most it may generate new conceptual problems in need of philosophical treatment. This idea underpins Wittgenstein's castigating psychology as a mixture of experimental methods and conceptual confusions (PI p. 232) or mathematics as a combination of calculations with 'gas'. To many philosophers, the advocacy of such views marks him out as a philosophical Luddite or philistine.

The diametrically opposed conception treats philosophy as the most general science, the supreme form of theory construction. On this view, nothing is in principle excluded as irrelevant for philosophical theorizing; neurophysiology, e.g., might well clarify semantics or the epistemology of perception. Indeed science may solve what seemed to be real philosophical problems. Such a millenarian vision inspires much contemporary philosophy.

Russell was both an advocate and a practitioner of this second conception of philosophy as the most general of the sciences. His remarks have a double importance for studying Wittgenstein's contrasting conception. First, they constitute a familiar and fully articulated account useful for highlighting features of Wittgenstein's. Secondly, they are something that Wittgenstein studied closely and reacted against, as it were constituting a centre of repulsion for his thought. Hence we begin with a brief survey of Russell's conception of philosophy.

Russell marched under the banner of 'the scientific method in philosophy'. What he aimed to accomplish was to effect a cure for the age-old scandal of philosophy, that it has made no visible progress (OK 13). This is a symptom that philosophers have been mistaken in their methods. The remedy is to emulate the method the sciences follow with such conspicuous success. If philosophers were to do so they too could expect parallel success in contributing to the gradual accumulation of genuine knowledge. The spectacle of scientific progress should be an inspiration for general imitation of its methods.

Russell advocated this conception of philosophy with evangelical fervour. He divided philosophers into two groups: those that were motivated by ethical and religious considerations (e.g. Plato, Spinoza, and Hegel) and those that drew their inspiration from science (e.g. Leibniz, Locke, and Hume). He roundly condemned the first group, observing 'that the ethical and religious motives . . . have been on the whole a hindrance to the progress of philosophy, and ought now to be consciously thrust aside by those who wish to discover philosophical truth' (ML 98).[1] What was particularly damaging in the work of these philosophers was the use to which they put logic. They treated logic as if it were 'constructive through negation'. 'Where a number of alternatives seem, at first sight, to be equally possible, logic is made to condemn all of them except one, and that one is then pronounced to be realized in the actual world . . . (whereas) the true function of logic is . . . exactly the opposite of this' (OK 18). The foundation of the scientific method in philosophy is the proper use of logic. Indeed, Russell summarized the difference between the new and the traditional conception of philosophy as the difference between the 'old logic' and the 'new logic'. 'The old logic put thought in fetters, while the new logic gives it wings' (OK 68). In the struggle between Darkness and Light, the champion of Light is logical 'pluralism' (ML 111).

What Russell urged was the transfer not of results, but of methods, from the sphere of the special sciences to that of philosophy (ML 98). The

----

[1] B. Russell, 'On Scientific Method in Philosophy', the Herbert Spencer Lecture, (ML 97–124).

aim is the dispassionate pursuit of philosophical tru   262   p'
achieved by philosophers should be impersonal and ob
traditional philosophy fails to meet this standard: it is
in intuition, and it is distorted by the hopes, fears, a
investigators. It is important to recognize that 'insight', untesu.
unsupported, is an insufficient guarantee of truth (OK 31). The
philosopher should see the world *sub specie aeternitatis*, 'as God might see,
without a *here* and *now*, without hopes and fears, without the trammels of
customary beliefs and traditional prejudices, calmly, dispassionately, in
the sole and exclusive desire of knowledge' (PP 160). Knowledge is most
apt to be achieved if philosophy is piecemeal, analytic, and tentative.
'Divide and conquer' is the maxim of success in philosophy, so that
the essential method of inquiry is analysis, not synthesis (ML 113). After
breaking down and isolating philosophical problems, we should proceed
to the invention of sober and tentative hypotheses as solutions to them,
hoping gradually to supplement and improve these hypotheses in the
light of further rigorous thinking. Only in this way can we ensure the
'possibility of successive approximations to the truth' (ML 113). This
piecemeal accumulation of philosophical wisdom will take such humble
forms as constructing catalogues of logical forms and inventories of
logical possibilities (OK 66–9; cf. 244 ff., LA 226 f.).

The appropriateness of scientific method for philosophy reflects the
fact that philosophy really is a form of science. It is a branch of science,
the essential function of which is the generation and inductive support of
explanations on the covering-law model. It consists of statements that
may stand in entailment relations. The construction of philosophical
theories is subject to the same intellectual constraints as the construction
of scientific ones: the aim in both cases is developing theories with the
maximum explanatory power using the minimum of assumptions
(primitive propositions) and theoretical concepts (primitive ideas). What
distinguishes philosophy from the special sciences? Russell gives four
answers to this question, assuming that they are at least extensionally
equivalent. First, generality: philosophy is the science of the general (ML
110), asking such questions as 'What is a number?' (OK 190 f.) or 'Is there
any knowledge in the world which is so certain that no reasonable man
could doubt it?' (PP 7). (Logic, the core of philosophy, consists of
completely general propositions.)[2] Secondly, necessity: all philosophical
propositions are necessary and *a priori* (OK 190; LA 199), belonging to
'the science of the possible' (ML 111). Thirdly, abstraction: philosophy
abstracts from all particular qualities and relations of particular things in
the pursuit of maximum generality (OK 189; PM i.2). Fourthly, form:

[2]This was Russell's view before he accepted Wittgenstein's thesis that logical propositions were tautologies: cf. PM i. 91, 77; PrM 7 (see also p. ix); ML 110, 112; LA 184, 239–41,
IMP 197, 204 f.

ilosophy is primarily concerned with formal questions; in aiming at generality by abstracting from all particularity, it confines 'attention entirely to the logical form of the facts concerned' (OK 190). That Russell takes these characteristics to be equivalent is most obvious in his account of logic, since logical propositions are alternatively characterized as being completely general, necessary, and as having truth-values determined by their logical forms alone (PrM 7; OK 67; ML 112; cf. IMP 199 f.). Philosophy then consists of propositions that are distinguished from those of the special sciences by their generality. It is governed by the ideal of axiomatic systematization. The ultimate achievement would be an arrangement of propositions 'into deductive chains, in which a certain number of initial propositions form a logical guarantee for all the rest' (OK 214).

Philosophy is one of the sciences, differing from the special sciences only in degree, not in kind (PP 149, cf. 154 f.). It is continuous with them. The pursuit of knowledge in science leads eventually into philosophy, since in seeking comprehensive explanations a scientist will raise ever more general and fundamental questions until finally he crosses the vague boundary that separates science from philosophy. Philosophy is the Queen of the Sciences, or perhaps more accurately the foundation of all the sciences (PP 154). Its question are fundamental, and its answers deeply important for science. It is indispensable to the achievement of a full theoretical understanding of the world. Philosophy differs from the special sciences only in the direction of movement of its thought and in the degree of generality of the truths that it seeks to establish (OK 185, cf. IMP 1).

Russell's conception of philosophy as a science is given a peculiar twist by his Eddingtonian view of science. This is reflected in a distinctive conception of the goals of philosophy, in the harnessing of certain negative goals to the obvious positive ones. The overarching positive goal is the attainment of a 'theoretical understanding of the world' (OK 36; ML 17). This has its corollary certain subsidiary aims whose achievement is necessary to controlled speculation in search of theoretical understanding. These include the constructions of catalogues of logical forms of propositions and of logical possibilities, and the careful assessment of the weight of inductive support for competing philosophical hypotheses. The most that can be claimed for a philosophical thesis is that 'it is a hypothesis which systematizes a vast body of facts and never leads to any consequences which there is any reason to think false' (OK 103). Its justification is not a matter of its being self-evident, but of its having strong inductive support (PM i. v, xiv, cf. 59, 62). The negative goal of philosophy is the destruction of dogmatism and of the pretensions of common sense. It aims to expose the hidden sense of apparent nonsense and the hidden nonsense of common sense. It makes apparent the gulf between appearance and reality. Its value lies 'largely in its very uncertainty; . . . it removes the somewhat arrogant dogmatism of those who have never travelled into the region of liberating doubt, and it keeps alive our sense of wonder by showing familiar things in an unfamiliar aspect' (PP 156 f.). In this respect too philosophy resembles science. The vulgar think that the physical world is composed of macroscopic objects having properties such as weight, colour, temperature, texture, and motion. Physics debunks this primitive outlook, revealing to the wondering onlooker that the world is really made up of submicroscopic objects (atoms) which have only the properties of mass, motion, and electric charge (PP 16, 35). Most amazing of all, what we naïvely think of as a solid object (e.g. a table top) is really nothing but a cloud of atoms widely separated from each other in space; it consists predominantly of empty space! The intellectual excitement of science, and much of its value, lies in the apparent paradoxicality of its hypotheses. It not only suggests the most fruitful hypotheses about particular aspects of the world, but also frees us from bondage to common sense. Philosophy aims at a similar inverting of preconceptions. Much of what we all think to be true is mere superstition and confusion, and many hypotheses whose truth seems inconceivable turn out to have very strong inductive support. '. . . [The] point of philosophy is to start with something so simple as not to seem worth stating and to end with something so paradoxical that no one will believe it' (LA 193).

In Russell's view the centre of gravity of philosophy lies within epistemology. The problem of philosophy is discovering and formulating the foundations of knowledge, i.e. the presentation of an axiomatic systematization of what can be known with certainty and a calculation of the degree of probability to be attached to propositions that cannot be supported by conclusive evidence (OK 214 f.). This primacy of epistemology is easily overlooked, particularly because of Russell's insistence on the importance of logic to philosophy. In his view, however, logic is important as a means, not as an end in itself. The correct account of the logical forms of propositions is necessary for identifying errors in traditional metaphysics and epistemology (OK 54). An inadequate account of logical form has 'vitiated almost everything that has hitherto been written on the theory of knowledge' (OK 68). Improvements in logic are a precondition of progress in epistemology. They are indispensable as tools in the search for the foundations of knowledge. Russell's focus on epistemology is evident in other ways. One manifestation is the role he assigns to Cartesian doubt and Occam's razor. Cartesian doubt is of the essence of philosophy just to the extent that the purpose of philosophical inquiry is the achievement of certainty. Occam's razor is given an epistemological justification by Russell: it reduces the risk of error by minimizing the number of hostages that a theory gives to fortune (LA 270 f., 280; ML 155). A second manifestation is his 'principle of acquaintance', i.e. the thesis that 'every proposition which we can understand must be composed wholly of constituents with which we are acquainted' (PP 58). Since the objects of acquaintance are the foundation of knowledge, the thrust of this principle is to guarantee that the analysis of a sentence is directly relevant to establishing its epistemological status. Indeed, the principle of acquaintance makes the theory of meaning logically subordinate to epistemology (cf. 'Logically proper names', pp. 129 f.). Another striking aspect of the primacy of epistemology is visible in Russell's conception of the direction of fit between logic and mathematics. His aim in reducing arithmetic to logic is to provide inductively supported foundations for logic. The support for his logical principles (especially for the theory of types and the axiom of reducibility) is parasitic on the justification for the truths of elementary arithmetic. The superstructure supports its 'foundations'.

Russell's conception of the relation of arithmetic to logic provides the paradigm underlying his conception of the theory of knowledge (PM i.3). At first sight his philosophy would seem to make room for revisionism, even for revolution. Might the results of our enquiry not be well-supported but barely credible hypotheses which overturn received wisdom by revealing 'all the vagueness and confusion that underlie our ordinary ideas' (PP 7)? Appearances here are somewhat deceptive. Any philosophical theory must ultimately fit the data of common knowledge; for these data 'can only be criticized by other data, not by an outside standard' (OK 74). Of course, the data must be given critical scrutiny. We must soak them in cynical acid to purify them of whatever is vague, confused, or doubtful. The result of this process will be to precipitate out of common opinion the 'hard' data, to separate this solid core of sense from the 'soft' data (OK 72 f., 77 ff.). The hard data are what any acceptable philosophical theory must fit. Therefore, they constitute the limits of revisionism. The most that philosophy can do is to 'examine and purify our common knowledge by an internal scrutiny' (OK 74). It has no authority 'to condemn the facts of experience and the laws of science'. If philosophy effects a revolution in our thinking, this is not accomplished by the results that it establishes, but by our interpretation of these results. Science, too, must fit the data of ordinary experience, but this does not make its theories uniformly dull or truistic. The deliverances of philosophy may be no less exciting, but no more subversive, than the revelation that solid objects consist of sprinklings of atoms in predominantly empty space! The hypotheses of philosophy give a rational reconstruction of the hard data winnowed out of common knowledge. Here, too, the logical foundations are supported by the superstructure. This scheme is the secret of Russell's vision that philosophy will enhance our sense of wonder in the very process of giving knowledge solid foundations.

2. Wittgenstein: the 'Preliminary' and Notebooks 1914–16

The 'Notes on Logic' of September 1913 outline the essential features of Wittgenstein's early conception of philosophy in what is printed as the 'Preliminary'.[3] Most of the central claims are embodied in the *Tractatus*; the salient ones characterize all his work. Although there are substantial changes in his conception of the methods and results which can be hoped for in philosophy, his view of the status of philosophy changes very little. This is one of the main threads of continuity in Wittgenstein's opera.

The first thesis is negative and limitative. Philosophy is to be sharply distinguished from science. It may be the Queen of the Sciences, or the under-labourer, but not, as it were, an ordinary citizen of the republic of ideas (Z §455). Philosophy is not a kind of science, distinguished by its dubiousness (LA 281) or generality. This claim already sharply differentiated Wittgenstein from Russell. Science, as Hertz[4] had shown, constructs pictures or models of reality. Philosophy does not, and it can neither confirm not confute scientific investigations. Nor can it provide the 'foundations of science'. A corollary is that in philosophy there are no deductions. In science we construct hypotheses from which, together with statements of empirical 'initial conditions', we deduce conclusions which are confirmed or confuted by experience. Philosophy, by contrast, is 'flat'. There are, *pace* Russell (ML 112), no *hypotheses* in philosophy. Nor are there in philosophy any 'primitive propositions' from which others follow deductively. It is not the task of philosophy to 'deduce' the existence of the external world (OK 80), God, or an eternal life. Logic likewise, *contra* Frege, is 'flat'. For there are no 'privileged' or 'primitive' propositions in logic.

The second, constructive, thesis is that philosophy is the doctrine of the logical form of 'scientific', i.e. empirical, propositions.[5] It consists of logic and metaphysics, the former its basis.[6] This 'structural' claim was *de facto* adhered to in the *Tractatus*' philosophy, but prohibited *de jure* by the account which limits philosophy to the analysis of 'what can be said'. (In the later philosophy the claim that metaphysics is 'based' on logic is eschewed in both forms since there are no ineffable metaphysical truths.

---

[3] The printed, so-called 'Costello version', is Russell's arrangement and, for the most part, translation from Wittgenstein's dictation and MSS. The remarks on philosophy all derive from the fourth MS (cf. B. McGuinness, 'Bertrand Russell and Ludwig Wittgenstein's "Notes on Logic"', *Revue internationale de Philosophie* 102 (1972), 444–60).

[4] H. Hertz, *The Principles of Mechanics*, tr. D. E. Jones and J. T. Walley (Macmillan, London, 1899), Introduction, p. 1.

[5] Here Wittgenstein and Russell are in apparent agreement, but only superficially, since they had very different conceptions of what logical form *is*.

[6] How, given that philosophy contains no deductions, metaphysics is 'based on' logic, is unclear.

Rather, the sibylline pronouncements of metaphysics are the distorted echoes of grammar.) Philosophy is, therefore, purely descriptive—a description of logical form. (Although the classical conception of logical form is later repudiated, the claim that philosophy is descriptive is an abiding element in Wittgenstein's thought.)

Wittgenstein lays down two further theses, one substantive, the other methodological. The substantive thesis is that propositions of logic, i.e. tautologies and contradictions (cf. TLP 6.112), must be accorded a unique position relative to all others. This requirement was to be faithfully fulfilled in the *Tractatus* analysis of senseless propositions. The methodological thesis is that 'distrust of grammar is the first requisite for philosophizing', an article of faith shared with both Frege and Russell. Surface grammar conceals logical form and makes totally distinct types of expression appear to belong to similar logico-synactical categories. (Later he will argue that similarity of form in surface grammar leads us to overlook radical diversity of use.)

Already here one can see the affinities, and even deeper disagreements, with Russell. The disagreements are sharpened in the course of the *Notebooks 1914–16*, and appear in their final form in the *Tractatus*. It is clear that Russell's conception of philosophy aroused Wittgenstein's ire even at this early stage. In May 1915 he was apparently reading Russell's *Our Knowledge of the External World*, for his notes of 1 May 1915 seem concerned with Chapter 3 of that book.[7] Russell there remarks that one of the access roads to philosophy 'is the road which leads through doubt as to the reality of the world of sense' (OK 70). To this Wittgenstein replies: '. . . doubt can only exist where a question exists; a question can only exist where an answer exists, and this can only exist where something *can* be *said*' (NB 44, cf. TLP 6.51). This Kantian strategy against scepticism was to remain with Wittgenstein all his life, and stands in striking contrast to Russell's classical empiricist stance. In the sequel Russell contends that philosophy should not follow Descartes and try doubting everything simultaneously: 'The reason for this abstention from a universal criticism is not any dogmatic confidence, but its exact opposite; it is not that common knowledge *must* be true, but that we possess no radically different kind of knowledge derived from some other source. Universal scepticism, though logically irrefutable is practically barren' (OK 74). To this Wittgenstein responds: 'Scepticism is *not* irrefutable, but *obvious nonsense* if it tries to doubt where no question can be asked.' Russell tempered scepticism with pragmatism: 'While admitting that doubt is possible with regard to all our common knowledge, we

---

[7] Von Wright suggests (in L. Wittgenstein, *Letters to Russell, Keynes and Moore*, ed. G. H. von Wright (Blackwell, Oxford, 1974), p. 83) that Wittgenstein did not have a copy of the book until 1920. In view of the internal evidence of NB one must conjecture that he did have a copy, or at least draft material of Chapter 3.

must nevertheless accept that knowledge in the main if philosophy is to be possible at all' (OK 73, cf. 78). Wittgenstein's dogmatic riposte is that 'All theories that say "This is how it must be, otherwise we could not philosophize" or "otherwise we surely could not live", etc., etc., must of course disappear.' But what is dogmatism here will be given a triumphant vindication in later years. Russell distinguishes 'hard' data from 'soft' data—the former being resistant to the acids of Cartesian doubt, the latter dissolving under their impact. Russell's method is to distinguish the two and isolate the hard data. 'My method', Wittgenstein replies, 'is not to sunder the hard from the soft, but to see the hardness of the soft.' He concludes his discussion abruptly and impatiently with the remark 'Russell's method in his "Scientific Method in Philosophy" is simply a retrogession from the method of physics' (NB 44).[8] He was not to change his mind on this important issue.

The central objections to Russell's conception of philosophy at this stage crystallize around his view that science and philosophy are akin in method and in product. For Russell, Cartesian doubt is a method of isolating the 'hard' from the 'soft' which will ensure epistemologically secure foundations; for Wittgenstein, Cartesian doubt is nonsensical. For Russell, Occam's razor is a methodological principle which will minimize epistemological risks; for Wittgenstein it is a logical principle which will eliminate redundancy (NB 42). For Russell, non-demonstrative support probabilifies philosophical conclusions; for Wittgenstein it is irrelevant since there can be nothing merely probable in philosophy. The differences in method, for Wittgenstein, reflect the differences in product. The method of science is hypothetico-deductive, but there can be no hypotheses in philosophy. A scientific hypothesis which is disproved by experience is false, but not nonsense. Philosophy, which plots the bounds of sense, cannot produce 'false' philosophical propositions; if it errs, then its product is not falsehood but nonsense. By the same token philosophy cannot produce, as Russell thought, 'partial and probably not wholly correct results' (ML 112). In philosophy we do not 'approximate' to empirical truths, and there is no *via media* between sense and nonsense. Finally, for similar reasons, there is no piecemeal advance in philosophy, for piecemeal progress is possible only where the links between the data are empirical. The adamantine web of logical forms is woven out of necessary links. A correct determination of any element requires a proper grasp of the whole.

[8] It might be thought that this must be a reference to the Herbert Spencer Lecture at Oxford, 18 November 1914 (ML pp. 97–124). This is not so. 'Scientific Method in Philosophy' is part of the title of OK, and is the page heading throughout the volume of the first edition. Moreover, the respective dates of the Lowell Lectures (delivered at Harvard, March–April 1914) and the Herbert Spencer Lecture make it more likely that Wittgenstein was acquainted with the former rather than the latter. The striking parallelisms between Wittgenstein's remarks and OK do not obtain with respect to the Herbert Spencer Lecture.

3. *The* Tractatus

The major innovation of the *Tractatus* relative to the preceding remarks on the nature of philosophy is the emergence of the doctrine of the ineffability of philosophy. This is a product of Wittgenstein's objections to Russell's theory of types. Its result is a distinction between the *de jure* contention that philosophy consists of no more than logical analysis of empirical propositions into their elementary constituents and the *de facto* status of the philosophy of the *Tractatus* itself, which self-confessedly violates the *de jure* limitations and consequently is strictly and literally nonsense.

The negative thesis of the 'Notes on Logic' remains: philosophy is wholly distinct from science, and its methods and products are not those of the sciences. The methodological thesis is likewise re-emphasized and further developed. Ordinary language is indeed misleading, for there is a yawning gulf between surface grammar and logical form. It is this which is the source of all philosophical problems. Yet, although deceptive, ordinary language is in good logical order. If it conveys a sense, it must comply with the 'laws of sense', i.e. the rules of logical syntax (TLP 5.4733, 5.5563). If it does not, it conveys no sense, and is not language. Here Wittgenstein again took issue with Russell, who thought that ordinary language was logically defective (and not merely deceptive), awaiting improvement (as opposed to mere elucidation) from an ideal language. But not only is ordinary language defective; ordinary thought, too, is deficient because of the faults of its vehicle. Our thoughts are confused and erroneous, needing replacement by precise and accurate formulations in an improved language which will spell out for the first time what we really know. Wittgenstein, however, argues that a perspicuous notation will not enable us to say something we could not say hitherto. It will not improve upon our thoughts or extend our knowledge. But it will enable us to make clear to ourselves what we said and knew before. If we have a perspicuous notation we can achieve a 'correct logical point of view'. For Russell logical forms are *discovered* and catalogued; for Wittgenstein they are given *ab initio*, calculated, not discovered. For Russell, new possibilities of fact and thought are revealed by philosophical work; for Wittgenstein every possibility is *necessarily* possible. For Russell, philosophy must emulate the methods of science to achieve tentative and constantly adjustable results of a progressive kind; for Wittgenstein, the task of philosophy can be (and in the *Tractatus* has been) definitively completed.

New ground is broken, or at least brought to light, by the Kantian claim that philosophy is a critique of language. The aim of the *Tractatus* is to set a limit to the expression of thoughts, to draw the bounds of sense

(TLP p. 3). This cannot legitimately be done by *describing* the limits of thought, for to do this what lies beyond the limits of thought would have to be thinkable, i.e. describable. But only nonsense lies beyond the limits of thought. Less metaphorically, a description of the limits of thought would, at the very least, involve the use of propositions that are necessary truths but not tautologies. This would involve violating the requirements of bipolarity as a condition of sense for atomic sentences. Likewise, it would require the use of formal pseudo-concepts as if they were genuine concepts. So the only legitimate form philosophy can take is to 'set limits to what cannot be thought by working outwards through what can be thought' (TLP 4.114). Philosophy 'will signify what cannot be said by presenting clearly what can be said' (TLP 4.115). It must confine itself to the 'clear presentation' of what can legitimately be said. It will consist of logical analysis of *empirical propositions*, but will not propound any philosophical propositions. Whenever anyone attempts to say something metaphysical or philosophical, the philosopher will patiently demonstrate that the bounds of sense have been transgressed, that certain signs in the putative philosophical proposition are illegitimate, lacking meaning (TLP 6.53).[9] The rationale for this radical claim is to be found in the very reasons for which the whole of the *Tractatus* is itself condemned as nonsense.

The path prescribed by the *Tractatus* is not the one it follows. For the *Tractatus* itself is a critique of language which attempts, by violating the rules of logical syntax, to *describe* the bounds of sense, to say what are the limits of what can be thought, rather than to show them. It stands condemned because it attempts to produce philosophical propositions whereas there are none. Why? Philosophy has traditionally attempted to describe the essence of reality. The accidental features of reality belong to the domain of empirical science; the necessary or structural features are, it is commonly thought, the concern of philosophy. Attempts to describe the essence of the world have done so by specifying formal, internal, properties or relations that constitute the essence of things (TLP 4.123). Such specifications employ categorial, or 'formal' concepts. Indeed the sibylline pronouncements of the *Tractatus*, e.g. 'objects are simple', 'the world is the totality of facts', etc., exemplify this philosophical endeavour. But formal concepts are not genuine concepts at all, but forms of concepts. Anything that philosophers attempt to say by means of formal concepts is in fact *shown* by the structure of ordinary empirical propositions.

---

[9] An even more explicit specification of this ideal of analysis is given in LF 163. Philosophy thus conceived is indeed *sui generis*, but not in virtue of producing, as the outcome of philosophical investigation, philosophical propositions which have a unique status. 'Philosophy is not a body of doctrine but an activity' (TLP 4.112), an analytical elucidation of non-philosophical propositions.

It follows that the propositions of the *Tractatus* are strictly nonsensical. They violate the rules of logical syntax by employing formal concepts as if they were genuine concepts. Consequently, logical form, contrary to the 'Preliminary', is indescribable. It can only be shown by philosophical analysis of the kind prescribed for future philosophy. Metaphysics is not a possible science, not even an *a priori* one. For 'metaphysical truths' cannot be stated in language, but only shown by ordinary propositions about empirical matters of fact. Metaphysics, as traditionally conceived, and as practised in the *Tractatus*, is not dismissed as illusory, but is consigned, together with ethics, aesthetics, and religion, to the domain of the ineffable.

4. *The later conception of philosophy*

In his post-1929 works Wittgenstein wrote more deeply upon the nature of philosophy than any other major philosopher since Kant; what he said is controversial and the subject of heated and bitter disagreement in the contemporary philosophical community; indeed, precisely what it is that he claimed, and what its implications are, is itself a matter of controversy.

The Source of Philosophical Problems

In the *Tractatus* Wittgenstein insisted, contrary to Frege and Russell, that ordinary language and ordinary thought are in good logical order. He never changed his mind on this matter. He later objected to Moore's idea that logical analysis will tell us what, if anything, we mean by sentences of ordinary language (WWK 129 f.). The truth is rather that we understand our sentences without being able to give their analysis. He stresses that philosophical analysis does not complete or add to our understanding of our language, at least not in the sense that philosophers understand English better than any other speakers of the language (PR 118). This theme persists: '. . . . every sentence in our language "is in order as it is"' (PI §98). Yet there is change even in the continuity, for his conception of good order changes.

Though ordinary language is in good order, it is the source of philosophical problems. This arises through the interaction of a number of factors. The aim of philosophy is stated in its most general, positive, form by Wittgenstein as the obtaining of an *Übersicht*, a surview, or perspicuous representation (cf. 'Übersicht', pp. 305 ff.) of a segment of our language. We strive to grasp the structure of our form of representation. But ordinary language is above all lacking in this kind of surveyability (PR 52; PI §122). The structure of our conceptual scheme is embedded in our dynamic linguistic practices, in the welter of grammatical rules and their methods of application which constitute the logical connections of language. These rules are not surveyable at a glance. An *Übersicht* is only obtainable by patient examination of how sentences and expressions are supposed to be applied (Z §272), and of their rule-governed connections with other sentences and expressions. But ordinary language puts many pitfalls in the way of the endeavour to achieve such a goal. For not only is it difficult to plot the rich, untidy, grammatical connections in language, but the 'surface grammar' of language is deeply deceptive. In the first place, ordinary language conceals deep differences in kinds of expression, their role and use, beneath superficial similarities of form. Numerals function as singular referring expressions, and we are tempted to conceive of them as proper names of abstract objects. Indexical expressions can occupy the place of names in certain contexts, so we may think that they are special kinds of names. Event-names or names of processes often behave superficially like names of objects. The plethora of analogies between very different kinds of expression is the source of endless philosophical mistakes and a barrier to philosophical understanding. Secondly, the deceptiveness of forms of words is paralleled by the deceptiveness of forms of sentences. Identity of grammatical mood is compatible with difference in use, and difference of mood consistent with similarity in use. Sentences with similar grammatical structure (e.g. the subject/predicate form) may have wholly different uses. Indeed, tokens of the same type-sentence may be employed quite differently. The forms of sentences can be taken in at a glance, their use is difficult to survey. Mesmerized by form we disregard use, and assimilate what should be kept apart, while sundering what should be kept together. Lack of surview of the uses of words and sentences alike leads us to raise typically philosophical questions and also to seek to resolve them in wrong ways.

Language, Philosophy, and Mythology

A second source of philosophical difficulty lies in what Wittgenstein called 'the mythology in the forms of our language' (BT 433).[10] 'A whole mythology', he remarked, 'is deposited in our language' (GB 35=BT 434). It is the task of philosophy to work against the myth-building tendency of our understanding (MS. 158, 28). The thought is rich in its implications, though Wittgenstein never developed it. The context of the remark is an indignant rejoinder to Frazer (*The Golden Bough*). Frazer fails to see that in his 'description' of the beliefs of savages he has at hand words which we do find perfectly intelligible, e.g. 'ghost' and 'shade'. These are not residues of bad science (like 'phlogiston') but living images. Do we not understand expressions like 'ghostly', and 'eerie'? If we describe a death with the phrase 'he gave up the ghost' do we show

---

[10] Wittgenstein here acknowledged his debt for this insight to Paul Ernst (cf. 'Übersicht', pp. 299 f.).

ourselves to be superstitious? Did Gothic painters who represented death
by a homunculus leaving the mouth of the deceased paint what they *saw*?
That these expressions are familiar to us shows, Wittgenstein stresses,
our kinship to the savages Frazer describes, and whose rites and myths he
wrongly represents as being uniformly proto-scientific beliefs.[11] No less
noteworthy is the fact that we use and understand expressions like 'soul'
and 'spirit'. Compared with this, Wittgenstein adds, the fact that we do
not believe that our soul eats and drinks is a minor detail.

It is impossible to be sure what Wittgenstein had in mind here, but
perhaps the following movement is in the right direction. Languages of
different cultures and different epochs[12] have embedded within them
different word-pictures of, e.g., the soul (the relation of mind to body, of
spirit to flesh). These pictures are a kind of myth, not a primitive science.
They fulfil a crucial role in the thought and imagination of a culture, a
role not unlike that of a form of representation. Whether the soul is
conceived as the 'form' of the body, or the body as the receptacle of the
soul—whether they are conceived as striving for total harmony, or as
involved in ceaseless strife—these mythical pictures embedded in language provide a repository of possibilities of expression for the culture.
In terms of such pictures, what is significant in human life, what is found
to be impressive, strange, or marvellous can be expressed. Other no less
important examples come readily to mind (e.g. Fate, Destiny, Doom).

Certainly Wittgenstein saw important analogies between ritual and
language. Ritual involves 'The use of a very highly developed gesture-
language' (GB 36), and the analogies between the structure of myth and
primitive rites on the one hand and our language on the other clearly
fascinated Wittgenstein. 'When I read Frazer, I keep wanting to say: All
these processes, these changes of meaning,—we have them here still in
our word-language. If what is hidden in the last sheaf is called the
Corn-wolf, but also the last sheaf itself and also the man who binds it, we
recognize in this a movement of language with which we are perfectly
familiar.' He does not say what kind of 'movement', but maybe the
following approximates to his thought: we speak of healthy people, but
also of healthy food and healthy exercise; we say that nettles are painful,
that wounds are painful and also that pains are painful.

All this may be interesting (or misguided) cultural anthropology, but
what does it have to do with philosophy? It connects up in at least two
important ways. First, the 'pictures' embedded in language, which bear a
kinship to myth, are not mistakes, but crucially important for the culture.

----

[11] Wittgenstein does not deny that some may be, rather he insists that not all are or *need
be* (M 315).

[12] Cf. Spengler, *Decline of the West*, Vol. I, pp. 117 f., 259, and, at p. 302: 'At any
particular time, therefore, the current image of the soul is a function of the *current language and
its inner symbolism.*'

We speak of time flying, of the stream of events, of time stopping still for a moment; we picture the mind as a place, space as a receptacle, mental images as pictures. The way these turns of phrases are employed causes us no more problems than talk of words being 'on the tip of the tongue'. But when doing philosophy there is a great temptation to misconstrue the 'picture', to take it as clear without *examining its application*. That is, we are prone to take the picture literally and then look for some way of applying it (by taking the 'picture' of numbers literally and inventing the 'myth' of a 'third world', neither temporal nor spatial, for these objects to reside in; or misunderstanding the 'picture' of mental *contents* and inventing the myth of the eye of the mind that introspects). 'In philosophy one is constantly tempted to invent a mythology of symbolism or of psychology, instead of simply saying what we know' (PG 56, cf. Z §211). We fail, in these kinds of cases, to do what needs to be done, namely to take the *sense* of the picture *from its actual application*.

The second point is a consequence of the first. Where our philosophical investigations lead us into such areas we are readily misled by the linguistic expressions, just as Frazer was misled by the practices he recorded into construing myth and rite as proto-science. Where language inclines us to look for a physical thing to correspond to an expression, and there is none, we postulate a spirit (PI §36). Contemporary philosophers in the new materialist vein speak of mentalistic expressions as constituting a *theory* which is in competition with neurophysiology! It is but a short step from here to the construction of a 'philosophical mythology'.

Wittgenstein remarked that Frazer, in his disdainful mein, forgets that we too have Plato and Schopenhauer. Platonism, idealism, the metaphysics of the *Tractatus*; all these, Wittgenstein seems to suggest, can be seen as kinds of mythology and magic lore.

> I think now that the right thing would be to start my book with remarks on metaphysics as a kind of magic.
> In which I must neither speak in favour of magic nor make fun of it.
> The deep character of magic would have to be preserved. (Vol. VI, 177, tr.
>   by Rhees in Introductory Note, GB 19.)

Wittgenstein did not try to develop this thought, perhaps advisedly. There are analogies, but also important disanalogies. Both myth and metaphysics have the character of profundity, command deep respect, and awaken fascination. Characteristic metaphysical movements often have counterparts in rite, magic, and myth, e.g. confusing identifiability-dependent characteristics with substances (in metaphysics: Hume's treatment of ideas; in magic and ritual: the scapegoat ceremony), or Platonic reification of abstract mass-nouns ('beauty' or 'death', conceived as names of abstract entities in a Platonic realm, and their mythical personification as gods), and even analogies between the role of God in metaphysics and myths (Berkeley's omnipercipient God who guarantees continuity of objects, and Zeus the 'all-seeing'). Nevertheless, there are great differences that should deter one from over-exploiting these analogies.

Some aspects of primitive practices are indeed primitive, erroneous, science. Metaphysics, although it often assumes the goals of a super-science, is *not* erroneous science, but nonsense. Ritual has a deep expressive role in the life of a community; metaphysics does not, in the same way, interlock with the forms of life of the culture in which it is rooted. Metaphysics offers pseudo-answers to misunderstood questions, and those questions, when correctly resolved, will undermine metaphysics. But although myth, ritual, and magic are underminded by the march of a technological civilization,[13] this is not because they are, in general, shown to be illusory or nonsensical. In their expressive aspect, they are not answers to questions at all, not even pseudo-questions. Metaphysics is an outgrowth of grammar; although it may express profound human aspirations, longings, and poetic visions, it is not itself symbolic. Myth and ritual, by contrast, although they *may be* erroneous proto-science, are frequently imaginative, expressive representations of fundamental features of human life and the world in which we seek to find a place.

The Nature of Philosophical Problems

Philosophers have often tried to characterize philosophy in terms of its subject-matter. Philosophy, it has sometimes been claimed, studies the ultimate nature of reality—in some sense in which science does not. This conception seemed particularly apt for metaphysics, and indeed fits the *de facto* philosophizing of the *Tractatus*. In the eighteenth and nineteenth centuries it was held (e.g. by Hume and the German and British psychological logicians) that philosophy was a kind of psychological anthropology, a science of the human mind. In the twentieth century, with the 'linguistic turn' in philosophy, some writers have at least given the impression that philosophy is about language, that it is, in some special way, a super-philology. These three conceptions characterize philosophy as a cognitive discipline, yielding, one hopes, true synthetic propositions. Two related conceptions are well known. According to the first (James, Russell), philosophy studies those problems as yet unamenable to scientific treatment, and its results are dubious and questionable. As soon as it makes genuine progress, it hands the subject-matter over to a new science (e.g. psychology and linguistics). According to the second

[13] Science and technology do create and contain their own mythology (a point emphasized by Paul Ernst and Wittgenstein alike). Whether these mythologies, however, have the power and expressive potentialities of those that have been destroyed is another matter.

(Russell), philosophy is characterized more or less formally by its high degree of generality and abstractness; it is simply the *most general* of the sciences.

A quite different trend is represented by the prescriptive conception of philosophy. Classically, philosophy was often conceived as the intellectual discipline which should discover how we ought to live. In a far lower key one branch of logico–linguistic analysis conceived of the task of philosophy as being to regiment, improve, and adapt our language. Philosophical propositions are not cognitive but stipulative (cf. Carnap and the logical positivists).

Wittgenstein will have no truck with this. The 'nature of reality' is studied by science, the 'nature of the mind' by psychology, and empirical linguistics is not philosophy. Some philosophical problems are general, but others (e.g. the problem of the inverted spectrum, the incongruity of counterparts, or colour-exclusion) are not at all so. It is true that astronomy and psychology developed out of speculations of philosopher-scientists, but that does not make their proto-scientific speculations philosophical any more than the genesis of dentistry makes it a kind of hairdressing. Nor is it the task of philosophy to tell us how to live or how to speak our own language better.

The *Tractatus* concluded that metaphysics is ineffable. Future philosophy was characterized as an elucidatory activity. The thesis of the ineffability of metaphysics is rejected as illusory in the later philosophy, but the clarificatory conception of the discipline is adhered to. Philosophy is not a cognitive pursuit; there are no new facts to be discovered by philosophy, only new insights into old facts (Foreword to PR; PG 256). There are no philosophical propositions; philosophy can only produce a distinctive kind of understanding of non-philosophical propositions, as well as a grasp of the illegitimacy of putative philosophical propositions. The distinctive understanding is a grasp of the grammar, the logical articulations of ordinary propositions, which will *dissolve* philosophical questions and put at rest philosophical worry. What is distinctive of philosophy is not its subject-matter, nor its cognitive product, but the nature of philosophical questions and their resolution.

Philosophers from Plato to Schopenhauer have located the source of philosophy in *wonder*. This, rightly interpreted, is true, and can be seen in the nature of philosophical questions. These do not express puzzlement about the causes and explanation of empirical facts. Nor do they concern themselves with the arcane and extraordinary. The wonder of philosophy is wonder about the commonplace and familiar. Nothing could be more ordinary than remembering the facts of yesteryear, but how is it possible to reproduce in memory what no longer exists? We order our lives by the clock, but how is it possible for us to measure time when the past is gone and the future has not yet arrived, and the present is an extensionless point? We know that objects continue to exist unperceived, but how can we know this when we cannot perceive that they exist unperceived? No one doubts that Achilles can overtake the tortoise, but how is it possible for him to do so, since he has to traverse an infinite number of spaces in a finite time? These typically philosophical worries express a puzzlement about the wholly familiar. They arise, in various ways, out of the structure of the language we employ in describing the mundane. Neither the phenomena nor the language are arcane, but the language is not readily surveyable. The task of philosophy is to dissolve the problems (not to *prove* that Achilles can overtake the tortoise, but to show what led us in the first place to wonder how it is possible for him to do so), and its methods are designed to give us a perspicuous representation of that segment of language which generated our confusion.

The contrast with Russell runs very deep here. On his view, common sense is a primitive insight into the nature of reality; philosophy gives a true, more profound insight into its nature, as does physics.

Philosophy and Common sense

This last remark raises a new issue. Some, Russell among them,[14] have thought that Wittgenstein's later philosophy consists in renunciation of intellectual responsibility by abject prostration before the pronouncements of the ignorant that are dignified by the name of 'Common Sense' and 'Common Usage'. But since common sense is no more than that set of beliefs unreflectively adopted by the bulk of society, it is a ragbag of obsolete science, misunderstood philosophy and prejudice. And common usage is frequently little more than the abuses of language committed by the ill-educated. How then can a self-respecting philosopher aim to defend common sense?

This objection to Wittgenstein rests on a twofold misunderstanding. First, he is not concerned to defend common-sense *beliefs* thus understood (nor to defend any other beliefs). It is no part of philosophy to defend the view that such-and-such 'stands to reason'. Questions of *opinion*, Wittgenstein stresses (LFM 103), are irrelevant to philosophy. But it is the task of philosophy to articulate and clarify grammatical connections that are embedded in common forms of speech and inference (e.g. 'How do you know it was red?'—'Because I could see it.'). Equally, some propositions that *philosophers* have presented as common-sense beliefs, and that may command the assent of the vulgar, are of philosophical concern (e.g. 'Material objects exist' or 'Things continue to exist unperceived'). But these are strictly grammatical propositions, not empirical, contingent, truths. Finally, there are many propositions, to

[14] E.g., Russell's 'The Cult of "Common Usage"', in *Portraits from Memory and Other Essays* (Allen and Unwin, London, 1956), or 'Philosophical Analysis', in *My Philosophical Development* (Allen and Unwin, London, 1959).

which Moore called attention, which could (misleadingly) be called 'common-sense propositions'. Propositions such as 'I have a body', 'I have been alive for a good number of years', or 'The world has existed for a long time', are of great philosophical interest. But *not* because they need defending! In these three kinds of case the sentences in question show something important about our form of representation. It is not the task of philosophy to justify or defend them, but to clarify their status and import.

Secondly, the requirement that we describe ordinary language and its use is not a canonization of its misuse. We possess criteria for correct and incorrect use of language. Nor does it preclude examination of relatively arcane reaches of language (e.g. mathematicians' descriptions of their activities). Most importantly, we do not examine ordinary language and its use in order to extract from it a *theory* about the world, the mind or anything else. 'For "naïve language", that is to say our naïve, normal way of expressing ourselves, does not contain any theory of seeing—does not show you a *theory* but only a *concept* of seeing' (Z §223). What is said here of seeing should be generalized. The examination of ordinary use will show us what our concepts are, not how we believe the world to be. Our form of representation is contained in our ordinary speech, and it is this which we must survey to clear away philosophical confusions. 'To philosophize is to reject false arguments' (BT 409); the task of philosophy is to show up the errors of philosophical speculation, to dissolve philosophical problems, not to set up new doctrines nor to found new philosophical schools of thought (BT 420). While Russell begins with common sense and ends with paradox, Wittgenstein works through paradox (e.g. imagining feeling pain in others' bodies, all objects losing their rigidity, people changing personality every day) to a perspicuous understanding of language, a surview of the grammar the use of which we know full well (cf. 'Übersicht', pp. 305 ff.). Russell hankers after novel truths, wonderful paradoxes, new discoveries of hitherto unheard of profundity. It is not surprising that he is disappointed in the apparently thin fare Wittgenstein offers. People who lack the need for transparency, perfect clarity, of argument, are lost to philosophy (BT 421).

The Status of Philosophy

Wittgenstein's opposition to the 'scientific' conception of philosophy remains constant. Philosophy is not a super-science, nor does it partake of the methods of the physical sciences. He draws four contrasts.

(i) In the sense in which science constructs theories, there are no theories in philosophy (PI §109, p. 230). Theories involve the construction of hypotheses which may be more or less correct, modifiable in the light of new facts, and achieve greater or lesser accuracy in predictive power. In philosophy there is nothing hypothetical.

(ii) Physics gives a simplified idealized description of natural phenomena, representing light rays as straight lines or bodies as point-masses; it abstracts from secondary factors, e.g. disregarding gravitational forces of distant stars in constructing terrestial mechanics. But there are no idealizations in philosophy. We can construct ideal languages for certain purposes, but their relation to ordinary language is not that of ideal-typical physical representations to physical reality (PG 77).

(iii) Physics searches for new truths about matter or energy and makes discoveries about the constitution of the atom or the nature of radiation. But there are no new discoveries in philosophy. Philosophical analysis is not a kind of chemical analysis (M 323, cf. CO 42 f. and 'Family resemblance', pp. 186 f.) which will reveal the hitherto unknown structure of human thought. All that analysis does is to remind us of articulations in grammar which permit the inter-substitutability of expressions in appropriate contexts. Wittgenstein criticizes the *Tractatus* on this count, for he had then thought that logical analysis would some day discover elementary propositions and their forms (cf. LF), but this was an error (WWK 182 f.). There is nothing new to find out in philosophy. So-called 'thought experiments' are not genuine experiments. Philosophers may think that it is a philosophical discovery or an important datum that, as a matter of fact, 'contrary to our preconceived ideas, it is possible to think such-and-such' (PI §109, cf. Z §272). This would be important if the rules of grammar followed from independent laws of thought, and we had access to the laws of thought by introspection, by noting what and how we think. For then we might claim that what can be thought can be said and what cannot be thought cannot be said (PLP 37 ff.). But whether we can or cannot 'think a particular thought' is not 'discovered' by strenuous mental endeavour. It is determined by whether a sentence has a sense, whether the rules of grammar permit a certain combination of words, whether we assign a sense to such a sentence. And *that* is not something we discover 'to our surprise'.

(iv) Science is progressive. It solves problems and moves ahead to new problems. One of the most striking features of philosophy is that almost all its problems are ancient ones. One reads '. . . philosophers are no nearer the meaning of "Reality" than Plato got . . .'. How remarkable! Wittgenstein exclaims, how extraordinary that Plato could get so far! Or that we cannot get farther! Is this, he queries ironically, because Plato was so gifted (BT 424)? The problems of philosophy remain much the same because our language has remained, in key respects, much the same. As long as there is a verb like 'to be' that seems to function like 'to eat', so long as there are adjectives such as 'identical', 'true', false', 'probable', so long as there is talk of the 'stream of time', 'the expansion of space', human beings will continue to run their heads up against the same baffling problems. Does this preclude progress? Cannot these nagging problems be resolved once and for all? In the 1930–3 lectures he spoke of his own philosophy as making possible, for the first time, the reduction of philosophizing to a skill (M 322).[15] He stressed that philosophy as he was now practising it was not merely a stage in the development of the subject, but a new subject. His work is one of the heirs of what used to be called philosophy (BB 28).[16] Does this imply the possibility of progress? Yes and No! Critically there can be progress; certain philosophical methods can be ruled out as illegitimate (e.g. psychologism in logic); certain philosophical 'doctrines' such as idealism or behaviourism can be shown to be nonsense. But if by 'progress' we mean accumulation of *knowledge*, discovery of new facts and construction of novel theories to explain them, then there is no progress in philosophy. Nevertheless, if philosophy aims at clarity, then as the monstrous chimeras and phantasmagoria of philosophy are displayed for what they are, something is achieved. An *Übersicht* can be obtained. To be sure, fresh puzzles and bafflement may arise as new 'pictures' are invoked by philosophers, frequently from other departments of intellectual endeavour, to shed light upon the structure of our thought. The same maladies in slightly different forms will crop up again and again, and there is no inoculation against them. The human intellect, it seems, tends to philosophical error as the human will inclines to sin. Intellectual sin, like moral sin, is not prevented by knowledge, but by understanding. To that extent philosophy cannot be completed. But at least some segments of our grammar can be definitively mapped for a given generation (cf. Exg. §92, 1.1). And this is, perhaps, the nearest we can get to applying the notion of progress to philosophy—the elimination of the clouds of confusion, and the achievement of the clarity of a surview.

We might be tempted to claim that although philosophy is sharply distinguished from physical science, nevertheless it is a cognitive discipline. It seeks to unravel *a priori* truths, and it is an *a priori* science. It is no coincidence that the great rationalist systems of metaphysics were couched *more geometrico*. Wittgenstein will have none of this. Necessary truths are a product of grammar, not descriptions of the structure of reality. There are no axioms in philosophy, no deductions, and no theorems. Philosophy does not seek to *prove* anything. Attempts to prove the existence of God by deductive argument, to demonstrate that there really are other minds, to deduce the objective existence of the 'material world' are chimerical. 'Proof, refutation, these are dying words

---

[15] This is a puzzling claim, never repeated again. Is the skill of philosophy the careful description and judicious selection of certain rules of linguistic use which will resolve philosophical problems?

[16] Presumably because it does not purport to prove anything (the existence of the external world, of God, etc.), nor to discover any metaphysical truths.

in philosophy, though G. E. Moore "proved" to a puzzled world that it exists. What can one say to this—save, perhaps, that he is a great prover before the Lord.'[17]

Though there are no proofs in philosophy, there are questions and there are arguments. But philosophical questions are not questions in search of an answer, but questions in search of a sense. For the task of arguments in many domains of philosophy is not to answer questions, but to show that they lack sense. Commonly the first mistake we make in a philosophical investigation lies in the philosophical question itself (MS. 124, 278).

Philosophy, Wittgenstein insists, *explains* nothing, but only *describes* (PI §126; BT 418 f.; PG 66; BB 18, 125). This must be understood in the context of the claim that 'everything lies open to view' (PI §126; PG 256; BT 418 f.; BB 6). In science there are new facts to find out the discovery of which will solve scientific problems. In philosophy we are moving within the domain of the grammar of our language; there is nothing new to be revealed. If there is anything concealed from us, unknown, it is irrelevant. For by token of being unknown, it can have no role in our rule-governed practice of using language. If we do not know it, it cannot be part of what we mean. If it is concealed from us, it cannot be the ground for saying what we say. We could not 'discover' a new rule of chess, we could only invent one, or discover that some other people play a game similar to chess but with slightly different rules. There is no discovery of new senses embedded in our propositions, for if there is a new sense, it is a different proposition.

'Every explanation is an hypothesis' (GB 30). *A propos* Frazer's explanations of magic, Wittgenstein remarks, 'I think one reason why the attempt to find an explanation is wrong is that we have only to put together in the right way what we *know* without adding anything, and the satisfaction we are trying to get from the explanation comes of itself.' This holds for philosophy too. There is nothing more dangerous than employing the word 'explanation' in logic (philosophy) in the sense in which it is used in physics (BT 418).

With due care, however, we may use the term 'explanation' in a different sense. It is surely true that Wittgenstein explains in unparalleled detail the sources of error and confusion in certain domains of philosophy. So too the claim that there are no deductions in philosophy is aimed at the hypothetico-deductive methods of science. Yet it surely follows[18] from the private language argument that, say, idealism and solipsism are misguided philosophies. The 'explanations' of philosophy, however, are 'explanations by description'. The correct description of our linguistic

---

[17] F. Waismann, *How I See Philosophy*, ed. R. Harré (Macmillan, London, 1968), p. 1.
[18] Though not by deductive inference! Solipsism and idealism are not false but nonsense!

practices will show where and why we have gone wrong in our philosophizing, reveal how we generated confusion and nonsense.

The claim that philosophy is purely descriptive raises a fresh problem. For if what philosophy does is to describe the workings of our language, then does this not make philosophy into an empirical science, a branch of linguistics? This is to confuse a method with the product. Philosophical problems are conceptual, not empirical. They are resolved by turning our attention towards the employment of words (Z §463). The description of our linguistic practices does not aim at an exhaustive empirical grammar of a language, but at the resolution of philosophical problems (PI §109). Our interest in rules of grammar is determined by, and limited by, the problems of philosophy. Just as many rules of law are only of interest to us when we are tempted to break them, so too certain grammatical rules only become philosophically interesting when philosophers are tempted to violate them (BT 425). These problems are resolved not by *answers*, not by philosophical propositions, but by the dissolution of the problems, often by means of further questions (RFM 147), or even by means of grammatical jokes.[19] By rearranging what we already know, by bringing into view trivial and well-known facts about our use of language, we untie the knots in our understanding which gave rise to the problems. When the over-familiar and the excessively obvious are illuminated and ordered, the depth of our philosophical pronouncements is seen to be illusory, the doubts with which the spectre of scepticism haunts us are seen to be groundless, and our scruples are seen to be misunderstandings. The grammarian is interested in exactness and comprehensiveness. Wittgenstein is interested in neither (Z §§464 f.); eliciting descriptions of grammar need only go so far as is necessary for the resolution of philosophical problems. He does not suggest that exactness and comprehensiveness are unattainable, merely that they are often irrelevant to philosophy.

The contrast between linguistics and philosophy, however, goes deeper. The differences are not merely those of purpose, exactitude, and comprehensiveness. Philosophy has a special concern with the limits of sense, and it describes the bounds of sense *from within*. By ordinary canons of grammaticality, typical philosophical assertions such as 'I cannot feel your pains' or 'I know that I am in pain' or 'I cannot know how you feel' are not ungrammatical. Equally, sentences such as 'It is five o'clock on the sun', 'It is (or is not) both red and green all over', 'One can (or cannot) trisect an angle with compass and rule', or 'The standard metre is one metre long' are not ungrammatical. Nor are such sentences of any particular interest to the grammarian. Yet they are typical sources of philosophical difficulties. Their surface grammar appears in order.

---

[19] N. Malcolm, *Ludwig Wittgenstein, a Memoir*, p. 29.

They look like well-formed meaningful sentences, being constructed on analogy with legitimate sentences, but in subtle ways they violate the rules of language. Where such sentences appear pregnant with philosophical implications, e.g. appear to state truths about the limits of knowledge or the essence of things, it is the task of philosophy to reveal why such combinations of words are illegitimate in our language. In this sense philosophy, with its 'descriptive' methods, has a concern with the *limits* of language, and the nature of the violation of those limits by the typical philosophical questions and their putative answers, which ordinary grammar does not. A further difference of importance is that philosophy describes language 'from within', whereas ordinary, empirical, linguistics describes language 'from without'. Although Wittgenstein does occasionally talk *about* words, e.g. pointing out that there are sometimes striking differences between first- and third-person uses of certain verbs or between the use of different tenses, his most common methods of argument do not involve ascent to the metalinguistic plane. The reason for this harks back to the *Tractatus* distinction between showing and saying. The bounds of sense cannot be *described*, for there is nothing beyond the bounds of sense to be described. If they could be described, then the negation of their description would make sense, but if it did then that description would not describe the bounds of sense. A statement that something cannot be, i.e. is logically impossible, is not a description of a possibility that is impossible—but nonsense. Ascent to the metalinguistic level is of no avail either. For to say that a certain sentence has no sense is not to say that its sense is nonsense. But if it is merely about signs and not about their meanings, then this at best merely describes the wholly contingent and alterable bounds of (say) English, not the necessary bounds of sense.

There are, then, no philosophical propositions. If there were *theses* in philosophy, they would be trivial; everyone would agree with them (BT 419; PI §127). That we know of the existence of 'external objects' because we perceive them is not a claim that one would proudly display as a philosophical thesis. That we know that things happened thus or otherwise because we recollect them so occurring is news from nowhere. Achievement in philosophy consists in sweeping away the monstrous impediments which stand in the way of these trivial assertions—but such achievement does not manifest itself in philosophical theses.

Philosophy, Wittgenstein insists, 'leaves everything as it is' (PI §124). This is a corollary of the claim that there are no discoveries in grammar, that 'Philosophy may in no way interfere with the actual use of language; it can in the end only describe it' (PI §124). It is not the task of philosophy to 'reform' language, nor to give language (or mathematics) foundations. Grammar is autonomous. Nevertheless, if the remark that philosophy leaves everything as it is is taken out of its argumentative context, it may mislead. Lack of a 'correct logical point of view' frequently infects empirical sciences and mathematics. There is extensive back-seepage of philosophy into these other disciplines. If Wittgenstein's critical investigations in philosophy of mind carry conviction, the implications for certain theories and branches of empirical psychology are very substantial indeed. So too, if his philosophy of mathematics is on target, it will curb mathematicians' gassing. It is true that what he has done (if his claims are right) is not to discover new facts, but to reveal the true face of nonsense. But it would be misleading to claim that the magus under whose touch what seemed to be gold is revealed to be tinsel 'leaves everything as it is' in this broader sense.

The Difficulty of Philosophy

Why then is philosophy so infernally difficult? Wittgenstein gives two attractive *general* answers.

In philosophy it is always a matter of the application of a series of utterly simple basic principles that any child knows, and the—enormous—difficulty is only one of applying these in the confusion our language creates. (PR 153 f.)

Why is philosophy so complicated? It ought, after all, to be *completely* simple. —Philosophy unties the knots in our thinking, which we have tangled up in an absurd way; but to do that, it must make movements which are just as complicated as the knots. Although the *result* of philosophy is simple, its methods for arriving there cannot be so. (PR 52; Z §452.)

What are the sources of the characteristic difficulties? We shall list some which Wittgenstein discusses. (i) *Analogies in surface grammar*: this phenomenon is the most important of all, for the grip of the analogy is extraordinarily difficult to shake. The grammar of material object words and sensation words, of colour-words and of 'names' of 'abstract entities', is both very similar and vastly different. Subject/predicate sentences have the same form, but they are used in countless different ways; declarative sentences share the same mood, but we must not let this blind us to the differences between various kinds of such sentences and their roles in language. All differences in logic are big differences. It is no easy matter to identify the small differences that make all the difference. Our choice of words in philosophy is so very important because the exact 'physiognomy' of the matter must be given, only the exactly right thought can move on the right path. A waggon has to be placed *absolutely exactly* on the rails if it is to be able to roll forward smoothly (BT 410). (ii) *The phenomenology of the use of language*: Wittgenstein dwells at length upon the nature of the experiences which accompany the use of language, for we are prone, in doing philosophy, to generate error by associating sense with the mental phenomena accompanying sensible utterance or thought. This is a common feature of psychologism in logic and endemic in philosophical reflection in epistemology, philosophy of mind, and metaphysics. Philosophers have tried to analyse logical connectives in terms of feelings of denial, or hesitation, or 'if-feelings', failing to see that the distinctive feelings are identifiable only because of their association with the independently meaningful symbols. In philosophy of mind we confuse concepts (e.g. pain) with the phenomena (pains), or emotions with their characteristic accompaniments; in epistemology we confuse knowledge with privacy, or groundlessness of assertion with indubitable evidence. (iii) *Pictures embedded in language*: grammatical problems are so difficult because they are connected with the oldest, most elementary habits of thought, i.e. with the oldest *pictures* embedded in language (BT 423). The correctness of the pictures is not in dispute, but their application is, and the difficulty in philosophy (e.g. in dealing with the 'inner/outer' picture of mind and body or the picture of time as a flowing river) is in unpacking the application of the picture and resisting the obscuring effect of the picture alone (PI §424). Often different pictures clash, and our puzzles are generated by the attempt to employ both pictures simultaneously. We sometimes think of time 'passing us by': it flows, and we stand still (in the 'eternal present'). At other times we think of ourselves 'swept along' upon the stream of time. Both pictures are attractive; both have their point. But if we attempt to apply them simultaneously we will produce a monstrous pastiche. (iv) *The model of science*: as we have seen, Wittgenstein thought that the archetype of explanation and intellectual progress that has been provided in the last four centuries by science wreaks havoc when applied to philosophy. For it inclines us to search for explanations instead of describing 'grammatical' conventions, to construct ideal languages instead of describing our own, to conceive of metaphysics as a kind of 'ultra-physics', to think of philosophical analysis as a kind of chemistry, and to blur the boundary between the empirical and the conceptual. (v) *Projecting grammar on to reality*: examples of this strange form of intellectual displacement behaviour abound in philosophy. The criterion-less application of the first-person pronoun 'I' is projected on to reality to yield the doctrine of the simplicity of the soul; the role of samples in explanation and application of certain predicates produces the grandiose doctrine of sempiternal simples; colour-exclusion is conceived as a super-physical necessity; our commitment to the rules of a calculus is projected on to a domain of supersensible objects standing in 'necessary' relations to each other. The modest sentence 'This is how things are' is magnified and projected to yield 'the general propositional form'. (vi) *Natural intellectual prejudices*: we tend to prefer the sharp to the vague, the systematic to the unruly, the infallible to the final. Thus we favour explanation of concepts by *Merkmale* rather than by family resemblance, we crave for maximum generality, brushing aside important differences as arbitrary impediments to the desired all-embracing generalization. We feel dissatisfied with the rules we have because we have an obscure (and wholly unjustified) feeling that the rules of grammar must not only do their job properly, but that it should be logically impossible that they should fail to do it properly. We suffer, in philosophy, from pathological doubt, feeling that mere quietening of actual doubt is trivial, since the very possibility of doubt is a kind of doubt. We find it extremely difficult to stop, to recognize as a solution what often looks as if it is merely a preliminary to one (Z §314), for at heart we persist in thinking that an explanation of grammar is both necessary and possible if philosophical problems are to be resolved, rather than recognizing that a careful description is all that is either possible or necessary. We constantly search for *grounds* (justifications), for we think that if there are no grounds we have uncovered a deep irrationality; but this use of 'irrational' is akin to that of 'fall' in the proposition 'if the earth were not somehow supported it would have to fall' (Vol. XII, 128). Logic (grammar) must speak for itself; there is no hidden substructure. Wittgenstein's insistence that in our impatience we often stumble past the point of resolution is a theme attractively illustrated by a simile of Boltzmann:

. . . many problems are like the question once put to the painter, what picture he was hiding behind the curtain, to which he replied 'the curtain *is* the picture'. For when requested to deceive experts by his art, he had painted a picture representing a curtain. Is not perhaps the veil that conceals the nature of things from us just like that painted curtain.[20]

Metaphysics is the attempt to peep behind the painted curtain. (vii) *Philosophical mythologies*: whole philosophical schools, grand philosophical 'theories' and 'doctrines' are myths of symbolism erected by philosophers. Thus Platonism, Cartesian dualism, idealism, logical atomism are philosophers' 'pictures', often growing out of the ordinary 'pictures' of language. They are mythological constructions resting upon misinterpretations of the grammar of language. Yet they captivate and fascinate, and are not easily shaken off.

Methods of Philosophy

Philosophy endeavours to achieve a surview of a segment of our language, a grasp of the logical network of concepts within a given

[20] Boltzmann, 'The Second Law of Thermodynamics', in *Ludwig Boltzmann: Theoretical Physics and Philosophical Problems*, p. 15. Boltzmann's painter is in fact Parrhasius, a painter of the fifth century B.C. The anecdote is in Pliny. Compare this with Goethe's remark: 'Do not I beg you look for anything behind phenomena. They are themselves their own lesson.' ('Man suche nur nichts hinter den Phänomen; sie selbst sind die Lehre.') (*Maximen und Reflexionen*, ed. Max Hacker (Weimar, 1907), no. 575.) Wittgenstein quotes this remark in MS. 134, under 3 March 1947; it is also quoted by Spengler, in *Decline of the West*, Vol. I, p. 156. Wittgenstein transposes this attitude towards nature to philosophy and grammar.

domain. The attainment of such a surview will, in Wittgenstein's opinion, dissolve philosophical problems. Philosophy seeks to establish 'an order in our knowledge of the use of language' (PI §132). The order it seeks is not the one and only proper order. The grammarian or philologist arranges linguistic data quite differently, for quite different purposes. The order philosophy seeks to establish is guided by the purpose of resolving philosophical, or conceptual, problems. Wittgenstein's later philosophy is as resolutely opposed to the scientific conception of philosophy as was his earlier. It is often thought that in the *Tractatus* he held that one could definitively resolve philosophical problems, whereas in the *Investigations* one could only obtain provisional solutions. This is a misinterpretation. It is true that *in a sense* the later philosophy is piecemeal and tentative, but not in the sense envisaged by Russell. It is piecemeal in the sense that achievement in philosophy consists in discerning the conceptual links that characterize a given domain of thought, not in grasping the whole vast network. The network of language does not possess the uniformity envisaged in the *Tractatus*, but is a patchwork of numerous different language-games. Wittgenstein compares the philosophical arrangement of concepts to the ordering of books in a library (BB 44). Philosophical achievement is comparable to seeing that two hitherto adjacent books should be on separate shelves, or that hitherto separated books belong together. Or, to vary the metaphor, it is comparable to finding that two pieces of a jigsaw fit smoothly together (BB 46); but the 'fit' between any given group of pieces does not contain the 'form of fit' for all other pieces: the way these pieces fit together is no guarantee that others will fit in the same way. The tentativeness of philosophy is not like that of science either: its results are not under constant reassessment, subject to the vicissitudes of new discoveries. It is rather that 'every new problem which arises may put in question the *position* which our previous partial results are to occupy in the final picture' (BB 44). The juxtaposition of books or of jigsaw pieces may be correct, but we may have to shift the whole group to a different position. To see the affinities between propositions of arithmetic and of geometry is an achievement, but whether they belong on the 'synthetic *a priori* shelf', on 'the analytic shelf', or 'in the archives' may still be unclear.

   The traditional conception of philosophy viewed the subject as the Queen of the Sciences, the most fundamental and profound inquiry into the nature of reality in which man can engage. One typical response to Wittgenstein's conception is to think that his later work trivializes philosophy.

Its positive doctrines seem to me trivial and its negative doctrines unfounded. I have not found in Wittgenstein's *Philosophical Investigations* anything that seemed to me interesting . . . [I]f it is true, philosophy is, at best, a slight help to lexicographers, and at worst, an idle tea-table amusement.[21]

This seems to illustrate Lichtenberg's aphorism: 'A book is a mirror: if an ass peers into it, you can't expect an apostle to look out.' Russell is like a man groping in a dark room who, when the light is switched on, complains that there is nothing interesting to see, forgetting that the achievement was to find the switch.[22]

(Der Mann, der sagte, man könne nicht zweimal in den gleichen Fluss steigen, sagte etwas Falsches; man *kann* zweimal in den gleichen Fluss steigen.—Und ein Gegenstand hört manchmal auf zu existieren, wenn ich aufhöre ihn zu sehen, und manchmal nicht.—Und wir *wissen* manchmal, welche Farbe der Andere sieht, wenn er diesen Gegenstand betrachtet, und manchmal nicht.) Und so sieht die Lösung aller philosophischen Schwierigkeiten aus. Unsere Antworten müssen, wenn sie richtig sind, gewöhnliche und triviale sein.—Denn diese Antworten machen sich gleichsam über die Fragen lustig. (PPI §111, cf. BT 412.)

((The man who says that one can't step twice into the same river says something false; one *can* step twice into the same river.—And an object sometimes ceases to exist when I cease to look at it, and sometimes not—And we do *know*, sometimes, what colour another person sees when he observes a given object, and sometimes we do not.) And this is what the solutions to all philosophical difficulties look like. Our answers, if they are correct, must be ordinary and trivial.—For these answers, as it were, make fun of the questions.)

In PPI(A) he added the sentence 'Nicht aber die Erklärungen, die die Probleme verständlich machen' ('But not the explanations [clarifications], which make the problem intelligible').

The confusions and endlessly baffling questions of philosophy are not trivial but deep; they stem from misconceptions about the structure of our thought. When they are resolved the structure of our thought is not altered, but understood. The illusions of philosophy are not trivial, they are not symptoms of stupidity, but rooted in fundamental features of our language, in structures of thought which determine the way in which we look at things, but which are extraordinarily difficult to survey.

It is characteristic of Wittgenstein's methods of philosophizing that he rarely attacks a philosophical position by frontal assault, preferring, like all great strategists, the 'indirect approach'. The diabolical fascination of the various forms of idealism will not be destroyed by detailed examination of its official doctrines, its outlying bastions as it were. For successful criticism will only lead to the erection of new lines of defence. Wittgenstein assails such philosophies by probing for the primitive *Urbild* which underlies them, often only implicitly. His criticism of logical atomism is

---

[21] Russell, *My Philosophical Development*, p. 216 f.
[22] Cf. BT 417: solving philosophical problems is like finding the right combination to the lock of a safe. Once this is found even a child can open the safe.

primarily in the form of an attack on the underlying 'Augustinian picture of language'. A similar strategy typifies his criticisms of solipsism and idealism. Wittgenstein is rarely satisfied with the revelation of one or two defects in a philosophical conception. He returns again and again from different angles to the same error, uncovering more and more fallacious presuppositions.

This is not mere obsessiveness, pedantry, or laudable thoroughness. It is an integral part of Wittgenstein's conception of the correct method of philosophy, and intimately related to the view that the actual solution to a problem often looks like a mere preliminary.

We must begin with the mistake and find out the truth in it.

That is, we must uncover the source of the error; otherwise hearing what is true won't help us. It cannot penetrate when something is taking its place.

To convince someone of what is true, it is not enough to state it; we must find the *road* from error to truth. (GB 28.)

Clarity will only come from an *Übersicht*. But to attain that, numerous misleading analogies must be brought to light, the sources of the misguided demands on language and reality must be laid bare, room must be made for philosophical understanding.

His strategy is attractively depicted by the metaphor of knotted strings:

You want to straighten out a knot by pulling at the ends of the string.—And as long as you pull, the knot can't come undone. You feel there is still a knot, so you pull. And the knot becomes smaller and harder.

One way of solving a philosophical problem is to tell yourself: *it is insoluble*. It isn't answerable or it would have been answered, you would have answered long ago. It's not a kink, it's a knot. Don't look for an answer, look for a cure. Don't try to pull it straight, try to unravel it. (MS. 158, 33 f. (in English).)

Though Wittgenstein declared proudly in the early 1930s that 'a new method' had been found (M 322), he insists in the *Investigations* that there is not a single method, but many different ones, like different therapies. The analogy with therapy is apt, and his philosophy—at least in its negative, critical, part—has often been referred to as a kind of philosophical therapeutics for conceptual neuroses. He recognized the similarity of method between his style of philosophy and psychoanalysis (BT 410; MS. 158, 34). The great methodological difference turns on the fact that psychoanalysis conceives itself to rest upon a theory about the nature of mental mechanisms. But the similarity is evident. Like the psychoanalyst, he merely makes the patient, the philosopher in the grip of a misguided picture, aware of what he is doing (WWK 186). Wittgenstein does not produce doctrines to counterbalance metaphysical theories, but merely shows how metaphysical doctrines stem from misuse of language. He arranges the grammatical rules which he elicits from the person who suffers from philosophical bafflement to reveal points of tension and to lay bare conflicting and illegitimate applications of language.[23]

Some of the typical methods Wittgenstein employs are worth mentioning. (i) Where analogies of surface grammar lead to philosophical error, he counteracts their effects by describing the uses of the expressions in question to reveal familiar but unnoticed differences. (ii) For similar purposes he invents a wealth of imaginary language-games, new uses of words, sometimes absurd ones, to help loosen the deceptive grip of customary forms of language (BB 28). (iii) Where our method of representation seems to mirror reality, to be justifiable by reference to the 'structure of reality', he instructs us to imagine perfectly conceivable changes of general facts of nature which would deprive our concepts in a given domain of their point and use. (iv) When the tantalizing pictures embedded in language mislead us, he directs our attention away from the pictures themselves and towards their applications. (v) Against our temptation to search for essences, to conceive of expressions as necessarily definable by reference to necessary and sufficient conditions, he insists upon detailed description of various cases. They may have no more unity than a rope has a single fibre. And if we *discover* a hidden unity, it cannot be this which led us to apply the one expression to the diverse phenomena. (vi) We are constantly tempted to 'mythologize' the mental to hypostatize mental mechanisms to resolve philosophical problems, to think that the mind, being 'mysterious', can accomplish so much more than mere symbols (BB 4). Wittgenstein recommends that we replace the mental mechanism by a physical substitute, for this will reveal how empty the 'retreat to the mental' was. The mind contains no such mystery; except perhaps this—that it can do what it can do without mystery. (vii) Against the psychologistic temptation to interpret meaning and understanding of symbols as a matter of psychological states or experiences accompanying the use of symbols, he invites us to detach the sign and try to think the sense without it. We will then see how irrelevant the psychological accompaniment (important though it is to us) is to understanding or meaning an expression. (viii) Where we fix our attention upon a captivating paradigm and try to force grammar into a

---

[23] Cf. Waismann, *How I See Philosophy*, p. 12; the point is an important one—Wittgenstein insists that he does not impose rules upon others, does not insist that a certain expression be used in such-and-such a way. All he does is to show the consequences of a commitment elicited from a philosophical confusion.

Related to the psychoanalytic analogy is Wittgenstein's insistence that underlying the intellectual confusion is the *will* to illusion. In MS. 158, 35 he alludes to Schopenhauer (in English): 'If you find yourself stumped trying to convince someone of something and not getting anywhere, tell yourself that it is the *will* and not the intellect you're up against' (cf. also BT 407,410).

predetermined mould, he produces a host of connecting links, some invented, to shake the grip of the paradigm. (ix) Where a particular form of words appears to reach deep into the structure of reality ('This is how things are' or 'The object has the property so-and-so'), he invites us to reflect on the origin of the form of words and its ordinary commonplace employment.

Is Systematic Philosophy Possible?

We have surveyed Wittgenstein's diatribes against treating philosophy as a kind of super-science or as methodologically akin to the empirical sciences. He insists that there are no theories, no explanations but only descriptions, and nothing hypothetical in philosophy. There are no philosophical propositions, hence no philosophical knowledge; there are no philosophical discoveries, for philosophy 'leaves everything as it is'. If there were any theses in philosophy they would be utterly trivial—things everyone knows.

These radical claims have seemed to many to be outrageous, to trivialize a profound subject and to place at peril its very existence as a respectable intellectual pursuit. It cannot be denied that it runs counter to deep-seated trends in contemporary philosophy. It is commonly argued that the existence of abstract entities must be accepted as an hypothesis, otherwise certain types of quantification would not be legitimate. Future ingenuity, it is thought, may enable us to dispense with these objects, but for the time being we must take their existence as a good *hypothesis*. Equally, epistemology is currently swamped with the doctrine of 'inference to the best explanation'. So the existence of other minds is thought to be the best explanation of the observed behaviour of human bodies, and the existence of objective particulars is thought to be the best available *hypothesis* to *explain* subjective perceptual experience. The model or picture upon which these philosophical claims are erected is self-consciously that of the advanced physical sciences. Other minds, objective particulars, even abstract entities, are comparable in cognitive status to hypothetical entities such as mesons and neutrinos. Ordinary language is frequently conceived to embody *theories* about the nature of reality, e.g. the language of mentality (i.e. discourse about sensations, perceptions, or experiences) is thought of as a *theory* about the mind or about human behaviour. So too teleological explanation of human conduct in terms of intentions, goals, and purposes is conceived of as an 'explanatory theory'. Contemporary materialists conceive of these 'theories' as in competition with physics or neurophysiology, in principle capable of being superseded by the truly cognitive advanced physical sciences.

Certainly Wittgenstein will have no truck with these claims. In his view such contentions are preposterous, based on misunderstandings about the nature of philosophy, misconstruals of grammar, misinterpretation of science and scientific method, and incomprehension of pictures embedded in language.

However, Wittgenstein's writings have also given rise to the impression that, if he is correct, no systematic methodical philosophy is possible at all. Philosophers commonly talk of 'constructing theories', in semantics or epistemology or philosophy of mind. But he prohibits theories in philosophy. Philosophy hankers after generalizations, but he condemns the 'contempt for the particular case'. Writers in philosophy strive after systematicity and comprehensiveness, he seems to dismiss this as either impossible or irrelevant. His interest in the anatomy of thought seems to be circumscribed by the needs of the pathology of the intellect. Many have felt uneasy about such restrictions, at least to the extent that they express more than personal predilection.

Some of the unease is misplaced, for it arguably depends upon misunderstanding. Wittgenstein's objection to 'theorizing' in philosophy is an objection to assimilating philosophy, whether in method or product, to a theoretical (super-physical) science. Philosophy is not hypothetico-deductive. But if thoroughgoing refutations of idealism, solipsism or behaviourism involve a 'theoretical' endeavour, Wittgenstein engages in it. If a careful, methodical, and systematic tabulation of similarities, differences, and characteristics of sensations, perceptions, and emotions is to be referred to as 'producing a theory of the mind', then he constructs a theory of the mind, is methodical and systematic (cf. esp. Z §§472 ff.), and points the way for subsequent philosophers of mind. For reasons already elaborated it is misleading to call this a 'theory', but the activity is legitimate—it is a description of the grammar of mental language. Wittgenstein said that he did not aim at comprehensiveness; but he did not either prohibit it or claim it to be impossible. At most he may have thought it uninteresting, irrelevant to philosophy, and possibly an impediment to surveyability. But, if philosophy is a quest for an *Übersicht*, then system there must be. For a surview does not consist of a haphazard collection of aperçus. If it is not comprehensive, at any rate it is systematic.

Recognition of family resemblance concepts in no way precludes systematic description of the conceptual phenomena. Although Wittgenstein warns against 'contempt for the particular case', it would be quite wrong to think that he conceived all generalization to be illegitimate; he himself makes claims such as 'Inner states stand in need of outer criteria', 'It is what justifies its assertion that constitutes the sense of a proposition', or 'Justification must be public'. To be sure, these are all 'grammatical' truths and strictly illegitimate, as were the propositions of the *Tractatus*. But their occurrence serves to dispel the confusion of the view that Wittgenstein rules out generalization.

Similar considerations apply to worries that arise from Wittgenstein's placing 'explanation' upon the Index. The sense in which this term has no place in philosophy is the sense in which it abounds in science, where one phenomenon is explained in terms of another, one fact explained by reference to new ones, and hypotheses adduced and tested to explain empirical facts. But need one deny a wider use to 'explain'? Indeed, if explanation is a correlate of understanding, must we not recognize such a use? To bring someone to understand a puzzling phenomenon by examining intermediate cases, tracing links, exploring analogies and disanalogies is surely as legitimate a form of 'explanation' as the distinctive hypothetico-deductive explanation of science. Philosophy, one might claim, explains by description whereas science explains by hypothesis. Philosophical explanation produces understanding by means of an *Übersicht*, scientific explanation produces new knowledge by constructing theories.

A final source of concern is the relationship between Wittgenstein's insistence that there are no theses in philosophy, that everything lies open to view, that any philosophical results are trivial and utterly uncontentious, and the no less indisputable fact that he propounds numerous apparently philosophical generalizations that are far from obvious, clearly non-trivial, and certainly highly contentious. He commits himself firmly to the Socratic method of bringing his hearers and readers to discern differences (and similarities) which are normally overlooked, yet which are crucially important for resolving philosophical confusion. But, he insists, he propounds no opinions (LFM 55), all he does is to ask 'Let's investigate whether so-and-so is the case'. How is this conflict to be resolved?

One must distinguish two kinds of cases. One kind of philosophical question takes the form of 'material questions'. Can one step into the same river twice? Do objects continue to exist unperceived? Do other human beings experience states of mind? To these the answers are indeed wholly trivial; and the work of philosophy does not consist in asserting the answers, but in disentangling the confusions that stand in the way of sound understanding.

The other kind of case concerns grammatical sentences. These are, of course, a mixed bunch. They are, however, all expressions of, or reflections of, grammatical rules. As such they are not, in Wittgenstein's view, genuine propositions, hence not genuine assertions. All one can do here, he insists, is to tabulate rules (WWK 184). These are elicited by detailed examination of typical philosophical problems. The rules thus elicited are implicit in our linguistic practices, and at no stage in the argument should anything contentious be passed over. Complete clarity must be obtained at each step (WWK 183). If contentions (pseudo-propositions) such as 'Inner states stand in need of outer criteria' seem disputable, that is because they are viewed outside the argumentative context which led up to them. If they are disputed, then the alternatives to them must be painstakingly explored; we must examine, e.g., the thought that one might possess a concept of an inner state divorced from behavioural criteria. If this is done properly it will be seen that these alternatives lead to incoherence.

If the line advanced captures correctly the structure of our form of representation, then indeed it is true *in a sense* that there can be nothing new and startling about telling us that mental states need behavioural criteria, that the sense of a wide range of declarative sentences is determined by assertion-conditions, that truth cannot intelligibly be transcendent. But it is also true that these apparent assertions are grammatical pseudo-propositions, expressions of conventional connections in language be-tween the use of certain words. If 'disputed', then further argument is necessary to show that it makes no sense to conceive of a mental state without behavioural criteria, to reveal that to conceive of truth independently of intelligible grounds of assertion is incoherent, and so forth.

Nevertheless, it would not be surprising to find the non-philosopher agreeing to some of these grammatical sentences as if to truisms, while philosophers, with a professional stake in 'theories of meaning' or 'truth-theories', respond with sound and fury. 'Philosophie versteht niemand. Entweder er versteht nicht was geschrieben ist, oder er versteht es: aber nicht, dass es Philosophie ist' (Vol. VI, 292). ('No one understands philosophy. Either he does not understand what is written, or he under-stands it, but not that it is philosophy.') For all that, it is misleading to claim that the particular conception of language (and philosophy) that Wittgenstein delineates is something we (philosophers) all knew perfectly well. While the pieces of the philosophical jigsaw are familiar, their arrangement is not. It may well be something that we can all *recognize* perfectly well (as a surview of our language), once we shed our blinkers. But it is certainly something we have never seen before in the light of day.

XIV

ÜBERSICHT

1. *Introduction*

The notion of *Übersichtlichkeit* is prominent in all Wittgenstein's later philosophy and is of paramount importance. It occurs on the second page of *Philosophical Remarks*, is discussed at some length in Vol. VI, hence too in the 'Big Typescript', and is a key to his conception of philosophy. It looms large in his philosophy of mathematics,[1] and is tacit in his fragmentary remarks on ethics and aesthetics. It is not, however, easy to capture its pervasive significance and its Protean forms. An *Übersicht* of Wittgenstein's concept of *Übersichtlichkeit* is no more readily available than is an *Übersicht* of any other problematic concept.

Notoriously, there is no happy way of translating 'Übersicht' and its cognates into English. We have seen that Wittgenstein himself had difficulties with the translation (cf. Exg. §92). His translators too have been unable to find a successful solution to the problem. Worse still, they have been unwilling to adopt a consistent one, thus obscuring the centrality of the idea in Wittgenstein's works. The translators of the *Remarks* use 'bird's eye view' to translate 'übersichtlich' and 'Übersichtlichkeit' (PR 52). 'Übersichtlichkeit' is rendered as 'perspicuity' (PI §122), but also as 'synoptic view' (Z §464); 'übersehbar' is translated as 'capable of being taken in' (RFM 170), 'übersehen' is given as 'command a clear view' (PI §122), 'Übersicht' is rendered as 'survey' (Z §273) and 'übersichtlich' as 'surveyable' (PI §92). While agreeing that there is no happy solution, we lay some store by consistency (as it were, in the interests of *Übersichtlichkeit*), and will either use the German word itself, or some cognate of 'survey' (including the archaic noun 'surview').

It would be partly true, but superficial, to claim that the concept of a surview is a direct descendant of the *Tractatus* conception of 'the correct logical point of view'. The partial truth lies in the fact that in the *Tractatus* philosophy is said to strive for a correct logical point of view, which is to be achieved by means of 'depth analysis', and in the *Investigations* it aims at a surview (perspicuous or surveyable representation), which is to be obtained by surveying all the uses and applications of words, phrases, and sentences in a given domain of thought which give rise to philosophical perplexity. The superficiality of this claim lies in its disregarding of the interconnections between surveyability and (i) the importance of seeing connecting links (and hence of imaginary

---

[1] We shall not discuss this aspect of the notion.

language-games), (ii) the repudiation of explanatory hypotheses in philosophy, (iii) the significance of seeing aspects and formal relations between concepts and phenomena (and *creating* such relations, and the importance which *that* has), (iv) family resemblance concepts, (v) scientific creativity, and the role of models in science, and (vi) coming to grips with what is impressive in ethics, aesthetics, and religion, ritual, and mythology, and what is *meaningful* in these aspects of human life. For surveyability, seeing connections which will alleviate a certain type of emotional and intellectual tension and discomfort (without *dissipating* it) and produce a deeper understanding, is not only the heir of 'the correct logical point of view', but also a descendant of the ineffability of 'the Mystical'.

There are two complementary ways to try to present the significance of an *Übersicht* in Wittgenstein's writings. One is quasi-historical, the other is to elaborate the connections which this concept has with related notions (just mentioned). They are complementary inasmuch as the first already points in the direction of the second. We shall attempt both routes.

2. *Precursors*

The quasi-historical route consists in bringing to light some of the self-avowed influences upon Wittgenstein's thought which contain seeds of the idea of surveyability and its importance. We must, however, stress that this mode of access is only *quasi*-historical. We are not claiming that Wittgenstein's conception actually derived from these sources—but only that it *could have* (cf. GB 41), not as an hypothesis, but as an internal relation between what predecessors who we know impressed him had to say on closely related matters (related, we may claim, partly by way of family resemblance) and his own developed views. Whether, *qua* historical hypotheses, our remarks are true, is, in the end, unimportant. After all, each writer creates his own precursors.

Frege (FA 5) wrote '. . . one of the requirements of reason . . . is . . . to embrace all first principles in a survey' ('das Bedürfnis der Vernunft nach Uebersichtlichkeit der ersten Grundlagen'). This conception contrasts with Wittgenstein's, both early and late. For Wittgenstein rejected the whole notion of 'first principles'. The idea that reason requires a surview of perplexing concepts is, however, a seed from which much may grow.

More significant, and well known, is the impact of Hertz's introduction to *The Principles of Mechanics*. The main feature here is Hertz's insight that some kinds of vexing problems are to be resolved, not by scientific explanation and hypotheses, but by clarification. Unclarity is often expressed by questions about the nature of a phenomenon, but what is needed, in some such cases, is not fresh information or sharper definitions, but a clearer understanding of existing information and definitions. In particular, the removal of contradictions between known relations and conceptual connections will alleviate discomfort. And then 'our minds, no longer vexed, will cease to ask illegitimate questions'.

Less well known, but no less important, are some of Boltzmann's remarks. In his youth Wittgenstein had wished to study under Boltzmann, though he did not do so. None the less, in 1931 he cited Boltzmann as a seminal influence upon his thought (cf. Exg. §122). This must allude to Boltzmann's writings, in particular perhaps to his emphasis upon surveyability, model-building, and the importance of analogy. Boltzmann explicitly relates models to surveyability:[2]

... [T]here is a need for making the utmost use of what powers of perception we possess, and since the eye allows us to take in the greatest store of facts at once (significantly enough we say 'survey'), this gives rise to the need to represent the results of calculations and that not only for the imagination but visibly for the eye and palpably for the hand, with cardboard and plaster.

He then elaborates a radical account of models in science. The beginnings of modern science conceived of achievement in terms of constructing explanatory hypotheses. But just when nineteenth-century science reached its apogee with Darwin's theory of evolution, physics, under the guidance of Kirchhoff, reversed its steps. It cannot be the task of theory to see through the mechanisms of nature, but only to set up the simplest possible differential equations to enable accurate calculation and prediction. Indeed, under Hertz's guidance, the attack on explanatory hypotheses went to extremes: hypotheses are mere colourful wrappings for bare equations. But others, especially fond of the 'colourful wrappings', while renouncing them as *hypotheses*, insisted on their importance as models and analogies (Faraday, Maxwell, Thomson). The mechanical models Maxwell presented in expounding his theories of electricity are not hypotheses, but *analogies*. The discovery of the great formulae was a consequence of the ingenuity and insight in creating fruitful mechanical analogies, a point missed by Hertz. Helmholtz's discussions of the mechanical analogies of the second law of thermodynamics,

... were more in tune with the spirit of science than the old hypotheses, besides being more convenient for the scientist himself. For the old hypotheses could be upheld only so long as everything went well; but now the occasional lack of agreement was no longer harmful, for one cannot reproach a mere analogy for being lame in some respects ...

---

[2] 'On the Methods of Theoretical Physics', in *Ludwig Boltzmann: Theoretical Physics and Philosophical Problems*, pp. 5 f. (Subsequent page references are to this volume.)

In the end, philosophy generalized Maxwell's ideas to the point of maintaining that knowledge itself is nothing else than the finding of analogies.[3]

The analogical approach to science, in Boltzmann's view, compensates for abandonment of complete congruence with nature by revealing more striking points of similarity. No doubt the future belongs to this new method, he concludes, although it would be wrong to *abandon* the old method completely.

The emphasis on analogical thought and its genuinely creative power is striking. No less so are passages, often echoing Hertz, in which Boltzmann warns against unnoticed but illegitimate extensions of concepts from one domain to another.[4] He stresses that the simplest preconditions of experience and laws of thought can only be *described* and that this description will dissolve apparent contradictions involved in philosophical puzzlement since it will show the nonsensicality of the questions.[5] He also emphasizes the importance of 'The overview of the whole, required for any mental activity aiming at discovering something essentially new or even just essentially new combinations of old ideas'.[6] This endorsement is coupled with a warning and a mention of Goethe: 'Only half of our experience is even experience, as Goethe says. The more general the overview one can win, the more surprising the facts one can discover but the more easily too one can fall into error.'[7]

Finally, Boltzmann recurrently emphasizes that the 'great problems' (why anything exists, why the law of cause and effect holds, what might be the true cause for the world to run as it does, etc.) are illusory. It is not the task of science to give ultimate explanations, but merely to construct fruitful models. Nor is it part of its role to 'solve the question as to the nature of matter, mass and force', but rather, as Hertz had suggested, to dissolve it.

My present theory is totally different from the view that certain questions fall outside the boundaries of human cognition. For according to that latter theory that is a defect or imperfection of man's cognitive capacity, whereas I regard the existence of these questions and problems themselves as an illusion. On superficial reflection it may of course be surprising that after recognition of the illusion the drive towards answering these questions does not cease . . .

. . . Only very slowly and gradually will all these illusions recede and I regard it as the central task of philosophy to give a clear account of the inappropriateness of this overshooting the mark on the part of our thinking habits . . .

If therefore philosophy were to succeed in creating a system such that in all

[3] ibid, p. 11.
[4] 'On the Question of the Objective Existence of Processes in Inanimate Nature', p. 67.
[5] ibid, p. 75; cf. Exg. §124.
[6] 'On the Development of the Methods of Theoretical Physics in Recent Times', p. 77.
[7] ibid., p. 96.

cases mentioned it stood out clearly when a question is not justified so that the drive towards asking it would gradually die away, we should at one stroke have resolved the most obscure riddles and philosophy would become worthy of the name of queen of the sciences.[8]

One could look upon the last paragraph as the embryonic programme which the *Tractatus*[9] pursued, the preceding one as representing part of the task of the *Investigations*.

Paul Ernst was a quite different source of inspiration. Wittgenstein expressed regret at not having acknowledged his influence in the Preface to the *Tractatus*. The essay of Ernst which impressed him was the *Nachwort* to Grimm's *Kinder-und Hausmärchen* (1910).[10] What are the main points in Ernst which parallel Wittgenstein's reflections?

First, Ernst emphasizes that myths, folk-tales and fairy-tales are a repository of mankind's moral beliefs. They express a world-picture and a fundamental belief in a moral world-order. They give a picture of the moral law, not by moralizing tales, but by poetic imagination, by exaggeration, by impossibilities, and by repetitions. It is a mistake to examine a folk-tale for 'internal explanation', i.e. for a chain of consequence and motivation. For that is not what a folk-tale, consciously or unconsciously, is trying to achieve.

Secondly, and consequently, Ernst sharply distinguishes the nature of understanding myth from scientific or historical explanation, and what is expressed by myth from what is aimed at by scientific understanding. To approach a myth or fairy-tale with questions such as 'Did it really happen?', 'How could this be?', is nonsensical. This is a misplaced rationalism. Science looks for explanations of facts, for a theory. But understanding of folk-tales is not to be sought thus. Poetic imagery and

---

[8] 'On Statistical Mechanics', p. 167.

[9] The impact of Boltzmann's writings on TLP is striking, especially, but not only, on the discussion of natural science in 6.3 ff. Thus compare 6.342 with Boltzmann, ibid., p. 106, 6.3611 (a) with p. 103, 6.371 with p. 104, the network analogy with pp. 118 f., and 5.1361 (b) (which should be translated 'Superstition is the belief in the causal nexus') with p. 139.

[10] Rhees reports (Introductory Note to GB, 18) that Wittgenstein said that he took the phrase, 'mythology in our language' from this essay. It does not occur there. Nietzsche, however, used the expression in *The Wanderer and his Shadow* §11: 'Through words and concepts we are now continually tempted to think of things as being simpler than they are, as separated from one another, as indivisible, each existing as and for itself. There is a philosophical mythology concealed in *language* . . .' Whether or not Wittgenstein read this work, he always conceived of the thoughts that language, in some sense, contains a mythology, and that philosophy itself bears a kinship to mythology as insights derived from Ernst. Ernst's phrase 'missverstandene Tendenz der Sprache', p. 273 (as well as 'eine spätere Zeit die Sprachlogik der Vergangenheit nicht mehr verstand . . .', p. 308) is the source of the phrase (and underlying conception) in TLP of 'a misunderstanding of the logic of our language'. In Vol. VI, 184 Wittgenstein remarks that when his book is published he must acknowledge his debt to Ernst, in particular for this latter phrase, which he should have acknowledged in TLP.

symbolism are part of the natural medium of folk-tale (it is natural to represent the common conception of the relation of body to soul as horse to rider, or servant to master). Historical explanation has a role in understanding folk-tales, not for purposes of historical understanding, but rather in so far as it illuminates an aesthetic understanding.

Thirdly, Ernst emphasizes that now that science (cognition) is no longer one with religion and poetry, the creative myth-making powers of mankind are split up. But science itself creates for itself a great mythology. Theories of history, Darwinism, the Kant-Laplace Theory, laws of gravitation, etc., all contain grandiose myths.

Where do we find the echoes of these remarks in Wittgenstein? In the *Tractatus*, we would conjecture, primarily in the remarks on ethics, aesthetics, and religion, as something that can be shown but not said. Also, no doubt, in the analogue between misunderstanding the logic of language in myth and folk-tale (where inanimate objects have souls, men have extraordinary powers of bodily transformation, etc.) and philosophical misunderstanding. But it is striking that Ernst's remarks resonate even more powerfully in Wittgenstein's later writings, particularly in the first set of 'Remarks on Frazer's "Golden Bough"' (derived from Vol. VI), which is the source of the main remarks on surveyability, and in the *Lectures on Aesthetics*. It is noteworthy that §93 (pp. 433–5) of the 'Big Typescript (the last section of the chapter 'Philosophie') is entitled 'Die Mythologie in den Formen unserer Sprache ((Paul Ernst))'.[11]

Frazer's approach to ritual and magic is not unlike the rationalist approach to myth and folk-tale. Wittgenstein's reaction to Frazer is akin to, though deeper than, Ernst's brief castigation of rationalist interpretations of myth. Wittgenstein's repudiation of explanation resembles Ernst's, and his search for understanding by means of a surview resembles Ernst's conception of poetic understanding. Wittgenstein's adamant insistence upon the autonomy of the aesthetic bears a kinship with Ernst's cast of mind. His pungent remark that Freud has not given an *explanation* of ancient myths (e.g. Oedipus), but propounded a new myth (LA 51), and his intimation that Darwinism was accepted, like Freudian psychoanalysis, not as a theory resting on very slender evidence but because of the charm of its unity (LA 26), are in marked agreement with Ernst on the myth-making of science.

In Vol. VIII, 235 (= EBT 518) Wittgenstein pointed out that the real achievement of a Copernicus or a Darwin is the discovery not of a true theory, but of a fruitful new aspect. This suggests an affinity with Boltzmann's remarks on the importance of analogical thought. Maxwell's analogical models were not mere colourful wrappings, but the creation of a fruitful analogy which would make possible a unified

---

[11] Cf. 'The nature of philosophy', pp. 271 ff.

'overview' of a domain of observation. Its fruitfulness was proved by the discovery of Maxwell's formulae, and from them flowed new and more surprising facts. Scientific creativity often consists in the choice or invention of a new form of representation which can fruitfully unify the facts.

The value and dangers of the passionate search for, and feeling that there must be, a unity amidst diversity of natural phenomena is beautifully brought out in Goethe's quest for the Primal Plant, under the guidance of the notion of a unity hidden beneath the diverse organs of the plant. Goethe's original inspiration for his botanical researches appears to have been a mixture of geneticism and analogical insight that might be put to work for purposes of comparative morphology. One can see the intermingling of the two in his remarks in *Italian Journey*;[12] on 27 September 1786 he writes:

> Here, where I am confronted with a great variety of plants my hypothesis that it might be possible to derive all plant forms from one original plant becomes clear to me and more exciting. Only when we have accepted this idea will it be possible to determine genera and species exactly.

On 17 April 1787 he writes in a striking passage:

> Among this multitude [of plants] might I not discover the Primal Plant? There certainly must be one. Otherwise, how could I recognize that this or that form *was* a plant if all were not built upon the same basic model [pattern]?

In a letter to Herder a month later (17 May 1787) he is still in the grip of his creative fantasies:

> The Primal Plant is going to be the strangest creature in the world, which Nature herself shall envy me. *With this model and the key to it, it will be possible to go on forever inventing plants and know their existence is logical; that is to say, if they do not actually exist, they could,* for they are not the shadowy phantoms of a vain imagination, but possess an inner necessity and truth. The same law will be applicable to all other living organisms. [Our italics.]

The real breakthrough, and partial emancipation from geneticism, came on 31 July 1787:

> While walking in the Public Gardens of Palermo, it came to me in a flash that in the organ of the plant which we are accustomed to call the *leaf* lies the true Proteus who can hide or reveal himself in all vegetal forms. From first to last, the plant is nothing but leaf, which is so inseparable from the future germ that one cannot think of one without the other.

Various strands come together here. First, note two elements that *can be* the source of endless confusion or of fruitful insight; namely, (i) the

[12] Goethe, *Italian Journey*, tr. W. H. Auden and Elizabeth Mayer (Penguin, Harmondsworth, 1970).

suggestion that only a hidden unity could justify the application of a single term to diverse phenomena, and (ii) that the unity must be genetic and developmental. Secondly, note how the former elements give way to *analogical* insight. Goethe expressed this in his criticism of Linnaeus who, in his view, made too much of superficial dissimilarities:

> For it is here that we hope the genius of the analogy may stand by us, as a guardian angel, so that we may not fail to recognize in a single doubtful case a truth which has stood the test in many other instances, but may instead pay due respect to the law, even when it seeks to elude us in the phenomenal world.[13]

Thirdly, note the striking phrasing that we have italicized in the letter to Herder. The 'model' of the Primal Plant is designed, as it were, to provide the 'logical space' for all possible plants.[14] What Goethe sought in nature he found *in a form of representation*. Hence the notorious shock he got from Schiller's perceptive response to Goethe's explanation of the metamorphosis of plants: 'That is no experience, that is an idea'.[15]

Goethe ultimately gave his insights a powerful expression in the poem 'Die Metamorphose der Pflanzen', which opens thus;

Dich verwirret, Geliebte, die tausendfältige Mischung
    Dieses Blumengewühls über dem Garten umher;
Viele Namen hörest du an, und immer verdränget
    Mit barbarischem Klang einer den andern im Ohr.
Alle Gestalten sind ähnlich, und keine gleichet der andern;
    Und so deutet das Chor auf ein geheimes Gesetz,
Auf ein heiliges Rätsel.

(You are confused, beloved, by the thousandfold mingled multitude of flowers all over the garden. You listen to their many names which are for ever, one after another, ringing outlandishly in your ears. All their shapes are similar, yet none is the same as the next; and thus the whole chorus of them suggests a secret law, a sacred riddle.)[16]

It is interesting that Spengler too compared *his* morphological method with Goethe's (rightly seeing the kinship with Leibniz). What both were seeking were the *morphologically necessary* interconnections, 'a physio-

---

[13] Goethe, *Die Schriften zur Naturwissenschaft* I, 10, p. 393, quoted and tr. H. B. Nisbet, *Goethe and the Scientific Tradition* (Institute of Germanic Studies, University of London, 1972), p. 15.

[14] There is a striking similarity, as well as difference, between Goethe's reflections and the ancient Principle of Plenitude, see A. O. Lovejoy, *The Great Chain of Being* (Harvard University Press, Cambridge, Mass., 1961), esp. Ch. IX.

[15] Schiller's remark is quoted by Wittgenstein in Vol. VI, 256 in the paragraph which precedes his quotation from 'Die Metamorphose der Pflanzen'. See p. 303 below and Exg. §97.

[16] Prose translation by D. Luke, *Goethe: selected verse* (Penguin, Harmondsworth, 1964), pp. 147 f.

gnomic that is precise, clear and sure of itself and its limits',[17] rather than a Darwinian causal hypothesis. It is also noteworthy that Waismann compares the method of philosophical clarification, of dissolution of puzzlement by juxtaposition, analogy and disanalogy, first with Boltzmann's remarks on models and then with Goethe's essay *Metamorphosis of Plants* (PLP Ch. IV, §2). He denies that the conception of the Primal Plant is a proto-Darwinian developmental hypothesis. It is a matter of *synoptic presentation*: 'Goethe's aphorism "All the organs of plants are leaves transformed" offers us a plan in which we may group the organs of plants according to their similarities as if around some natural centre' (PLP 81). Comparison of our language (or parts of it) with invented calculi or language-games serves a similar function, i.e. to obtain a synoptic view. The point is not *explanation*, but the easing of perplexity by a surview.

It is, of course, impossible to prove whether this was, at one stage, Wittgenstein's opinion or merely Waismann's own view. However, it seems misleading. The function of invented calculi or language-games is not akin to a fruitful morphological form of representation for a systematic typology of richly diverse natural phenomena (cf. Exg. §§130–1). We must distinguish (i) developmental hypotheses, (ii) organizing models for the production of fruitful empirical theories or typologies (and here Boltzmann and Goethe are akin), (iii) a synoptic view of an *a priori* structure, which is what we seek in philosophy. This in no way diminishes the importance of the relation between the need for an *Übersicht* in science and the analogous need in philosophy. In both cases the significance of analogical insight is emphasized. But in the case of science the insight is creative, in philosophy it is purely descriptive.

This is perhaps confirmed by Wittgenstein's 'Remarks on Frazer's "Golden Bough"', in which he quotes Goethe's poem:[18]

'And so the chorus indicates a hidden law' is what we feel like saying of Frazer's collection of facts. I *can* set out this law in an hypothesis of development, or again, in analogy with the schema of a plant I can give it in the schema of a religious ceremony, but I can also do it just by arranging the factual material so that we can easily pass from one part to another and have a clear view of it—showing it in '*perspicuous*' way. (GB 34.)

Here we are clearly offered three possibilities. There are two further important points. First, Wittgenstein is emphasizing that for *some* purposes, an understanding of a feature of a ritual or religious practice may be produced by the very method characteristic of philosophical

---

[17] Spengler, *Decline of the West*, Vol. I, p. 105.
[18] W. quotes the same line, 'Und so deutet das Chor auf ein geheimes Gesetz', in MS. 156(a), 49 and comments on it. It is not a law that we perceive but something that might be called the presentiment or idea of a law.

understanding. In particular this is the case when we wish to fathom our own reaction to a ritual ceremony (e.g. a sense of awe or horror—the resonance of the rite in what we know of humanity and of ourselves). Secondly, Wittgenstein stresses that what *looks* like a hypothetical link or developmental hypothesis may be no more than a way of presenting similarities and analogies, to sharpen our eye to a *formal connection* (e.g. the 'generation' of an ellipse from a circle).

In the case of science, whether at the early classificatory stage or at the stage of explanation and discovery, a paradigmatic schema or model may, by *creating* internal relations, afford such insights as will yield a surview and hence a fruitful morphological, explanatory, or predictive theory. This, as Boltzmann warned, is a dangerous step into unknown territory. It may be fruitful, or disastrous. When it misfires, it is prone to create scientific mythology. Psychoanalysis, as an example of a model that becomes a prison, fascinated Wittgenstein. Here the primary schema was the libidinal origin of all motivation, the picture of all anxiety as a repetition of the anxiety of the birth trauma (akin to the 'Urszene' (LA 51)), or the representation of all dreams as forms of wish-fulfilment. This Wittgenstein considered to possess a strange attractiveness and strength —the power of a mythology rather than of a plausible scientific theory.

Having looked at these various discussions we may attempt to draw our material together by juxtaposing the foregoing with some of Wittgenstein's other remarks. In his *Lectures on Aesthetics* (LA 28), Wittgenstein emphasized that he was trying to effect a change in style of thought. It is plausible to take this as a pointer to the significance of analogical thinking, produced by comprehensive survey of similarities (and dissimilarities), and a repudiation of the ubiquity of causal or genetic explanation. Equally, it points to a rejection of false idols, whether those of science or of mathematics (e.g. Cantor). Wittgenstein's scanty remarks on science suggest that he accepted Boltzmann's emphasis upon the importance of analogical thought as the source of creative models from which testable theories may be constructed. Similarly, he saw in Freudian theory a misuse of analogies in the generation of a scientific mythology. Surveyability, in understanding ritual and religious symbolism, plays a crucial role, in Wittgenstein's view, in producing an understanding of what, at first sight, seems bizarre. Just because ritual is *symbolic*, an *Übersicht* of that 'highly developed gesture-language' (GB 36) can resolve perplexity in a way in which a developmental hypothesis cannot.[19]

[19] Note that Wittgenstein does not repudiate the possibility of causal explanations in anthropology. He merely denies their ubiquitous applicability to all questions. How a ritual ceremony developed is one question, what it means is another. And why it is 'impressive', 'terrible' (perhaps only to *us*, the non-participants) is yet a third. The latter is not answered merely by a surview of the data, but by the connection of the surview, the analogies and similarities with 'the thought of man and his past . . . the strangeness of what I see in myself and in others, what I have seen and have heard.' (GB 41.)

Developmental hypotheses have their place, but that which is most deeply perplexing and disturbing is not to be resolved thus, although it is easy to be fooled into thinking that it is. And *this* is important, for when genetic explanation overreaches itself, it can deprive us of an important bewilderment and rob us of the drive to understand.[20] The same point holds in the domain of aesthetics: genetic, causal explanations cannot touch the heart of aesthetic impressiveness. Aesthetics, like language, is autonomous. Explanation in aesthetics is commonly a matter of 'certain comparisons—grouping together of certain cases' (LA 29). Causal explanation does not drain the aesthetic of its power, it simply passes it by.

Each of these bold methodological claims is contentious and important. Each deserves careful scrutiny. We shall not, however, undertake this here. We have raised these matters in order to show that Wittgenstein's remark 'The concept of a surveyable representation is of fundamental significance for us' belongs to a certain cultural tradition, and that in his own thought its implications reach well beyond the boundaries of philosophy.

3. *The surveyability of grammar*

Philosophical problems are not resolved by adducing new facts or discovering new truths. 'We want to *understand* something that is already in plain view' (PI §89). But what is it that a person who lacks a surview fails to understand? What did Augustine not understand about the nature of time? For, to be sure, in his extra-philosophical discourse a person puzzled by the nature of time, the existence of unperceived objects, or memory knows how to use temporal expressions, refers correctly to objects left locked in a cupboard and makes ordinary memory statements just as we all do. He does understand the language which gives rise to the puzzlement in so far as he uses it correctly and can, if asked, give ordinary explanations of terms like 'yesterday', 'tomorrow', 'next year'. So in what sense is lack of an *Übersicht* a failure of understanding?

The failure of understanding expresses itself in various ways: (i) in asking questions ('What is time?' 'What is mind?' 'How is it possible to remember the past?') which appear to call out for arcane answers or sharp definitions, but which are in fact resolved by an arrangement of what one knows; (ii) in answering such questions in the wrong way, e.g. by the construction of pseudo-theories (giving a 'logical reconstruction of the world', putting mathematics on a 'firm foundation' or 'proving' that the

---

[20] 'My talent consists in being capable of being puzzled when the puzzlement has glided off your mind. I am able to hold the puzzlement when it has slipped through your hands (and you therefore think you are clear).

The art of the philosopher is not to be cheated of his puzzlement before it is really cleared up.' (MS. 157(b), 31.)

mind is identical with the brain); (iii) propounding grammatical propositions (often incorrect ones) as if they were metaphysical ('super-
physical') truths about the ultimate nature of reality (e.g. 'One *cannot*
know anything about the future', or 'One *cannot* know what another
person's experiences are' (or worse—'. . . are really like'), or 'objects
don't continue to exist unperceived'); (iv) consequently propounding
false empirical statements which, outside the philosopher's study, would
betoken lack of mastery of language, but within the confines of the
magical circle of madness display lack of an *Übersicht* ('I don't *know*
whether the sun will rise tomorrow' or 'I don't know what your pains
are *really* like').

A surview of the segment of language that surrounds the confusion
will dissolve it. It removes those *misunderstandings* which stem from false
analogies, misdirected questions, and failure to apprehend the status of
grammatical sentences. The aim of a surview is to be able to 'take in at a
glance' a segment of grammar, so that one will not be misled by surface
grammar, false analogies, or pictures embedded in language which,
considered independently of their application, mislead us. But our
grammar, or those crucial parts of it that give rise to philosophical
problems, is not readily surveyable. It is embodied in our dynamic
linguistic practices, not in a concretized 'frozen' structure.

In 1929–30 Wittgenstein suggested representing a segment of grammar
by means of a readily surveyable 'concretized model' (cf. Boltzmann's
remark, quoted p. 297 above). His example was the colour octahedron as
a model for part of the grammar of colour words. This idea vanishes in
his later writing. At best, one might say, it is a rare case of no great use in
general philosophical method. But perhaps one should go further—it is
positively misleading: one can construct a model for a physical theory,
but not for grammar. The colour octahedron is merely another complex
symbol, not a model of a phenomenon. It is akin to a change of notation,
not to a description (let alone a 'theoretical representation') of a notation.
It may illuminate what puzzles us about a notation by way of contrast
and difference (as the decimal notation may help explain some puzzling
feature of the rationals).

Be that as it may, it is not normally possible to give a representation of
a segment of grammar that can be 'taken in at a glance'. There is, as it
were, no aerial photography in grammar. We must find our way through
the maze of language by trial and error. It is noteworthy that Wittgenstein's efforts to obtain a surview of one or other segment of grammar are
frequently concerned with showing that attractive and *prima facia* promising branches of the maze are in fact dead-ends. It is only by coming to
recognize all the wrong turnings that we will really have an *Übersicht* of
the maze.

Wittgenstein emphasizes the importance of finding and inventing connecting links (PI §122). In the case of family resemblance concepts the terrible urge to find a hidden essence expressible in a *Merkmal-definition* can be alleviated by patient description of the overlapping members of the family. For one will then realize that the unity of the family lies in chains of analogy and resemblance rather than in a concealed essence awaiting discovery. We have here a *created* unity amidst diversity, not a mythical 'natural kind'. *Inventing* connecting links (e.g. imaginary language-games) has a crucial role in relieving the pressure of grammatical paradigms, bringing to light the fact that the apparent adamantine web of logical necessity is the product of our steely determination. As we envisage different possible necessities of form, different conventions of grammar, we come to realize that the transcendence of logic is the intangibility of shadows, that like the desert mirage the forms of thought shimmer, waver, and change in the light of history.

In general, what is necessary is to obtain a kind of synoptic view without getting lost in the details which would produce completeness. A surview must delineate the salient logical articulations forged by grammar, the central structure of the net of language, not the local refinements. Some of the lavish detail of an Austin's descriptions of features of English grammar would, one suspects, strike Wittgenstein as philosophically fairly pointless. Worse still, it may, by its very complexity (like a 'proof' in the notation of *Principia Mathematica* that $28 + 41 = 69$) defeat our efforts to obtain a surview.

How holistic, then, is a surview? Is there any hope for a single unified *Übersicht* of language as a whole? Undoubtedly it is a holistic notion; we are striving to take in *as a whole* a segment of grammar, to grasp the environs of a concept. Certainly one of the tasks of the *Investigations* is to give us a surview of the concept of a *language*, which had so misled Wittgenstein when he wrote the *Tractatus*. But although the concept of a language is, and must be, surveyable, language as a whole cannot be taken in at a glance. It is here that piecemeal (but not unsystematic) work is all that can be hoped for. Problems are tackled as they arise, segments of grammar surveyed, but the *totality* cannot be grasped at once. With time, a total picture may emerge (all the books in the library may be in the right place (BB 44)). But, it does not follow that the total picture can itself be readily surveyed. Secondly, even a total arrangement may only be correct for a given epoch: as the organic forms of language change, new adjustments will be necessary. Moreover, new questions may always arise, new analogies and new illusions may always crop up, requiring philosophy to plough over the ground yet again.

If a surview of a part of language is obtained, the philosopher is saved from misunderstanding, will recognize the sources of ridiculous empirical statements in misunderstood metaphysical expressions, and see correct grammatical sentences for what they are. Is this a mere negative

achievement? Is philosophy merely a prophylactic? Despite Wittgenstein's occasional intimations to this effect, the answer is surely—No! (see
'The nature of philosophy', pp. 488ff.). To obtain a surview is a positive
achievement, a mark of successful performance of an activity (note the
continuity here with the claim in the *Tractatus* that philosophy is an
activity, not a body of doctrine). What it produces is a distinctive type of
understanding—hence just as ordinary understanding of language has
criteria and is connected with explanation—so too is the philosophical
understanding that consists in achieving a surview. Of course, philosophical understanding does not tell us what we mean by the language
we speak. But it is produced, *inter alia*, by a systematic arrangement of
our common explanations of meanings, and by an examination of the
ordinary uses of expressions. One could say that we obtain an understanding of our understanding. One might also attempt a metaphor to
capture the deeper aspect of the matter. When we have an *Übersicht* we do
not merely see the world *by means* of the network of language, but we see
the world through the network of language (cf. PPI §97).

What, then, are the criteria for possession of philosophical understanding, for obtaining a surview of parts of grammar? First, the successful
elucidatory activity of untying knots in our understanding and resolving
philosophical perplexity; secondly, the skill manifest in marshalling
analogies, disanalogies, and actual or invented intermediate cases that
will illuminate the network of our grammar (perhaps *this* is what
Wittgenstein meant in his remark that philosophy has at last become a
matter of skill); finally, and above all, clarity and perspicuity in *description*
of those grammatical articulations which, because of their placement,
produce, like the Hall of Mirrors at a fair, ghastly distortions, monstrous
shapes, or illusory echoing depths. Possessed by philosophy, but lacking
an *Übersicht*, we get lost in such a maze of mirrors; bewitched by the
illusion of depth, we lose the understanding—and hence the depth—for
which we search.

The surveyability which Wittgenstein exhorts us to pursue is no will o'
the wisp. It is not a *contingent* feature of language that its grammar is
surveyable. That it must be possible in one way or another to describe
our use of language and to remind ourselves of the grammatical
explanations which we normally accept as criteria of understanding is a
reflection of the contention that a person's conduct cannot be described
as rule-governed unless he himself sees it as rule-governed. There can be
no question of a chess-player discovering new rules, or discovering that
unbeknownst to him he has been playing according to a rule (as opposed
to a strategy) of which he was unaware. For if he is 'unaware of the rule'
to which his behaviour unwittingly conforms, then we have a mere
regularity, uninformed by a norm. Hence the surveyability of grammar is
a corollary of the claim that there are no *discoveries* in philosophical

grammar, no surprises in logic. Consequently, the outcome of a surview of a segment of grammar is not a *theory* (a 'theory of truth' or a 'theory of the mind' in philosophy is nonsense) nor an *explanation* (of why there are so-and-so many primary colours). Nor are any novel truth-claims made (only idols are destroyed). Rather we obtain understanding, not discovery, insight, not information, clarity, not novelty.

XV

THE GENERAL PROPOSITIONAL FORM

1. '. . . *a picture held us captive* . . .' (PI §115)

In 1915 Wittgenstein wrote, 'My *whole* task consists in explaining the nature of the proposition, i.e. in giving the nature of all facts, whose picture the proposition *is*. In giving the nature of all being' (NB 39). This vastly ambitious conception of the task of philosophy was carried through in the picture theory of meaning. The complex doctrine of isomorphism underpins the contention that the essence of the proposition gives the essence of the world (TLP 5.4711). The conception of the 'essence of the proposition' is elaborated in the doctrine of the general propositional form. The ramifications of this doctrine are staggering. For it was Wittgenstein's contention that the whole of logic is contained within the elementary but rich conception of a proposition as such. 'The description of the general propositional form is the description of the one and only general primitive sign in logic' (TLP 5.472). The general propositional form is given by a 'description' of the essential features of the propositions of any sign-language (TLP 4.5).

Why should there be any such common features? Why should all the multifarious propositions of the various languages of humanity share a common essence, an underlying form? There must be a general propositional form because there cannot be a proposition whose form could not be foreseen, i.e. constructed (TLP 4.5). This brief answer condenses an earlier argument (NB 75, 89): there must be a general propositional form because the possible forms of propositions must be *a priori* (and what the various possible forms have in common is the general propositional form). This claim is tantamount to the claim that it is unintelligible that we should come across a form of words which we could recognize as expressing a sense, but of which we could also say that it could *not* be *foreseen* that such an expression constitutes a proposition, i.e. that *this* is a proposition is not implicit in the rules of logical syntax. This *is* unintelligible, since it would mean that in order to recognize this new logical form as a form of proposition, as expressing a sense, one would have to have some unique experience, a 'logical experience', in virtue of which one recognized that this unforeseeable expression is a proposition. But that would render logic dependent upon experience, whereas logic is wholly independent of whatever is the case or not the case.

What then is the general propositional form? Wittgenstein's answer (TLP 4.5), seemingly empty and mysterious, is that the general propositional form is: 'Es verhält sich so und so'. ('This is how things stand' or

'This is how things are' do not always capture the German. In some contexts 'Such-and-such is the case' or 'Things are thus-and-so' are preferable.) This captures well the form of elementary propositions (TLP 4.51), from which *all* propositions are constructed. It satisfies the requirement that the general propositional form 'must be contained in all propositions in some way or other' (PT 4.4303).

An elementary proposition asserts the existence of a state of affairs (TLP 4.21). What is involved in 'asserting the existence of a state of affairs' is sketched in the theory of the elementary proposition as a concatenation of simple names combined according to logical syntax, individually standing for their meanings ('objects') and conjointly representing a state of affairs (possible combination of objects) which may or may not obtain, independently of whatever else is the case. Hence every elementary proposition asserts that things (objects) are concatenated thus-and-so.

What more is added to the general doctrines of the elementary proposition by the claims about the general propositional form? Primarily the thesis of extensionality. The thesis is: 'All propositions are results of truth-operations on elementary propositions' (TLP 5.3). Wittgenstein equates the general propositional form with the general form of a truth-function $[\bar{p}, \bar{\xi}, N (\bar{\xi})]$ (TLP 6). Given that an elementary proposition is a truth-function of itself (TLP 5), then what the general propositional form shows is that all propositions can be generated out of elementary propositions by successive applications of the operation of joint negation.

We can then summarize the doctrine of the general propositional form in the following theses. (i) The general form of the proposition is given by the expression 'Things are thus-and-so'. (ii) This is a variable. (iii) It has a determinate range. (iv) The essence of the elementary proposition is to assert the existence of a state of affairs, as explained by the picture theory of the proposition. (v) The general propositional form expresses the necessity that every proposition is a truth-function of elementary propositions.

2. *'We want to replace wild conjectures and explanations by quiet weighing of linguistic facts'* (Z §447)

The criticisms in the *Investigations* of the notion of the general propositional form can be separated under three headings. First, Wittgenstein examines with a critical eye what kind of error was involved in dubbing 'Es verhält sich so und so' the expression of the general form of a proposition. Secondly, he argues that contrary to his early preconceptions there is no such thing as 'the general propositional form'. Our concept of a proposition is not an ineffable, super-categorial one, nor do we define it by *Merkmale*; it is, rather, a family resemblance concept. Thirdly, arguing that all that was really captured by his early formulation of the essence of the proposition was that a proposition is whatever is true or false, he examines the relationship between 'proposition' and 'true' and 'false' in order to establish whether the concepts of truth and falsehood can give us a non-trivial means of circumscribing (defining) our concept of a proposition. Although Wittgenstein also criticized the thesis of extensionality, the issue is not linked, in the *Investigations*, with the criticism of the general propositional form.

Wittgenstein came to think that the conception of the general proposi-tional form was a typical philosophical illusion (cf. Exg. §104). All propositions, it had seemed, were to be compared with reality for truth or falsehood; they provided yardsticks by which to measure reality. So, it had seemed to follow, the possibility of agreement or disagreement must be part of the general propositional form. Every proposition was conceived as a description of a state of affairs, and since the essence of the proposition was the essence of a state of affairs, the understanding of the one seemed to constitute the understanding of the essence of reality. But this was merely to project our form of representation on to reality. Our grammar permits us to represent sentences as a network of names linked by logical ties. Instead of 'The bottle is blue', we may say 'The bottle has the property blue'; instead of 'The bottle is to the right of the glass' we may say 'The bottle stands to the glass in the relation to-the-right-of'. But to project this on to reality as Wittgenstein did in the *Tractatus* is a grievous error, akin to that of the spectacle-wearer who thinks that all objects are surrounded by plastic frames. The conception of the general propositional form as asserting the existence of a state of affairs con-ceived as a concatenation of objects is part of this illusion.

'Such-and-such is the case' or 'Things are thus-and-so' are English sentences. But does everything that counts as a sentence expressing a sense say that things are arranged (concatenated) thus-and-so? Does 'It is raining' say that things are arranged in a certain way (Z §448)? Could one say 'It has the property raining'? What is it that has this property? And what of 'No. I won't', 'It hurts', '2 + 2 = 4', or 'Time passes'? A multitude of sentences, many of which apparently express genuine propositions, do not say 'Things are thus-and-so'.

A second feature of our favoured sentence-form is that it has a subject and predicate. To be sure, it is easy to conceive of all elementary sentences as attributing a characteristic to an object. Indeed, Wittgenstein stresses that when we say that such-and-such is the case ('. . . dass es sich so und so verhält . . .') we mean that *such-and-such* is *so-and-so* ('. . . dass das und das—so und so—ist'((PI §95). Nevertheless, first, there are many elementary sentences (e.g. 'It is raining', 'I am tired') which do not attribute characteristics to objects identified by a subject term. Secondly, there is no such thing as *the* subject/predicate form. The superficial grammatical distinction conceals countless different logical forms (PG 202 ff.). The subject/predicate form is our primary norm of representation within which we conceal innumerable kinds of methods of projection and diverse methods of application of expressions. (This point holds whatever the magnitude of the conceptual utility of the subject/predicate norm of representation.)

To say that 'Things are thus-and-so' expresses the general propositional form is akin to saying that 'thing' expresses the general form of a name (and hence of any object). The analogy is instructive. For this analogous move evidently obscures the actual use of the English word 'thing'. We say that there are some things to eat in the cupboard, thus referring to edible objects for which names are available. But we also say that some interesting things happened in Parliament today, referring to events which are not objects at all. Many bearers of genuine names are not things. People are paradigm name-bearers, and also paradigmatically not things. We confer names on directions ('North'), winds ('Boreas'), locations ('North Pole'), etc., none of which would we call things. Formal logic contains name variables; ordinary language contains the term 'thing', which *inter alia* has a function akin to that of a name variable. But to jump to the conclusion that it is 'the general form of a name' is to assume that the structure of ordinary language is that of formal logic. That is an illegitimate conclusion. It distorts the use of useful term 'thing'. We must let ordinary language and its structure speak for themselves. So we must examine the actual use of 'thing'. And what goes for 'thing' goes for 'Such-and-such is the case', or 'This is how things are'.

'This is how things are' is an English sentence which is applied as a propositional schema (variable), capable of picking up reference to an antecedent or subsequent statement. We may say, 'He explained his position to me, said that this was how things were, and that therefore he needed an advance' (PI §134). But it has this role only because it has the structure of an English sentence. We would not feel at ease with 'He said: "*p*, and therefore I need an advance"', nor would we ever be tempted to say that 'p' expresses the general propositional form. One can imagine such a convention replacing ours. But then one can imagine a sentence with sense functioning, in the appropriate context, as a propositional variable. So we might use 'The sky is blue' thus (PPI §117), and say 'He explained his position to me, said that the sky is blue, and that therefore he needed a loan'. (If this seems bizarre, reflect on the use of 'That's the way the cookie crumbles' in American slang. For we could indeed say 'He explained his position to me, said that that's the way the cookie crumbles, and that therefore he needed an advance'. But would anyone claim that 'That's the way the cookie crumbles' expresses the general propositional form?)

The use of 'This is how things are' is indeed distinctive. It is employed primarily to pick up a previous explicit or implicit statement. In this respect it is *like* a propositional variable, but it lacks what seemed to be an essential feature of the proposition, namely agreement or disagreement with reality. In taking this form of words as expressing the general propositional form, Wittgenstein sublimed an expression which has an ordinary use in our language into a *form* which thereby lacks any legitimate use. 'This is how things are' is a proposition used as a propositional schema, but not because it ineffably contains the essential characteristics of propositionhood (e.g. agreement or disagreement with reality). Rather, what gives it its character as a proposition is primarily that it *sounds like a proposition*, is a sentence of English, and hence we use it to fulfil its particular role.

3. '. . . *do we have a* single *concept of proposition?*' (PG 112)

One feature of our concept of a proposition (a sentence with sense) is a certain characteristic ring, intonation, and rhythm. But this is neither necessary nor sufficient, even though it was important in explaining the captivating charms of 'This is how things are' as an expression of general propositional form. It is not necessary since we can readily conceive of a language which differed from English only in inverting the word-order. This would be completely lacking in the characteristic propositional ring but since it would possess the identical logical multiplicity of English its sentences could express propositions nevertheless. If we were to learn it, its sentences might assume a characteristic intonation. But they might not; and even if they did, it would not be as a consequence of this that we attribute propositional status to such strings of symbols. *Satzklang* is not sufficient for propositionhood either, since we talk of insignificant sentences as well as of significant ones. Many sentences that have the right 'ring' do not express propositions, but are rather nonsense strings of words. In Wittgenstein's view many strings of words do indeed look like, and sound like, propositions, but are not. *But*, if we disregard the matter of 'sounding like a proposition', do we still have *any* general concept of a proposition?

Wittgenstein's answer is clearly negative (PG 112; BT 61). The concepts 'proposition', 'language', lack the formal unity ascribed to them in the *Tractatus*. They are rather a family of structures related to one another in complex ways (PI §108). This is evident from the fact that we explain the concept 'proposition' by means of examples (PG 112). Our practice of explaining what a proposition is does not include genuine

Merkmal-definitions (cf. Exg. §136). For this reason we might say that 'proposition', like 'number', is not sharply defined. We could give it sharp boundaries if we wished. But we do not do so—for we have no need to (PG 117). Lack of sharp boundaries does not infect the centre with uncertainty.

But if the boundaries of the concept of a proposition are indeterminate, how do we determine, of a new proposition, that it is a *proposition* (PG 113)? Only by analogy; and nothing forces our hand! Singular observation statements, psychological statements, first-person psychological attributions, mathematical equations, statements of applied mathematics, statements of laws of physics, tautologies, or contradictions, these and numerous other categories are related by a web of similarities and analogies which could not be constructed or predicted in advance (PG 117). Indeed, when Wittgenstein's strictures fall upon some category or other, e.g. tautologies, 'grammatical sentences', or the result of prefixing 'I know' to an avowal, what he is doing is simply stressing *disanalogies* commonly unnoticed by philosophers who want to draw special philosophical conclusions from such apparent propositions. The disanalogies provide a ground for challenging those conclusions. Thus, if one takes 'I have toothache' to express a proposition, one will infer that it is an object of knowledge. Consequently, one will conclude that 'I know I have toothache' has a sense and means something different from 'I have toothache'. The numerous disanalogies between avowals and other sentences with a superficially similar grammar are introduced in order to cast doubt upon such inferences.

'Proposition', like 'number', is not defined once and for all by drawing sharp boundaries. Nor does our explanation of the meaning of 'proposition' have to distinguish propositions from everything else, including cabbages and kings. A definition of 'number' which does not rule out Julius Caesar from being a number is not, *pace* Frege, therefore defective. We must not confuse Julius Caesar with a number, or a cabbage with a proposition, but we do not need a definition to stop us from so doing. We do need, occasionally, to distinguish one type of proposition from another and to explain why we distinguish them. This we can generally do; (e.g. we may distinguish tautologies from non-tautologous propositions; the concept of a tautology, like that of cardinal number, may be said to be rigorously circumscribed). Sometimes, especially in philosophy, we need to distinguish a proposition from a sentence which lacks a sense. This too can be done, but often only with difficulty, for it requires a careful examination of analogies and disanalogies of precisely the kind Wittgenstein engages in so frequently. Moreover, one cannot *prove* that a 'metaphysical sentence' is only a pseudo-proposition; one can only persuade its propounder to examine the ordinary use of that sentence or its constituents to the point at which he is willing to give it up.

4. '. . . *the use of the words "true" and "false"* . . . belongs *to our concept "proposition" but does not "fit" it* . . .' (PI §136)

One obvious objection to the contention that proposition is a family resemblance concept is examined by Wittgenstein. For surely, it might be argued, it is of the essence of a proposition to be true or false. So why cannot the concept be sharply circumscribed in terms of the property of bearing truth-values?

Wittgenstein links this issue with the conception of the general propositional form as well as with the redundancy account of truth. The *Tractatus* conception of the general propositional form, expressed by 'such-and-such is the case', was, Wittgenstein concludes, a confused way of saying that a proposition is whatever is true or false, i.e. an argument in the calculus of truth-functions. For instead of saying 'Such-and-such is the case' gives the general propositional form, he could have cited the sentence 'Such-and-such is true', for the latter fulfils much the same function as the former.

Against this move to delimit propositions in terms of truth and falsehood Wittgenstein deploys the following argument. First, he very briefly propounds the redundancy 'theory' of truth: '"p" is true' is equivalent in sense to 'p', and '"p" is false' is equivalent to 'not-p'. When attributions of truth occur without mention of a proposition, the equivalence is given by means of an expression employed as a propositional variable. Thus 'What he says is true' is equivalent in sense to 'Things are as he says'. Wittgenstein never developed this analysis, nor did he discuss possible counter-arguments.[1] His purpose in thus briefly propounding it seems to be negative and twofold. First, he aimed to repudiate the correspondence theory of truth which is central to the picture theory of meaning. As the doctrine of the general propositional form suggests, a proposition is true if objects are, in reality, concatenated in the way represented by their proxies (names) in the proposition being arranged (according to logical syntax) as they are. The redundancy analysis reduces the notion of correspondence to triviality (i.e. to say that 'p' is true is to say that things are as 'p' describes them as being). So to characterize the proposition as whatever is true or false is not to say anything *more* than that we call something a proposition when we apply the calculus of truth-functions to it. His second negative purpose was to deny that the notions of truth and falsity can help us determine the essence of a proposition, as was implied in Frege's theory (but not in the *Tractatus*). We do not have a concept of truth (and falsehood) which is independent of our concept of a proposition and so could be used to

[1] Cf. A. N. Prior, *Objects of Thought*, (Clarendon Press, Oxford, 1971), Ch. 1–2.

determine whether something is or is not a proposition. One cannot put words together, and then add 'is true' as an experiment, so that if the result makes sense then the combination of words expresses a proposition (PG 124). For in order for 'is true' to have a meaning, we must give it a meaning and this is not something to be discovered by experiment. A proposition is what is true or false, but since truth and falsity are not independent of propositionhood, that tells us no more than that, given a proposition, it makes sense to attribute truth or falsity to it. It gives us no means for determining what things are propositions.

Wittgenstein spells out an analogy: it is as if we were to say, 'The king in chess is *the* piece one can check'. But this is useless unless we have an independent way of determining the application of check (which we obviously do not) or of identifying the king (which we do, but not by reference to being checkable). To think that truth and falsity give the essence of the proposition, and hence disprove that it is a family resemblance concept, is akin to thinking that one gives the essence of games by saying that one plays them.

There are, or course, many other ways in which philosophers have tried to give the essence of the proposition. The *Tractatus* had tried to capture it by means of the notion of a logical picture of a state of affairs. But that contention depended upon the complex doctrines of isomorphism and logico-metaphysical atomism which Wittgenstein later repudiated. All that is left of the picture theory of the proposition is the problem of the pictoriality of the proposition, but that was the very problem which the picture theory set out to solve. A proposition can be said to be a picture of a state of affairs. The proposition that p is a picture of the state of affairs that p. But this gives us no means of determining what things are propositions. Just as the attempt to characterize propositions in terms of truth fails because it rests on an equivalence between 'p' and '"p" is true', so too characterizing propositions in terms of pictoriality merely signifies an articulation in grammar. 'The proposition that p' is equivalent to 'The proposition that the fact p makes true' (PG 161). What we have here is an internal grammatical relation set up in language, not a relation between language and an extra-linguistic reality which obtains independently of the grammatical articulation. Propositions and states of affairs 'belong' to, but do not 'fit', each other.

Similar considerations would apply to characterizing propositions as objects of knowledge or belief. A proposition, one might say, is what one believes. But all that amounts to is that substitutions such as 'He believes that p' = 'He believes the proposition that p', or 'What he believes is that p' = 'The proposition that he believes is p' are permissible in our grammar. Again, it might seem that one could characterize the proposition as that which can be asserted or denied (PLP 298). But this too merely points to further intra-linguistic connections. Instead of 'He asserted that p', we can write 'He asserted the proposition that p', instead of 'He asserted that p is true' we can say 'He asserted that the proposition that p is true'. Nevertheless, one might object, does not the notion of assertion give us a handle upon that of a proposition? A proposition, we say, is what can be asserted or denied. But now, is not assertion (or denial) a speech-act identifiable by description of circumstances of utterance? Indeed, but only on the condition that what is asserted *is* a proposition. One cannot identify an utterance as an assertion in advance of grasping it as expressing a proposition. An assertion is a particular use of a proposition, so to say that a proposition is what is asserted amounts to no more than that a proposition is what is used as a proposition is used.

What a proposition (*Satz*) is, Wittgenstein concludes, is in one sense determined by the rules of sentence-formation in the given language (which determine the *Satzklang*). But this is of no interest to us. In another sense, what a proposition is is determined by the use of the sign (propositional sign) in language-games. Certainly 'true' and 'false' are part of the language-games with 'proposition', but they 'belong' to it, and do not 'fit' it, i.e. provide no independent test of propositionhood. And if we examine the use of 'proposition' in our language we will see no more than a network of more or less remote similarities and analogies, without any single central core that can be given in terms of any expression of general propositional form.

XVI

UNDERSTANDING AND ABILITY

1. *Introduction*

Meaning, explanation of meaning and understanding are a triad of concepts whose interconnections are the focus of the *Investigations*. Each requires separate scrutiny, and the network of relationships between them needs to be displayed. Our discussion hitherto has concentrated upon meaning and explanation. Now understanding must be examined. For understanding is internally related both to meaning and explanation of meaning. Meaning is the content of understanding and understanding is the correlate of explanation (PG 45, 60). Hence unclarity about understanding is apt to lead to misconceptions about meaning and explanation.

The central theme of *Investigations* §§143–242 is the nature of understanding. Wittgenstein analyses the relationship between understanding and such categories as states, processes, events, and abilities, pointing out the many pitfalls that lie here in the path to a philosophical grasp of language and meaning. The thread of his argument leads ultimately to the culmination of these sections, namely the nature of rules, normative determination and rule-following (cf. Volume 2). In this essay we provide only a further link in the chain—a clarification of understanding.

2. *'We regard understanding as the essential thing, and signs as something inessential'* (PG 39)

Wittgenstein invokes a familiar picture:

It seems that there are *certain definite* mental processes bound up with the working of language, processes through which alone language can function. I mean the processes of understanding and meaning. The signs of our language seem dead without these mental processes . . . We are tempted to think that the action of language consists of two parts; an inorganic part, the handling of signs, and an organic part, which we may call understanding these signs, meaning them, interpreting them, thinking. These latter activities seem to take place in a queer kind of medium, the mind; and the mechanism of the mind, the nature of which, it seems, we don't quite understand, can bring about effects which no material mechanism could. (BB 3.)

This idea is most natural and widespread. We can imagine the non-existent, expect things which have not happened, think of things which might have happened, and mean (by a remark about a person) someone who is thousands of miles away or who died thousands of years ago. What a remarkable thing is the mind! For signs alone surely could not do this.

This picture is reinforced by obvious reflections. Signs are arbitrary and conventional. Replacing 'p' by 't' in 'chap' produces a sign with a quite different meaning, but it is arbitrary that we should employ one sign to signify thus and the other to signify otherwise, rather than vice versa. Again, 'chat' in English has one meaning, in French another—but the signs alone, the marks upon the paper, are quite dead. What gives them meaning, it seems, is what goes on in the mind when they are read, heard, or uttered. It is our meaning and understanding them which gives them life. Furthermore, when one does not understand a sentence nothing is missing with respect to the sign; one has the sign, what is lacking is the understanding that must accompany it, and which is its mental correlate. Similarly, when a parrot squawks an English sentence, perhaps even on an appropriate occasion, we do not say that it can speak English, for it neither means nor understands what it says. Yet another consideration derives from reflection upon the antecedents of utterance, especially in one's own case. I know what I mean to say, we are inclined to think, before I say it. But I do not parade the words in my mind before putting them on public display. On the contrary, I use the words in order to convey my meaning to another, to bring before his mind what is already before mine. Signs, it thus seems, are the public code whereby meanings are conveyed in discourse.

The most noble and profitable invention of all other was that of SPEECH, consisting of *names* or appellations, and their connection; whereby men register their thoughts; recall them when they are past; and also declare them to one another for mutual utility and conversation . . . The general use of speech is to transfer our mental discourse into verbal; or the train of our thoughts, into a train of words.[1]

Finally, we may note that many explanations of meaning do not lay forth the whole use of the word explained. What the explanation does, it seems, is to provide the stimulus for a mental process which produces an understanding of meaning.

3. *Meaning and understanding as mental phenomena*

These elementary observations incline us to think of meaning and understanding as mental phenomena. This inclination is reinforced by further considerations.

First, I cannot *observe* the understanding of another, but only the

---

[1] Hobbes, *Leviathan*, Ch. IV.

behaviour that manifests understanding. If I order someone to do something, I can observe his compliance, but not his understanding of the order, which seems a prerequisite for his compliance. Since he may understand without complying, it seems to follow that the behaviour is one thing, the understanding another. Understanding is then conceived as the underlying mental phenomenon of which the behaviour is a symptom. Indeed, we may sometimes be inclined to think that only the subject of understanding really knows whether he understands. For our 'access' to his understanding is only by inductive or analogical inference, whereas he has 'direct (privileged) access' to his own mental life.

Secondly, we are familiar with the experience of suddenly understanding something (e.g. suddenly seeing that the rule of the series 1, 5, 11, 19, 29 . . . is given by '$a_n = n^2 + n - 1$'). We naturally speak here of a sudden 'flash of understanding' and readily employ metaphors of 'mental illumination' to describe the distinctive experience. We say, after the matter has thus become clear, 'Now I understand', and we do so *because* we understand. So it seems our utterance is a consequence, or even a report of, a mental phenomenon.

Thirdly, the experiential difference between understanding and not understanding something that is temporally extended (e.g. a speech, a lecture, or a piece of music) is distinctive. Listening to a lecture one does not understand, overhearing a conversation in a foreign language one does not know or only imperfectly knows, involve a very different succession of experiences from following a lecture or conversation one does understand. For someone accustomed to classical music the experience of listening to Stockhausen is distinctive, he feels that he cannot follow the music. Understanding, it seems, is a mental phenomenon that accompanies the hearing. Likewise, when one reads an obscure text parrot-wise, what is lacking is the accompanying mental understanding.

Finally, having used a pronoun to refer to a person, one may clarify the reference by saying 'I meant A', and one assures another that his remark is clear by saying 'Yes, I understood you'. The past tense of these verbs seems to report specific past events, like 'I pointed at A', or 'I touched you', only mental events rather than physical ones, since we have to ask the speaker whom he meant or whether he understood.

4. Understanding as a state, process, activity, or experience

We are inclined, when reflecting upon the various things signified by verbs, to classify them as belonging to very general categories. Some verbs or verb phrases seem to describe experiential events such as hearing a gunshot or catching sight of something. Others, however, describe activities or processes which go on in time, such as listening or searching,

singing. Yet a third kind seem to describe states which obtain
.g. being agitated, feeling ill or well, being relaxed or tense.
sifications are not illegitimate. To the extent that we have
clear notions of states of mind or body, activities or performances, etc.,
we can classify accordingly some of what we describe by means of verbs.
However, philosophical confusions lurk in the background. Grammarians distinguish between dynamic and static (or stative) verbs.[2]
Dynamic verbs are held to refer to activities, processes, and events. Static
verbs are commonly held to 'refer to a state of affairs, rather than to an
action, event or process',[3] to distinguish states from activities.[4]
Philosophers, however, are prone to elevate the (largely syntactical)
distinction between kinds of verbs into an ontological distinction.[5]
Disregarding the humdrum uses of 'state', 'activity', and 'performance',
they conceive of a state, activity, or performance as what corresponds,
respectively, to a static verb, activity verb, or performance verb. These
concepts are thus elevated to the status of 'super-concepts' (cf. PI §97). A
state, e.g., is conceived as the correlate of the 'general form' of static
verbs, just as, in a widespread view, an object is whatever is designated
by a Fregean proper name. This procedure is perilous. In the first place,
the various lists of static verbs given by grammarians and philosophers
prove to be extraordinarily heterogeneous, often including what by no
stretch of the imagination one would classify under the ordinary notion
of a state. Moreover, many verbs that occur on these lists only
imperfectly satisfy the criteria for being static verbs. In particular, it
transpires that it is misleading to classify verbs as static or dynamic, but
rather there are, in many cases, static and dynamic *uses* of one and the
same verb (e.g. 'think', 'am thinking'; 'smell', 'am smelling'; 'has', 'is
having'; 'love', 'is loving'; 'be', 'is being'). If so, it becomes increasingly
doubtful whether the syntactical category wears the trousers; instead, the
grammarian seems to rely on his intuitive grasp of the common-or-
garden notions of act, activity, and state in order to distinguish between
static and dynamic uses of a verb. Secondly, we do have an ordinary
notion of a state in contrast with an activity or action. However vague
and crude they may be, the words 'state', or 'activity' are in circulation as
part of the currency of our language. It is evident that our ordinary

[2] R. Quirk, S. Greenbaum, G. Leech, J. Svartvik, *A Grammar of Contemporary English* (Longman, London, 1974), pp. 39 f., 92 ff.

[3] J. Lyons, *Introduction to Theoretical Linguistics* (Cambridge University Press, Cambridge, 1968), p. 315.

[4] Ibid., p. 316; cf. F. R. Palmer, *The English Verb* (Longman, London, 1974). pp. 70 ff. Palmer subdivides non-progressive verbs into (i) private verbs: 'those that refer to states or activities that the speaker alone is aware of' and (ii) verbs of state: 'which refer not to an activity but to a state or condition'.

[5] See, e.g., A. J. P. Kenny, *Action, Emotion and the Will* (Routledge and Kegan Paul, London, 1963), pp. 171 ff.

notion of a state is not defined as the correlate of a static verb, nor is that of an activity defined as the correlate of a dynamic verb. Thus, e.g., many states are referred to by adjectives prefixed to 'state', as in 'gaseous state', 'crystalline state'; also by an abstract noun inserted in the expression 'a state of ξ', as in 'a state of exhaustion', 'a state of depression'. Conversely, 'sleep' satisfies the criteria for dynamic verbs, but sleeping is not an activity (cf. PI §47), nor is rising in price an activity of butter (PI §693), even though butter does rise in price and 'rise' is a progressive verb. The philosopher may, of course, deny that the notion of state which he introduces as the correlate of static verbs has anything to do with our ordinary notion of state, except *per accidens*. If so, the onus of proof is upon him to introduce and explain this term of art, using the materials supplied by the (as yet) imprecise notion of a static verb or static use of a verb. This task remains to be done, as is evident from closer scrutiny of current discussion of static verbs.

This class of verbs is generally characterized in terms of lack of a progressive aspect (continuous tense) and imperative mood. Other supplementary criteria are also cited by some authors. Static verbs (i) cannot form a pseudo-cleft sentence with a Do pro-form (i.e. 'what I did was to Φ . . .'); (ii) cannot be qualified by manner adverbs such as 'quickly', 'slowly', 'reluctantly'; (iii) the present tense is not frequenta-tive; (iv) 'A has Φd' implies 'A Φs'. The result of applying these criteria is both bizarre and puzzling. It is puzzling in so far as many of the verbs commonly identified by these writers as static verbs do not in fact satisfy the requisite criteria. Thus, e.g., 'perceive', 'hear', 'see', 'smell', 'taste' are held to be static verbs. But one would not think that to see a flash, hear a rustle, taste a wine, or feel the roughness of some cloth, is to be in a state of any kind. Moreover, 'smell', 'taste', and 'feel' do have continuous and imperative forms, can be qualified by 'slowly' and 'quickly', and can form a pseudo-cleft sentence with a Do pro-form. Similarly, it is generally agreed that some verbs of emotion are static verbs, e.g. 'love', 'fear', 'hate'. This too is curious, for while they are non-progressives, they do have an imperative form ('Love they neighbour as thyself; fear God; hate evil!'). To love, hate, or fear are emotions, not states of mind. They have a greater kinship with attitudes and dispositions than with *emotional states* such as agitation, anxiety, excitement. Also among psychological static verbs by common consensus are 'mean', 'mind', 'know', 'remember', 'forget', 'intend'. Although one might classify these as verbs of cogni-tion, they do not pick out cognitive states. One may be in a state of agitation, but not in a state of knowing, remembering, or forgetting. Moreover, although they are non-progressives, at least some do have imperative forms (e.g. 'Know thyself!', 'Remember me!', 'Forget that it ever happened!', 'Mind your step!'). Finally, the non-psychological static verbs constitute a very odd bunch, e.g. 'exist', 'be', 'have', 'consist of', 'contain', 'include', 'belong to', 'own', 'possess', 'involve', 'depend on', 'cost', 'deserve', 'fit', 'be blue', 'be taller than'. It is counter-intuitive to embed *any* of these verbs in the contexts 'X was in the state of ζing', 'X was in a ζ state', or to think, e.g., of owning, possessing, belonging, having as *states* of anything.

Side by side with these counter-intuitive claims comes disregard of the ordinary use of 'state', both with respect to states of objects in general, and with respect to states of mind in particular.[6]

With respect to types of matter or stuff we have at least some clear and uncontroversial applications of 'state'. Being solid, liquid, or gaseous are three standard states of matter. Being molten is a state of aluminium, being frozen a state of water. But while it is true that bronze *consists* of copper and tin, and that high-octane petrol *contains* lead, consisting of copper and tin, or containing lead, are not, respectively, states of bronze or petrol. Equally, we speak of the state of a house (e.g. 'in a dilapidated state'), of a garden ('well kept') or of a room ('untidy'). But owning a house, possessing a garden, a room's belonging to a person, are neither states of the house, garden, or room, nor of its owner.

We do have a notion of psychological states (see p. 335 below), but knowing, meaning, intending, forgetting, remembering, etc., are not such states. Nor, as will become clear, is understanding. We speak of being in a state of intense excitement, deep depression, joyful anticipation, fearful trepidation, irrepressible cheerfulness, etc., but not of being in a state of hating, loving, or fearing, let alone of meaning, intending, or minding. To introduce a technical notion of state which assimilates these various phenomena is confusing, at least prior to further refinement of the simple notion of the correlate of a static verb. First, we need a sharper specification of this term of art. Secondly, unless the term of art can be shown to be a refinement of our ordinary notion of state, it is ill advised to use the term 'state' for the preferred category. Thirdly, it is confusing to assimilate into one category phenomena as diverse as dispositions or quasi-dispositions, emotional states or occurrent moods, and abilities or powers, whether passive or active. Although they share the negative feature of *not being* acts or activities, this does not justify uniting them under the concept of a state.

When we attempt to classify understanding or meaning, we find, at least upon superficial reflection, that we are tempted in different directions. On the one hand, understanding seems to be a distinctive experience. This is marked out by the 'experience' of suddenly understanding something or of seeing the multiple aspects of something

---

[6] This is not to say that the ordinary notion is so sharp and systematic as to guarantee classificatory usefulness. But investigation must surely *start* there, and, if necessary, sharpen our common concept, rather than assume that a syntactical classification can readily be sublimed into an ontological one.

(especially where the object is symbolic, e.g. the ambiguity of a pun). Like James, we might ask ourselves: 'What is that first instantaneous glimpse of someone's meaning which we have, when in vulgar phrase we say we "twig" it? Surely an altogether specific affection of our mind.'[7] Similarly, past-tense reports of meaning and understanding seem to be reports of experiences.

However, there is an equally strong temptation to conceive of understanding as a process or activity which goes on in time, has different phases, and may be interrupted. Understanding readily appears to be a complex mental process accompanying the spoken (heard) sentences. James had this conception too:

> I believe that in all cases where the words are *understood*, the total idea may be and usually is present not only before and after the phrase has been spoken, but also whilst each word is uttered. It is the overtone, halo, or fringe of the word, *as spoken in that sentence*. It is never absent; no word in an understood sentence comes to consciousness as a mere noise. We feel its meaning as it passes.[8]

This temptation is reinforced by reflecting upon the way one follows a speech, lecture, or piece of music, with understanding—which seems to accompany the aural stimuli step by step, sometimes faltering or stumbling, sometimes anticipating what is yet to come, and thus 'clearly' a process or activity. And it is this process or activity, we think, that is so obviously missing when we listen without understanding.

Nevertheless, there are yet other factors, apparently conflicting with the foregoing data, which point to understanding's being a state of the mind rather than an activity of the mind. The manifestations of understanding are a finite array of performances, but a word, which I understand, has an indefinitely large range of combinatorial possibilities and applications, some of which I may never utilize; so too a rule for the expansion of a series of numbers has an infinite range of applications, not all of which can be manifested in a person's behaviour, even though we say that he has grasped the rule of the series. Consequently, one is inclined to think that understanding must be a specific state of mind from which the finite performances manifesting it flow like water from a reservoir. This is reinforced by further facts. To know the meaning of a word involves knowing how to use the word in discourse. But when I suddenly understand a word (when it 'dawns on me' that 'caldo' in Italian means 'hot' not 'cold'), I don't have an instantaneous representation of all the possible applications of the word. So my knowledge must be a state from which the applications follow, e.g. a mental correlate of a rule of a series from which the numbers of the series follow.

Furthermore, both understanding and meaning, like intending, have

---

[7] W. James, *The Principles of Psychology*, Vol. I, p. 253.
[8] Ibid., p. 281.

the peculiarity of anticipating the future, of applying both to the present moment and to what will only later occur. When I teach a child to write down a series of numbers (say +2), he will, if properly taught, start '0, 2, 4, . . .'. But already now I mean him to continue past 1000 by writing '1002, 1004, . . .' and not '1004, 1008 . . .'. Likewise, if I understand the rules of chess, my understanding reaches forward to future applications of them. This seems to imply that understanding is a state of mind from which the future applications of understanding follow.

5. Resultant philosophical confusions

The preceding reflections bring us to the brink of philosophical confusions of a deeper kind. One more step, and mystification and mythology ensue. If understanding and meaning are mental processes, experiences, or states, then they should be accessible to introspection, as is hearing, listening, or suffering.

It needs only brief reflection, at a superficial level, to abjure the idea of inner accessibility. First, we are sometimes mistaken in thinking we understand; so the object of this introspection must be singularly elusive. Secondly, it proves very difficult to capture the specific quality of mental experience, process, or state which 'understanding' apparently names. The experiences accompanying understanding seem diverse and differ from one occasion to another. Do they have a common essence? It is difficult to say. Our first inclination is to suggest that these mental phenomena are only imperfectly accessible to introspection, for they are too quick to be captured by the eye of the mind (like the racing needle of a sewing machine).

Let anyone try to cut a thought across in the middle and get a look at its section, and he will see how difficult the introspective observation . . . is. The rush of thought is so headlong that it almost always brings us up at the conclusion before we can arrest it. Or if our purpose is nimble enough and we do arrest it, it ceases forthwith to be itself. . . [T]he attempt at introspective analysis in these cases is in fact like seizing a spinning top.[9]

Alternatively, if we convince ourselves that at least in some cases we can slow things down to an introspectively perceptible speed, we may be prone to complain that 'our psychological vocabulary is wholly inadequate to name the differences that exist'.[10]

Many thinkers, however, find the picture of the mind thus depicted highly implausible. In particular, if the conception of meaning and understanding as states of mind is the dominant one, we may be inclined

[9] Ibid., p. 244.
[10] Ibid., p. 251.

to affirm that these phenomena are mental, but deny that they are conscious or introspectible.

Two lines of argument then open up, a weak one and a strong one. The weaker line is to argue that understanding is an hypothesis. One may be further pushed in this direction by the additional consideration that we may err in thinking we understand. For this error shows itself in our future linguistic behaviour, our use of an expression, and our responses to others' use of it. But if future behaviour can disconfirm understanding, then surely current behaviour can only probabilify the assertion that a person understands an expression. Therefore, on this conception an assertion of understanding is only an hypothesis about a mental phenomenon (PG 82).

The stronger line involves a dissatisfaction, partly semantic, partly scientific, with the mere idea of an hypothesis which never goes so far as to explain what it is that the behavioural evidence is evidence for. For the weak line merely stresses that the evidence for understanding falls short of incontrovertibly establishing understanding (since it does not entail understanding) and is always open to subsequent disconfirmation. But if this is so, what *is* the hypothesized understanding for which the evidence is evidence, and how does it *work*? If these questions are taken seriously, can we avoid conceiving of understanding as a hypothetical mental *mechanism*?

. . . it is hard to see how one can seriously doubt . . . that language is both used and learned in accordance with strict principles of mental organization, largely inaccessible to introspection, but in principle at least, open to investigation in more indirect ways.[11]

Since the correlation between mind and brain is (on this view) as yet imperfectly understood, the most we can do for the moment is try to develop an abstract structural model of such an hypothesized mental organization.

It seems to me that the most hopeful approach to-day is to describe the phenomena of language and of mental activity as accurately as possible, to try to develop an abstract theoretical apparatus that will, as far as possible, account for these phenomena and reveal the principles of their organisation and functioning, without attempting, for the present, to relate the postulated mental structures and processes to any physiological mechanism or to interpret mental functions in terms of 'physical causes'.[12]

---

[11] N. Chomsky, 'Some Empirical Assumptions in Modern Philosophy of Language', in *Philosophy, Science and Method, Essays in Honour of Ernest Nagel*, ed. S. Morgenbesser, P. Suppes, and M. White (St Martin's Press, New York, 1969), p. 277.
[12] N. Chomsky, *Language and Mind* (Harcourt, Brace and World, New York, 1968), p. 12.

One of the many difficulties of this gambit consists in the notion of mental structures. To be sure, not all structures need to be embodied. We speak freely of logical or mathematical structures without committing ourselves to Platonist reification. But just because of this, the 'structures' we have in mind are those of a calculus, a set of formal relations constituted by rules for the use of a symbolism. Similarly, we speak of the structure of a sonnet or novel, but here too there is no question of the structures being embodied in anything other than the writings of which they are the structure. In such contexts it makes no sense to suppose that anything is 'hidden' or 'mysterious', awaiting future scientific discovery. The obvious danger of talking of *mental* structures is the temptation to think of the mind as a mysterious, imperfectly understood, *medium*. If overt behaviour is mere empirical evidence for as yet inaccessible and unknown mental mechanisms, it will be entirely natural to wonder what these are. Furthermore, Wittgenstein's failure to construct hypotheses about these inner structures will seem bizarre. One will be struck by '. . . the curious, and I believe stultifying, decisions to concentrate on evidence . . . putting aside the question of what the evidence is evidence for. The traditional answer to this question was that the observed phenomena are evidence for an underlying mental reality . . ..'[13] But, of course, the traditional answer conceived of the 'underlying mental reality' as a peculiar type of substance, standing in contrast to material substance, but none the less substance for all its mentality. Consequently, the 'structure of the mind' thus conceived was taken to be the structure of such an ethereal (and mysterious) mental stuff. Indeed, James at one point suggests 'The consciousness of the "idea" and that of the words are thus consubstantial. They are made of the same "mind-stuff", and form an unbroken stream.'[14]

Taken thus to its limits, this gambit is not attractive to all. But many philosophers have taken the final plunge, namely to identify mental states, processes, and experiences with states of the brain. Thus, Central State Materialism explicitly construes mental states, processes, and experiences as states of a person 'apt for bringing about a certain sort of behaviour'.[15] Such states 'actually stand *behind* their manifestations' and are conceived of as causally responsible for the behaviour that manifests them. Thus, the behaviour that we identify as a manifestation of meaning and understanding is indeed a symptom of the 'underlying mental reality'. However, unlike the classical dualist conception of the mind, the Central State Materialist contends,

[13] N. Chomsky, 'Some Empirical Assumptions in Modern Philosophy of Language', in *Philosophy Science and Method*, p. 281. (This is part of his criticism of Wittgenstein's 'behaviourism'.)

[14] W. James, *The Principles of Psychology*, Vol. I, pp. 281 f.

[15] See, e.g. D. M. Armstrong, *A Materialist Theory of the Mind* (Routledge and Kegan Paul, London, 1968), pp. 82 ff.

It may now be asserted that, once it be granted that the concept of a mental state is the concept of a state of a person apt for the production of certain sorts of behaviour, the identification of these states with physico-chemical states of the brain is, in the present state of knowledge, nearly as good a bet as the identification of the gene with the DNA molecule.[16]

Nor is it only philosophers who are inclined to think that what is obscure about meaning and understanding will only be finally clarified by neurophysiology. The idea penetrates into linguistics and psychology:

Whatever it is that represents . . . past and future or imagined events in our mind is the main part, if not the whole, of reality as we grasp it. The link to meaning is there—beyond the reach of any instruments we now have. As one team of psychologists sees it, meaning is the part of language that is least understood 'because in all probability it reflects the principles of neural organization in the cerebral hemisphere'.[17]

But is it really true that meaning is thus mysterious and least understood? If it seems so, it is because we have a false picture of what it is to understand meaning.

6. *Understanding and meaning are not processes, experiences, or mental states*

All the pictures of understanding and meaning thus far elaborated are sketched out by Wittgenstein as part of the conceptual pathology so pervasive in philosophical reflection upon language and mind. Although the various phenomena which constitute part of the 'data' from which such philosophical castles of cards are built are genuine enough, they are, in his view, misconstrued. His task is to rid us of such misconceptions. It is because we have a distorted view of grammar that we concoct mysteries. To disperse the clouds of mystery we must, therefore, examine the way we speak of understanding and meaning.

For the purposes of our studies it can never be essential that a symbolic phenomenon occurs in the mind and not on paper so that others can see it. One is constantly tempted to explain a symbolic process by a special psychological process; as if the mind 'could do much more in these matters' than signs can.
    We are misled by the idea of a mechanism that works in special media and so can explain special movements. (PG 99.)

Contrary to what is suggested by some of the phenomena of meaning and understanding, meaning and understanding are *not* experiences. Of course, there is such a thing as the experience of suddenly understanding.

[16] Ibid., p. 90.
[17] D. Bolinger, *Aspects of Language*, 2nd edition (Harcourt, Brace, Jovanovich, New York, 1975), p. 187. (quoting S. Locke, D. Caplan, and L. Kellar, *A Study in Neurolinguistics*, p. 10).

But the experience is not the understanding, and a description of the experience does not give the essence of understanding. What does happen when one suddenly understands? Surely many things *may* happen: one may have various mental images, say certain things to oneself, experience a certain tensing of the muscles—or one may not. When one suddenly grasps the rule of a series one may exclaim 'Now I can go on!', one's face may light up, one suddenly changes one's rhythm of breathing. But one may have all these experiences and manifest all these subtle behavioural changes, and yet not understand, not be able to continue the series correctly (PI §§151 ff.). Conversely, one may continue the series without having any of these experiences; if asked 'What happened when you understood?', one may answer blankly 'Well—I continued the series—nothing else happened'. The experiences are neither necessary nor sufficient for understanding. The criteria for understanding lie in performances. The pupil understands the rule of the series when he goes on to expand the series correctly, no matter what experiences accompany his correct performance.

Of course, often prior to going on to expand a series according to a rule, the thought of the rule of the series may occur to one. But 'Now I can go on!' does not mean 'The formula has occurred to me' (PI §152; BB 113). Nor does one exclaim 'Now I understand!' because the formula has occurred to one and because one has noticed in the past that one was able to go on correctly whenever the formula had occurred to one. For the formula may indeed occur to one, yet one may not understand. For one must *apply* the formula correctly. Of course, there is a connection between the formula occurring to one and going on correctly. And the pupil uses the words 'Now I understand!' with justice when the formula occurs to him, given the *circumstances* that he has learnt algebra, expanded such series before, etc., and his making this avowal is a *criterion of his understanding*. But the words are not a description of the circumstances in which they are rightly used. The circumstances are the stage-setting of the language-game with such expressions of understanding. When a pupil *in such circumstances* evinces such expressions, then he satisfies *criteria* for saying *of him* that he understands, and he is justified in his utterance (i.e. uses it with right, cf. Exg. §155), not by his experiences, but by the circumstances of his utterance. For *inter alia*, he may exclaim 'Now I can go on!' even though the thought of the formula has not crossed his mind, and, in appropriate circumstances, we should agree that he has understood (PI §179). We persist in thinking that when we say 'Now I understand!', we say so *because* we understand, and *therefore* our words are a report of an introspectible experience. We should rather consider the exclamation to be a *signal* of understanding, which is judged to be correctly employed by what the pupil goes on to do (PI §§180, 323). This is broadly correct, yet one must distinguish different cases.

There are occasions when one rightly says 'I understand, now I can go on', and then, when asked to go on (continue the series, whistle the theme, etc.), one suddenly finds one cannot. Does this inevitably mean that one was wrong in saying that one understood? Clearly not—no more than when one says 'I can lift that heavy weight', and then bends down clumsily and slips a disc so that one cannot lift it. We make room for *losing an ability* between avowal and performance, and sometimes agree, on the basis of further criteria, that when a person said he could . . . he could, even though he was subsequently unable to. (Other possibilities can be envisaged too.)

The classical conception, according to which understanding the meaning of a word is having the experience of imagining its denotation, is likewise misconceived. It may be that when one orders a person to pick a yellow marble from a pile, he has an image of yellow when he understands the order. But his understanding does not consist in having such an image, and the temptation to think so is lessened by reflecting on the order 'Imagine a yellow patch!' (BB 12). Indeed, one's inclination to 'locate' understanding in the on-goings of ethereal images is also lessened when one reflects that a yellow piece of paper in one's pocket is no less serviceable than an image of yellow in one's mind (indeed, in many ways more so, since one can look at it in different lights, hold it up next to other objects for match or mismatch) (BB 4). If one objects that one may forget what colour the piece of paper is (i.e. that *this* is called 'yellow'), one should reflect that one may equally forget of what colour one's mental image is an image.

Moreover, the criteria for having a mental image differ from the criteria for understanding. My sincere avowal concerning my mental imagery is authoritative, but my avowal concerning my understanding may be undermined by my subsequent performances manifesting misunderstanding. This may appear to confirm the 'weak hypothesis' conception of understanding. But it only so appears as long as the incoherence of the hypothesis-relation thus conceived is not laid bare. And the illusory appearance vanishes when one grasps that the avowal, in these circumstances, is a *criterion* of understanding. It is, of course, defeasible. But if it is not *defeated* it confers certainty.

A further point against the imagist conception is that the criteria for having images presupposes the criteria for understanding inasmuch as a person, when asked what images he has, must understand the question (hence satisfy the criteria for understanding) and the words he uses to answer it. One can keep an image in mind for five minutes, but it makes no sense to talk of 'keeping one's understanding in mind (before one's mind) for five minutes' (PI p. 176). The grammar of 'understanding' and of 'having images' is totally different. Understanding the meaning of a word or sentence is not a matter of having images. We do not deny that a person understands a sentence because he cannot draw a sketch from it. Why should we suppose that he must draw a mental sketch (PI §396)?

Finally, we are wrong to suppose that 'I meant so-and-so when . . .' is a report like 'I kicked so-and-so', only about the mind rather than the feet. When asked 'By "Napoleon" did you mean the victor of Austerlitz?', one's affirmative reply may indeed be correct, but not like the report of a pain; rather, like 'I knew that 6×6 = 36' (PG 103). To say 'I'm sure I meant him to write 10,000 and not 20,000 when he came to square 100' is like saying 'I'm sure I should have jumped into the water if Arabella had fallen in' (LFM 28).

However, if meaning and understanding are not experiences, neither are they activities or processes in the mind. To call understanding a process is as misleading as calling 3 an object (PG 85). To call meaning an activity is as wrongheaded as thinking that rising in price is an activity of butter—only the latter absurdity, unlike the former, leads to no philosophical confusions (PI §693).

Processes take time (go on), and so have a beginning, middle, and end, consisting of various phases. As such they are clockable on a stop-watch, they can be interrupted, and sometimes resumed at the point of interruption. Wittgenstein does not deny that there are mental processes. They share the generic character of processes, but are distinguished by their mentality, i.e. the fact that they can (commonly) be concealed, that their owner's avowal has a privileged status, that their specific identity is logically dependent upon that of their owner, etc. Humming a tune 'silently', reciting poetry 'in one's head', and saying the alphabet or counting one's steps to oneself are mental processes.

However, understanding is not a mental process. It is true that when one listens to a lecture or watches a game of chess *with understanding*, one has a distinctive series of experiences, different from those which accompany uncomprehending attention. But the experiences vary from case to case, as well as from person to person. So understanding cannot be identified by reference to *Merkmale* given by such a process. Moreover, even if perchance the process were uniform, it would not constitute understanding, for we do not determine whether someone understands by discovering what processes accompanied his listening. No matter what mental processes accompany understanding, they are neither necessary nor sufficient for it. Whether a person understands a lecture is determined by whether he can recount it, answer questions about it, and evaluate it intelligently. Whether a person understands music is shown by how he plays it, how he talks about it, or what aspects of it he appreciates. If someone were to insist that with him understanding is a mental process, we should draw his attention to the differences between the criteria for mental processes and the criteria for understanding (PI p. 181). Understanding chess, understanding German, or understanding

Bach are not interruptable as is a mental recitation of a poem. An 'interruption' of understanding is a loss of understanding, or failure of understanding, not a hiatus in a process resulting from withdrawal of attention (Z §85). Suddenly understanding the rule of a series is not something that goes on, lasts as long as, or longer than, the noise of the passing traffic. Understanding the multiplication tables is not a process with a beginning, middle, and end, but a gradually acquired ability to operate a calculus. Understanding what someone says is not an articulated process like the utterance of the sentence, nor yet an unarticulated process, for it is not a process at all.

Is understanding, then, a mental state? Certainly the verb 'to understand' is non-progressive and is commonly said to lack an imperative form,[18] it cannot form a pseudo-cleft sentence with a Do pro-form, its present tense is non-frequentative and 'I have understood' implies 'I understand' (but one can understand slowly or quickly). Nevertheless, it is misleading to conceive of understanding as a state of mind in the accepted sense of the term. Psychological states, Wittgenstein stresses, have *genuine duration* (Z §§76 ff., cf. Z §488). One can typically ascertain, as it were, by spot check, whether they are still *going on* (Z §72). Where there is genuine duration, the enduring phenomenon can typically be observed, continuously or intermittently (Z §76), but there is no such thing as an uninterrupted observation of my capacity to multiply (Z §77) or my understanding of arithmetic. One can determine, e.g., the duration of an impression on a stop-watch, but not the 'duration' of knowledge, ability, or understanding (Z §82). Genuine states of mind typically run a course, flaring up, abating, and vanishing (cf. Z §488) (hence one must distinguish emotions or emotional dispositions from emotional states (Z §491)). They are subject to degrees of intensity. If one is in a state of extreme agitation from three o'clock to four o'clock, then at any intervening time one is agitated. If one is anxious from five o'clock until six o'clock, then one is anxious *continuously*. One can interrupt, break into, or disturb a psychological state, which may subsequently be resumed, as when one breaks off one's intense concentration to deal with a trifle, and then resumes one's work, or as when one calms a friend's acute anxiety only to find that he lapses into the same state later. Loss of consciousness is incompatible with the continuity of a psychological state, hence it is 'Sleep that knits up the ravell'd sleave of care, The death of each day's life, sore labour's bath, Balm of hurt minds . . .'. Understanding is not a mental state. There is no such thing as being in a state of understanding. One may understand something *from* a certain time (the time at which one learnt or understood it) *for* a certain time (as long as one passes 'tests' of understanding, i.e. satisfies criteria of understanding),

---

[18] But what of 'Understand this: as long as I am in charge, there will be no squabbling!'?

i.e. until one forgets or ceases to be able to do such-and-such. But one does not understand it *continuously* from the time one came to understand it until one ceases (PI p. 59 n.), as one is in a state of acute anxiety continuously from the time one hears that one's child is missing until, some hours later, one hears that all is well. One's intense concentration may be interrupted, but not one's profound understanding. One may suddenly lose one's understanding (one's 'grasp') of a problem, and then equally suddenly regain it. But this is not akin to the sudden abating of an acute pain and its subsequent resumption when the analgesic wears off. It is rather like suddenly forgetting and then subsequently recollecting (PI p. 59 n.; Z §85). One may cease to understand a theorem, a person, a language, etc., but that is not the termination of a particular psychological state. Nor is one's understanding 'interrupted' or 'terminated' by falling asleep. One may (misleadingly) call 'having a rule in mind' a mental state, and when one understands the expansion of a series one may have a rule in mind, yet this understanding is not a state but an ability. So if understanding were a state, it would have to be a hypothetical state or a state of a *hypothetical* (non-introspectible) mechanism, either mental but hidden, or neural and awaiting the discovery of a future super-science. Hence one is led so readily to concoct philosophical 'theories' in preparation for future science.

In all these cases, sharp categorial differences distinguish meaning and understanding from mental states, processes and experiences. We find it difficult to pinpoint the nature of meaning and understanding; hence we are tempted to claim that their nature is evident in introspection, but is nevertheless ineffable (Z §86). But this is only because we have a false picture of what their nature should be.

7. Understanding and ability

The thrust of the argument thus far points in the direction of equating understanding with an ability. To understand a rule of a series is to be able to expand the series correctly in accordance with the rule; to understand a sentence is, *inter alia*, to be able to apply it; to understand a word is to be able to use it correctly. We may acknowledge that for some cases of 'understand' this is a move in the right direction. However, before pursuing it further we must first scrutinize the concept of an ability, for it presents distinctive pitfalls.

The concepts of potentiality, power, and ability, so central to Aristotelian and medieval scholastic philosophy, were subsequently neglected almost completely. In recent years a revival of philosophical interest in powers and abilities has occurred,[19] stimulated by Wittgenstein and Ryle.

A power must be distinguished both from its exercise and from its vehicle, *a fortiori* from the structure of its vehicle. That an ability is categorially distinct from its exercise should be obvious: the electric kettle I buy (cold and empty) can heat water (otherwise I should not buy it); the car in my garage can do 70 m.p.h. (otherwise I should take it to be repaired); a man can speak even though he is silent, can do arithmetic even though he is not calculating, can read and write even though playing cricket (although he cannot read or write while playing cricket, i.e. one cannot exercise both the ability to write and the ability to play cricket on the same occasion).

The distinction[20] between an ability and its vehicle is no less evident. A book can fit into a drawer (and indeed one can *see*, not its ability, but *that* it has it). The vehicle of its ability to do so is its shape, but its shape is distinct from its ability. One can measure its shape, but not its ability to fit. Whisky can intoxicate. The vehicle of its ability is the alcohol it contains, but the alcohol is not identical with the intoxicating power. One can weigh the alcohol, but not the ability to intoxicate. If an ability is distinct from its vehicle, *a fortiori* it is distinct from the structure of its vehicle which may explain the ability. A pianola can play certain tunes. The vehicle of its ability is the mechanism of drums, pins, and wheels. Their structure, the physical interrelation of parts, explains how the pianola can play, but is not identical with that ability. Science explains powers by discovering underlying structures, but it is a mistake to think that it *reduces* powers to the structure of their vehicle. Hemlock possesses the power to poison; the vehicle of its power is coniine; the molecular structure of that chemical, i.e. 2n-propylpiperidine, in conjunction with principles of physiology and biochemistry, explains how hemlock poisons. But its power to poison is categorially distinct from its chemical structure.

By exploiting later systematizations of philosophical misconceptions about abilities, one can clarify and extend Wittgenstein's critical remarks. One tempting misconception is transcendentalism, i.e. the fallacious reification of powers, according to which they are conceived as occult entities mysteriously contained within the possessor of the power. Wittgenstein discusses this: the action of a machine seems to be in it from the start, i.e. we are inclined to compare the future movements of a machine to objects already lying in a drawer which we then take out: the possible movements of the machine are already in it in some mysterious

---

[19] See in particular M. Ayers, *The Refutation of Determinism* (Methuen, London, 1968); A. J. P. Kenny, *Will, Freedom and Power* (Blackwell, Oxford, 1976); A. White, *Modal Notions* (Blackwell, Oxford, 1976).

[20] The distinction is Kenny's in *Will, Freedom and Power*, p. 10.

way (PI §194). The possible movements are not, of course, the actual movements (they may never occur), nor the physical conditions for moving either (for we say, of these conditions—'Experience will show whether this gives the pin this possibility of movement', but not 'Experience will show whether this *is* the possibility of movement'). So we conceive of the possibility of movement as a kind of shadow of the movement itself. But powers are not invisible, sensible properties—they are categorially distinct from actualities, and the categorial distinction is not captured by supposing potentialities to differ from actualities in virtue of being invisible or occult (even though it is true that one cannot see the horse-power under the bonnet of the car). We establish the existence of powers and abilities in diverse ways, some of which may reinforce our proneness to fallacy. We establish that the car can do 100 m.p.h. by driving it fast, i.e. observing its performance. The transcendentalist may think that our inference from its performance to 'a power capable of producing it'[21] is one from effect to cause, a thought reinforcing the conception of power as an occult entity. But the inference from 'AΦs' to 'A has the power to Φ' is not such an inference. There are diverse grammatical grounds, criteria—not inductive evidence, for ascription of different powers and abilities (BB 100–25).

In reaction to the sins of transcendentalism two forms of reductionism have evolved. The first is the reduction of ability to its exercise, whose most famous proponent was Hume: 'The distinction which we often make betwixt *power* and the exercise of it is . . . without foundation', and 'is entirely frivolous'.[22] Wittgenstein does not discuss this form of reductionism at any length. Rather, having surveyed, in elaborate detail, the variety of grounds for attribution of abilities by means of a large number of imaginary language-games which differently 'segment' the use of 'can' and 'is able to', he envisages a language-game in which doing a thing is the only justification for saying that one can do it. Of this he simply remarks that there is no *metaphysical* difference between such a linguistic practice and others in which a wide variety of justifications for attribution of ability are accepted. To adopt Humean reductionism looks like accepting as a ground for attribution of ability only the strongest possible evidence—which is then held to be identical with the ability. Note that there are two moves here, first, a *grading* of evidential support (i.e. the suggestion that Φing is the best possible evidence for being able to Φ) and, secondly, a *reduction* of ability to performance. Both moves are mistaken. First, the fact that a *person* Φs no more incontrovertibly establishes that he *has the ability* to Φ than any other evidence; his performance may have been a fluke, a matter of beginner's luck (this being one of the many differences between human and natural abilities).

[21] Hume, *Treatise*, Bk. I, Pt. iii, Sect. xiv.
[22] Ibid., Sect. xiv.

Secondly, sometimes our justified attributions of potentialities do not wait upon actual past, present or future performance at all. A round peg (of a given size) can fit into a round hole (of a given diameter) and cannot fit into a square hole (of a given area). It may be prevented from being inserted in the hole, but not through lack of power, rather by circumstances which do not defeat the attribution of power. Thirdly, once the illusion of privileged status of current performance is thus revealed, it is evident that the other and various kinds of evidence we take as justification for attribution of ability are not in principle weaker than, nor metaphysically different from, current performance *qua* evidence. And this is precisely Wittgenstein's point. They only seem metaphysically inferior because one notices the categorial difference between power and sensible property, one is sceptical (possibly, as in Hume's case, because of scepticism about induction) about the validity of any evidence other than actual performance, so one equates the power with the current exercise of it and projects the categorial difference between power and exercise on to the difference between current exercise and other kinds of grounds for ascribing a power. But there is no such difference between the evidence of present and past performance; both are, in different ways, defeasible criteria. Observation of the vehicle of an ability is not necessarily or even generally evidence inferior to that of current performance. Where the nexus between power and vehicle is conceptual (with round pegs and round holes), observation of the vehicle often suffices without testing (although here too the power does not entail its exercise). Where the nexus is empirical (as in the case of feeling the muscles of the javelin thrower), observation plus knowledge of the activity are perfectly adequate.

As regards the actual reductionism, Aristotle's arguments[23] already suffice to give Hume his quietus. If a person cannot do something when he is not doing it, then it is senseless to speak of chess-players, linguists, translators, riders, runners, or swimmers. For a person who cannot Φ is not a Φer. So all attributions of skill are ruled out. Similarly, with skill disappear the notions of learning and forgetting how to do something. For if an activity must be learnt, yet one cannot do it when one is not doing it, then as soon as one stops one forgets, and one only learns when one engages in it. Moreover, perceptual powers (the ability to see, hear, or taste) will be lost when not exercised, so one will be held to go blind when not seeing and deaf when not hearing. So reduction of ability to its exercise is absurd.

A different kind of reductionism is the reduction of an ability to its vehicle or the structure of its vehicle. It is not surprising to find this thesis prominent in Descartes, for as the father of the philosophy of the new

---

[23] Aristotle, *Metaphysics* (Theta); discussed in Kenny, *Will, Freedom and Power*, p. 126.

sciences he saw quite clearly that one form of scientific *explanation* is by reference to structures. He mistakenly thought that explanation is reduction and held that the geometrical properties (the spatial structure) of material objects not only explained but constituted its powers (and that all its 'remaining properties' were only effects of its structure upon percipients). Wittgenstein's discussion of transcendentalism applies equally to vehicle-reductionism. The possibility of the machine's movement is no more identical with the machine itself or its structure than it is with an occult shadow. We construct the machine in order to give it the possibility of such-and-such a movement. We do not construct the possibility of the movement.

Vehicle-reductionism, however, is particularly relevant to fallacies concerning mental abilities in general and understanding in particular. We have already surveyed the temptation to conceive of understanding as a mental state. Wittgenstein's discussion points towards an analysis of understanding as an ability. But in a perverse way this may, if care is not taken, reinforce the fallacious conception of understanding as a state. For one of the standard pitfalls in philosophical analysis of ability is to think that an ability is itself a kind of state.

> There are . . . various reasons which incline us to look at the fact of something being possible, someone being able to do something, etc., as the fact that he or it is in a particular state. Roughly speaking, this comes to saying that 'A is in the state of being able to do something' is the form of representation we are most strongly tempted to adopt; or, as one could also put it, we are strongly inclined to use the metaphor of something being in a peculiar state for saying that something can behave in a particular way. And this way of representation, or this metaphor, is embodied in the expression 'He is capable of . . .', 'He is able to multiply large numbers in his head', 'He can play chess': in these sentences the verb is used in the *present tense*, suggesting that the phrases are descriptions of states which exist at the moment when we speak.
>
> The same tendency shows itself in our calling the ability to solve a mathematical problem, the ability to enjoy a piece of music, etc., certain states of mind; we don't mean by this expression 'conscious mental phenomena'. Rather, a state of mind in this sense is the state of a hypothetical mechanism, a mind model meant to explain the conscious mental phenomena . . . In this way also we can hardly help conceiving of memory as a kind of storehouse. Note also how sure people are that to the ability to add or to multiply or to say a poem by heart, etc., there *must* correspond a peculiar state of the person's brain, although on the other hand they know next to nothing about such psycho-physiological correspondences. We regard these phenomena as manifestations of this mechanism, and their possibility is the particular construction of the mechanism itself. (BB 117 f.)

Abilities, powers, capacities, and dispositions, though they may be acquired, possessed for a time, and perhaps later lost, are not states. A new car can do 120 m.p.h. (even though its owner is not so rash as to drive it at that speed), but it is not in a state of being able to do 120 m.p.h. An old car, by being overhauled, may be brought into a state in which it can, again, do 120 m.p.h., but its being able to go that speed is not a state of the car. Rubber, in its solid state, is elastic, but its being elastic (unlike its being compressed) is not a state of the lump of rubber. Burning rubber is in a state of combustion, yet being combustible is not a state of rubber but a passive power or disposition of rubber. Sugar is soluble, but solubility is not a state of sugar.

So too with psychological dispositions, powers, and abilities. Being able to speak French, play chess, or conjugate Latin irregular verbs are not states of a person. Being clever, intelligent, charming, or dull are not kinds of mental states, nor are understanding, knowing, or remembering. One may interrupt a person's exercise of his intelligence or manifestation of his understanding, but not his intelligence or his understanding. One may, through senility, cease to be intelligent and no longer understand some complex mathematical theorem. But loss of intelligence or understanding is not termination of a state. Dispositions, powers, and abilities, though possessed for a time, do not have genuine duration. One may continue to possess (and exercise) them, but they are not continuous anythings.

We have already seen the temptations of conceiving of the mind as a hypothetical mental structure, and of literally identifying mental abilities with neural states. To be sure, one can infer from the operations of a machine, whose mechanism is concealed in a casing, what its hidden structure is. But a literal structure must be the structure of something or other, made of some stuff or other. Yet the mind is neither a substance, nor made of a substance. If we speak of the structure of the mind we can only sensibly mean the formal relations between the concepts in terms of which we describe the mind, or the formal relations between elements of symbolisms used by creatures who have minds. Yet such structures are neither hypotheses nor mental mechanisms in a hypothetical sense. Although behaviour manifesting understanding is not itself understanding, but evidence for it, what this is evidence for is an ability, not a state, i.e. not a persisting mental structure in an ethereal medium. Moreover, the evidence is *criterial*, not inductive, not deductive, nor *a priori* probabilifying evidence. This point is *absolutely crucial*.

Central State Materialism is more radical, both in its materialism and its explicit reductionism. According to its view of dispositions,

. . . to speak of an object's having a dispositional property entails that the object is in some non-dispositional state or that it has some property (there exists a 'categorical basis') which is responsible for the object manifesting certain behaviour in certain circumstances . . . [I]f brittleness can be identified with an actual *state* of the glass, then we can think of it as a cause, or, more vaguely, a causal factor, in the process that brings about the breaking. Dispositions are seen to be states that actually *stand behind* their manifestations. It is simply that the states are *identified* in terms of their manifestations in suitable conditions, rather than in terms of their intrinsic nature.

Our argument for a 'Realist' account of dispositions can equally be applied to capacities and powers. They, too, must be conceived of as states of the object that has the capacity or power.[24]

There is a puzzle about this confusion. We are not tempted to identify the horse-power of our car with a state of its engine, although the car has such-and-such horse-power because of the state (structure) of its engine. We do not identify the possibility of a machine's movements with its structure which explains them. So why is vehicle-reductionism so tempting in the case of mental powers (or indeed molecular structures—as in the case of brittleness)? The reason, perhaps, is a miscegenous crossing of transcendentalism and reductionism. There is a sense in which we cannot observe powers, but only their manifestations. Yet, we contend, the manifestation occurs *because* the object has the relevant power or ability. The transcendentalist conceives of the power as an invisible entity within the object (a kind of elementary or even inanimate soul) which causes the manifestation. Science explains how objects can do what they can do by discovering underlying structures. Where the structure is visible (as in the case of the internal combustion engine) we are not greatly inclined to identify the power with the structure. But where the structure is invisible, as in the case of the molecular structure of brittle objects, the transcendentalist picture more readily intervenes, inclining us to identify the disposition (passive power) with the (no longer occult but still unobservable) structure which explains it, and hence to conceive of the disposition as the *cause* of its manifestation. *A fortiori*, in the case of mental powers and abilities such as understanding, we note that the manifestation of understanding is distinct from understanding. We are already inclined to think of understanding as a state, and consequently we jump to the wholly erroneous conclusion that it is a state of the brain which is the hypothetical cause of manifestations of an ability. But an ability is not a state, nor is it the cause of its manifestations; it is not a visible entity with an observable structure, but neither is it an invisible entity with an unobservable structure.

Such category mistakes as are committed by vehicle-reductionism do not show that mental abilities do not have an explanation by reference to neural structures. It merely shows that they are not identical with such hypothesized structures which may explain their exercise. But it also suggests that the view that there *must* be such a 'categorical basis' is a piece of mythology.

---

[24] D. M. Armstrong, *A Materialist Theory of the Mind*, pp. 86, 88.

No supposition seems to me more natural than that there is no process in the brain correlated with associating or with thinking; so that it would be impossible to read off thought-processes from brain-processes . . .

It is thus perfectly possible that certain psychological phenomena *cannot* be investigated physiologically, because physiologically nothing corresponds to them.

I saw this man years ago: now I have seen him again, I recognize him, I remember his name. And why does there have to be a cause of this remembering in my nervous system? Why must something or other, whatever it may be, be stored up there *in any form*? Why *must* a trace have been left behind? Why should there not be a psychological regularity to which *no* physiological regularity corresponds? If this upsets our concept of causality then it is high time it was upset. (Z §§608–10.)

Whether there are or are not such underlying neural structures which will causally explain manifestations of understanding or meaning remains to be discovered. We simply do not know. But, of course, it in no way follows that we do not know what understanding or meaning something really are. Our ignorance of the structure of the possible vehicle of an ability is not an ignorance of the character of the ability. Equally, psycholinguists' mystification of the concept of meaning in a language, and their attribution of this pseudo-mystery to ignorance of neural organization which it allegedly reflects, stems from semiconscious illegitimate vehicle-reductionism.

8. *Understanding as a family-resemblance concept*

Understanding seems to be an ability. A person who understands something is able to do certain things. Nevertheless, the equation of understanding and ability is misleading. It leads to errors in an account of understanding language and its uses, and also to parallel errors about other forms of understanding. It is more correct to say that understanding is akin to an ability, or that in its dominant uses 'understanding' denotes an ability. Why adopt this cautious formulation?

The first point to stress is the *diffuseness* of understanding in comparison with the generality of practical abilities. This is visible in the following features.

(i) If understanding is an ability, it is not an ability to do, for every item one understands, one single type of thing or uniform class of things. This distinguishes understanding from many, though by no means all, kinds of practical abilities. A person who understands a sentence of his native tongue can do many things, e.g. paraphrase it, explain it at length, use it in appropriate contexts, respond to it in appropriate ways. A person who understands children can get on well with them, make himself loved by them, communicate his sympathy to them, play with them to their delight, grasp (understand) their motives and their complex symbolic behaviour (in particular their displacement behaviour), and so on. This large variety of abilities of which different understandings may consist does not merely reflect the multiple criteria for understanding. After all, pain has multiple criteria, but lacks the inherent complexity and richness of the concept of understanding. It reflects the fact that understanding is a family resemblance concept.

(ii) Understanding, over a wide range of its objects, seems intuitively more passive than *some* of the abilities which are associated with such objects. Understanding German is not the same as being able to speak German, since one may understand yet be unable to speak (although one can say what a German sentence means). Understanding music is not the same as being able to play or compose, nor is understanding art being able to paint or sculpt. Moreover, understanding how to do something is not in general the same as being able to do it.

(iii) There are different kinds of understanding which do not correspond in any straightforward way to different kinds of abilities. Compare understanding an order, understanding a calculus or a proof in a calculus, understanding a person, understanding a late Beethoven string quartet, and understanding (as Augustine could not) how it is possible to measure time. Of course, in each case there are certain things which we are inclined to say that a person who understands such-and-such may do, for it is those things, which, if done, constitute the criteria for understanding. But although doing so-and-so may be a criterion of understanding such-and-such, one must not jump to the conclusion that the understanding *is* the ability to do so-and-so. One may well have the ability long before the understanding that manifests itself in the exercise of the ability.

If one understands a calculus then one is able to operate it. But understanding women is not at all like understanding a calculus. In what sense does a person who understands women have an ability which the person who does not understand them lacks, other than the ability to understand women? The quest for philosophical understanding is not obviously best described as an attempt to acquire an ability to *do* something.

A second point of contrast is that there are degrees of understanding which are not reflected in the degrees to which a given ability is possessed. Abilities are often capable of degrees: the more able one is to do such-and-such, the more excellent one's performances are likely to be. But degrees of understanding do not always result in a more skilful execution of some act or activity. We may speak of a deepening of our understanding of a late Beethoven string quartet, although there may be little if anything that we can do as a result. Criteria for the change may lie in the way we listen and the delight we take in the music. It is very often our *attitudes* that change with the deepening of our understanding, not our abilities. The deepening of our understanding for a person may amount to no more than a more generous empathy or effort of imagination. And lest it be thought that this depth is uncharacteristic of understanding language, reflect on the deepening of understanding of literature with maturity.

A third point concerns the relation of explanation of meaning to understanding an expression. If a person understands the explanation of 'x', then he understands 'x'. This is a general feature of understanding language—namely that explanation is internally related to meaning and understanding. But it is not, in general, a feature of practical abilities. There is, all too frequently, a wide gap between understanding the explanation of how to Φ (e.g. ride a bicycle) and being able to Φ. Where Φing is such an activity, it is not a criterion for not having understood the explanation of how to Φ that one should fail to go on to Φ. But a criterion for my not understanding a grammatical explanation of 'x' is that I do not use 'x' correctly.

A fourth point concerns different kinds of understanding of language. Reflect on the differences between understanding a nonsense poem (by Carroll or Lear), understanding an English sentence out of context, and understanding the same sentence in the context of a novel. We might say, again, that these are different kinds of understandings of sentences or that one understands them in a quite different sense (PG 43). Similarly, what ability does a person have who understands the epigram 'Architecture is frozen music'? Is it that he can sincerely say 'That is a powerful picture'?

Finally, reflect on different types of lack of understanding manifest in the following sentences (cf. PLP 347):

I cannot understand you, you must speak louder.
I cannot understand you, that is sheer nonsense.
I cannot understand you, I don't speak German.
I cannot understand you, what you said was too complicated to follow.
I cannot understand you, I don't see why you want . . .

Similarly, one must note that although some types of understandings are contrasted with an absence of understanding which consists in lack of certain kinds of ability, room must also be made for misunderstanding. Someone misunderstands an order, e.g., not if he merely is unable to say what it means, but if he acts on it *wrongly*.

These different features of the grammar of 'understand' are confusing. They may lead one to conclude that 'understand' is ambiguous just as the kinship between various phenomena of understanding and the categories of experience, process, state, and activity may lead one to think that 'understanding' in some of its uses denotes an experience, in others a state or process. In view of this it is instructive to note the development of Wittgenstein's thoughts on the issue.

In the *Grammar* his position is equivocal. He contends that in certain of its applications 'understand' refers to a psychological reaction that occurs while hearing or reading a sentence (PG 41). Later on, distinguishing understanding from its behavioural manifestation which is a symptom (*Anzeichen*) of understanding, he suggests that understanding is a state (PG 84). Although he correlates understanding with ability (PG 47) and remarks that calling understanding a process produces a false grammatical attitude to understanding (PG 85), he does himself call understanding a process, and distinguishes the processes that are criteria for understanding from the process of understanding (PG 82). He does indeed note that 'understanding' is not the name of a single process accompanying reading or hearing sentences, but argues that it is the name of more or less interrelated processes in the context of the use of language. From this he concludes that 'understanding' is a family resemblance term, naming a family of processes (PG 74). Yet earlier, in a discussion of understanding chess, he remarked that here 'we can again observe the ambiguity of the word "understanding"' (PG 49).

This unsatisfactory position is mirrored in Waismann's contention that in one of its uses 'understand' stands for a mental reaction, but in others understanding is not an experience but a disposition, or merely a piece of behaviour appropriate to a sentence (PLP 347 f). He argues that the word 'understanding' was gradually extended from a core of characteristic cases to others more or less akin to it, concluding that it is ambiguous. Understanding consists of 'a whole bundle of processes, dispositions, experiences, patterns of behaviour which are bound together by language into a sort of unity' (PLP 348).

The *Investigations* irons out most of these wrinkles. Understanding, Wittgenstein now argues, is not an experience (PI §153), a mental process (PI §§152, 154), or a mental state (PI p. 59 n.(a), §149), although it has a certain kinship with each of these. Nor is he any longer inclined to speak of the ambiguity of the word 'understand'. 'I would rather say that these kinds of uses of "understanding" make up its meaning, make up my *concept* of understanding. For I *want* to apply the word "understanding" to all this' (PI §532).

Is understanding, then, an ability? Perhaps one can best encapsulate the truth in a metaphor (cf. PLP 346): the grammar of 'understands' and 'is able to' run for a stretch over parallel tracks (cf. PI p. 192).

XVII

MEANING AND UNDERSTANDING

1. *Introduction*

The concept of meaning is complicated and many-faceted. It plays a role in a wide variety of contexts, both within and outside philosophy, and it interlocks with many other concepts. It is connected with the notion of significance, as when we speak of ethical meaning or of the meaning of life, and with that of signifying, as when we speak of clouds meaning rain. It is connected with the idea of intending, for people mean to do or say certain things. Our concern here is solely with the notion of linguistic meaning. The meaning of a word is intimately related to its denotation, the idea expressed by it, grounds for its application, justification and criticism of its use, definitions or explanations of it, and what is understood or communicated by its use. Similarly, the meaning of a sentence is connected with the notions of truth and falsity, proof and evidence, certainty and probability, necessity and possibility, belief and other 'propositional attitudes', assertion and other 'speech-acts', explanation, communication, understanding, and meaning something. Finally, these internal connections are multiplied many-fold in virtue of the relations between the meaning of a sentence and the meanings of the expressions of which it is composed. The concept of meaning is intended to give the solution to a huge array of simultaneous equations.

The aim of a philosophical investigation of meaning is to reveal, or perhaps to introduce some order into this apparent chaos, i.e. to survey and organize the multiple applications of the concept of meaning and the welter of conceptual connections between meaning and other notions. An obvious technique is to begin with some simplification or schematization of the concept of meaning and then to progress by successive approximations towards a complete analysis of the concept. By treating one or a few conceptual connections as basic, we might well hope to exhibit the rest as their consequences. The ideal would be to produce an analysis of the concept of meaning that would manifestly be a solution to the whole set of 'equations' into which this concept enters. All of the important internal relations between meaning and other notions (denotation, truth, evidence, explanation, communication, etc.) would flow from this analysis. Whether or not they are intended to be executions of this programme, most philosophical 'theories of meaning' conform to it.

Were a philosopher to start from scratch according to this strategy, he would immediately be faced with bewildering choices. There is wide latitude as to which conceptual connections are to be treated as basic and which should be left for the final theory to account for; moreover, there seem to be no principles that might inform his choice, since he could not know in advance of attempting to construct a full theory that choice of a particular basis would not succeed. The difficulty would be to know how to make a rational beginning. Providentially, nobody finds himself in this distressing situation. From the beginning, philosophical reflection on meaning is informed by certain preconceptions; these provide the starting point of inquiry and shape the subsequent elaboration of the theory. Augustine's picture of language is what Wittgenstein identifies as the proto-picture underlying the development of the important modern philosophical theories of meaning. The foundation of this speculation is the thesis that words are names, i.e. that meaning is essentially a matter of correlating words with objects. Meaning consists in the relation of words to things. All other internal relations with meaning must be shown to conform with this conception, and if possible they must be shown to flow from the correlations of words with things. Augustine's proto-picture informs all standard modern theories of meaning, even those appearing to have nothing in common, e.g. causal theories, imagism, accounts of meaning in terms of speaker's intentions, and verification-ism.

Frege's achievement was to promote the prospects for constructing a complete analysis of meaning in conformity with Augustine's proto-picture. He introduced sophistication and subtlety into the dominant framework of thought about meaning. First, by distinguishing sense from reference, he multiplied the correlations of words with things and thereby provided solutions to perennial problems. Secondly, by careful attention to the forms of sentences, he made more plausible the idea that the meaning of a sentence is composed of the meanings of the words of which this sentence itself is composed. Frege's work has deeply influenced most subsequent investigation of meaning. Much of the philosophy of language consists of relatively minor extensions, refinements, and modifications of his pioneering theorizing.

The consequences of this outlook on meaning are profound. Two are so entrenched in our thinking that they are scarcely detectable. First, only simple internal connections are recognized. We assume that proof, evidence, and verification have nothing to do with the meaning of a sentence unless they determine its meaning quite straightforwardly; either understanding a sentence is knowing how to verify it or else verification is irrelevant to meaning. Similarly, we assume that complete mystery is the only alternative to acknowledging that the meaning of a sentence is composed out of the meanings of its constituents in accordance with its logical form. We are tempted to assert that explaining the meaning of a sentence *must* take the form of describing its truth-conditions; that explaining the meaning of a word *must* take the form of stating conditions necessary and sufficient for its application; and that giving a correct explanation of a word is a sufficient condition for using it correctly. *Simplex sigillum veri* is an unshakable article of faith. It even thrives on the recalcitrance of the 'data', and it tempts us to forgo close scrutiny of plausible theories. Communication requires shared understanding; this requirement is met provided a sentence used to communicate is correlated with an abstract object (its sense) that can be apprehended by different persons; details of this apprehension and of how it facilitates communication are apparently of no concern. A second consequence is the circumscription of the science of semantics and its separation from the other sciences of language, syntax and pragmatics. Semantics studies the correlations of words with things, whereas syntax focuses on correlations of expressions with each other and pragmatics on the correlation of words with behaviour and attitudes. Only what falls within the purview of semantics is thought to be relevant to meaning; neither syntax nor pragmatics contributes to a 'theory of meaning'. The fundamental notion in semantics is that of truth under an interpretation, where by 'interpretation' is meant an assignment of objects, properties, relations, etc., to words of the appropriate logical type. The thesis that semantics is the scientific investigation of *meaning* encapsulates and builds on Augustine's proto-picture of language.

Wittgenstein's thorough criticism of the Augustinian picture involves a repudiation of this traditional strategy for philosophical investigation of meaning. Any elaboration of Augustine's proto-picture distorts the concept of meaning in fundamental ways. This is the thrust of the barrage of arguments in the *Investigations* §§1–142. In particular, Wittgenstein criticizes both of the major consequences of the traditional outlook on meaning. First, the internal connections between meaning and related notions are mostly far from simple. There are many different kinds of explanations both of words and of sentences. Giving a correct explanation manifests, but does not guarantee, understanding, nor does it constitute a sufficient condition for using a word or sentence correctly. Similarly, describing how to verify a sentence in many cases is a contribution to its grammar (PI §353), though in other cases there is no such thing as verifying or giving grounds for a statement (cf. PI §377 ff.). A proper conception of such internal relations shows them to be complex, to vary from case to case, and to depend on circumstances. Secondly, both the characterization of semantics and the demarcation between semantics and syntax or pragmatics are faulty. Even ostensive definition should not be construed as correlating words with things, but rather as correlating words with other signs (cf. 'Ostensive definition and its ramifications', pp. 96 f.). Any explanation explains something only *within* language. This undermines the rationale for distinguishing semantics from syntax and pragmatics. In particular, assigning truth-values to assertions is only one among many ways of reacting to the use of sentences, and others equally manifest understanding or lack of understanding of the sentence used. Similarly, gestures, samples, and features of the context may play a role in explanations of meaning or in the applications of language, and hence they are essential elements in the characterization of meaning. The very idea of semantics is a major obstacle to the philosophical clarification of the concept of meaning.

If these critical arguments are cogent, we must make a complete break with tradition and start afresh in thinking about meaning. But what positive guidance does Wittgenstein offer? What is the key to a proper investigation of meaning? The answer, as we have repeatedly insisted, lies in the notions of understanding and explanation. Philosophical puzzles or confusion about meaning can be traced to lack of an *Übersicht* of the varied criteria for understanding expressions and of the relationships among these criteria. Others stem from failing to appreciate the normative status of explanations of meaning as standards of correct use. The proper strategy is to focus on explanation and understanding and on the relation between them. In particular, giving a correct explanation is a criterion of understanding, while the explanation given is a standard for the correct use of the expression explained. Correspondingly, using an expression in accordance with correct explanations of it is a criterion of understanding, while understanding an expression presupposes the ability to explain it.

In effect, Wittgenstein reverses the traditional direction of fit between meaning and understanding. The Augustinian picture tailors the accounts of understanding, explanation, and communication to the conception that meaning consists in correlations of words with things. Inverting this procedure requires investigation of what it is to understand an expression, what it is to explain it, and what is involved in communication. The concept of meaning must be shaped according to these constraints. Clarification of the appropriate criteria of understanding will dissolve the philosophical problems for which the Augustinian picture of language, in more or less sophisticated forms, provides the solutions. Consequently, any need for that conception of meaning will disappear.

Just how radical is Wittgenstein's break with philosophical tradition can be gauged by contrasting the conception of understanding implicit in influential theories of meaning with his own account of the criteria of understanding. While most contemporary discussions of meaning are rooted in the theories propounded by Frege, Russell, and the *Tractatus*, Wittgenstein noted that some of the deep distortions of meaning, explanation, and understanding originate with Plato. Our examination accordingly starts with the dawn of error and then moves immediately to its zenith.

2. Plato

Plato's best-known dialogues are debates on 'big' questions, e.g. 'What is justice?' They proceed by the Socratic method of questioning purported answers and raising objections against putative solutions. These works are the seeds of the dominant conception of philosophy as arguments about very general questions. What is less obvious, but equally influential, is Plato's tacit conception of meaning, explanation, and understanding. His ideas have shaped the thoughts of many generations of philosophers.

In the more Socratic dialogues, Plato gives a negative characterization of understanding. Interlocutors unable to give satisfactory general definitions of such terms as 'virtue', 'justice', 'piety' are said not to understand these terms or not to know what virtue, justice, and piety are. Socrates' self-appointed mission was to convict people of ignorance of these important matters. His method was to take inability to define a word as proof of failure to understand it. Wittgenstein termed this argument 'Plato's method' ('Platos Betrachtungsweise' (C8, 75)), and he criticizes it as fallacious (PPI §67, cf. Exg. §70). Plato misrepresents our criteria of understanding in claiming that a person who cannot *define* a word does not know what he is talking about in using it (PI §70, cf. §§79 f.). The 'Socratic fallacy' is exposed by the fact that there are criteria for understanding a word other than giving a definition of it; someone's use of it may manifest his understanding it independently of whether he defines it. Moreover, his failing to give a preferred *form* of explanation of it on request does not defeat such an attribution of understanding to him. None the less, the idea lingers on that inability to give a definition in answer to a Socratic question is a scandalous demonstration of ignorance (e.g. FA p. ii), and it supports the insistent demand for *Merkmal*-definitions of concept-words used for any serious scientific purposes (cf. 'Family resemblance', pp. 189 f.).

This account of the 'Socratic fallacy' reveals only part of Plato's distortion of the concept of understanding. The rest, though operative in the early dialogues, becomes more prominent in the later ones, particularly in discussions of the Theory of Forms. Socrates' searches for definitions are motivated, often explicitly, by the desire to establish a standard of correctness for applying expressions the applications of which are frequently controversial. Plato's Forms are meant to fulfil this role. The Form of Justice, e.g., is a standard or measure of what is just; by looking at it or by making use of it we can authoritatively determine whether particular actions or agents are rightly called just. Although Forms are transcendent abstract entities, they are similar to samples in functioning as standards of comparison for applying words. The fact that

Forms provide the answers to Socratic questions itself reveals important aspects of Plato's conception of understanding and explanation. Understanding 'X' consists in acquaintance with the Form of X-ness, and this manifests itself in the ability to give an explanation (λόγον διδόναι) of what X-ness is. From this conception can be extracted Plato's criteria for adequacy of explanation. First, an answer to 'What is X-ness?' must provide an objective standard of correctness for applications of the term 'X'; independently of our judgements, it must settle whether any application is correct or not. Its crucial function is normative. Secondly, explanation of what X-ness is must lay out a general rationale for applying 'X' to whatever falls under this concept; presumably it must exhibit conditions necessary and sufficient for applying 'X' to an arbitrary object. (Both of these criteria of adequacy are conspicuous in Socrates' arguments criticizing and repudiating putative definitions of words.)

These observations suggest alternative ways to characterize the 'Socratic fallacy' or the mistakes embodied in 'Plato's method'. First, we could credit Plato with the insight that understanding a word presupposes the ability to explain it, but accuse him of distorting this by invoking too restricted a conception of what it is to explain a word. His error is the refusal to acknowledge anything as a correct *explanation* other than a *definition* in terms of necessary and sufficient conditions of application (cf. Exg. §70). He wrongly rejects as explanations accounts of how to use a word which consist of lists of examples of its correct application (cf. PG 119 ff.; BB 196; PLP 84) or accounts which would be inapplicable or mistaken in bizarre circumstances, e.g. in respect of dealings with homicidal maniacs (cf. BB 26 f.). Plato's distortion of understanding is thus exhibited as the consequence of a misconception about explanation. Secondly, we could trace this misconception itself to the insight that correct explanations of meaning have a normative status with respect to applications of the explanandum. Plato's error was to suppose that any sentence having this function must have a particular form, viz. that it must be couched as a general rule licensing or forbidding the application of the explained term in certain specified circumstances. Given this preconception, Plato takes it to be obvious that no adequate explanation can consist of a list of examples, or a specification of conditions *defeasibly* justifying (or prohibiting) application of a term. According to this diagnosis, the root of his misrepresentation of understanding and explanation is a deep-seated illusion about normativity manifested in the idea that every genuine rule must have a certain form.

However he analysed it, Wittgenstein thought that 'Plato's method' was influential and deeply misconceived. He exposes its misconception of understanding, explanation, and the normativity of rules. On the other hand, it is a congeries of misconceptions organized around a fundamental insight, viz. that understanding presupposes the ability to justify and criticize applications of a word and that an explanation provides a standard of correctness for the use of an expression. Plato's errors contain much truth.

3. *Frege*

The concept of sense (*Sinn*) as standardly interpreted has a dual role: it is intended as an elucidation or explication of the everyday notion of meaning (as applied to expressions in language), and it is related to understanding in so far as the sense of an expression is presented as the content of a person's understanding of this expression. Thus with the concept of sense Frege appears to link meaning with understanding. Indeed, both his explanation of 'sense' and his distinction of sense from reference are thought to turn on issues about understanding and other 'cognitive states', e.g. belief. He aims to resolve five important perplexities. (i) How is it possible to understand a singular referring expression ('proper name') that refers to nothing? (ii) How is it possible to understand a sentence that lacks a truth-value (e.g. a sentence from fiction)? (iii) How is it possible to understand two proper names each of which in fact refers to the same object without knowing that they refer to the same object (e.g. 'the Morning Star' and 'the Evening Star')? (iv) How is it possible to understand two sentences one of which is derived from the other by substitution according to a true identity-statement without knowing that their truth-values are the same? (v) How is it possible to understand two sentences each of which is in fact true without knowing that they have the same truth-value? Answers to the first pair of questions invoke the possibility that an expression may have sense without having reference. Answers to the other three rest on the idea that the road from sense to reference runs via facts, viz. that ignorance of fact makes grasping the sense of an expression compatible with ignorance of its actual reference. This evidence apparently justifies the contention that Frege's account of sense focuses on the connection between meaning and understanding.

Frege's thinking about meaning betrays the influence of 'Plato's method' in two respects. First, the inability of the ordinary person and even of the typical mathematician to give a satisfactory definition of the number one or the concept number is equated with lack of understanding of concepts that are the foundation of the whole structure of arithmetic (FA pp. i f.). Adequate definitions are essential for the justification of arithmetical statements, indeed even for demarcating the subject-matter of the science of arithmetic. Secondly, the sense of a word resembles a Platonic Form. It is an abstract entity that exists independently of being conceived or thought of (cf. NS 149). A word is given meaning by being correlated with such an entity. Its meaning is its sense, i.e. an entity, and this entity determines to what things the word can correctly be applied. The sense of a word, if expressible, will be expressed in a definition stating the complete rationale for its application, i.e. necessary and sufficient conditions for its correct use. Hence only such a definition constitutes an adequate specification of a word's sense. Understanding an expression consists in apprehending its sense, and mutual understanding consists in joint apprehension of the same transcendent entities. Senses of words are Forms stripped of their metaphysical functions. The fact that the sense of an expression is an abstract entity, and the corollary that understanding consists in correlating words with such entities, reveal Frege's account of meaning to be a sophisticated version of the Augustinian picture of language.

In virtue of its affinities with Plato's method, Frege's account of sense similarly distorts the concepts of understanding and explanation as well as the nature of justifications for the use of expressions. Inability to define an expression is not a criterion for failing to understand it; an adequate explanation need not take the form of a *Merkmal*-definition; and justification for the use of an expression need not be couched as a general rule stating sufficient conditions for its applicability. In addition to these mistakes, Frege's account contains certain mysteries equally characteristic of Plato's thought. No clarification is forthcoming of the criteria for grasping a sense (or a Form); using a term correctly is not treated as such a criterion since this is compatible with ignorance of its sense—the situation characteristic of most mathematicians according to Frege (and Plato). A parallel difficulty is Frege's notorious failure to specify clear criteria for identity of sense. Obscurity enshrouds the connection between apprehending its sense and either the ability to give a definition of an expression or the ability to apply it correctly. Consequently, both the possibility of apprehending a sense and the consequences of doing so seem problematic (cf. NS 157). It is equally mysterious how an *entity* can have the normative functions of a rule; i.e. how the *thing* which is the sense of a concept-word can justify the application of this word to an object. These crucial unclarities threaten to deprive sense of both its normative role in justifying the use of expressions and its explanatory role in demonstrating the possibility of communication.

Frege's misconceptions about understanding, explanation, and justification of use are not three independent gratuitous blunders, but rather a set of mutually supporting distortions. According to his views about meaning, clarification or analysis of the concept of understanding must itself incorporate a *Merkmal*-definition of the phrase 'to understand "X"'. Relying on the idea that giving an explanation manifests understanding, we might try to specify adequacy of an explanation of 'X' in terms of a rule knowledge of which would be a sufficient condition for understanding 'X'. If such a rule stated conditions that jointly were weaker than a sufficient condition for the correct application of 'X', then his knowledge of it would not be a sufficient condition for a person's having the ability to apply 'X' correctly; and if the conditions enumerated were not individually necessary for the correct application of 'X', then his knowledge of it would not be a sufficient condition for his having the ability to avoid mistakes in applying 'X'. Consequently, it seems, only knowledge of a *Merkmal*-definition of 'X' could appear as one constituent in the analysis of what it is to understand 'X'. Conversely, knowing a rule explicitly stating the *Merkmale* of 'X' itself seems to be a sufficient condition for having the ability to apply 'X' correctly; it would make the task of applying 'X' completely 'mechanical'. The proper analysis of understanding apparently gives *Merkmal*-definitions a privileged role among explanations, while the possibility of *Merkmal*-definitions seems to vindicate the *Merkmal*-analysis of understanding itself. A parallel nexus links *Merkmal*-definitions with a misconception of the normative role of explanations. It is natural to restrict attention to rules of use that state *conclusive* reasons for or against the application of an expression 'X', i.e. rules that firmly establish the fact of the matter about applications of 'X'. For this purpose, nothing other than conditions individually necessary and jointly sufficient for the application of 'X' will apparently suffice, and such rules do serve this function. Consequently, *Merkmal*-definitions alone seem to meet the conditions of adequacy for explanations imposed by taking seriously their normative role in justifying and criticizing applications of words.

Impressed by Frege's misconceptions about understanding, explanations, and justification of use, one might conclude that he altogether fails to relate meaning to understanding in his account of sense. Indeed, the distortions of the concept of understanding shared by Frege and the Platonic tradition suggest a neglect to consider what it is to understand an expression. The motto of his investigations into meaning seems to be 'Take care of the sense, and leave understanding to take care of itself'. In this respect we fall victim to an illusion if we characterize the notion of understanding as central to his theory of meaning. Less misleading would be the contention that it drops out of his considerations.

This reassessment of Frege's account of sense is supported by a careful inspection of his writings. Everyday explanations of words are given short shrift (cf. FA pp. i f.); they do not meet the standards of completeness requisite for any adequate explanation (GA ii. §56; FC 33). As a consequence, Frege ignores their role in justifying or criticizing applications of words and in providing grounds for or against holding judgements to be true. He concentrates exclusively on the 'ultimate grounds' for applications of words or for holding judgements to be true (cf. FA §3; GA ii. §56). Even understanding is rarely mentioned explicitly. It is common to construe his idea that sense determines reference (SR 58) as the claim that understanding a word involves possession of a means for settling what its reference is, but Frege himself does not add this gloss. Although he ultimately relates the thesis that the sense of a sentence is composed of the senses of its constituents to the claim that understanding any sentence is a matter of understanding its constituents and its structure, this is done belatedly and the principles connecting senses are conceived Platonistically as laws of super-physics. Even when he speaks of grasping a thought this phenomenon is far removed from the humdrum understanding of a sentence; it is mistakenly conceived as a mental act, perhaps the most mysterious of all such acts since it stands at the very limit of mental phenomena (NS 157). Frege's disdain for considering understanding is most conspicuous in his purely formal arguments for difference of sense or inadequacy of definitions. Two names 'A' and 'B' differ in sense provided that there is some pair of sentences '$\Phi(A)$' and '$\Phi(B)$' that might differ (or be judged to differ) in truth-value (FC 29; SR 62). Similarly, the definition of identity of courses of values in terms of the extensional equivalence of their defining concepts is incomplete because it is possible to construct a function X (ξ) admitting courses of values for arguments, satisfying the condition X $(\dot{\varepsilon}\,\Phi(\varepsilon)\,) = $ X $(\dot{\alpha}\,\Psi(\alpha))$ if and only if $\neg^{a}\!\!\!\frown \Phi(a) = \Psi(a)$, and differing from the identity function (GA i. §10). Although considera-tions about understanding can be read into many of Frege's texts, they are explicit in very few.

This reinterpretation is also supported by reflection both on Frege's programme and on his methods for carrying it out. His ultimate purpose is to vindicate the philosophical thesis that all truths of arithmetic are analytic. His technique is not to scrutinize actual explanations of number-words, signs for numerical operations, or rules of inference, but rather to reconstruct the language of arithmetic on more rigorous foundations. He replaces our explanations of adjectival uses of numerals in sentences by translating sentences of the form 'There are n F's' into sentences involving quantifiers and identity; and he replaces our explana-tions of substantival uses of numerals by such definitions as '0 = the extension of the concept "is equi-numerous with the concept x $\neq$ x"'. Similarly, his redefinition of 'number' has the consequence that mathematical induction can be proved not to be a form of inference exclusive to arithmetic, but rather to be a logical inference in a deceptive guise (FA pp. iii f.). Frege's account of the sense of words and sentences in arithmetic replaces ordinary explanations and inference-rules with a calculus expressed in the symbolism of his concept-script. He purports to demonstrate that the analogue within this calculus for every truth of arithmetic can be derived from the basic logical laws by means of the definitions of the constituents. The sense of an arithmetical statement is far removed from what we understand and what we explain. Indeed, it is so far removed that, even if Frege's proof of the analyticity of arithmetic were formally sound, this could not be claimed to illuminate an aspect of the meaning of arithmetical statements, i.e. what we understand in understanding arithmetic. Paradoxically, this divorce of sense from understanding might appear to be a strength in Frege's justification of arithmetic. If sense is to provide an objective standard of correctness of application, it must settle whether a word is correctly used independently of whether we take it to be. Paradoxically, this desideratum will be partly secured if in our practices we never judge correctness of use by reference to the formulation of the sense of an expression. In this way the normative role assigned to sense pulls Frege towards treating sense as something transcendent, and this in turn tends to disengage sense from understanding.

Far from emphasizing understanding, Frege's theory of meaning has an opposing thrust. Thus is reflected in his status in the recent history of philosophy, viz. as the Father of Philosophical Semantics. He pointed the way to this paradise by adumbrating an account of meaning which can be *reconstructed* around the notion of reference or truth under an interpretation. Puzzles about Frege's notion of sense can be cleared up by concentrating on this idea, not by seeking to demonstrate a closer link between sense and understanding than is apparent in his writings. The germ of this reconstruction is that two expressions have the same sense if and only if they have the same reference under every admissible interpretation. Since 'numbers are objects', the sentence '4>3' has the same logical form as 'Smith is taller than Jones', and hence it is immediately obvious that '4 = 2^2' differs in sense from '4 = 3+1' and equally that '2^2' differs in sense from '2+2' and '4' provided that indefinable expressions are dissociated from their intended interpretation and treated instead as the atoms for constructing alternative interpretations. This way of presenting Frege's account of sense clarifies his failure to discuss the sense of indefinables, his commitment to contextualism even prior to the generative account of understanding, his restrictions on definitions, and the non-triviality of identity statements, even in arithmetic. Frege's primary legacy lies in the growth of systems of formal semantics, which are not concerned with understanding. It is true that his idea of a generative theory of understanding has been developed by later theorists, but only under the aegis of a misguided conception of understanding.

4. *Russell*

One of the foundations of Russell's reflections on meaning is the empiricist thesis that all ideas are ultimately derived from experience. Understanding an indefinable expression consists in acquaintance with what it stands for. The analysis of a definable expression shows how to construct its meaning from the meanings of other expressions; a complete analysis would define it in terms of indefinables and thus reveal how its meaning is derived from acquaintance. The complete analysis of a sentence would exhibit it as a construction out of atomic sentences by means of logical operators—a construction in which each atomic sentence would contain only indefinables. Formulated as the principle of acquaintance, this conception seems to enthrone understanding as the central notion in the development of his account of meaning.

Although Russell views understanding as having such a central role, his conception of understanding is itself so distorted that he is not in a position to reap the harvest of his insight. This appears most conspicuously from considering three ideas fundamental to his thought about meaning.

(i) Russell's whole account is a rigorous working out of Augustine's proto-picture of language in a pure, simple, form. Every expression left as the residue of logical analysis will be a name whose meaning is the object that it names, and every analysed sentence will consist solely of names. This vision motivates his theory of definite descriptions and his multiple-relations theory of judgement or belief. It also warps his account of logical forms and molecular propositions. Aware of the importance of form or structure in understanding sentences, he attempted to incorporate the form of a sentence as one constituent in its analysis; he treated the form of a two-term relation, e.g., as a logical object, acquaintance with which was one ingredient in understanding an atomic sentence the 'relating relation' of which was a two-term relation ('Theory of Knowledge', pp. 185 f., 204 ff., 217 f., 242 ff.). Similarly, until persuaded by Wittgenstein to treat them as syncategoremata, Russell construed logical operators as names for logical objects ('Theory of Knowledge', p. 186). The corollary of adherence to this stark Augustinian picture of language is the thesis that a complete understanding of any expression consists in acquaintance with the named object, if the expression is indefinable, or in knowing its analysis into indefinables, if the expression is analysable. Russell is thus committed to a mistaken account of the criteria of understanding and of failing to understand expressions, as well as a too restrictive conception of the adequacy of explanations. Finally, he leaves mysterious the connection between understanding an expression and knowing how to use it, notably so in the case of indefinables.

(ii) Russell conceives of understanding as a mental act whose nature is known by introspection. This is clear in his discussion of indefinables. In this case, understanding consists in acquaintance, i.e. in immediate awareness of an object. Verdicts that certain expressions are not indefinables are often supported by the observation that careful introspection discloses no objects correlated in our minds with these words (e.g. 'Theory of Knowledge', pp. 295, 300). Russell's discussion of analysable expressions rests on the same conception of understanding. This is clear in his principle of acquaintance. This contextual principle is advanced as an analysis of what it is to understand a sentence. This complex mental act is broken down into constituent acts of acquaintance. A correct analysis of the act of 'understanding a proposition' is very complex and depends on the form of the proposition understood. Its complexity suggests that it must be treated as an explanatory hypothesis, i.e. as something only capable of inductive justification by appeal to data from introspection. There is an unresolved tension between Russell's conceiving of understanding as a mental act and his taking understanding a proposition to be an explanatory hypothesis. But both strands of his thought are incompatible with the correct account of understanding.

(iii) Russell's account of meaning has the function of a scientific theory; it is a *theory* of meaning. The root ideas are offered as the minimal theoretical apparatus necessary for explaining how language works: the meaning of an indefinable is the object named, and the meaning of any complex expression is composed out of the meanings of its simple constituents. Russell's purpose is to marshal inductive support for the theory of meaning that flows from this pair of explanatory hypotheses. They are shown to explain the possibility of understanding the sentences of our language and the possibility of communication; they suffice for the construction of the science of logic and the whole edifice of classical mathematics. This is the justification of the method of logical analysis and of logical atomism as a theory of meaning. This conception of the inductive justification of an account of meaning is in sharp contrast with Frege's ideas and with the whole Platonic tradition. It involves, as it were, a total eclipse of the normative functions of meaning and explanations of meaning. Far from having a role in justifying or criticizing applications of expressions, Russellian analyses presuppose our already possessing standards of correctness; an analysis must conform to our practice of using an expression, not vice versa. Ordinary explanations of meaning alone provide standards of correctness, and hence they alone have a part in delineation of criteria of understanding expressions. If Russell's theory of meaning is claimed to expose the foundations of our understanding of language, then it must be remembered that these foundations rest on what they are said to support, since his analyses are not explanations of meaning at all, but explanatory hypotheses in a new science of language.

Russell's theory of meaning could be criticized for distorting the concepts of understanding and explanation. Alternatively, it could be said to redefine 'understand' for his scientific purposes. In either case, he does not relate meaning to understanding.

5. *The* Tractatus

Wittgenstein's logical atomism amalgamates important elements drawn from Frege and Russell. The result is an account of meaning distinctively different from both of its immediate ancestors. From Russell the *Tractatus* took over the simple version of the Augustinian picture, viz. the principles that the meaning of a name (simple sign) is the object named and that the meaning of a sentence is a function of its constituent expressions. In addition, Wittgenstein accepted and further elaborated the idea that sentences are not names, i.e. that there is no such entity as a proposition to function as the object of such propositional attitudes as belief, supposition, or understanding. From Frege the young Wittgenstein absorbed opposition to intrusion of psychology into logic. Antipsychologism requires the exclusion from an account of meaning of any consideration of how expressions are actually taught, learned, or explained, how they are understood, or what are cited as grounds justifying or criticizing particular uses of them; *a fortiori*, this attitude condemns the empiricist principle that understanding has its origins in acquaintance as *irrelevant for the logic of language*. The upshot of combining these ideas is a version of the Augustinian picture resembling Russell's in its stark simplicity and Frege's in its pure formalism.

When re-examined in the light of Wittgenstein's later conception of meaning, the sweeping anti-psychologism of the *Tractatus* must be regarded as a fundamental weakness. Exclusion of consideration of explanation and understanding then appears as a grave lacuna in its whole account of meaning, threatening the very idea that the *Tractatus* gives a philosophical account of *meaning*. When Wittgenstein criticized the conception of understanding in the *Tractatus*, his target was not the explicit content of his logical atomism, but rather a revision of its theses incorporating an account of understanding which preserved its essential contentions about sense. The *Tractatus* does not *state* that understanding a name consists in acquaintance with the object named, nor that ostensive definition is the fundamental form of explanation for names, nor that understanding a sentence is operating a calculus according to definite rules (PI § 81). These are, however, the only accounts of explanation and understanding that conform with Wittgenstein's logical atomism. Independently of them, there would be nothing in the *Tractatus* deserving of attention as an account of meaning. But adding them leaves the book open to an equally damning verdict.

6. *Umblick*

Concentration on the relation of meaning to explanation and understanding is the conceptual backdrop to Wittgenstein's criticisms of the Augustinian picture of language. This setting provides the dramatic unity to what might otherwise appear to be disjointed comments about random points in the *Tractatus* and in the work of Frege and Russell. A carefully organized recapitulation of critical points already discussed may help to draw together the threads of the *Investigations*, thereby making both its plot and the deficiencies of the Augustinian picture more perspicuous and surveyable.

There are four ideas related to explanation and understanding which serve as foci of Wittgenstein's thought.

(i) *Criteria of understanding*: there are multiple kinds of criteria of understanding expressions, whether words or sentences, and many criteria of each kind. The general error of philosophical accounts of meaning is to distort the criteria for understanding expressions by elevating some into entailments and neglecting others altogether. This involves a double oversimplification: first, an unwarranted restriction on what is treated as internally related to a person's understanding an expression, and secondly, the replacement of defeasible, circumstance-dependent inference-rules by deductively valid ones. In fact, criteria of understanding are diverse, equipollent, defeasible (both positively and negatively), and laid down in grammar. Various versions of the Augustinian picture distort criteria of understanding in different ways.

(a) Giving an explanation of an expression in accord with the practice of explaining it is a criterion of understanding it. This principle is contravened if one argues that ostensive definitions or explanations by examples are not explanations at all, or that giving any explanation is merely a symptom of understanding because this only inductively supports the prediction that the expression will be used correctly. The same principle is infringed by the common ban on multiple explanations of terms and by the idea that the practice of explaining certain expressions may be incoherent.

(b) Using an expression in accord with the practice of using (and explaining) it is a criterion of understanding it. This truth of grammar is denied if one argues that there is no such thing as using or failing to use an expression in accord with an explanation or a pattern of use. It is also denied if correct use is treated merely as a symptom of understanding either because understanding consists in an independent mental event or state (e.g. acquaintance with an object) or because understanding an expression entails using it correctly at all times, including future ones.

(c) Appropriately producing or reacting to a sentence is a criterion of understanding it (and so too is explaining in what circumstances it is appropriate to utter it and how it is appropriate to react to it). This principle is conspicuously neglected by the Augustinian contention that all sentences are descriptions, also by the widespread idea that the meaning of a word is exhausted by its contribution to the truth-conditions of sentences in which it occurs, as if the essential function of speech were the conveying of information.

(d) The relations between different criteria for understanding an expression are contingent. What connects the practice of explaining an expression with the practice of using it correctly are patterns of behaviour normal for those who speak the language. This is distorted in the Fregean idea that giving an explanation establishes understanding of an expression only if the explanation given states sufficient conditions for applying the defined expression. A similar sublimation typifies the weak cluster theory of proper names (cf. 'Proper names', p. 237). Contingent regularities also link the various explanations comprising the practice of explaining an expression, or, equally, the various ways of using an expression comprising the practice of using it. These too are frequently sublimed (cf. 'The standard metre', pp. 173 f., and 'The uses of sentences', pp. 72 ff.).

(ii) *Standards of correctness*: we distinguish between correct and incorrect explanations of expressions, also between correct and incorrect uses of expressions. We may appeal to standards of correctness in justifying judgements about correctness; in particular, we often cite explanations in justifying or criticizing applications of expressions. A general mistake in philosophical accounts of meaning is to caricature standards of correctness of explanation and use, as well as the connections between these standards. These distortions too are apparent in various versions of the Augustinian picture.

(a) The possibility of making an objective distinction between correct and incorrect explanations does not presuppose the existence of a general invariable standard of correctness of explanation, but merely the existence, relative to each expression explained, of fairly definite practices of explaining expressions ('agreement in definitions') (PI §242)). Failure to appreciate this manifests itself in the idea that standard explanations are not really explanations at all. Thus, e.g., since the acceptability of an ostensive 'explanation' of 'red' rests on whether the object employed as a sample really is red, it seems that the putative explanation presupposes an independent genuine, explanation of 'red'. Philosophers often provide spurious standards of correctness. One common idea is that an explanation is correct only if it is 'complete', i.e. only if it expressly states how to use the explained expression in every possible circumstance (cf. 'Explanation', pp. 38 ff.). Another related idea is that the correctness of a definition must itself be independent of circumstances; if, for whatever reason, an explanation is ever inadequate, it is always so. Finally, philosophers' explanations of meaning are totally divorced from ordinary practices of explaining meanings of words, and are treated as explanatory hypotheses. The correctness of such explanations is held to be independent of any normative role in our practices. All these strands of thought suggest that only definitions by necessary and sufficient conditions qualify as genuine explanations.

(b) The possibility of an objective distinction between correct and incorrect uses of expressions also seems to presuppose the existence of general invariable standards of correctness relative to each expression, but in fact presupposes only the existence of tolerably definite practices of using expressions ('agreement in judgements' (PI §242)). Failure to appreciate this launches the Platonic search for answers to the question what X really is. The aim of much philosophical inquiry into meaning is the discovery or construction of a rationale for the use of each expression. This is typically conceived as a set of general rules stating conditions *indefeasibly* licensing (or prohibiting) the application of any particular expression. These strands of thought converge in the idea that only a rule stating necessary and sufficient conditions for applying a term makes possible an objective distinction between correct and incorrect uses of this term. Philosophical analysis aims to provide for this need.

(c) A correct explanation of an expression is a standard of correctness for the use of the expression explained; it is a rule for the use of this expression. Given the previous misconception that only rules of a certain form can function as standards of correctness, philosophers infer from the normative status of explanations both that every correct explanation must have the form of a formal definition and that many so-called explanations, e.g. ostensive definitions and explanations by example, are not correct explanations. This involves a distortion of the concept of a rule and an oversimplification of the connection between rules and their applications. Rules, hence explanations too, may have *many* forms (cf. 'Explanation', pp. 37 ff.). Recognition of this truism is blocked by fascination with the illusory ideal of rules so framed that they 'contain' their own applications, for this seems to require that a proper rule describe all the conditions in which it is to be applied and also state its verdict for every case. What connects a rule with its application is never the form or 'geometry' of the rule-formulation, but rather the practice of applying rules of this kind and the criteria for following this particular rule (cf. Volume 2). In developing theories of meaning, philosophers treat the formulation of meaning-rules satisfying certain constraints as the terminus of their inquiries, as if these gave the foundations of language. Instead, they should remind themselves that in the beginning was not the rule, but the practice (the deed).

(iii) *System*: the notions of system and structure are readily applicable to language. Indeed, a language is often characterized as a system of communication, while sentences used to make moves in the language-game are typically complex and have various structures. It is tempting to relate these notions to the concept of meaning. Philosophers typically do so. This is a conspicuous feature of the *Tractatus* and of Frege's account of meaning. The various versions of the Augustinian picture drive towards the idea that individual words are atoms of language each of whose combinatorial possibilities and significance are completely determined by a single complex meaning-rule which is one fragment of a vast calculus. This involves exaggeration of the extent to which language is systematic and structured.

(a) The contextual principle that the meaning of a sentence is composed out of the meanings of its parts in accordance with its structure is an essential component of the Augustinian picture. It is correlated with an unduly restrictive conception of explaining the meaning of a sentence, and it thus misrepresents the criteria of understanding sentences. Furthermore, its defence leads to the sublimation of the notions of sentence-structure and of explaining the meanings of words and phrases; as a consequence, there is distortion of the criteria for understanding subsentential expressions and of the criteria for understanding sentence-structure.

(b) The idea of system supports the standard philosophical argument establishing difference of meaning. If two sentences differing in meaning differ in only one constituent (e.g. if the truth-conditions of '$\Phi(A)$' differ from those of '$\Phi(B)$'), then the two substituends for this constituent must differ in meaning (viz. the names 'A' and 'B' must differ in meaning). Conversely, if two expressions ever differ in meaning, then they always do; and consequently, so too do complex expressions in which they occur (except if the differences cancel out). Since, e.g., 'He has established his base camp on Mount Everest' is not equivalent with 'He has established his base camp on top of Mount Everest', the expressions 'on' and 'on top of' differ in meaning, and therefore so too must the sentences 'The calendar is on the table' and 'The calendar is on top of the table'. (Parallel arguments are employed in segregating expressions into logical categories: in particular, if there is any context in which one expression can significantly occur but another cannot, then they differ in category.) Such absurdity can be avoided by de-emphasizing system and allowing discussion of identity and difference of meaning, explanations, and understanding relative to particular contexts (cf. BB 115).

(c) The ideal of demonstrating that all inference is logical inference informs the delineation and differentiation of logical forms in philosophical accounts of meaning. In fact, failure to exhibit familiar modes of inference in the form of sound logical inferences is often treated as tantamount to failure to discern the logical form of the statements involved (e.g. sentences incorporating adverbs). Philosophical analysis will furnish a theoretical unification of all legitimate modes of reasoning. These regimented explanations are not correlates of understanding and do not reflect what we ordinarily mean. Neither Frege's explanation of multiply quantified sentences nor Russell's explanation of the word 'the' *was* a correct explanation of these expressions; nor was giving either of these 'explanations' a criterion for understanding the explained expressions. Even if such analyses were shown to be extensionally equivalent to ordinary explanations of these expressions, this would not prove that we have all along, unbeknownst to ourselves, been *following* these rules. (Indeed, the proof of extensional equivalence would presuppose that we possessed and followed rules of use independent of the analyses.) Our language does not have this uniform inferential structure, though it might be so reconstructed that its replacement did.

(d) Bewitchment with the idea that language is systematic is manifested too in undue emphasis on the forms of expressions. It supports the illusion that identity of grammatical form betokens identity in the uses that we make of expressions; e.g. that the mood of the main verb or word-order fixes the use of a sentence. Typically there are many more uses of expressions than there are distinct grammatical forms, and the correspondence between form and use is seldom better than very rough.

(iv) *Normativity*: explanations of the meanings of expressions have normative roles. They are rules for the correct use of the explained expressions or standards of correctness. Not only do philosophers commonly deny that statements actually having this role in our linguistic practice are genuine explanations, but also they affirm that statements 'analysing' or 'giving the meaning' of expressions in our language are the only genuine explanations in spite of their not having this normative function in our practice. This distortion is apparent in all versions of the Augustinian picture and particularly virulent in contemporary theories of meaning.

(a) The method of analysis inverts the direction of fit between 'explanations' and use. The analysis of an expression, far from serving as a standard of correct use, has the status of an explanatory hypothesis to be tested against the independently recognized pattern of correct use of this expression. Any discrepancy is a reason for modifying the proffered analysis, not the use of the analysandum.

(b) Unless the 'explanation' of an expression has the appropriate normative role, giving it does not have the status of a criterion of understanding the 'explained' expression, nor is the 'explanation' itself part of the grammar of this expression. The analyses desiderated in many accounts of meaning would not be better explanations than the everyday ones, nor would they give better understanding of the expressions that we commonly use; neither an analysis in the manner of logical atomism nor a definition made complete according to Frege's specifications would be an *explanation* at all. (At best it would be a stipulative sharpening of a concept that we might profitably use in place of our ordinary less sharp concept for certain purposes (cf. Exg. §§76 f.).) Similarly, only in special circumstances does correlating a word with an object constitute an explanation of this word.

(c) We not only act in accord with rules, but we also follow them. There are criteria for following particular rules, e.g. the rule 'add 2'. It is possible to establish with certainty what rule someone is following (even though this inference is defeasible). Among the indefinitely many possible rules to which someone's use of a word conforms, there is typically one privileged one, viz. the explanation that he is following. Only by ignoring the distinction between conforming with and following a rule, together with neglecting the normativity of explanations, does the underdetermination of explanatory hypotheses by observational data even appear to have any relevance for an account of meaning.

(d) Explanatory hypotheses are deductively linked with the observations that they explain. Consequently, if an analysis of the meaning of an expression is thus to explain its use, it must state general conditions for the correct use of the analysandum, and hence there must be an internal relation between a formulation of the analysis and a description of any circumstances in which the analysandum is correctly used. This misrepresents the relation between an explanation and the use of an expression. There is no necessity for this kind of internal connection between a correct explanation and the circumstances for correct use of this explanandum. The relation is justificatory, not hypothetico–deductive, and the justificatory role of an explanation is compatible with its having any form whatever, e.g. an ostensive gesture together with a sample, or a list of paradigmatic examples.

7. *Überblick*

In breaking off at *Investigations* §189(a), the 'Proto-Investigations' left a great lacuna to be filled. Two topics in particular had still to be covered to complete Wittgenstein's general account of meaning and its connections with understanding and explanation. First, the characterization of explanations as rules of use calls for a clarification of the concept of a rule and of the concept of following or applying a rule, for, as we have seen, philosophers' vision of these matters is obscured by dense clouds of dust. Secondly, the strategy of relating meaning to criteria of understanding requires further clarification of the concepts of understanding and meaning something as well as elucidation of the notion of a criterion itself. All three of Wittgenstein's known attempts to extend the argument of the *Investigations* §§1–189 continued with a discussion of rules and rule-following; this material is linked with consideration of fundamental questions in the philosophy of mathematics, and hence it provides one proof of the connection between his remarks on mathematics and remarks about meaning and the mind (cf. PI p. 232). The final (published) version of the *Investigations* supplements the earlier remarks on understanding with fuller discussion of related issues in the philosophy of mind, thus clarifying the notion of criteria of understanding and the importance of the notion of criteria. This provides a link between his remarks on the 'philosophy of psychology' and his account of meaning. Whether or not he was successful, he did at least make a sustained attempt to complete the argument laid out in the 'Proto-Investigations'.

Wittgenstein's conception of meaning and his perception of his task in giving a philosophical clarification of meaning implies a picture of philosophy that contrasts sharply with contemporary orthodoxy. Many are inclined to think that an account of meaning is fundamental to progress in any branch of philosophy; central issues in ethics, epistemology, the philosophy of mind, etc., all wait on a correct conception of meaning. Some optimists even believe that a proper theory of meaning would finally settle all major problems in philosophy. Wittgenstein's conception of philosophy is just the opposite. Discussion of issues concerning meaning ramify into problems in the philosophy of mind and the philosophy of mathematics; hence they cannot be settled on their own prior to wider-ranging philosophical investigations. The connection of meaning with understanding and with rule-following shows that the philosophy of mind and the study of normative phenomena are just as central to philosophy as 'philosophical semantics'. As is evident from our earlier scrutiny of Frege, Russell, and the *Tractatus*, misconceptions about meaning are misconceptions about understanding, explanation, rule-following, justification by rules, etc. Hence clarification of the concept of meaning will come only as a result of simultaneous advances on many fronts.

This conception of philosophy has two important corollaries.

(i) It spotlights Frege as the great myth-maker of contemporary philosophy. Descartes's sway remained unbroken for nearly three centuries. The problem of securing the foundations of knowledge and the examination of the varieties of scepticism obsessed these generations of philosophers; epistemology was deemed the centre of gravity. Frege's influence has gradually transformed the whole climate of philosophy, with momentous assistance from Russell and the young Wittgenstein. He made giant strides towards the construction of a science of logic and of language. His account of meaning seems not only systematic, rigorous, and elegant, but also suggested apparently definitive solutions of long-standing puzzles, especially about the nature of language. His methods and theory of sense are the foundations of modern philosophical semantics. His vision inspires most philosophers with the idea that the study of meaning is the gateway to truth in philosophy. Frege thus stands at the opposite end of the spectrum from Descartes. Under his influence we have accepted the tyranny of semantics in place of enslavement to epistemology.

(ii) To the extent that Wittgenstein's philosophy is systematic, this characteristic is a result of his pursuing certain methods in dissolving philosophical perplexity. In two respects his purposes were incompatible with producing philosophical remarks that have the features characteristic of a *system of thought*. First, he eschews the construction of explanatory hypotheses that might unify the descriptions appropriate for philosophical clarification. Secondly, he implies that there is no division of the branches of philosophy into the central and the peripheral, hence that there is no coherent programme for tackling the big problems and leaving the lesser ones to be tidied up later. The body philosophical is neither a despotism nor an oligarchy, but a pure democracy. The absence of hierarchical structure is lack of one kind of system, though it would be erroneous to identify this lack of system with anarchy.

Although it lacks features of both content and form that typify system-building, the *Investigations* is not a random collection of remarks without internal unity. Rather the source of its unity is in its method. The aim is always to generate an *Übersicht* of parts of the grammar of language that give rise to puzzlement, and the method is to explore and describe the criteria of understanding the relevant expressions (or kinds of expressions). The products of these inquiries may look very different from each other since criteria of understanding various kinds of expressions ramify in diverse directions. Yet the underlying purpose and method is constant. In Wittgenstein's view, the most important product of the *Investigations* is the method (cf. PI §133).

The primary ingredient in Wittgenstein's method is the notion of criteria of understanding. This motivates and unifies his criticisms of the Augustinian picture of language. It informs his important discussions of ostensive definitions, samples, explanation, family resemblance, determinancy of sense, and understanding itself. Finally, it resolves apparent conflicts in his own thought. In particular, Wittgenstein advances a bewildering variety of seemingly irreconcilable dicta about meaning. The meaning of a word is its use in a language (PG 60; PI §43); its use in practice (BB 69); its role in the language-game; its place in grammar

(PG 59). The meaning of a word is what is explained in explanations of its meaning (PG 59; BB 1). The meaning of a word is its purpose (PR 59, cf. PLP 157 f.). The meaning of a sentence is its use (PI §421); its method of verification (WWK 47, 243 ff.; PR 200 f., 289; BT §60; PG 127; cf. PI §353); what is explained in explaining its sense (PG 131). The justification or grounds of an assertion constitute its sense (PG 81, cf. Z §437). Most of these slogans have the form of identity-statements. Since what is equated with meaning differs from one to the next, it seems either that Wittgenstein's conception of meaning is incoherent or that the term 'meaning' is radically ambiguous in his work. Either verdict is superficial. The apparently conflicting slogans are intelligible and unproblematic when expanded as remarks about criteria of understanding. Each calls attention to one among the many kinds of criteria for understanding words or sentences, and none is intended to make an exclusionary claim that only criteria of the one mentioned kind really qualify as criteria of understanding.

The landscape traversed by Wittgenstein in the course of his philosophical investigations is vast. Following him closely, keeping our eyes on his tracks, we get the impression that the terrain is rough and that many of its features are shrouded in gloom. It is difficult either to get our bearings or to anticipate the movements of his thought. We need to lift our gaze and look around in order to find our way about. Only thus can we identify the landmarks that guide his course and come to recognize previously encountered features when seen from a new angle. With progressive loss of the feeling of disorientation, we may find that the light will dawn gradually over the whole landscape. In this volume we have attempted to draw back the veil from the sources of light—the three beacons of meaning, explanation, and understanding. They illuminate the terrain so far traversed, and, as we shall argue, their powerful rays penetrate even to the uttermost limits of Wittgenstein's *Philosophical Investigations*.

INDEX